STAYING WEST

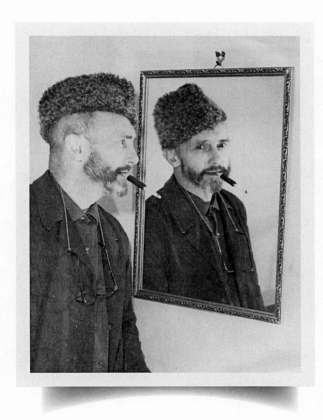

STAYING WEST

The Writing Life of Anthony C. West

Audrey Stockin Eyler
Emeritus Professor of English
Pacific Lutheran University

Cover and interior book design by Scot McDonald

Cover and frontispiece: A. C. West in his "oul karakul." Photo by Emlyn C. Baylis, Llanberis, c. 1968. Used by permission of the photographer and Miriam West. Cover photos, front (derived from same photo as for frontispiece) and back (the author, Audrey Stockin Eyler. Photo by John M. Eyler, 2014).

Manufactured in the United States of America

1 3 5 7 9 10 8 6 4 2

Library of Congress Control Number:

ISBN 978-1-942661-03-0

Published by Kitsap Publishing
www.KitsapPublishing.com

To John

Foreword

WHEN ANTHONY C. WEST'S first collection, *River's End and Other Stories*, appeared, the reviewer in the *Oxford Mail* (August 11, 1960) described reading it as "quite an experience. Like a kick in the guts from a jack-booted leprechaun." The image is apt. West powerfully united violence, decay, and corruption with natural, fanciful, poetic, and spiritual beauty. The combination is the complex, contradictory texture of life itself, of course, and West had a genius for making the reader see and feel it. Through the senses he reached for the head and the heart. Like his literary countrymen Bernard Shaw, W. B. Yeats, and Sean O'Casey, West offered a complete world view. Parts of that view were esoterically Christian; all of it was socially munificent, and most of it was ahead of its time in being ecologically responsible.

Receiving highest praise, his work was in print for fifty consecutive years: *The Native Moment, Rebel to Judgment, The Ferret Fancier, As Towns with Fire*, miscellaneous poems, essays, and a dozen or more short stories. For recent decades, however, it has seen neglect. Attempting to repair this loss, Eyler explores West's critical reception, his auto-fictive method and other mysteries about his writing life. She has discovered among his papers other novels, promised but never published, and she brings to light his surprisingly feminist magnum opus, The Lady Actaeon, which occupied him over six decades.

West's remarkable life (1910-1988) became the material for his ever-developing art: his childhood spent between big house and peasant fields in Down and Cavan, his hobo years in the United States during the Great Depression, his Royal Air Force Pathfinder navigating in the bombing of Germany, his experiments in communal farming, his role as father of eleven children, and his own spiritual development. This narrative he steadily mined for his separate but cohering fictions. Through the fiction—especially through Actaeon—and through his letters and interviews, Eyler investigates the special proximity of West's life to his fiction and finds a way to let the writer tell his own amazing story of fidelity to his art.

Contents

PREFACE

Anthony C. West (1910-1988) was a brilliant and prolific Irish writer. Sean O'Faolain discovered him. *Esquire* promoted him. Reviewers hailed his originality and depth. His Irish editor wrote to him, "What is so exciting about your work is that not only can you out-write the majority of the so-called professional boyos as a user of words but also you are writing at a level of experience and thought which so very few of them even know exists." The corpus of published work ultimately was small—a few poems and essays, four novels, a couple of novellas, and about a dozen short stories. Censors sometimes protested his language. Reading fashions, tastes, and tolerances changed. Critical interests shifted. Though he was in print for fifty years of the twentieth century, his work has since become hard to find; even literary scholars now say "Who? Should I know him?" Furthermore, West kept a low personal profile, increasing the challenge for appreciating this talented artist's unusual story. Yet he deserves new readers and renewed critical attention.

Initially captivated by his short stories in 1981, I read on through his longer fiction and had written much of *Celtic Christian Socialist* before a first interview with West, himself. As our acquaintance grew through interviews and letters, it became apparent that West's own story demanded a telling. Discoveries about his prolixity, his depth, and his struggle to get that Yeatsian "balloon of the mind into its narrow shed" astonished me, held me, and have led gradually to this book. I offer it as a mapping of a territory, with West himself being a narrating guide. I hope that having more of his primary text and details of his writing life available rewards his existing enthusiasts, creates more readers of West, and aids future West scholars.

From the first, readers have suspected proximity between West's fiction and his life. When, fulfilling his request, I assumed after his death the responsibility for sorting his literary papers and could read the pages evidencing his efforts and achievements, I could confirm the spiritually motivated application of his life to his art. I was transfixed.

i

As scrupulously as Yeats, West made the phases of his life as he experienced them—physically and intellectually—the material for his art. His "auto-fiction" makes it possible now, when West's publications are widely unavailable, to offer not only a biographical acquaintance, but also a representative portion of the literary rest of West.

Intent on showing this dynamic record of West's mind and art, I offer extended passages from West's own fiction, published and unpublished, these sometimes strung to advance the autobiographical thread, sometimes to illustrate a critical point. I have made selections from thousands of pages of his fiction, which embody the developing mind of West, to present this writer at his long, transcribed, transcending work. Through these inserted pieces from the auto-fiction, this transmutation of experience, the stream of whose (mostly unpublished) pages accumulates and winds like a glacier through his decades, the reader can discover this indefatigable artist at the deeply creative and productive, but normally hidden, parts of the writer's life. Especially, extended excerpts from the unpublished novel that grew over six decades from a short story to fifteen hundred pages, his *magnum opus*, help to make it possible. Among the distinctions of this novel, *The Lady Actaeon* is West's only work with a female (and, it will be a double surprise to his critics, feminist) protagonist.

Certain features of his story strongly resist a biographer's usual chronological approach; such are strategically revisited to accommodate their "staying" nature. There is, for example, West's unceasing revision of his work. He particularly felt unfinished with his earliest years. He resisted "hardening off," as he called it. Biographers typically have little to say about the subject's childhood: The baby arrives—it might well have been delivered by stork; the biographer remembers the child in a few straggling episodes between ages one and eighteen or thirty-five, episodes thus made unjustly significant. The subject naturally takes over the biographer's real interest only in maturity. West's childhood, however, remains one of his more revisited sources for his fictions, all of which, furthermore, are preoccupied with some spiritual stage of growing up. West recognized a fundamental evolution of spirit: A person's spiritual growth is naturally impeded by ego; the developing human must steadily deny this egotism, if one would move toward individualism, equality, and freedom. The same goes for mankind. Simple chronology then becomes inconsistent with his implicated cosmological stance.

Nevertheless, presenting an overview in the introductory and summary chapters, and moving throughout the book between the biographical past and a literary present, I depend for clarity upon a chronological chapter outline, the chapters anchored by his eight decades and his geographical movement. The reader will also be assisted by complementary photographs within the text, and by the appendix, which includes lists of West's published and unpublished works, cited characters, and major biographical events. In my culling among his paragraphs, I have usually retained his Irish-English spellings and his distinctive punctuation (sometimes it is central to characterizations); I've made occasional clarifying insertions or silently corrected the typing. Through strategies of typeface and spacing I attempt to preserve both clarity in reference and narrative fluidity among the sources and to reduce my own narrative presence. His, after all, is the word-magic.

For expediency's sake in the summer of 1989 when I was sorting and organizing the more than 30,000 pages in West's London study— necessarily a cursory process within six weeks–I arbitrarily assigned each recognizable version of *Actaeon*, as they kept turning up, a letter of the alphabet. The versions—or parts of them—were in no perceptible order. Recognizing them, dating them, discovering their internal chronology, even identifying some more of them since then, has been and remains a challenge. I defend studied guesses about them here, advising readers that the alphabet does not signify the writing chronology of the versions. To save worse confusion in the future I retained, in referencing my photocopied set, all those letter assignments I made to the original West papers, which his family first placed at St. Mary's, Strawberry Hill, University of Sussex, in Twickenham.

His papers have since been transferred to Ulster's Linen Hall Library, and in the Ulster Museum hangs the engaging portrait of A. C. West by Ross Wilson. West never realized his plan to move back to Ireland in the later years of his life, but in these honoring respects, and I hope through some contributions of this book, the "son for Éiru" has made it safely home.

ACKNOWLEDGMENTS

Many people, too many of them, alas, no longer living, have helped me in this project of decades. My deepest gratitude goes with the dedication to my husband, historian of medicine John M. Eyler, companion, critic, photographer, and often my rescuer in computer difficulties. To the West family my debt is huge. I began serious study of West's fiction when Poolbeg issued *All the King's Horses* in 1981, and had much of *Celtic, Christian, Socialist* drafted when I met the author and his wife mid-decade in their London flat. West responded kindly to my questions and wrote me helpful letters thereafter. Eventually he asked me to look after his papers at his death. When that sad time came, I was honored to assume the task, but I could not have managed it without Olive West's extraordinary help, hospitality, and photocopying permission for my subsequent study. Thanks to all the Wests I met in London and Ireland, the children following their parents' generous and hospitable lead, especially Stephanie, who went many extra miles on my account. Jocelyn and her daughter, Sarah, supplied photos and Sarah's letter of welcome from her grandfather. Mary, Miriam, Kathy, and Simon also produced photographs, documents, and memories, as did West's Woolsey relatives in Derry, George and Teresa, Vanya, and Muriel Woolsey Darling.

* * *

Pacific Lutheran University was generous in helping to fund my research through several Regency grants, travel grants, and sabbaticals. Administrators, faculty, and staff offered invaluable support. Members of my department and division, especially those in the offices of chair and dean, helped to make this work possible. Megan Benton was an invaluable reader and consultant. Jack Cady and Marjorie Rommel shared their writerly insights. Wayne Carp of the Department of History helpfully empathized over biographical research. Pacific Lutheran University librarians Laura Lewis and Gail Egbers, along with archivist Kerstin

Ringdahl and photographer Kenneth Dunmire, were faithful resources.

Colleagues in the American Conference for Irish Studies have been a critical audience for the parts of this study that I have given as conference papers; many gave me practical information and criticism. Sean White, years ago, kindly initiated my contact with West, and Blackstaff publishers, especially Anne Tannahill, eventually secured it. Thomas Dillon Redshaw and James Rogers promoted my work through *Eire-Ireland*; Robert Lowery of the *Irish Literary Supplement* started the whole West project more than three decades ago through assigning me a review of *All the King's Horses*; numerous other colleagues from the American Conference for Irish Studies, especially Robert Tracy, Robert Garratt, James MacKillop, James Cahalan, Stephen Arkin, Robert Mahony, John Harrington, Maureen Murphy, Mary Helen Thuente, Bonnie Kime Scott, and Charlotte Headrick, also deserve thanks for leads or critical insight. Nor can I neglect to credit my colleagues in our Western regional chapter of ACIS for decades of personal interest and professional support.

Numerous people in Ireland and the United Kingdom offered direction, memories, and hospitality: Frank and Alice Prochaska in England; Hugh and Margaret Richardson and family of Moyallon; the clerk of the Friends' Meeting of Moyallon; Philip and Lorraine Wilson, Susan, and Linda, of Portadown and the Craigavon project; Gordon and Carol Nicholson, Paddy Mack, Peter and Helen Lotz, and Marion Moore when I visited Farnham; Ted Hickey and Elizabeth Crum, Kenneth Anderson, Patricia McLean, and other helpful staff at Ulster's Museum; Ciarin O'Keeffe in the Glenveagh National Park Office; Sophie Hillan King and John Cronin of The Queen's University, Belfast; Tim and Mairead Robinson of Folding Landscapes in Galway; Brendan Barrington of Penguin. Maurice Leitch and Michael Longley kindly consented to interviews. Two public librarians in Cavan, Malachy Doherty and Brian Connolly, located West's books in the restricted cupboard for me. Thanks go to Alice Prochaska and Sally Brown at the British Library; to staff at the Public Record Office and at the Ministry of Defence; to Sheila Kent and Clare Ryder, librarians of St. Mary's University College, University of Surrey, at Strawberry Hill; to Marie Rooney at The Gate

Theater in Dublin; to Colette O'Flaherty of the National Library of Ireland; to West's friends, Jake Bush in Wales and Ormond Edwards in Scotland.

Additionally, I owe many thanks to the Yeadells, widow of West's skilled Pathfinder pilot, and their son, Michael, along with Christopher Webb of Romford, Essex, whose father, Alan, was also a member of RAF Squadron 627 and compiled *At First Sight* (1991). They generously supplied information, direction, and pertinent photocopies. I thank the people at the Mosquito Aircraft Museum at London Colney; Royal Air Force Flight Lieutenant Mary Hudson at Bentley Priory; Group Captain J. R. Goodman of Kingsbridge, Devon; Christine Gregory and Joanne Ratcliffe of the Royal Air Force Museum, Hendon; Group Captain Goodman; Mary Hugh of the Air Historical Branch 2 (RAF), Ministry of Defence; and Janice I. Mullen and staff at the Imperial War Museums. They aided my efforts to discover copyright ownership of the military photos.

Stateside, thanks go to others who have at various stages most helpfully read, listened, or offered service: Alan Graebner, Lora Beth Norton, Judith Lynip Shadford, Gene Shadford, Nancy Leigh Suksi, Annie Ludlum, Ruth McRee, Florence Sandler, Gloria and Dennis Martin, Dolores Schaefer, Noni Dworkin, and Patty Cumbie. Thanks are due to Dorothy O'Connor's family—Floyd, Sharon, and especially Dorothy's sister, Marilu Cooper; to C.C. Clawson who made a pilgrimage for me in Custer, South Dakota; and to my family, especially in-laws Marvin and Catherine Eyler, who went on several West errands in Washington, D. C. Thanks to Devin-Adair Company; to staff—including James Cellan, John Davenport, and Anne Kenne—at the University of St. Thomas; to staff of the University of Minnesota's Wilson Library and to Robin Overmeier and Elaine Challacombe of the Wangensteen Library; to Rosemary Furtak of the Walker Art Center in Minneapolis; to staff at the Minnesota Historical Archives; to the U. S. Navy archivists at the Smithsonian, to Roslyn Goldman, to Cheryl E. West of Gales Ferry, Connecticut, Arthur Schlesinger, Jr. in New York, and to writer Jack Curtis of Big Sur.

Thanks are due to my students at PLU who have read, written about, and discussed West's fiction with me. Kay Whitford typed the R text onto a disk. The members of three senior seminars in biographical writing were helpfully critical and encouraging, as they realized their teacher's own engagement with the assignments. Neighbor Amanda Hawkinson helped with filing. Kathleen Prevost offered critical insight, technical help, and superb traveling company one working summer; Seth Graebner was an able assistant in another. The most recent contributors to this project have been my book's designer, Scot McDonald, Pat Schmidt, and author Karen Robbins of Gig Harbor, WA, and the Kitsap Publishing team.

The long look required by this study could not help but increase awareness of the connectedness among my own opportunities to learn. One's love for words originates, of course, where she begins to hear them, and I owe this start to my parents, classicist F. G. Stockin, Jr. and painter Marjorie Ortlip Stockin. I also wish to thank my teachers, those responsible for kindling and sustaining my enthusiasm for formal study of English literature and writing from my first day of school through graduate studies: At Caneadea #6, grades 1–3: E. Beach; 4–6: B. Lombard; at Fillmore Central, 7: R. Kleinspehn; at Houghton Academy, 8–12: R. Hess, R. Hutton, B. Keith, D. Rowe, L. Smith, D. Wells, S. Wright; at Houghton College: A. Campbell, C. Davis, R. Fair, S. Foster, W. Greenway, R. Hazlitt, A. Lynip, S. MacLean, J. Rickard; at Alfred University: M. Bernstein, E. Curry, E. Finch, D. McKenzie, D. O'Hara; at the University of Wisconsin-Madison: T. Bender, M. Eccles, B. Friedman, S. Henning, L. Kapell, W. Nelson, C. Pondrom, J. Wiesenfarth; at the University of Minnesota in Minneapolis: C. Anderson, M. Hancher, D. Hurrell, W. Josal, A. MacLeish, L. Mitchell, G. O'Brien, M. Steinmann, E. Stekert, L. Unger. I wish to credit here, finally, Leland Shaw, an exemplary senior colleague, who in his fourth decade of college teaching and I in my first year of it, magnanimously shared with me his office. For years thereafter, until his death in his mid-nineties, he offered his friendship, his library, his invaluable insights from Milton College classrooms and from his quiet, exemplary commitment to the vocation of handing things on.

PERMISSIONS

Permissions to use published materials, private letters, and photographs were generously granted by the following: Emlyn C. Baylis, of Gwynedd, North Wales, for the photo of West in his "oul karakul"; Condé Nast Publications Limited through Harriet Wilson, Director of Editorial Administration and Rights, for portions of "The After Vacancy," from *Vogue* (London), December 1969; *Eire-Ireland*, a journal of The Irish American Cultural Institute, and John P. Walsh for use of two essays: "Piques in Darien: Anthony C. West and his American Publishers," Fall, 1992, 49–66, and "The Old Made New Again: Imagery in Two Stories by Anthony C. West," Fall 1985, 52–64; Floyd J. O'Connor of Taos, New Mexico, for Dorothy's dancing dream; T. Pakenham of Tullynally, Castle Pollard, Co. Westmeath, for the letters to West from Christine Countess of Longford; Lily West for the use of Anthony West's letter to Anthony C. West; the West family for the pictures from their archive; Joan Yeadell for parts of a letter from her late husband, Wilfred Yeadell to West, 18 December 1976.

Photographs:
George and Ellen West family: 39, 67
Moyallon estate: 40, 44, 46, 50
Farnham estate: 61, 67, 68, 69, 71, 73, 74, 75
A. C. West singles: 84, 127, 154, 159, 307, 309, 311
Olive Burr West: 125, 157, 187, 189
West children: 157, 187, 189
Royal Airforce images: 127
Actaeon typescript stack: 289

CHAPTER ONE

OVERVIEW:
A SON FOR ÉIRU

[May 1956]
Boulder Farm
North Stonington,
Connecticut

Dear Mr. Anthony West,

    A few weeks ago I was very much taken aback when a friend of
mine who had just been to see the Editor of Esquire *told me how . . .*
glad he [the editor] was to be buying three stories from me. As I hadn't
sent him any I was very much surprised. . . . When my agent called
up . . . and asked with more asperity how Esquire *had got the stories*
without her knowledge . . . I explained as much as I knew. . . . So far
the inconveniences have all been mine, and they have been minor
ones. But presently you will find yourself troubled with this kind of
thing. . . .

    I think I can justifiably say that I am an established writer in this
country. I also think I am justified in saying that there is no precedent
for a new writer coming onto the scene and using the name of an
established writer.

*I hope you won't think I intend anything impertinent or deroga-
tory when I suggest that we should come to some sort of agreement on
this matter. The Churchills were able to agree to become Winston C
and Winston S. Churchill, and when G. H. Wells began to write in the
twenties my father H. G. Wells managed to persuade him to change
his name to avoid just the sort of confusions that lie before us. . . . I
hope we can agree on something of the kind. I think I can legitimately
ask you to make the change as my first published work appeared
in England in the* New Statesman *in 1938–39, ahead of your first
publication dates I believe. I realise that you have an absolute right to
use your name as you choose but I think it would be fair if you were to
either drop the "h" from Anthony, or change the Christian name, or
the surname, or to insert an initial between them, when you publish in
America where my efforts are concentrated. I have been successful in
making the name quite a valuable property and I think I am entitled
to enjoy the benefit of it, if you will forgive my putting the matter as
crudely as that. . . .*

*I hope you will have every success here with your writing, and I
would be glad to give you any advice or assistance that I can. . . . But
I also hope that you will recognise the awkward situations that may
come up in future if it is not recognised that there are two of us . . . I
find it universally assumed here that I wrote your story in* Esquire, *and
I am going to get the credit for the other stories as they come out unless
you take steps to establish your own identity. Half the effect of your successful entry into this field, or perhaps more than half, has been lost . . .*

I am, also I am sorry to say, yours,

Anthony West

When he received this letter from the son of H. G. Wells and Rebecca
West, Cathcart Anthony Muir West was understandably distressed. It was
1956, and he had begun to write seriously twenty-five years before, when
he was twenty-one.[1] Not that he was well known or that he had done
nothing else: six nomadic years in the States, censorship, exile, marriage,
service in a world war, farming, and nine children had intervened. But

he had just sold some impressive stories, and a prodigious, renewed effort in the last few years seemed finally to be paying off. That spring *Esquire* had sent him $500 for "Not Isaac." Another story, "Narcissus unto Echo," had won him much attention in the preparation for the May issue whose ink was hardly dry. "The Turning Page," which as "Myself and Some Ducks" had been aborted by censors of *The Bell* fourteen years earlier, would come out in December. Ironically, he formerly had been published under pen names (as "Michael MacGrian" in *The Bell*); now in *Esquire* he had agreed to use his own. Although his first story had appeared in 1937, actually before the American Anthony West's, that had been under another pseudonym, Terence O'Reilly.[2] Other such names appeared on agricultural or local press contributions and on manuscript drafts and submissions.[3] West quickly wrote to *Esquire*:

> I received a long letter yesterday morning from an Anthony West living in America telling me about himself and his work, a son of H. G. Wells. It is quite a blow to me, especially as he states you bought my three tales on the strength of his good name and reputation. I crawled into the doghouse and started to think it over.
>
> Firstly, I knew vaguely there was another person writing named Anthony West. Some five or six years ago a friend wrote me about a novel under the name. I have never read anything this man has written, as I seldom read novels. And certainly I had no idea that he was an American or was writing in America or that he was so well-known and established. In fact, from what he tells me, he is somewhere near the top of the tree.
>
> But on third thoughts I found it increasingly difficult to accept that you misread the name, unless our respective life-approaches and styles are almost identical. There are many points......[West's own signal for a trailing thought] I am here in shadow and he is there in limelight; my letters to you suggested a totally different background—I am a soil-son and he was born with a golden pen in his mouth; there are his novels, his established New Yorker work, and his employment of an agent, while I have no agent: there are numerous reasons why something so well-informed and so acute as the community of brains that is Esquire would hardly unknowingly confuse identities: and surely, you would have

written me had you any doubts? Or have I been existing on a marsh-gas bubble of another man's hardwon work and reputation?

    West realises he cannot prohibit me from using 'our' name but claims he has made it a commodity of value which on the strength of his letter I fully admit, and I have no wish to cause 'us' embarrassment. Personalities apart, he has obviously earned his name and place by hard work. You are the professionals and know your way about—what hell does one do in such a case. If you are going to publish the Duck and the Sheep stories, maybe it would be possible to insert a note in your magazine?

    If in your eyes my work stands up without a name I am quite willing to call myself something else. I'd like CLEMENTS West. Clements was my mother's maiden name. As regards pseudonyms: I publish for reasons of privacy some agricultural articles under Tom Whitfield. Also for reasons of privacy I published in the beginning under Michael MacGrian, but all my friends objected to the Celtic Twilit flavour and prevailed upon me to use my own name; and also, Irish material in England does not seem to be very popular at this time. I work here quite on my own and have no contacts with the literary worlds of England and America, save through the Writers and Artists Year Book. *Until recently, in fact until you bought my three stories, my life and mind as a writer have always been kept well under the table.*[4]

"Stay West, young man" counseled *Esquire*'s editor, Arnold Gingrich.[5] But what might that provoke? What had these editors intended? Surely they anticipated such problems? Did they count on readers' fast and false assumptions to stimulate sales? Was there some grudge against the other, well-established West? Gingrich assured West that a mix-up had no part in their evaluation of his work. While an addition of a distinguishing initial was an "American barbarism" they normally tried to avoid, it would be fair and appropriate here, he told Anthony C. About other West authors—this Anthony, Geoffrey West (the pseudonym selected, incidentally, by G. H. Wells when H. G. Wells persuaded him to change his name for the same reasons[6]), Sackville-West, Rebecca, or Nathanael, Gingrich refused to worry.[7] Meanwhile, he telegrammed that

Esquire was accepting "River's End."[8] In his letter of 9 July, he continued to be "wildly enthusiastic":

> *I intend to say in the magazine itself as much as I possibly can about the rare quality of this story, so I won't go on with a lot of extra compliments now. I simply think it's the best story we've had in twenty-three years of publishing* Esquire, *better than the "Snows of Kilimanjaro . . ."—but there I go.*

West grew even more nervous about the name. On 16 July he thanked Gingrich for explaining his point of view,[9] yet he remained fearful:

> *. . . While Anthony West (American) can look after himself, the similarity of names plus possibly a difference in styles and viewpoints might well embarrass both Wests in time to come and bring irritation and annoyance to their respective publishers, agents, and camp-followers.*
>
> *Provided my stuff stands, I don't really care one way or another. I'm no pen prima donna. But West did write me and somehow I cannot offend him in cold blood. Esquire is a powerful publication and is obviously read around the world by reasonably intelligent people, and that West would have to swallow and deny the River story under your tremendous patronage would be a bitter pill for him as man and writer.*
>
> *Any chance in letting Echo go to Wests 1 and 2; say nothing about Ducks save a quiet name-change; and then sail under full canvas with the River? Three stages with Echo published May 1956, almost a year before? What do you think?*
>
> *Or else—leave West and Anthony out of it and give me a new name altogether; and leave Echo behind? A quick new snappy name? <u>JOHN KELLS</u>? (Kells in Gaelic is associated with 'head'. There are only six Kells in the London Directory. And John goes back as far as mankind. And, indeed, anonymity suits me better. I can live and write quietly.*[10]

"I see your point about giving offense," Gingrich replied, ". . . so we'll run the December story . . .as being by Anthony C. West."[11] He thus seemed deftly to comply with his writer's request and simultaneously to dismiss it.

For that year, Anthony C. West appears to have been thought hot property. Film and literary agents inquired. Jacques Chambrun had recently negotiated the sale of *Peyton Place* to Twentieth Century Fox for $125,000, he reported to West in January 1957 in a second attempt to attach himself to this potentially prosperous writer. He had offered his service to West in November, after reading "The Turning Page," and in his courteous, noncommittal reply, West mentioned a recent fizzle of an ABC film contract.[12] But this time Chambrun extended a compliment to his potential writer's mother on *The Fountain Overflows*.[13] This "name business has cropped up again," West lamented to Gingrich, as he appealed to the *Esquire* editor for a way to save Chambrun embarrassment.[14] West never could lay aside niggling doubts about Gingrich's decision and the effects other writing Wests may have had on his own career.

> . . . *Very funny—I got my name in wedlock! . . . I was sorry about the whole thing but couldn't stop* Esquire *ploughing on and I don't suppose the Madison Avenue cynics would believe me when I said I just didn't know that Anthony West was a novelist.*[15] *But, overall, I have to accept this as an act of destiny which forces me further out on my own limb, underwriting my detachment from any literary cultus or cabal and, anyway, . . . as a writer I'm content with an artisan's wage with the great luxury of being my own boss, malice to none.*[16]

He stayed West, nevertheless, and with four novels, at least a dozen incidental stories and two collections of them, numerous re-issuings, and some translations thereafter, he remained continuously in print for fifty years. It remained an unfortunate coincidence of names. As one reviewer of West's last published novel, *As Towns with Fire* (1968), commented, "With all the Wests in the literary world today who write interminable and pretentious novels, it may be that readers have confused Anthony C. West . . . [who] may have written one of the best novels of this year, or perhaps this decade . . ."[17]

Yet the challenges of self-definition, of staying West, carried their consequence in more than appellation. The occurrence of this coincidence at the very moment of what appeared to be an auspiciously turning fate, the contrastive responses of the two Anthony Wests to their situation, the wry humor Anthony C finds in it, the Irishman's hazy awareness of another writing West, and the apparent acquiescence to his peculiar destiny all make this introductory episode representative—a quintessence of Anthony C. West's personal, professional story.

Focusing on *As Towns with Fire* in his recent history of the Irish novel, George O'Brien has rightly appreciated West's pitting individual identity against the collective, celebrating its substance and viability.[18] Such loneliness is the modern reality, as West explicitly observed in his first letter to Christine Countess of Longford (see chapter 8). Just how comprehensively West explored this theme, neither O'Brien nor West's other readers have had sources to understand until now. With a gift approaching total recall, West accepted every experience, he said, as "grist for his mill." Fragments of this story he has acknowledged directly, and some fictionalized aspects of it have been published. The bulk of it, however, which he steadily built into a vast and artful narrative structure, has never, before *Staying West*, appeared—either as autobiography or as fiction.

In "The Self as History" Alfred Kazin observes that in the hands of the novelist "fiction is never simply autobiography." Nor, of course, is autobiography unfictionalized. When the experience and the art are known to be proximate they become especially compelling and complex. Kazin has also contended that "for the nonfiction writer personal history writing is an effort to find salvation, to make one's own experience come out right." Finding salvation can as well be a motive for writing fiction. The novelist knows that "man in the mass will never order existence."[19] Ordering therefore must be done privately, by the individual, through creative imagination. There are many artists intent on ordering parts of experience for the self, truth with a small "t"; a few, however, consciously position the self to serve an ordering that is transcendent—even to the point of subsuming that self. Anthony C. West is this kind of writer. In his fiction and in his life West relentlessly probes the self-defining (and self-abnegating) Hamlet/Christ theme—whether and how to be, to do, to love, to earn, to spend, to act; whether merely to prefer or to initiate; whether thinking and being actually are doing; and what should be the relationship between the thinker-doer—the individual—and the other.[20]

The reader is held by West's insightful questioning and by his commitment; parts of his own pattern he bestows upon numerous protagonists. West reads voraciously. He rewrites. He has tantalizing success, over and over again astonishing editors and publishers by the fecundity and depth of his words. For over six decades the pages stream out— thousands and thousands of them, many of them shimmering with that extraordinary quality that is the light of genius. Sometimes his vision and dedication recall George Eliot's Lydgate and Dorothea, as West labors passionately to delineate the spiritual tissue of human existence and validates through his own experience art's potential to teach. Of course, with every rereading of *Middlemarch*, the reader hopes for Dorothea's reform. Oh why can she not see that the minotaur Causabon would eat her? How can Lydgate be so stupid about women? There is no reordering of their lives. The reader may fantasize that this time through the plot Dorothea and Lydgate won't be quite so blind, but every time they must obey Eliot's uncompromising truth to character. Taking in the evidence of this artist's struggle, the reader may similarly want West to reap more practical success in the narrative of his life. Could he not satisfy that editor by making the plot tighter? Could he not provide for that audience a leaner, less meditative, less poetic prose?[21] Letters from commercial publishers advise him to probe more secular questions, more conventional questions, or to ask questions with shorter answers. Could he not be more sympathetic to modern impatience? Contracted to a retrospective travel piece, for example, why does he find it impossible to put aside his research into Irish religious history? He often frustrates publishers by something that will not let him produce exactly what they can sell. He frequently addresses newspaper editors on political, educational, agricultural, or religious topics: why can he not develop a pragmatic writing skill to keep the family's pot boiling more vigorously? Growing acquainted with West, the reader wants "that man who types all night" to be to his own children the wiser father he knows his fictional Simon Green needs; the husband to be more empathetic and loving than Christopher MacMannan is to Molly Chester.[22] If only. West, enormously more talented and more devoted than most, unflagging in his spiritual quest, nevertheless human and vulnerable, stays West with cost. One reads his *oeuvre* with dismay as well as sympathy, held by the power of a gargantuan ur narrative that becomes both his art and his life.

Yeats suggested there may be one myth underlying a person's existence and that if people could find it, it would permit understanding all that individual did and thought. West is consciously held by more than one myth, the first being the tale of Narcissus. His personal favorite among his published stories bears the name "Narcissus unto Echo," a phrase which West's readers gradually begin to appreciate.[23] Narcissus, in the cautionary Greek account, is by love's generous standard a failure. Ignoring the cries of Echo, who adores him, he becomes so infatuated with his own reflection in the pool that he falls in and drowns. To understand West's application of the image, we must regard several additional metaphors he invokes. In one autobiographical essay he calls himself a "long distance" runner, "the track the length of my life."[24] The record also implicates West the writer variously as a questor, a Grail-seeker, the doomed-to-tell Ancient Mariner, and fated Actaeon, who paid for gazing upon divinity. All his life he grows to understand this quest and the liabilities by recalling the egotistic danger of the pool-gazing to the ever-extending narrative.

He works faithfully, filing or embroidering facts, imagining potentialities, recasting his experience in this vast and continuous fiction, reorganizing and separating parts of it in light of reading, reason, spiritual insight, dreams, and artistic forms. He puts his discoveries into letters written by his characters, as well as into actual letters to close friends or sympathetic correspondents, making them repositories of an evocative record. He introduces Menippean dialogues between protagonists and antagonists to expose and explain and transcend such antinomies as Protestant and Catholic. He tries first-person accounts; he works with selective and omniscient third. He even experiments with intercalary arrangements of silent and spoken thoughts of the protagonist—the strategy on which he settles for *The Native Moment* (1959). At one level, of course, any writer must be narrowly focused, attentive to the artist within. Narcissus-like, West studies the whole reflection of his life, which art permits him to capture, but wisely cautioned, he also stands out-side the myth. Unlike Narcissus, he remains self-aware, seeing the man looking at the man (his favorite story's title perhaps suggests this redemp-tive attention). Thereby an artist can resist the self-absorption, the vanity, that arrogance that paralyzed and destroyed Echo's beloved.

The ur narrative West creates in the process of looking depends highly upon autobiographical event. He confronts his life as sacred mys-tery — sees the artist's obligation in a pilgrim's progress — and throughout the ur he takes his place with unfeigned humility. The protagonist's name may change; with moves in time or geography, West artfully imposes structural tangents and even tentative closures, but the original, underlying spiritual search resumes and remains on-going and depend-ently autobiographical. So West keeps adding to this huge ur narrative, raiding and rearranging, embellishing sections of it as he has need or inspiration. Such is his artistic methodology: vast, conscientious, integra-tive. He imagines a similar pattern on a cosmic scale:

> The gods made man and put a little poem in his hand and the devil tore the poem up and flung it on the wind. Now and again, a poet finds a bit; some are fortunate enough to find two or three bits. Probably Shakespeare and Goethe and Blake, to mention three poets, found half a dozen bits. In fact, it could be that all the bits have now been found and are scattered about the world. . . . The modern man must now set forth to find all the pieces . . . and finally put the poem together again (Room without a Door, #5, 995).

The same early protagonist from Room without a Door cites the spiritual consciousness of Tolstoy in *Anna Karenina* and concludes to his friend, "I walk with the great ones, Adam, in my own very small way. I can begin to understand their language" (995). As artist, West describes the objective and the journey. He had not lived very far into life's experi-ence himself before he began depicting this comparable pilgrim, exag-gerating some autobiographical traits, adding or deleting others. He became serious about the writer's life at twenty-one, beginning systematic composition at least as early as nineteen-thirty. He wrote his first stories, he says, at sixteen. He was still writing at his death more than six decades later.

Many—perhaps even most—pivotal aspects of this ur tale West lived, beginning at the geographic level. Physical journey lies at its auto-biographical heart. Settings of West's childhood in Down and Cavan are evoked in *Rebel to Judgment* (1962), *The Ferret Fancier* (1963), Wall, and *As Towns with Fire* (1968). His teenage years in Cavan form the setting for Jonty's life in The Casual Comedy.[25] West's North American years were nineteen to twenty-five (1930–1936); Naked to Laughter and many novella versions of a narrative called Embryon, as well as the published novellas *Swineherd* and *The Monocrats*, grow from them. West returned to Ireland and lived for a time on the money he made trapping and selling eels, an experience that anchors *The Native Moment* (1959). Giving up the eel business for ecological and humane reasons, he hoofed and biked around Ireland, from Donegal to Kerry to Dublin. From these places come other parts of Wall, Comedy, and all of Room. The island of Sark for a summer, London before and during the War, Ulster before his enlistment; South Africa for Royal Air Force training, and the English Midlands' military life all appear in *As Towns with Fire*. His nearly three decades in Wales support some of the short stories and an unpublished novella usually called The Jewel in the Snout or Circe, a Hitchcockian murder-mystery that gains much of its plausibility from West's knowledge of pig-farming and from his eye-witness of war's damages to human sensibilities. Sections of this ur narrative West thus isolates and enlarges; they become stories or novels that stand alone on internal and self-supporting plots. Some of them are his published works. An evolving relatedness of the published novels has been demonstrated in *Celtic, Christian, Socialist*.[26] My study of West's unpublished fiction since then reveals, however, that the four published novels are not just the visible parts of an iceberg; they are small extracted chunks from an enormous glacier.[27]

He was intently shaping a whole of his life and art, by simultaneously extracting and shaping pieces from that whole. West thought few sections of his ur ready for publication.[28] The sections that form the unpublished

Room give clues to his method and this hesitancy through numerous vignettes of the writer describing a writer. Protagonist Stephen Muir stores in ponderous letters—especially in letters to his artistic friend Adam in California—the ideas he wants to mine later on. West the writer and Stephen the future writer both recognize that no narrative line can support such discursive weight as presently exists in these accounts.

> I have been writing down my year in order to bury it and have a terrible pile of notes now—all corpses. . . . May I burden further your good patience by directly recording some of my main ideas and opinions at some length? I'll try to write carefully. You need not feel you ought to read them but do keep 'em in case........This method kills two birds and also, having to write to a living conscious person makes me more careful . . .

"Don't bother to read this if you don't want to," Stephen in effect tells Adam: "It's for me more than for you. It helps me to think ideas through, if I try to clarify them for someone else." This is good pedagogy for learning what he must, as every teacher knows. Stephen continues:

> You may find it boring. Nevertheless, just in case you, too, are interested in saving your soul, as godknows we wish more people were, I'll gladly give you all benefit of my own search and growing insight (Room without a Door, 992).

Although the egocentric (not egotistical) immaturity of his statement may prompt a smile, his purpose is serious. Stephen's experience here illuminates the troubles West soon encountered with the New York editors who took him up after *Esquire*. Protagonists Stephen, Adam, and Christopher are all socially unpretentious young Irishmen from a modest, rural background like West's own. Of course each of these pilgrims is not West in every detail as he develops their stories; West does make fiction from the experiences he selects. Yet very many circumstances of West's own life match the surface pictures in the pool, and the Narcissus-figure is both West and Everysoul in mental and spiritual potentiality, certainly in the fundamental, all-important quest.

West sometimes seems to play in the ur narrative with roads-not-taken. What, for example, if he had married X? The unpublished A Son For Éiru is premised upon Stephen Muir's having married the dutiful, bourgeoise Vuya (a character further developed in the published *Native Moment*) and settled down to conscientious farming in Ireland. He scrupulously, indefatigably nurtures the soil, raises livestock for breeding rather than for slaughter, aerates the land, and proves the neighbors wrong about "Folly Farm." Stephen—West renames him Conor—is by this time fifty-five, father of seven grown daughters. Unlike West himself, he has no sons. The daughters and sons-in-law don't want his farm, so he intends to write up his experiment, explaining details of his agricultural success, hoping to attract idealistic buyers who are also pragmatic workers. Giving a five-hour preamble, in which he reveals a spiritual cost in his marriage to a generous but materialistic woman like Vuya, Conor puts down his pen to drive to the station to pick up his youngest daughter, due home for the holiday. Swerving to avoid a tinker, he hits a bridge and fatally rolls his car over the embankment. Part two follows Conor's spirit as it revisits the points of choice in his youth and encounters again the people who represented alternatives. West believed deeply enough in spiritual reality that he wouldn't have thought a disembodied narrator an insurmountable obstacle to a transcendent design, yet still another version of Room makes Stephen a deceased veteran whose diaries are discovered.

Just how freely does West move the material from life to art? Readily and adaptively, without vulnerability to suit. For illustration of West's typical artistic adaptation of incident, it is instructive to consider a paragraph whose central experience West has used in more than one fiction, one of them published. It appears on page two of *Rebel to Judgment* (1962):

> On the way to the marsh, down Mallow Bray, I see two gray-green migrants. They have a magical smallness and perfection. The female is on the ground below a hawthorn still stark in the armor of its polished purple thorns. She is crying plaintively, with great loudness although

the cry is smaller than the squeak of a shrew. It fills the hollows of the woods. Her tail is lifted, her wings hunting. The male sits on a twig, singing. Still singing, he rises and drops hummingbird-lightly and hovers over the female, lowering himself slowly, carrying himself on unseen wings and mating her, so swiftly and so gently that it might not have happened. He flies back to his perch, singing a greater song. The little gray female ceases her poignant calling and pecks about for makebelieve food as if she has no knowledge at all of what has been done.

In Room without a Door this experience is reported in a letter Stephen writes to his friend, Paula, in the States:

I watched two little birds the other day, I think they were migrant warblers of some kind. The female was on the ground, her tail lifted and uttering a plaintive single luring cry with constantly fluttering wings. The male was up in a yew bush singing his heart out. Still singing, he dropped down to the female. She never moved, keeping up the cry and wing-fluttering. The male was very excited, keeping up his song and flying around her. Then, in the middle of the singing and without ceasing he gently lowered himself unto his wife, supporting himself with winging, and mated her in a flash. And if he sung before, he anthemed after it and the little grey slut of a wife became quite matter-of-fact and pecked around on the ground for make-believe food as if her mate had never accomplished this unearthly song-filled union. I felt guilty watching it with cruel eyes. And that's probably damned near the ideal only I can't sing (3A, 479).

West also uses it in A Son for Éiru:

One day he watched two little birds, two very small grey-green migrants. He did not know their names. The female was on the ground below a bush, her tail lifted and uttering a plaintive single luring cry that was full of a delicate piercing pain, her wings constantly fluttering. The male was up in the bush, singing his heart out. Still singing, he dropped down as though on a piece of elastic and hovered over the excited female.

She quickened her cry against the male's singing and without breaking his song, he lowered himself gently unto her and wifed her, supporting himself with winging. And if he had sung before, he anthemed afterwards. But the little grey wife stopped calling and became matter-of-fact, pecking about for makebelieve food as if she had never shared in the unearthly song-filled union. Watching all this, he was ashamed. It seemed a ritual fit only to be observed by spring..........(72–73)

Biographical dating of this experience is likely unimportant: whether West uses it in 1922, 1936, or 1962, he makes appropriate changes in date and place, adapting the incident to each narrator's developing sensitivities. The first telling reflects the wonder of a pubescent boy in the spring of the Cavan lakes, the second the experience of a twenty-six-year-old in the spring near the Curragh. The innocence of the first boy stands in dramatic contrast to the edgy, female-demeaning, grudging sexual frustration of the second. Young Adam of *Rebel* does not identify the kind of bird, though he is aware that it is not common. The woods are new and magical. Sound and motion entrance him. The birds' innocence matches his own. Eden is still undisturbed.

In the second account, however, while the reader is clearly invited to see the same birds, now identified as warblers, West has employed them to show the jeopardy for this young adult mind. Stephen is reporting this mating to a friend whom he has considered marrying. He has confided the possibility of this marriage to another friend most casually, telling him not to share the thought with Paula because she might burn her boats and begin to count on him! By this time the reader has watched enough of Stephen's amours to become quite annoyed at his heart-battering insensitivity. "Little grey slut of a wife"? "Damned near" the marital *ideal*? West makes Stephen's attitude deny his stated insistence on equality of male and female souls. The young man's fine philosophical talk is not matching his self-indulgent emotions. He has much to learn.

The third use of the birds emphasizes the adult protagonist's disenchantment. The "delicate piercing pain" and subsequent matter-of-factness and separation of the female contrast to the male's intense effort, his "singing his heart out," and the human watcher is so acutely reminded of his own malaise as to be ashamed to be implicated. The third viewer of the birds, pained by his own experience, can hardly watch at all.

Several versions and parts of Room without a Door exist, and a comparison here also helps to illustrate this relationship between author and protagonist. West employs a third-person, limited omniscience that accounts for some of that what-will-be-will-be optimism about the future that Stephen Muir enjoys. It provides a counterpoint to the simultaneous and earnest questing. The reader knows no more than Stephen how his life will turn out. The second version imagines another possible end for the pilgrim and the ur-text (West poses numerous others; the death by auto-accident was an early example). It posits Stephen's death through war, his manuscripts and diaries now having been collected and edited by the unnamed narrator of the introduction. Making the reader emphatically aware how the author separates himself from his protagonist, "Narcissus unto Echo" gives the death event in a hospital room, Stephen apparently among other veterans (the published short story makes only the most oblique hints about the circumstances). Christopher MacMannan's death in a plane crash offers in *As Towns with Fire* another fate for this picaresque questor. Any one of these fates was a potential for West himself, a navigator in a marking Mozzie with the Pathfinders of the Royal Air Force.

These imaginings also permit West to underscore the fictional and autobiographical distinctions being observed. To the skip-reader, to the impatient critic, as to the outsider, Lucinda Sault's initial assessment of MacMannan is attractive because it seems so succinct, and it suggests traits of West, himself, but it is beguiling to take as West's last word about either:

> Your highly developed maleness is your worst stumbling block . . .
> Together with your artistic sensibility and your contradictory child-
> likeness — everything utterly complicated by your idealism and Celtic
> intuitions, together with your stubborn christianity and religious patrio-
> tism — my God, but you are a difficult person (*As Towns with Fire*,
> Blackstaff, 323).

Her own vanity affronted, Lucinda becomes dismissive and eventually vindictive toward Christopher.

Readers can become more generous when seeing similar complexity in the writer's direct records of the same idealism, of Celtic intuitions, and of Christian sympathies. Meanwhile, it is instructive to see the differences between Christopher and Conor of A Son for Éiru, responsible father and innovative farmer of Irish land who Conor is. While tension may well have been keen at the time between West and his wife, Olive, Vuya's easy financial status and her happiness with domestic conventions can never have described Olive Burr West or the Wests' progeny and circumstances. The Wests had four sons besides the seven daughters, and a productive, biodynamic farm remained pie in an ever-lowering sky. None of West's children wanted his farm in the sense of following his writing life, but in making these deviations echo his real situation, West suggests through Conor the farmer, the questing writer. The artist's imaginative interest in a problem is, of course, likely to be ultimately more important than his experience of it.

Yet it is instructive to ask in what ways and at how much variance with the biographical detail is this particular image of Narcissus? One cannot be certain when West wrote A Son for Éiru. Its discontents are those of physically comfortable, economically successful middle age. At fifty-five (1965) West was facing some of the hardest of writing and domestic times, and he never did experience material luxury in his seventy-eight years. He never earned enough after the war to pay income tax, nor did he ever see sustained royalties or taxable income from his writing.[29] His pleasure in remembering the time he made enough money to offer small loans to a couple of his grown children underscored how accustomed he was to having nothing extra.[30] He appears to have kept no conventional journal or diary, although he is often autobiographical in letters. There are a few filed pages of direct talk about his life, some of them the solicited blurbs for publishers, but responding to these requests made him so uncomfortable, he said, that he sometimes asked Olive to write them for him. Formal autobiographical statements seemed self-indulgent. What records were important, on the other hand—spiritual investment of his talent, development of his writing skills, the storing

of impressions and experience, and the pursuit of ideas—were all available to him through this autobiographically inspired and continuous ur
fiction.

In Room without a Door West also has Stephen writing a play—The
Apple Tree, whose three-hundred-seventy-five unpublished pages sit in
West's own files. (West later re-titled this play The Mowin' Man, although
he never published it.) Was West writing Apple when he was trapping
eels in Irish lakes during the late thirties before he went to London? Or
before that, when he roamed North America and wrote two early novels
(lost?) that publishers returned? From the address on the typescript of
the play, it is apparent that he was working on it at Albrighton, where
he lived between 1947 and 1950, but perhaps he was renewing an effort
begun before the war. It seems not to include the prison-situation of The
Window—the play (lost?) that was headed for production, but canceled
when London was bombed. Maybe he was drafting The Apple Tree
during the months of hiking and biking around Ireland after his years
in North America, continuing both Apple and Room later, in the fifties,
as suggested by the dated one (1955) of two versions of Room's chapter
one. As immaturity in technique often corresponds to the pica imprint
of his early typewriter and the state of the paper, there is encouragement
to date A Son for Éiru fifteen years later, in 1970.

While his readers may never be absolute about all the dates and
versions, they are afforded plausible suppositions about the life and
development of West's artistry. To stay West meant the development
of a style that can be partly described by the overused term, "Romantic
Realism," though he achieved it well before twentieth-century critics
began to exploit the words. Detailing scrupulously the people, language,
practices, and landscapes he observes, this Grail-seeker is at the same
time passionately expressive about beauty. He is nostalgic without being
sentimental: he looks at an ancient past where he thinks spiritual understanding for humans was more accessible.[31] He articulates for humanity
an evolutionary potential that gives him hope for the future. This simultaneous handling of the transcendent with the gritty realism shows in this
episode from As Towns with Fire:

The bombers began their bombing. MacMannan could see the sticks falling away and plunging down, the island seeming to shake like a jelly, the impacts rippling the sea. Someone grossly overshot and dropped a bomb in a little harbour on the mainland, momentarily emptying the water out of it in a great circular wave. The next time round MacMannan saw several small boats sitting on the tops of the houses, the harbour-water still boiling. When the bombing finished Gillespie flew low over the island, now jubilant and relaxed. The surface was honeycombed with a mass of craters without a sign of life.

No one might have been killed. MacMannan knew that these islands usually had steep cliffs rising sheer from the sea and in all probability the Germans had tunnelled out deep shelters and ammunition cellars in the rocks. Apart from Gillespie's face-saving choler it had all been detached and toy-like, a lilliputian happening in silence on the immemorial edge of the great Atlantic, where history had fought fleets, deciding evolution for thousands of years: the big bombers floating in the air like a shoal of fish in a lazy sea, a kind of illusion, a pageant—one small scene from a vast epic . . . (Blackstaff, 399–400).

The importance and lure of critical inquiry into his output accepted, West poses both familiar and unconventional challenges for the literary biographer. Why did he employ more than twenty pseudonyms? Why has he seemed so elusive, maybe evasive? Why are the existing biographical releases often inaccurate and vague? Who would believe that a writer so generously lent his last copies, even to strangers, that there were times when he could not have produced a single copy of his published novels in his own house? Why would he spend years producing a 1500-page novel, send off the typescript, uninsured, to a potential publisher, and never retain a copy? Why, after losing such a manuscript, would he do the same thing again? Why did he send such mixed signals in his presentation of women, his characterizations of them often arguably demeaning, although he would defend gender equality? Such questions naturally emerge, and with patient exploration here and on his terms, so do many of the answers.

Had he no achievement as a writer, West would still arrest attention for unusual features of his life, which was never easy, even when it appeared quiet and reclusive. He was born a late and last child in an unhappy household, where he had been conceived by an invalid mother who by the time of his conception could not walk. She had been a governess; his father was valet and butler to a linen lord in County Down. Seeing life among both peasants and gentry, he also saw more than one side of Ireland's religious and political divisions. Here, West says, he lived among intolerant Orangemen, rigid Calvinists and revivalist Quakers.[32] When that linen lord, Wakefield Richardson, fatally threw himself onto the iron palings from the window of his London hotel, George West again took a butler's post—for the Maxwells of Farnham House in Cavan, giving his young son the company of Catholic schoolmates for his second decade—for his late childhood and early adolescence. Experience with sadistic authority in the classroom nearly cost the child his sanity. At fourteen, furious with the teacher he later vilified as Master Rainey in *The Ferret Fancier*, he walked out of the school, assuring his mother he would read on his own. He did. Eventually he took a job in a Cavan law office.

At nineteen he emigrated to New York, but not for money—looking for Whitman's ghost, he said.[33] He bummed and thumbed his way across the United States and Canada at the nadir of the Great Depression. Returning to Ireland after six years, he found an atmosphere oppressive to a young writer. At first he gave managerial retail in Cavan a try. Then he tramped and cycled the length and breadth of his island. He spent a summer writing in Sark; finally he emigrated again, to London.

War erupted. In London during the Blitz, he worked with an ambulance crew. He married an English girl, Olive Burr, and they returned briefly to Ireland and to Belfast. To stop Nazis as well as to support an increasing family, he joined the Royal Air Force. Training in South Africa, he became a navigator in a Mosquito, marking for raids that included Dresden, Hamburg, and Oslo. He was a long time struggling to write the war experience under control (*As Towns with Fire* appeared in 1968), though a Rockefeller Award in 1946 had been an encouragement to the artist immediately after he was commissioned and demobilized. Supported by his farm and laboring skills and Olive's cafes and shops and secretarial jobs, the Wests reared their eleven children, most of the time in Wales. The odd sale of a story—especially the six to *Esquire* in the middle of the century—and bursary grants from the English and Northern Irish Arts Councils helped in some of the many lean years to sustain his writing. He was made a member of the Irish academy, Aosdana, in 1981.

In July 1982 the Wests moved to London to be near to some of their offspring. After forty years with at least one child in the house, now all of them were adult and nearly independent. A slight stroke and, in 1984, a fractured left femur confined West to their flat in the Oakfield Road in Penge. Although his mind was not impaired, and he continued to write, his movement was drastically slowed. He died of heart failure on 19 November 1988.

Among his natural gifts, West possessed not only an extraordinary memory; he also held certain extra-sensory faculties. An intensely spiritual, life-long quest for skill at what he calls "in-seeing" was joined to his recall, enabling him to mine his childhood and adolescent experience in unusual ways. Keenly aware of these advantages along with spiritual obligations, he felt nevertheless that his artistry was slow to mature. He admitted that the lack of formal education handicapped him in the marketplace and cost him developmental time; yet he recognized that part of his originality lay in his chosen separation from schools and coteries.

He tried to let criticism help him; in fact, he sought it, but he never let it dissuade his effort. As much as he appreciated the hospitality of arts organizations that honored him on several occasions, he had no taste for "schmoozing." Through corresponding he could have company on his own terms, have only as much of it as he chose to embrace. This strategy gave him less distraction from study and writing. "I'm isolated here, by choice, and have no contact with anyone in the literary dogfight," he explained to a publisher.[34] Isolation, however, had its price. It is true there were visits from friends like Christian Community priest and friend Ormond Edwards; Olive's London-based school chum, journalist Gerda Massey and her husband Rex; local school teacher and poet Peter Grwffyd[35] and his wife, Beryl, whose informed essay about *As Towns with Fire* rests among West's papers[36]; or New Yorker Jacob Bush, expatriated writer in Wales. Representatives from various publishing houses who had corresponded sometimes looked him up. His day-to-day contacts were not literary, however, and he preferred it that way. He was happy not to be widely identified as a writer among his rural neighbors, pseudonyms protecting him, yet naturally enough he needed collegial, intellectual exchange. Editorials or other articles in the papers or journals he read[37] were likely to prompt a written response. He clipped columns and made comments in margins, and he wrote to other authors and editors. Sometimes letters became his way of jump-starting the fiction-writing. As he explained to novelist-producer Maurice Leitch,

> *If any time you're stuck, try writing a letter about what you want to write,*
> *to a close friend. Sometimes that works, sets the mill grinding. Sleep well*
> *and don't talk or discuss anything for an hour after you wake, don't get*
> *sidetracked. Talk's wasteful, cheap, horribly expendable.*[38]

West's letters, like his fiction, bear a remarkable blend of the Elizabethan poetic and his contemporary country-raw. "Our hills are hugely white unto winter" can comfortably follow "Mulligan's crusty sow." The voice is distinctively artistic, whether the subject be typescript or bank account, whether he is revitalizing a cliché about the weather or lamenting the state of Ireland. In his correspondence, he tosses out phrase after startling image that most writers would have hoarded for a greater occasion or would at least have used again, but West, while he might return to the same vein, regularly finds new gold. One is reminded of young John Ruskin recognizing his own similar ability to run on like a ball with no friction to stop him. The letters show that when he has the facts, West cites them; when he has only a considered position, he is clear about that condition. He can be strong, deferential, or tentative. He is never Narcissus the blind egotist. As he notes in this example, the challenge to another author was rare; the texture here, however, is characteristic West:

Messrs Chatto & Windus.

Dear Sirs:

I was looking at Pierre Clostermann's 'Flames in the Sky' which one of the children brought home.

On page 155, last paragraph, there is mentioned the destruction of the Gestapo HQ, Oslo.

Now, I happened to be in the second Mozzie on that raid. As far as I know, the HQ was not destroyed. A streetcar full of Norwegians was destroyed. The raid, as a raid, was a fiasco, from beginning to end. The then wing commander of 627 Squadron, PFF, was gong-greedy; he had a couple of previous VC's to emulate. I believe he was killed after the war, slow-rolling a Mosquito on the deck. Nevertheless, from Clostermann's point of view, regarding the durability of the Mosquito, the raid again proved the aircraft's excellence. Every aircraft with the exception of W Willie, the one I was in, came back to Peterhead holed, and one, under Flight Lieutenant Mallender, had a gaping hole in the starboard leading edge and landed safely at 175 knots on a shortish runway. There were only two 2000-lb HE bombs dropped, the CO's and W Willie's. The raid was on the 31ˢᵗ December 1944. All the Gestapo were out of the building and hitting up New Year's Eve. FW190's could have easily jumped us, but refrained, for some reason. A little later, a coastal strike of Mosquitoes was jumped by FW 190's and practically wiped out.

At the same time, myself a writer, I feel that Clostermann treads queachy ground in this retracing of war heroics; one has to be very careful about mere militaristic chauvinism. I've never yet been able to use my war experiences, unsure of my ultimate aim.

As a PS: I don't normally attempt to correct other writers.

Yours very truly,
Anthony C. West
ex F/O and Navigator and Air Observer
627 Mosquito PFF Night-Marking Squadron.[39]

He talks on paper at great length with people like his agent or his editor or with associates who share his philosophical interests: sometimes six, single-spaced, A4 pages with very small margins. A typical letter, however, offers six to ten inches of lively and idiosyncratic prose in massive, single-spaced paragraphs, or like the one above, several short paragraphs flanking one large block addressing the chief topic. Often there appears some self-deprecating comment, which in West is not false modesty. Sometimes this candor must have worked against him; in failing to emphasize the positive, he certainly defies the contemporary counsel on the resumé. Here is an Eeyore-excerpt from his response to the compilers of *Contemporary Fiction in America and England: 1950–1970*:[40]

> *I'm not of much help, I'm afraid. There may have been comments on my work, apart from review mentions in the US and here. . . .*
>
> *I'm working now on an Irish novel, having received a grant from the Northern Ireland Arts Council.*
>
> *I've lost three years working on a huge 'play-novel' which, according to several professional opinions, is a failure.*

The letters are never vain. He does not indulge in talk flattering to himself, inclining on the subject of his successes to be brief. He too readily apologizes for gaps created by his self-education, and yet, because he recognizes that this very isolation from schools and coteries accounts for part of his artistic distinction, he also defends it. When a school official wrote to the Wests about a possible Harrow Scholarship for son Jeremy, West responded with an appreciative letter that shows this ambivalence. The additional cost he envisions makes the whole thing doubtful in the first place, but West goes on to rationalize it:

> *On the other hand, if a boy is prepared to work, he can get as far from the [local school] as he can from Harrow. By and large, there is no great difference in instruction value. As you will know, we, ourselves, put little or no weight on the snob-values concerned. . . .*
>
> *However, if you like, sir, see what the position promises to be. If in the next twelve months we came up, the picture might be different. I*

have a book [The Native Moment] *coming out this spring—never know!
altho', god knows, it's not very Harrovian in its general approach to life.*[41]

He sometimes did entertain second thoughts about his career-long
writing strategy, but without complaining or recanting. Like others of
his literary countrymen—Shaw, Yeats, and O'Casey, for examples—
West held a formally structured view of individual and social progress
that informs his writing. He studied humankind's development in its
ecologic-economical, civic-legal, and spiritual-cultural aspects[42] and
perceived special continuities between the past and the future. He did
not retract earlier claims, but he re-evaluated choices from another perspective, one that these years of study had given him, when he said he
sometimes wished he had published just one book.[43]

Writing one book, however, is in effect what he did. Faithful to an
all-encompassing spiritual objective, his experimentation with form
not interrupting his study of this cosmic system or the development of
his artistry through this ur narrative, he steadily transposed to narrative
all the stages of his experience—physical and cerebral. In the last one,
whose title recalls the Greco-Roman goddess of the hunt, Artemis /
Diana, who punished the voyeur Actaeon by turning him into a stag
then brought down by his own hounds, West takes on his greatest artistic
challenges. Concluding, as the title suggests, with a violent cost, The
Lady Actaeon is the most important work to derive from the ur. Here
West probes both the upper and lower strata of Ireland's population, from
the well-off and highly educated O'Dea Russel and aristocratic English
poet Diana Hauley to their antitheses, dispossessed Denis Dempsey the
tinker and his wife Delia. West makes the interior monologue as well as
dialogue carry the heavy freight of questing analytic and poetic minds.
He addresses the history and politics of Ireland. And he does what he
has done with no other section of the ur narrative: he creates a female,
feminist narrator.

Does the title also carry ironic reference to himself as an invader?
Does it offer the ironic implication of Diana's destructive force against
the author's own prejudices? West had said early in his career that he
couldn't write about women,[44] nor in the published sections of the ur

does he try. Yet all the time in Actaeon he was experimenting with a female sensibility; here the artist was freeing his anima. Though he may in a moment of writerly frustration or in a tone of macho-fraternity to editor or agent refer to Diana Hauley as witch or bitch,[45] he comes to reject that term for her, as over the decades he develops her into a subtle and sympathetic woman.[46] Such metaphoric references to his manuscript would suggest the tale's power to hold him against rationality and will. Neither the prophet nor the artist has the luxury of retiring the quest. West, like Coleridge's Mariner, felt divinely compelled, and he accepted that if he grew ancient in the reiteration of his tale, such was his karma.

As indicated, autobiographical aspects of West's ur tale include the geophysical and intellectual, the emotional and psychic, and the artistic. The aspiring writer at work has already been shown in Room's Stephen Muir. An unpublished 700-page extraction called Wall lies between Stephen and the appearance of O'Dea Russel of Actaeon. (By the typeface and by the address, 22 Park Road, on the cover sheet it dates from West's Air Raid Patrol days in London before he was married.) Although she appears in another early story, Lady Diana is not yet a figure in Wall, but her husband O'Dea is featured at a much less intellectualized stage of the Everypoet's artistic evolution. Wall opens in the life of O'Dea's poet-mother, who in all the subsequent treatments of Actaeon is only an important memory. Caitlín O'Mara settles in Dublin for love of her adoring husband and his business, but her heart remains in her native Kerry, where she descended from Mithraic worshipers of the sun-god. Her small son accompanies her in daily walks on the sea wall. When the weather permits they swim. One day she leaves him sitting on the rocks with her clothes and her ring when she dives into the water and never surfaces.

The novel follows O'Dea's growing up among a retinue of servants and governesses, some of them reliable, some of them rascals. The child weathers them all with the disincarnate help of his mother, whose spirit is visible to him. Eventually his father marries again—an entirely worthy Jane Eyre among the staff—and O'Dea, to his delight, is transplanted to her farm home in Corran. Anthony C. West was literally no orphan, however alienated he may have become from his parents, but in this

fictionalized Corran farm and rural village the reader recognizes the
deliberately mixed autobiographical material from Moyallon in County
Down and Farnham in Cavan, which West later drew on for *Moment*,
Rebel, *Ferret*, *Towns*, and several published short stories.

O'Dea's artistic proclivity matures, and the story grows out of his
development—here as a painter. By the time he emerges in Actaeon and
Diana has joined the novel, O'Dea has shed his rural and artistic identities. The artistic-creative abilities eventually become Diana's poetic ones.
Corran is dropped. O'Dea takes on the soul's development at stages
beyond the childhood of *Ferret*, the late adolescence of *Moment*, or
the young adulthood of *Towns*.[47] The soul-progress for O'Dea becomes
increasingly abstract—religious, historical, sociological, and theological,
as West's autobiography may be charted in it. Each time West resumes
the challenge of Actaeon, the story demands a fabrication of events that
will accommodate the full soaring of his poetic spirit and the equally full
employment of his spiritual studies. Artistically and philosophically, it
treats not a final, but an ever-evolving, yet markedly adult stage.

O'Dea of Actaeon unsentimentally (and insensitively) recalls to his
bride this mother who was early reclaimed by the sea (O'Mara, after
all, was her name), and he also tells Diana about the servants who initiated him to sexual awareness. In this novel the redeeming governess has
disappeared; O'Dea's father has withdrawn in grief and died. No significant imagery of the Corran farm life or of the painter remains. O'Dea
becomes an unconventional Church of Ireland clergyman, pleased to
be in an isolated Irish parish. Apart from his appreciation of art's sanctity,
O'Dea's applied role as artist has been transferred to Diana.

Diana's evolution is exceptionally intriguing. From the selfish original of early versions she grows into a responsible and sympathetic character. Diana and O'Dea meet and marry at nearly forty. He has refused
to settle for a comfortable government appointment after receiving a
medal for heroism as a prisoner of war; instead, he follows a spiritual
leading to a rectory in West Meath. O'Dea has met Diana among dinner
guests assembled in a London socialite's home to honor him. An early
Diana story, The Garden Party, sketches the occasion: celebrated for her
poetry, acceptable by her social position, but too old—her hostess naively

thinks—for the marriage competition, Diana Hauley appears to be the
ideal foil to show off that hostess's own husband-hunting daughter. Of
course her strategies prove superbly futile.

Thus the English aristocrat finds herself married to a rural Irish
parish. Although there are colorful local characters and plausible effects
of such a union one can readily picture and appreciate, significant
interest lies in the emergence of West's female narrator. Diana's mind
becomes ironic and supple. She does not know her husband well, of
course, and in the less successful and very short versions of the tale—
early and late—she never does learn much about him, the shared relationship ending on the honeymoon in Kerry with his accidental death.
In most versions Diana has conceived on that honeymoon, and in a
number the Russels' child survives to become a participant in the telling
of the story. Sometimes this child is male. Several versions include an
explanatory postscript, extending the fiction about the narrator; others
lead the reader to an appropriate conclusion by an authorial pseudonym.
Although in all the short versions (usually titled Memento Mori), as in
some of the longer ones, O'Dea Russel (Rex in the early drafts) is the
one killed in an accident, in most among the long versions, the death
is Diana's.

In the growth of the long novel, Diana's characterization evolves.
From the earliest to latest versions, Diana is the professionally successful woman who had thought herself forever happily independent
of family, sex, church, and debilitating national prejudice, yet gradually
she must confront the prejudices she has denied. She finds her new life
in rural Ireland stifling to her artistic, cerebrating, feminist identity, and
she feigns no acceptance of the traditional role of a rector's wife. Her
awakened sexuality, her admiration for her husband, her adjustments
to parish people and their ways, as well as her spiritual and intellectual
discontents are all filtered through her highly poetic imagination. She
becomes—perhaps with some initial technical credit to Molly Bloom,
to whom she refers—steadily more intriguing. Pregnancy—unwanted
but not carefully prevented—eventually seems to derange her. Diana
wanders off into the fields like a Joycean Ophelia, where in her labor she
is raped and her baby is perilously delivered at a tinker-midwife's fire. In

its most successful versions, the story emerges through a combination of Diana's diary and her child's grown-up reconstruction of Diana's last twelve hours when she was without it.

Both Diana and O'Dea are mouthpieces for ideas—there's no getting around this feature in West, any more than in the plays of Shaw.

> I tried to portray the clash (soul-body, man-woman, old-new, feudalism-modern progressive . . .). What we have yet as living 'allowance' is no more than a crudely transformed feudalism and that includes all forms of Marxism. It will probably take us another two thousand years to evolve, through reformation and not by mere transposition, to a truly human attitude.[48]

As the characterizations develop, however, especially as Diana through internal monologue becomes the chief teller of the story, the work's narrative subtlety grows.

Parts of more than twenty drafts of Actaeon exist—short stories to novels, typescripts of twenty to fifteen-hundred pages. Its titles also vary, including The Stone and the Ring, Ring Around Stone, The Stone in the Ring, Naked to Laughter, and of course, The Lady Actaeon and Memento Mori. West tries different narrators, different structural modes, different resolutions to the plot. Actaeon gives him a place to examine and present unpopular ideas, like the equality of men and women, their equally deserving artistry, and their equal intellects; like women's sexual needs; like sympathetic lesbian love, or like a reciprocally respectful relationship between England and Ireland.

Diana's thought becomes increasingly intricate, funnier, more poetic, more free, more likable. The reader sees West coping in explicit, self-conscious ways with her feminism. Here, for example, in what is probably an early version (E), Diana challenges O'Dea, who is speaking generically of artists:

> . . .The valid artist has never been so rich in raw material as now, he has never had so many extraneities to overcome, against the dearth of public discernment.

He....? she queried, with a whimsical smile.

Yes, he, he said. An artist must effect some sort of hermaphroditic equilibrium . . . (E, 709)

By later versions, although discussion of the topic certainly does not disappear, the issues have become more integrated with the characterization of Diana as poet:

I can't live in poetry as Dea lives in his priest, all practical priest, man as priest and priest as man, stirred by his basic faith-cum-knowledge, his mind made up, god in some heaven, Christ as Christ or carpenter his mentor providing endless pentecost of light; acting out this complex, living by it, his life on a different level, higher perhaps or, perhaps, one just more abstract . . . the final truth unsayable, like his nonexplanation of the resurrection, the paradox maintained . . .(R, 389; R disk, 315).

I can understand a little better why I married him while marriage, *per se*, may still bear doubt. I want to be a free wife and it's implied I'm wife and free and yet, must also be a mother. I don't want to play a poetic Donne to his reasoning priest while I must intuit as he must reason and, anyway, Donne's dead and gone and done, his loves and Jacobean prayers as dust.

This pregnancy's like thinking with a hand tied behind my back.

I walk slowly up to the old graveyard, welcoming the quiet dusk with a kind of nervousness as if it were a closure on my life, Monday further than the stars (S, 302).

Women: when will we be free from ignorance, sex-spite and the mime of lust to which our physiology willingly condemns us? Half-creatures, our sexuality our cross. Laws and wedlocks, promises and undertakings, the difference between mistress, wife and whore a spider's gossamer. Ana [their maid-Pygmalion project] returns to bed and I read again the marriage service and fume: a woman could contract to marry a blackguard or a drunkard and, once tied, society commandeers her boats and would watch her sink till drowning (S, 345).

Diana's reflection grows more sardonic, as she predicts her husband's martyrdom at the tongues of this congregation:

> I'll give 'em a year to crack your crook, my dear, to tame you. They'll mob you with synodal whispers, piss wiss hiss, I said he said. They'll gather faggots for your barbecue, ambush you at night with low church orange peels and trip you with potato skins. They don't think, my dear, they instinct ancestrally, their brains comfortably ingrown.
>
> O love that foremost . . . that soupy hymn, Miss Thomas sticking to her romantic favourites. She'll win. They'll all win. They all must win by doing nothing long enough, their water harder than your stone. I know. My facts are facts, albeit bitch-facts but suitable for this manger, their smiles their bites, sans antidote and sans appeal. . . (S, 119–120).

As her delivery date approaches, emotional and mental distress obviously threaten her equilibrium, but the reader can never put her insight aside.

> [Dea] knows old Greece like the back of his Irish hand, how thinking was first made, how intelligence set men free and how it now threatens to enthrall them like children with sharp knives; how the caesarean syndrome poisoned Europe, throttles thought, creates abstract authority, makes herds, spawns bureaucracies, claques, compromises, temporizes, twists and turns, lies, bluffs, fornicates for power and maintains dead attitudes and habits for its own emolument. . .
>
> Hail, Caesar's ghost!
>
> Ill-met at Philippi and Hitler hail, kiss Roman toe, say majesty to transient kings, worship dictators, blow Marxist tunes on Tory bugles, maintain divine demonic rights and privileges . . .
>
> Democracy, your other name is perfidy (S, 399).

It's midnight and the dark is very still, expectant, frost: night's a real thing, more real than day. I open the halldoor and inspect the shivering stars, the coldness draughting past me, shaping my body. Old Taurus paws the skies, hay on his jeweled horns. In a month or so, spring will bury him.

The plough's half-hidden by a northern hill. I find the Pole and set course for bed, nodding the night goodnight, the same for self in all the mirrors, weeing a drop in hope I won't dream. Junior awakes for his nightly dozen. I feel what must be a head for feet are kicking the other end.

All nights are rather similar (S, 411–412).

This hideous heaviness round about me heaped in darksome glades. . . .

Or:

Gorgonius suits abdominous and wan like a fat squab on a Chinese fan. . . .

I half-remember lines and forget the poets. Forgetment worries me a little, willfully or fortuitously, half-remembering everything, the other half this fetal incubus that kicks impatiently to get out and yet won't leave. Talk about sexophrenia—I'm not, this child has taken over—a nameless ageless sexless turbulent lump: pupa and I, puparious. It'll burst me open, then slough me off, a wrinkled coat of skin (S, 412).

Even without West's explanations, or without seeing the length and breadth of the whole corpus, his professional readers could immediately appreciate West's artistic experimentation, his great love for words, and his vocabulary—"one of the most extensive and poetic treasuries of our day . . . brilliant and absolutely right use of stunningly poetic expressions."[49]

Actaeon's deliberate challenge to West's own original sense of narrative impossibility contributes to an organic, Protean quality of this book, which is in other ways, as well, the manifesting of West's personal, ever-evolving intellectual, spiritual, and artistic self. With English Diana and Irish O'Dea, he exchanges the gender-roles of the iconic John Bull and Caitlín ní Houlihan. Mythic prototypes are evoked and fused to help the writer and the reader understand the scope and challenge. The goddess demands the fealty of the Ancient Mariner. Actaeon looked on divinity and perished for it. The writer may fare little better, en route risking distraction by the Narcissistic ego, even if he has, like the Mariner, committed to the quest. Through sections from Actaeon and through other parts of the ur narrative, through published and unpublished work, one hears the personal echo of this provocative and maverick Irish writer. An unorthodox spiritual and aesthetic vision, challenging arrogance, ambition, or vanity recalls this Narcissus when he confronts his image in the water; the vision commands and defines his staying West.

ENDNOTES

1   The earliest published piece of writing by ACW appears to have been an essay on Bishop William Bedell of Kilmore and Ardagh, 1629–1642, in *Ardagh and Elphin Gazette* of Kilmore parish: "The Personality of Bedell" by Anthony West, fragment with inscribed date: September 1935, courtesy of West's niece, Muriel Woolsey Darling, November 1992.

2   "The Scythe," *Ireland Today*, II, 5 (May 1937), 43–47.

3   These include John and Tom Whitfield, Trefwr, John Mongan Russel, Mary Mongan Russel, Brigid Russel, Adam McAdam, Michael Maturin, Anthony Morris, and John Dreame.

4   ACW to Bruce Colen, 2 June 1956, *Esquire*.

5   Arnold Gingrich to ACW, 30 July 1956, *Esquire*.

6   Anthony West offers this information as an aside in his third paragraph.

7   AG to ACW, 7 June 1956, *Esquire*.

8   AG to ACW, 10 July 1956. Gingrich had wisely suggested in his letter of the ninth the name change from "River Rendezvous."

9   He refers to another letter from Gingrich of the 12th, one missing from the collection, which (further?) explained Gingrich's "point of view." Is this a mistake in citing dates? Perhaps Gingrich's letter of 7 July arrived on the 12th?

10   ACW to AG, 16 July 1956, *Esquire*.

11   AG to ACW, 30 July 1956, *Esquire*.

12   ACW to JC, 31 December 1956.

13   Jacque Chambrun to ACW, 3 January 1957.

14   ACW to AG, 7 January 1957.

15   West likely had read none of Anthony West's work and was but dimly aware of his existence.

16   ACW to William Bittner, nd [November 1970?]. See also ACW to Charles Davy, c.15 May 1961.

17   John Berthelsen, "An Irish West Rises As Novelist" Sacramento, 19 April 1970.

18   George O'Brien, *The Irish Novel, 1960–2010* (Cork University Press, 2012), 28–30.

19   "The Self As History" Alfred Kazin, 78–79, in *Telling Lives: The Biographer's Art*, ed. Marc Pachter, University of Pennsylvania Press, 1981.

20   West said that before he began writing, he made notes for himself and did his research. Then he closed them to write, looking back only to confirm pertinent facts (ACW to AE, 31 January 1987). His notes may be numbered, unconnected paragraphs or factoids, hundreds of them, or they may take form as an essay. From such prose statements, he more clearly understood and controlled the effects upon characters and plots. Such notes follow the heading "Erosion— Short Story—by Anthony C. West—Notes for a Short Novel on a Katabolic Theme—Half-conscious Origins (Blind Roots and Mycorrizal Associations)." No text accompanies Erosion; it may appear under another title.

21   Agent John Schaffner takes West to task about jargon or obsolete terms that suddenly violate his transcendent prose, JS to ACW, 27 January 1958. West responds, "I suppose I can't use words which have endured changed associations, but I do feel and see them, sometimes, in their pristine meaning or half-meaning" (ACW to JS, 4 February 1958).

22   Simon of *The Ferret Fancier*, 1963, and Christopher of *As Towns with Fire*, 1968.

23   Audrey S. Eyler, "The Old Made New Again: Imagery in Two Stories by Anthony C. West," *Eire-Ireland*, Fall 1985, 52–64.

24   ACW, "The After Vacancy," *Vogue* (London), December, 1969, 63–79.

25   Only a small part of this novel appeared in *The Honest Ulsterman*, number 57, 1977, page 69, anticipating publication that never occurred.

26   Fairleigh Dickinson University Press, 1993. At that time, not yet having examined all of the nearly 35,000 pages West left, I was unaware of the scope of this ur narrative.

27   There are, it is true, a few (as far as I know, unpublished) stories in the file that seem to have no demonstrable connection, topical or chronological, to this autobiographical ur, pieces that seem not to be embroidered or reconstructed parts of his experience. These may represent a brief commercial effort at television script. He knew he was less successful at such fabrication, his soul not being in it. The four published novels, the *River's End* stories, and most of the unpublished fictions make the heavy use of autobiography here described; thousands of other, unpublished pages image even more comprehensively the Narcissus figure in the pool.

28   Though he was naturally grateful for the sale, he was also dismayed when Ivan Obolensky of Obolensky and McDowell, Inc. did some editing and rushed *The Native Moment* and *Rebel to Judgment* to print. He had sent them along with

other typescripts, including Actaeon, apparently with the expectation of getting critical help, and having been told they needed revision, was waiting for their return, ACW to John Schaffner, [June] 1959 and 23 May 1959.

29   ACW to Mgr. Depart. of Health & Social Security, Saint Andrews' House, Bury Saint Edmunds, Suffolk. 19 March 1977.

30   ACW to Mr. Hughes, Midland Bank Manager, 10 March 1971.

31   Irish scholars often remark the ancient proximity of the sacred and secular. For a recent example, see Colm Lennon, *Sixteenth Century Ireland: The Incomplete Conquest.* Gill and Macmillan, 1994, p. 133; cited by Kevin Williams, *The Irish Literary Supplement*, Spring 1995, p. 13). West takes this idea very seriously.

32   ACW, "Questionaire [sic] on Anthony C West,"nd, Letters A–C and Interviews.

33   ACW, questionnaire from Rhiwlas, 1. See Letters A–C and Interviews.

34   ACW to A. F. Rosa and A. Escholz, University of Vermont, 30 November 1972, for *Contemporary Fiction in America and England: 1950–1970.* See Letters A–C, Biographical.

35   Peter and West collaborated on a story that was never published: "The Sequestered." West similarly and separately collaborated on stories with friends Trevor Ravenscroft and Fasil Haeri.

36   Beatrice Bracken, "Man in Armour." See Reviews and Notices to *ATWF* in box 19.

37   Besides Anthroposophical and Christian Community journals, West subscribed to *The Manchester Guardian.* He frequently marked, annotated, or clipped pieces that interested him. Agents and publishers and friends appear to have sent him the reviews of his own work; I have found no record of research on his part to obtain them.

38   ACW to Maurice Leitch, 8 December 1965, BBC.

39   ACW to Chatto & Windus, 20 April 1964.

40   30 November 1972, ACW interviews.

41   ACW to Mr. Anthony, 7 February 61, Children's education.

42   This three-fold plan was anthroposophical.

43   ACW in taped interview by ASE, June 1986. Here he says he never fulfilled his potential.

44   West talks at length in letters to his American friend, Dorothy O'Connor, about Diana's characterization.

45   ACW to JS, 25 August 1962.

46   ACW to Dorothy O'Connor, c. 22 July 1958.

47   See *Celtic Christian Socialist* for an exploration of these stages as West understood them.

48   ACW to John Schaffner, 28 November 1958,

49   John Schaffner to ACW, 1959.

CHAPTER 2

1910 MOYALLON: THE BIRTH BRIDGE

ALTHOUGH THE CLERK erroneously reported it as the first of August, and West himself sometimes forgot the date,[1] Cathcart Anthony Muir West was born July 1, 1910, to Ellen Clements West, a former governess, and George West, steward and valet to Wakefield Richardson of Moyallon House, near Gilford, on the edge of County Down. The baby was named for three sisters—Catherine, Anne, and Muriel—of the big house family, which, like others of the area, made its fortune in linen and, before the American Civil War, cotton.[2] Catherine, Anne, and especially Muriel indicated an intention to sponsor this fifth and late child[3] of the butler, born some years after his mother had been confined to a wheel chair with a paralysis, which had been slowly developing since the hard and forced birth of her first infant. They decided, however, to give only one pound to the child every Christmas until he was twenty-one, and even that plan was shortly interrupted.[4] Wakefield's sudden death put an end to all possibilities; from the sisters the boy carried no further endowment than his name. Yet from the Richardson estate he took an inheritance of memories and mined them, particularly for *Rebel to Judgment,* as well as for aspects of the childhoods described in *The Ferret Fancier*, in *As Towns with Fire*, and in sections of the unpublished ur narrative from which we can now see his published fictions have been cut and shaped.

> *I was born on the very border between Down and Armagh, in Moyallon, near Gilford, in a wee thatched cottage[5] at the end of a short loanen, and Harvey's river ran past the bottom of the garden, and I could stradleg the stream, one foot in Down and the other in Armagh; and the bridge is still there on which my mother said I had been found by my father, a legend I've never been able to disbelieve and one which has had a powerful emancipating effect on me all my life: a kind of arrogant, aristocratic hope when the going was hard. . . .*
>
> *The river ran on sweetly, under a pine wood and through several pleasant fields, joining the noble Bann. I often dream of watching fish there to this day, waking with a mixture of sadness and relief. The Bann was lovely there, trees hanging over it, shallowed by summers, trout hovering, and in winter a powerful fat black force racing to its inland sea that was Lough Neagh.[6]*

To his agent, West recounted the same matter of the bridge, noting that the later move to Cavan was a symbolic bridging, and added

> *I should mention that my mother was an invalid and that I never saw her walking; consequently, I never completely lost my stream.[7]*

The imagery of bridging continued to serve West throughout his writing life, working beside his mythic motifs like the Narcissus. It was particularly useful for addressing his child-consciousness. Early stories from the ur show him bringing together, bridge like, especially the highly contrastive features of his unusual childhood. Such bridging imagery functions also at the center of the very adult Actaeon, with its connecting of genders, nations, social classes, rural and urban sensibilities, head and heart.

This image has both visual and aural effect when West gives the myth of his bridge birth to the protagonist poet in *Rebel to*

George and Ellen (Clements) West with their first four children: l-r Harold, Jack, Eileen, Dorothy. WEST FAMILY COLLECTION, PHOTOGRAPHER UNKNOWN.

Judgment—appropriately heightened. Adam is symbolically framed against the crossroads (read also: "Cross" with roads) of the judging, parliament-community, while the feature of the literal birth-bridge remains autobiographically familiar:

> While the infant poet in me fully accepted her story that I had been found by my father on the wall of the old stone bridge over the Aoine one green and gold July morning, I assiduously attended the bawdy sessions of the crossroads' parliament, overhearing and illhearing the continual debates. . . .And it was a long time before I was willing . . . to accept that the bridge of my birth was a biased myth (*Rebel to Judgment, 14–15*).

West experimented at length with this recollected child's world. It formed a part of The Casual Comedy, a novel MacGibbon & Kee had scheduled for publication in the late seventies but withdrew when Simon and Schuster decided not to share the cost. Let Sorrow Say is an unpublished story from this larger block of the ur, a fragment of fifty-some

"The infant poet in me fully accepted her story that I had been found by my father on the wall of the old stone bridge over the Aoine one green and gold July morning . . ." Rebel to Judgment, 1962, 14. *The bridge over the Bann behind Moyallon (Audrey Eyler with Philip Wilson of the Craigavon project, Portadown).* PHOTO BY JOHN M. EYLER, 1995.

West at four, ". . . always seeming to be preoccupied, making them worry about him. He couldn't explain that he had watched the very grass growing." Let Sorrow Say, *7 (unpublished).*

pages, in which Jonty (Jonathan) the protagonist, a child under seven, perceives the colors, dancing lights, and supernatural beings—little people, as well as larger and shadowy human forms—who, unseen by most adults, animate the world:

> Billie Parr the Press was a tall powerful man with a loud voice, his colours jagged and dark red, his little people surly and unpleasant (15); Blackjack Flannigan was another large man with a bushy black beard. He carried a carving knife and roamed over Ireland looking for the man who had stolen his wife. He made Jonty queasy for there always seemed to be a grey shadow behind him and Blackjack seemed to know it was there for he jerked his head and muttered over his shoulder (16).

> Talking about his growing as families do, they said he had remained a slow and withdrawn child, seemingly quite unaware of his surroundings and always seeming to be preoccupied, making them worry about him. He couldn't explain that he had watched the very grass growing. People began to comment that he was becoming a handsome boy and praised his large grey eyes. His mother frequently warned him that it wasn't good manners to stare at folk so. He said he was only looking at the colours they made [his mother's were "all mixed up"; his father's were "angry"] (7).

> His world [was] new and shining, a rotting piece of wood a kind of precious thing, common stones gleaming like fairymen's gold, the flying birds wearing spears of golden light on their heads, the big bullocks grazing in Pagett's field attired in glowing skins of light, creation an iridescent psalm of joy singing the heavens.
> He didn't talk for a long time, save in his own vernacular, a kind of heart language with sounds that serviced many things with differing intensity. Sometimes his sister Vicky . . . seemed able to interpret what he said. Vicky was closer to him, warmer and more sympathetic than his parents who were vaguely embarrassed by his belated arrival, Saul his father seeing him as another mouth to feed and back to clothe . . . (3).

I needed a so-called accident to provoke Jonty's will to walk. When [he was] almost two, his sister Vicky, seven years older, had taken him for a walk down the Lake Avenue with a friend. The two girls argued as they went over possession of the pram handles and at the edge of Rossmore Lake, above a steep grassy terrace, their difference of opinion became a physical struggle. He remembered being shaken about, the girls' faces like flaming torches as each one tried to prise the other's hands off the handle. They had forgotten to brake the pram and it got away from them, plunging down the terrace and cowping on its side in the lake, Jonty hanging half in the water by the straps. He didn't cry and could remember the translucent coldness of the water on his face and then the hot waves of the girls' anxiety as they waded into the lake to rescue him. Thick as thieves again, they raced him home, smuggling him into the house and changing his wet clothes (3).

Unwittingly, Jonty changed as the quintessential intensity of his natal insights diminished, the material environment moving slowly into human view so that for a time he was confused in himself between the two worlds until, quite suddenly, as a fledgling falls from its protecting nest, like the turning of a glove right side out, he crossed the bridge between creation and the self, Egypt behind and wilderness ahead, reaching the first point of essential human loneliness one autumn afternoon with his sister on the Chestnut Avenue under an ominous autumnal sky, a chill haze hiding the distance as the painted trees shed sadly their pink and golden offerings to the year's end (6).

Having known this strange prescience in the pram, West also says he registered the distinction of his gender at a remarkably early age.

I returned to Moyallon four years ago and recognized the trees I climbed and saw myself as I was then, recognizing the place where I experienced my first sexual orgasm when I was five with a little friend. I was aware of sex when I was two, which may have been a good or bad thing.[8]

The experience surfaces in more than one fictionalized work, including an unpublished story titled Initiation.

At the end of August, the year he [Jonty] was seven, the Lady Penelope told him that she was going away to a private school in Switzerland, Henny, as she called Miss Henderson, going with her. . . . You see, you've only to grow up. I've got to do it properly.

How? he asked.

Oh, lots of ways, silly! . . .

I'll be missing you...he muttered shyly . . .

Well, Penelope was explaining, you're male and I'm female. It's in the bible, too. A cow is female an' a bull male. You can easily see the difference because males have what's called a penis. . . . Henny told me all about it an' how it works. I'll have to have babies when I grow up to make heirs—that is, when I marry somebody.

How do you make hairs? he asked, entirely out of his depth. . . .

She took up a rotten twig and broke it into little bits and there was a long silence. She was wearing a creamy dress with puffy shoulders, dozens of small pink flowers needleworked across the bodice, her feet in brown sandals and creamy socks, her big eyes darkly luminous in the green sunlight, the red-gold hair in two tapering plaits with creamy bows hanging down either side of her face like ropes. Jonty? . . . I—I want you to love me.

He nodded, meaning that he did.

Well will you? she asked.

How? he asked.

I know, she said. I can show you. Henny showed me how. . .

It has to be stiff, she said. Make it stiff.

Whether he did so or not, her magical touch made the cock spigot-stiff in seconds and spread pleasant sensations all over his body . . . He stared down at her, the leaf-muted sunlight gleaming on the web of pale hairs on her legs and thighs, the smooth wax-pale thighs darkening into the sunburned legs, the little pursed mouth at the bottom of her belly like a wound. It goes in here...she instructed. . . .

He hesitated, loath to lie on her and she pulled him down and more

"Linen was king . . . The last 50 years of the 19th century marked its hey-day." ACW to ASE, December 1987. Moyallon: Front gate and entrance. PHOTO BY JOHN M. EYLER, 1988.

George West and his family were among the first occupants of these (new c.1908–1909) houses, built for Moyallon's staff. PHOTO BY JOHN M. EYLER, 1995

by accident than skill the union happened, the physical sensation a soft hot fire, all his five senses seeming to rush into his cock, the sixth one floating above them in a soaring dream, sound rushing past his eardrums, the trees threshing in sudden storm that tossed him high above the valley (Initiation, 1, 6–10).

West's memories of his childhood are rich in details that help to account for the amazing texture of the stories that feature rural life in Corran. Not the least advantage of this experience was his position between the staging arenas for aristocratic and peasant activities.

My father was the butler, a finicky, responsible job. He had to know all about wines, clothes, accoutrements. He had started when he was twelve, as a pantry-boy, working from six in the morning to eleven at night. With this post he got free coal and could eat either at home or in the House.

Saul Darcy had several pantries as they were called, with cupboards and drawers lined with green baize, full of cutlery and silver trays and plates all wearing the Rossmore crest. There was even a set of gleaming golden plates and cutlery in a big safe for special guests which Penelope said were worth thousands of pounds. Saul had another pantry upstairs behind the great diningroom with more bells and cupboards full of shining glassware, next to the gunroom with its baize-lined glass-faced cupboards holding . . . even old blunderbuses and muzzle-loaders which one of the keepers cleaned and oiled every day, no smoking painted in red on the walls and on the outside door. . . . Outside the doors of the kitchen yard was the larder with its hundreds of hooks on wooden racks and a big bin for the feathers, and a butcher's block for killing and cutting up sheep and cattle. For Jonty, this larder was the most unpleasant place on the estate. It scared him, oozing violence and blind fear and filled with twining vegetation and strange fern-like forms like frost-flowers on a windowpane, the chewed blood-stained block like an altar in some obscene temple. Penelope laughed at his reactions, asking why, but he could only say he didn't like the place. (Let Sorrow Say, 29–30).

"On the manor's other side . . . coach-houses and harness rooms, the latter full of shining saddles and sets of silver and brass-mounted harness, all smelling comfortably of leather, all the metal parts glowing, the silver moon-bright and the brass as gold." Let Sorrow Say, 31–32 (unpublished). The coach house behind Moyallon. PHOTO BY JOHN M. EYLER, 1995.

Not only did he straddle the stream with one foot in each county and with eyes on such contrastive spaces as pantry and stable, but the bridge of his birth stationed him to observe two historical eras—of agriculture and of industry—and the separated classes who populated the plantation.[9]

Linen was king . . . The last 50 years of the 19th century marked its hey-day. It had a brief hey-day during the first World War when it was used to cover the fuselage of the then aeroplane. (My time). . . . I remember farms with working looms. . . . Many of the poor augmented their wages by drawing the threads of the fine lawn handkerchiefs which the finishing mills delivered and collected in bundles by the gross—piecework for a pittance. . . . I remember, when driving to Gilford in our pony and trap with my mother, seeing hordes of shawlies issuing from the factories at quitting time. . . . I remember the lighters going along [the Newry Canal to]. . . Portadown . . .a mile or two from the southern edge of Lough Neagh. Linen industrialized the counties of Down, Armagh, and Antrim, Belfast increasing its size a thousand times.[10]

On the manor's other side, behind the lawns and shrubberies, there was another town of stables, dog-kennels, coach-houses and harness rooms, the latter full of shining saddles and sets of silver and brass-mounted harness, all smelling comfortably of leather, all the metal parts glowing, the silver moon-bright and the brass as gold. The coach-houses had carriages of all shapes and sizes — traps, gigs, go-carts and the big brake that took the servants to Lilouley Church (Let Sorrow Say, 31–32).

Wakefield Richardson wasn't an evil man. As a youth and young man he had been wild, following the beagles for miles and womanizing in pubs all over the county. Sometime then he had caught syphilis. . . . An only son, he was 'officered' by three sisters. The merest mention of sexuality forbidden, he was treated with mercurial cure-alls. . . . My father was his valet, friend and nurse. He slept on a trucklebed in his bedroom to be on hand during his nightmares. My father was the only person he trusted. . . . Although his sisters knew that his illness was sinful and incurable, they found a woman to marry him on the count that a married sinner saved the appearances. . . . The 'wife' was really his warden. She never slept with him.

I remember her as a beautiful scented being with lovely violet eyes and I was in love with her. . . . My father and others knew that she had a lover, a handsome RIC sergeant from Gilford who visited her at night when patrolling the manor. I think Wakefield knew. In his wilder healthier days he had a local mistress, a 'widow' called Doak with one daughter who resembled him. . . . He liked shooting and fishing and used to go to a property near Bessbrook for weeks, my father with him. . . . Finally, his sisters booked a consultation with a London psychoanalyst, the vogue of the time, to whom he was supposed to tell everything that had ever happened to him, which was supposed to cure him. He wanted my father to go with him but this wasn't allowed. He told my father that

he wasn't going to go through with it and jumped from the third story of
a London hotel onto the iron railings.[11]

I used to go up to the big house every evening for the quart of milk. I
was supposed to go round by the road but usually sneaked past the front
of the house in the dusk because it was less lonely. The lady saw me going
one evening and waited for my return, ghosting out from behind a shrub-
bery in a beautiful cream dress, jewels round her white neck catching on
the last lights, her perfume in the wet air rich as Mahomet's paradise.
She scared me, scolding me for going this way, examining the can in case
I was having more than [our] due. She always carried a little peke on
her arm like a muff. She told me among other things that God wouldn't
approve of my coming this way.[12]

Near hand she's the loveliest woman I've ever looked upon. From her
little brown shoes to her nut-brown hair she is nurtured with gentle lovely
life, smelling like honeysuckle and ferns and that sweet flesh-scent roses
have; the milk-white neck, the high breasts she wears proudly for their
beauty, not like the bloody parish-women who only have breasts to hide
with a kind of peephole shame (*Rebel to Judgment*, 4).

For him, the Manor's private preserves were a kind of Tir-na-nOg, a
guarded place of ease, refinement and plenty where poverty and struggle
never showed their weary faces; elysian lawns soft as lambswool to the
foot that stepped down terrace by terrace to a sunken garden with its big
stone-rimmed pool with a merry fountain shining the sun in the middle
and waterlilies and clumps of iris, the fat goldfish tame to the hand as
chickens; rustic paths through shrubberies with foliage like flowers and
rare high trees he had never seen before; great banks of flowers tossing
their fires of colour into the air so he could scarcely distinguish between
flower and butterfly, the colours floating over the beds, myriad bright
beings surging through them, their sweet scents soaking the air; the
weedless gravelled paths, clipped yew hedges and the big circular sum-
merhouse on wheels that could be made to follow the turning sun from
morning till night, inside a fine room with furniture in bright chintzes;

the gazebo smothered in honeysuckle and climbing roses and the big domed conservatory with its strange palms and tropical plants thriving in steamy acrid warmth . . . (Let Sorrow Say, 29).

When they were on the farm and I was a baby, my mother took on an illiterate day-woman for half-a-crown a week, plus meals, as much to help her as to get work out of her: Emma Doak, who couldn't spell swan on a box of matches. . . . She lived with her half-blind aged mother in a pretty two-roomed thatched mudwall cottage under a thicket of damson bushes at the end of a long winding lane. . . . Mrs. Doake was bent double over a heavy stick, with an age-leathered face, a brown mole on her left cheekbone big as a threepenny bit; a wise old rook of a woman in her black skirt, blouse and shawl. . . . Now and again the gossips when short of a livelier topic hinted carefully that Dilemma might be the half-sister of the ruling landlord (As Towns with Fire , Knopf 15–17).

He had gone to London to see a special sort of doctor who, the parish said, had expected him to confess everything he had ever done or thought, a prospect that gave every sound parishman nightmares. One morning he had jumped from a window, falling several stories and impaling himself on the spears of an iron fence. His wife had had her child, a son, and came back to live in the Manor and married again to a young Englishman (Rebel to Judgment, 149).

Here on the Richardson estate until he was ten, Cathcart Anthony Muir West took in things that not only shaped his attitudes but became, themselves, sensorily and intellectually reconstituted in his fiction. Here he first assimilated the detail of rural life and landscape and experienced nature's spiritual mediumship. His treatment of nature, evident in the passages just quoted, becomes one of the striking features of his prose. In Down, as shown through mostly natural and religious imagery, he "crossed the bridge between creation and the self, Egypt behind and wilderness ahead," like Jonty, "reaching the first point of essential human loneliness."

*Mrs. Wakefield's Sunday School: ". . . With Sunday School mornings, church
at eleven and Sunday School afternoons I had plenty of religion between five
and eleven and could find my way around the Bible, Prayer Book and hymnal.
. . ." ACW to ASE, November 1987. Quaker Meeting House, Moyallon.* PHOTO
BY JOHN M. EYLER, 1995.

Here his instruction by Victorian parents with severe Calvinist habits
of thought and practice was augmented by the Sunday School enthusiasm of the landlord's wife. She built a meeting house, adopting and
enforcing a Quaker authority. West's early experience with Christian
thought matures and expands. At first constrictive, it became preparatory
for the adult's passionate, lifelong study of christology, a visible influence
on life and text.

*I believe Wakefield's father, John Grubb Richardson, was a Quaker, from
Quaker-Hugenot stock. The Quakers had built a large meeting-house
above the Bann, about a mile from the (later) Moyallon House. . . . The
Quakerism of my generation of Richardsons had decayed into revival-
istic and intolerant Christianity similar to presentday sects in America.*

It decreed that all employees on the estate should be Christians, which meant Orangemen. . . .

At five, I was made attend the C[hurch] of I[reland] Sunday School in Gilford. . . . As well, I had to attend Mrs. Wakefield's Sunday School in the afternoon, in the Meeting House she had built for revival meetings for the 'saved.' With Sunday School mornings, church at eleven and Sunday School afternoons I had plenty of religion between five and eleven and could find my way around the Bible, Prayer Book and hymnal, God watching my every action and hearing my every thought for I took the God-stuff seriously.[13]

As simple sunday jesus-christians and six-day practical heathens, Kilainey's parishioners were full of blind unchristian fear, the old Irish avatars all dead, the new god an idol with an appetite like a concrete mixer; they put more faith in gossip and in pseudo-gospel hymns that invoked bull-fight emotion than in that awful cross-carrying road to Golgotha and quite willfully they preferred the artificially formed religious habit for the *content* of their faith, which they thought they could answer with home-made notions concerning conscience and divinity (As *Towns with Fire*, Blackstaff, 20).

I concentrate on the bell booming distantly in its high stone tower and listen to the rippling rings that spread across the parish's silent pool, catching the elusive strike-note falling its harmonics down the cool woods, the sounds like sunlight seeping everywhere. It is the first time I've really listened to the bell that has named all the heavy Sundays of my years. Each strike is a chord, insistent and demanding, intonement for hereafter. O worship and fall down, death lurking in tomorrow and tomorrow (As *Towns with Fire*, Blackstaff, 52).

This childhood acquaintance with religious forms he found oppressive invests West's adult decisions about faith and practice with credibility. The family had been long settled in the area south of Belfast and reflected many of the religious conventions of their neighbors. A letter of introduction West apparently carried with him to America vouched for

the "sober, honest, industrious, . . . adaptable and genial" character of
this young man with "a standard of intelligence and alertness very much
above the average," and certified that his "very respectable parents [had]
resided in the vicinity of Portadown for upwards of thirty years, during
which time they enjoyed the confidence and esteem of the entire community."[14] A great-grandmother, Margaret, seems to have come from
Kilkeel, daughter of Susan Lindsay Aberdeen and a fisherman who,
perhaps, with the Kilkeel schooners followed the herring shoals.[15] West's
father, George, had been born in Cavan.

> *I know almost nothing of my father's parents at all. William West, my*
> *grandfather, lived in Kilmore, a proper Victorian. My grandmother bore*
> *him thirteen children.*[16]

MacMannan made his way to the sergeant's mess, feeling relieved and
thinking about his grey female erk: his mother's grandmother, Susan
Lindsay had been born in this locality, a MacDonald from County
Down; a half-freebooter, had abducted her in his lugger the time of
the Napoleonic wars and had given her twelve children, MacMannan's
grandmother marrying a second cousin of the same name. They were a
close clannish lot who fought between themselves but always presented
a united front to society. Susan Lindsay, a young girl of fifteen lifted on
to a wild man's lugger, swallowing the story the spider told the fly . . .
(*As Towns with Fire*, Blackstaff, 465).

> *My mother came from Poyntz Pass, around Loughbrickland, Patrick*
> *Bronte's country, one of five sisters and one son. Extraordinary clan*
> *they were. My mother was a governess, extremely learned. She had an*
> *extraordinary mind, so powerful she could follow you with it; she might*
> *as well be standing over you. It took me a long time to break that. She*
> *was a typical Protestant intellectual: she wanted to be something instead*
> *of becoming something. My mother had regrets. She thought she should*
> *have done better, but the fact is she married my father and had five chil-*
> *dren. She was intellectually his superior; she didn't give him any initia-*
> *tive at all. My parents were ambitious—not snobbish ambitious, but*

anything common, vulgar, offended them.[It was] an uneasy marriage . . .
no mean factor in my education.

    Father was an Orangeman, pro-Ulster. My brother Jack married a
Catholic girl and my father cried. I was afraid of my father in the early
days and kept out of his way. He horsewhipped my brother Harold when
he was twenty-one, home on leave from an academy in Dublin. He was
taking a girl out, a respectable girl, a doctor's daughter, and he was very
smart in uniform. My father was a jealous, married man. He met him,
sent the girl packing, took a stick out of the hedge and beat him.[17]

. . . Her learning hadn't made her marriage any easier since Conor
lacked the means to value it. She married against her family's wishes
and they ignored her. . . . He had come almost ten years after Agatha,
when Ellen's ailment had already made her walking difficult and later,
he realised that his loud aunts had been accusing Conor of downright
lechery, blaming Ellen as an accomplice and himself as a kind of sin's
evidence (*The Ferret Fancier* , O'Brien, 29).

    For the first eleven years of my life, race-consciousness didn't enter
into living at all. We were all one, in this; and all protestants in that
area, racism as such moving over into religion so that protestantism
seemed to be a race! Taking a radius of about three miles around my
birthplace, I only remember one Roman Catholic family, which was
looked upon as outcast. Their nearest church was a couple of miles from
them and they went to Mass on Sundays across the fields, to avoid any
possible trouble on the roads. That part of Down was a hot Orange-
Protestant enclave; our childhood folksongs were Orange songs and to
hell with the pope. Until we moved south, I don't think I ever talked to a
Roman Catholic. The local politics were feudal-Tory with the inevitable
religious colouring: God was an Orange-Protestant gentleman, who
made it his business to see that workers worked and asked no questions.
The naive and ignorant neighbors were latter-day Puritans, pure and
simple, with all the associated self-righteousness and envy, complicated
by the unrelenting economic pressures under which men become disloyal
to one another — informing a kind of one-upmanship. In this sense the

environment was very frightening for an imaginative boy, especially as
God was over all, the wealthy His appointed executives on earth. My
father would have agreed, but my mother fought back, protectively.

. . . Fortunately, my mother was a fine nature-lover, early on imbuing
me with affection and respect for the natural environment, so that at an
early age I could get something from a sunset, or a moonlit night, which
the neighbours' children never saw or acquired.[18]

Perhaps more than anything else the habit of critical observation he
acquired from his mother helped to widen his social sympathy, helped
him gain tolerance and understanding in a new religious exposure to
Roman Catholics occasioned by the family's move to Cavan. The move
would significantly advance the socio-religious bridging in the second
decade of his life.

I mind a decent hardworking man, one Tommy Macreedy, the carpenter
and a good one. He was a thin brown man with a big moustache and
had six or seven small children. Mrs. Macreedy was a loose-fleshed
ginger woman with grey-blue lovely eyes. She eked out the wages by
eternally hem-stitching or 'drawing' stacks of linen handkerchiefs and
her long skirt and blouse [were] always snagged with the white threads.
I played with little Brian Macreedy; he is probably about to this day if
the war didn't get him. Tommie lost his job with an hour's notice because
someone reported that he had been seen going into the Railway Hotel in
Portadown for a pint on his way home one Saturday night. He, wife and
family used to walk, carry, and push themselves the three long miles there
and back every Saturday evening. Tommy was moving on the Monday
morning, dunno where he was going. Mrs. Macreedy was holding her last
wain. It was bawling its head off and she was crying to herself with the
worry, the other children hanging on her skirt with its decoration of loose
threads, her hand under the baby's bare ass. To sooth it, she opened her
blouse and pulled out a big breast and the bawling suddenly ceased and
there was uncanny quiet.[19]

. . . Walking up a steep brae he heard the honest clip-clop of a horse's feet and a tinker's caravan crept over the brow, a contraption like a big cask on wheels, a kind of pumpkin rig silhouetted against the apocalyptic furnace of the sky, a thin pipe sticking out of the side of it and smoking.

His heart turned over: he couldn't mistake the strong squat form with the square soldier's shoulders, the old hat pressing out the ears and the pipe with more smoke to it than the chimney. Jack Smart, himself, walking at the old horse's head, a nag Quixote could have swopped for Rosinante with a tenner for luck. Were Jack riding the horse he could have looked like the pale man in Revelation.

Suddenly shy to pass them, Simon kept to his side of the road and hardly glanced over as Jack went past, a sudden rise of old shamedness in him for his past employment of them.But, as usual, Jack was buried in his own meditations. Mrs. Jameson was perched up on the driver's box, the three small ones beside her and nursing her latest wain as she smiled round the land like the Queen of Connaught as if it were her own and agreed with every stone and straw of it; dressed for her part—a pink scarf on her head and a good blue rug wrapped round her shoulders, the baby inside it warm and safe against her breasts. Tinker Madonna . . . (*The Ferret Fancier*, O'Brien, 21).

ENDNOTES

1 1910 See his application to the C. Day Lewis Fellowships, for example, 2 March 1978, Arts II.

2 Philip B. Wilson, through diaries kindly supplied by Hugh Richardson of Moyallon, provided this observation, 1910, by one Muriel Harris, close family friend and a sister-in-law of Gertrude Richardson, the fourth daughter, who married Frederick Leverton Harris: "During these days several items of minor interest have occurred. Nellie [Ellen] West's youngest, having unfortunately turned out to be a boy, not a girl (had it been a girl it was to have been called Cathleen Annie Muriel in remembrance of the trio) has been christened Cathcart Anthony Muir, a brilliant suggestion of Anne's, on the spur of the moment, apropos of which Nellie said "Well, Miss Muriel, if Miss Anne has not hit it, she's staggered it!"

3 George and Ellen two decades earlier had four children: Harold, Jack, Eileen,
   and Dorothy. Eileen eventually moved to Australia and did not keep in touch
   with her family. West remained loyal to Dorothy, visiting her for the last time in
   1982.

4 West's annotation on a chronology I submitted to him for verification, 2
   December 1987.

5 The original cottage has been torn down. West's niece, Muriel Darling, suspects
   the thatching on this "wee cottage" is an example of poetic license. Contrastive
   paper drafts of this biographical account confirm artistic revisions that support
   her, and in a letter of 14 December 1987, West enclosed a newspaper photo,
   likely one Muriel had sent him of the house, marking the cottage (built, he says,
   by Wakefield Richardson "about 1908/9"). Could he have been conceived in the
   thatched cottage before his parents moved to the new housing, or was the Wests'
   moving delayed or progressive?

6 ACW to John Boyd, 4 October 1962, BBC.

7 ACW to John Schaffner, Biographical Sketch, January 1959; ACW Interviews.

8 ACW to Audrey Eyler, 17 May 1987.

9 See the introductory pages of *Celtic Christian Socialist*.

10 ACW to AE, nd, rec'd 2 December 1987.

11 ACW to AE, 17 May 1987.

12 ACW to John Boyd, 4 October 1962, BBC.

13 ACW to AE, November 1987.

14 Herbert Sewell, Town Clerk and Executive Sanitary Officer of the Urban District
    of Portadown, County Armagh, to All Whom It May Concern, 3 April 1930.
    ACW Interviews.

15 An unidentified correspondent to ACW from Belfast c/o Ms. Fannin, re: his sister
    Dorothy and their grandparents, great-grandparents. See Autobiography.

16 ACW in taped interview with AE, July 1987.

17 ACW in taped interview with AE, July 1987.

18 Undated questionnaire on ACW, 1–2. See Letters and interviews, A–C.

19 ACW to John Boyd, 4 October 1962, BBC.

CHAPTER THREE

1920 FARNHAM: THE UNSETTLING OF OLD WAYS

As WEST PERCEIVED his position, he stood from birth like a bridge between extremes: his ill-matched parents, Big House and peasant company, mill and farm, nature's mentoring and the landlady's Quaker Sunday school, North and South, Protestant and Catholic. When, after the death of Wakefield Richardson, George West assumed a similar post for Lord Farnham of Cavan, the contrasts were exacerbated, especially in giving the boy new political and religious awareness. The change was eventually liberating to his spirit, but the process was at first torturous.

> In the middle of the Irish Trouble, my family moved down into the 'rebel' south, when I was eleven. . . . This move gave me the opportunity to see how both kinds of Irishmen existed.[1]

In a published reminiscence called "The After Vacancy,"[2] West reviews these difficult years:

> We, my family and our neighbours, the protestant poor, were a minority within a catholic majority and although only a minority of catholics were active rebels, we kept our heads down and mouths mum. Primed

*or poisoned by decades of Orange protestant propaganda, we watched
the developments with anxious fear, hearsay not short of stories about
previous Irish eruptions. England's protecting Tans roared at all hours
round the narrow parish roads in their swift Crossley tenders, tipsy on
whiskey commandeered from rebel pubs; dusty or rain-soaked British
Army columns passed through the parish, on horseback or on foot, the
men singing, whistling, wryly joking and complaining and generally
satiating my youthful lust for strong oaths. . . . There had been many a
night when my parents had packed their most valued possessions and
had dozed until dawn in their clothes, in expectation of a rumoured raid
and eviction, my mother asking: "Do you think they'll let us get the furniture out," my father, not now so brave as he usually was with me, roaring
back: "How the hell do I know!"*

*My home, such as it was, was my home, protection, womb: to think
of leaving it in the middle of a blind unchristian night was a kind of
stupifying fear that changed my known world to wilderness in which no
custom or possession could be secure (66, 70).*

Oddly enough the next four years or so now seem uneventful although
they contained the Rebellion and its peculiar conclusion. Kilainey itself
was fairly quiet, most of the protestants keeping their heads down and
content to let the Black and Tans and British Army do the fighting. I
seemed to have been wholly involved in the business of staying out of
parish trouble, with self-survival, telling self-protective lies when necessary. I was a beautiful liar. I was still small for my age, neither child nor
boy and so could escape censure under the law of pardon for children
and fools (*As Towns with Fire*, Blackstaff, 46).

War over the world, civil war at home and nationalist rebels drilling
at the catholic end of the parish, Ulster Volunteers at the other and
the Kilainey estate fouled by rumour and trouble makers religious
and profane, who daily launched canards to draw the hungry hunt
off their own tracks. This was my first fool's paradise into which I was
slowly maturing with a schoolmaster doing his best to teach me respect
for God along with all the mental tricks necessary for the worship of

Mammon, half my mind already leery and deceitful as old Fagin's and quite proficient in the saving art of the hangman adult lie (*As Towns with Fire*, Blackstaff, 34–35).

It is true that West was too young at the time of the Troubles to be seriously involved with the armament of any group, but he was watching. He uses his childhood memories of political hostilities in the environs of Moyallon and Farnham to supplement his research for writing The Casual Comedy. Five nearly complete versions exist, with fragments that indicate there were others including the history of ancient Breffni, presented in Comedy as the Glennmore estate, parish of Kilainey. He uses much of this background for O'Dea's parish of Kilsuan in Actaeon as well, the setting gradually evolving in the complexity of its historical detail and political implication.

The Casual Comedy addresses irresponsible landlordism in this place. Its protagonist, Jonty Darcy, born in 1902 to the familiar bigoted butler and his regretful Victorian wife, would have been the age of West's next older sibling. Jonty moves uneasily into his adulthood among representative participants in the Troubles, where Britain's introduction of the Black-and-Tans into post war unrest escalates rather than subdues violence. Jonty's grandfather is a Lambeg-drum maker; Jonty's most admired friends include a Rebel leader, Sean Rua Fitzpatrick, and a gentle schoolteacher, Molloy. Patriotism is exposed as a thin cause no matter the side, too many people turning the system's deficiencies into private opportunity. Jonty does not escape the hurtful effects, but he must learn to transcend them and protect a socially responsible individualism. Sean and Master Molloy hold deep affection for each other, although they espouse different approaches to solving the country's problems. Both become mentors to Jonty, Sean an active Sinn Feiner, and the Master a tolerant, articulate pacifist. Jonty listens to their debate:

> . . . You, an' the same goes for the Ulsterman, are matching the politics of emotion against the cold British politics of power and what you all lack is the politics of tolerance.
>
> I know how you feel about tolerance, Master, but—

I don't feel tolerance, Sean, I think it and try to act it. Pearse conjures
up an Ireland that never was. She was finished in 1172, after maybe five
thousand years of high culture, her mysteries silent an' Celtic Christianity a flickering light when once it was a European bonfire. It's the
Reformation Pearse is talking about, along with the Ulsterman. I'm
sorry, Sean, an' sorry for all the waste of life and property and sorry too,
as an Irishman, that you haven't been more successful.

At least, Master, we've started something, Sean said.

That you have, that you have...the Master agreed. Violent shortcuts
in politics, Sean, are only illusions. Like the funeral, politics' shortest
road is the longest way round (The Casual Comedy, #1, circled 5, 219).

For some time at Farnham the Wests lived above the dairy;³ subsequently they moved to the house in the old wall of the estate. West
describes the fears it nurtured in the unpublished Deliriums, Dreams,
and Realities, another story excerpted from The Casual Comedy.

*The house we lived in then was a square three-story building on a bald
drumlin, the four sides facing the four winds of heaven. It was supposed
to be the remains of a seventeenth-century semi-fortified farmhouse built
by a Protestant planter against the dispossessed native, with six-foot-thick
stone walls and a blocked tunnel, possibly an escape route, leading out of
the cellar in which there was a circular well, its deep water answering a
light like a glassy cyclopean eye. . . .*

*Neighbours said that the house was haunted by the shades of the
occupants who had been killed in the 1642 Rebellion. A local wise-
woman swore she heard roaring shouts and shots on certain nights of the
year with, for me, the implication that let alone the living, even the long
dead refused to forgive each other. . . . My delirium outdid the spae-wife,
her shouts and shots a harmless pantomime compared to my hallucina-
tions. The six steep flights of stairs from my topmost room to the cellar
became a compulsive treadmill of terror, the stairs themselves turned into
white bone and sticking up in the air without wall or protecting baluster,
the vertiginous descents as fearful as the dank claustration below where,
again and again, my body fell down the deep well-shaft and through the*

The Wests lived a number of years in the far house pictured here, the remaining one of four such structures built into the original wall of the estate. PHOTO BY JOHN M. EYLER, 1988..

"The house . . . was a square three-story building . . . with six-foot-thick stone walls and a blocked tunnel, possibly an escape route. . . .The six steep flights of stairs from my topmost room to the cellar became a compulsive treadmill of terror, the stairs themselves turned into white bone and sticking up in the air . . . .Deliriums, Dreams, and Realities, 3, excerpted story from The Casual Comedy (both unpublished). PHOTO BY JOHN M. EYLER, 1988.

smothering water, under which I found temporary peace until the whole
business started all over again. But this was only an apprenticeship to
fear (3).

The well here, although it is anticipated in a terrifying fall, already
images at least a temporary relief. Its ultimate peace is described in "Narcissus unto Echo," where the well-eye fuses hopefully with the wheel
of sun and seasons and reincarnation, as Stephen's soul reaches its rest.

West's works suggest that the child's experience was rich in human
variety encountered among the wealthy owners of the estate and the
poor peasants who worked it. His position as offspring of the butler could
have made him a natural study to his father for pantry boy, but the strong
influence of his mother, his own great intelligence, and his tempera-
mental independence, plus the tensions of the times, marked West for
quite another future. Such a transition could hardly be smooth: the
unsettling of old ways affected him and shows in the work at many levels.
As he perceived it, while traditional hypocrisy, greed, and want of charity
obtained, religion and politics became ever more muddled. Ireland
was divided. Europe was geographically re-described by the two world
wars. Great technological change was taking place, as the boy excitedly
watched cars replace horses.

Wakefield Richardson . . . introduce[d] the automobile. In summer, it
created clouds of dust which covered the green hedgerows — a horseless
carriage I thought was wonderful. Heretofore all the work had been done
by horses. . . . That was the end of 6000 years of horse civilization, since
the time of the first Pharaohs. I remember the long convoys of huge shire
horses pulling heavily laden carts passing my home, going between the
mills from Newry to Belfast. . . . I was born at the transition of a new
world-economy.[4]

Eddy was the estate coachman's daughter. Old Paine was really a chauffeur now but was still called coachman. . . .He was a fresh man, on
seventy. He could only wash a car by fooling himself it was a horse,
walking wide with soothing whoas round the back in case it kicked. .

. . The Paines lived in the coachyard. Their house still smelled kindly of the fusty, oak-acrid tang of leather, and harness racks and saddle maidens were still on their kitchen walls . . . (*Rebel to Judgment*, Obolensky, 7,9,12).

A man like Paine also lacks spiritual resources that could help him cope, as the narrator observes.

Then the mare kicked Paine in the head, in the stable. It was I who discovered him. I was in the stableyard looking for Eddy and heard his mumbling groans, immediately suspecting her, the groan sound like the heated objections to love I'd overheard on other occasions.

  I found Paine half conscious on his backside behind the tightly haltered horse, his big hands on his thighs, the pair of blue women [the tattoos on Paine's arms] doing their little dance, a step-ladder lying behind the mare's heels. I ran for help (*Rebel to Judgment*, Obolensky, 57–58).

Old Paine was real. He did actually try and buck a mare and she kicked him on the head—in Cavan, that was. He tried to serve her in the stable from a stepladder. . . . Paine was a great orangeman, very saved, God save us.[5]

Paine was very great with the landlord, to whom he had been groom or batman in the Boer War, each one having saved the other's life, apparently, on two tight occasions. Before that they had wrangled about the world together for several years (Rebel to Judgment, 11).

The Casual Comedy's plot, his "Troubles yarn," is more tightly woven than that of *Towns*, which offers comparable length, and its threads are intricately knotted. Of course West's ultimate interest, as is typical, lies in the spiritual development of its protagonist, Jonty Darcy, within the political context with its wide sociological implication. A wide and well-developed cast of supporting characters contributes to a full sense of parish life and personality. The poignant case of Tom Mor illustrates such effect. First West shows the risks of materially elevating the individual without educating him. Learning his house duties in the sudden environment of affluence, the youth wants money that is not his. Of course his contentment with his station is destroyed, but there is neither foresight nor forgiveness in the landlord. Temptation overwhelms Tom. When he is sacked for helping himself to unearned coins, he reacts by committing a major burglary against the estate-agent and absconds to England with the funds.

Tom's story, however, does not end here. Its lessons are more complex. Jonty takes the Rector Willoughby's sermon on charity and the Lord Glenmore's[6] reading of the Corinthian love chapter at their word and, remembering Tom's gradeschool kindness toward him as evidence of a goodness that might be redeemed through mercy, pleads for leniency in Tom's case. They refuse, and Tom thanks Jonty for the noble try by naming him an accomplice. Tom also deserts a poor and pregnant lover: Harriet loses her job as maid at the rectory and later, when the child is still-born, dies of hemorrhage, unwept by the parish. Values are so perverted that when word comes back that Tom has died for England in the trenches of battle, his crimes are forgotten. Lady Glenmore pays a call on his mother and offers her more compensatory coins than Tom stole, somehow forgetting that her own prosecution instead of a forgiving instruction in his case had sent him off the premises in the first place. A stone is put up in Tom's honor and only Jonty puzzles why Harriet didn't more justly receive the monument.

In Actaeon, West uses the same incident, featuring the injustices toward women in the blame and in the penalties. Perhaps this time there is some mollifying of the male's stance in the implication that Clegg suicided. The episode haunts Diana Hauley's memories of home, where the servant girl hemorrhaged to death in her attic room; Diana recalls the conversation about it with her Welsh nurse, and her review also discloses her current attitude toward pregnancy.

> I come-to with a start, thinking suddenly of poor Helen Dungworthy, the pretty maid with odorous name who bled to death in a Hauleyford attic, alone. That dull brown stain on my bedroom ceiling like an anguished face, the men chipping it away and making a patch like a coffin-lid.

Nain, what made Helly die?
>She died with a baba, Di Back.
>Do babies make people die?
>Sometimes, cariad, sometimes.
>They'll never make me die.
>Ust, ust...
>Why did Clegg die?
>Remorse, annwyl. A terrible thing.
Compunction kills.
It would be a miracle. I haven't laid an egg in years . . .
(Actaeon, R, 77).

Jonty's spiritual development has consciously begun with his epiph-anal lesson in the Greek word *entelechy*: *entos*, within; *echo*, I have; and *telos*, purpose. "I am my purpose" (The Circus and the Crust, circled 2, 70). He gradually sifts through his options. Sean Rua is killed in a raid, perhaps through the cowardice of his companions. Molloy dies mailing a letter, shot for no reason by a Tan on a drunken rampage. Mindful of their influence and instruction, Jonty will make his own way through the besetting problems of this modern world and maybe even offer a contribution toward diminishing them through his studies of history, myth, literature, and religion.

> *There was a [another] legend about Farnham. The lord in my time wasn't supposed to be heir, but his brother died suddenly, and his own son was killed in Egypt in the War. They said there's no two generations in succession would inherit the estate.*[7]
>
> *In my time Cavan was a small county town with a population of three or four thousand, a good market town and reasonably prosperous, serving a large agricultural region. The surrounding region is one of subsistence farms and several landlords' estates, many of which were burned out in the twenties Troubles. The district has a strong Orange/ Protestant minority established by the Ulster Plantation under James I. In the 1640s Cromwell's army settled more Protestants, dispossessing native Irish. Formerly, the district had been the seat of the O'Reillys,*

princes of East Breffni, descendants of Niall of the Nine Hostages. . . .Its
lakes belong to the Erne Valley system and go back to the stone and iron
ages, the Erne waters being a cultural and cultic strom.[8]
    This unhappy island! Oh, the drums, the parades, the hard hats,
and the walking sticks. When I got to Cavan I escaped that, although the
Orange Order was quite strong. I was suddenly in a society where there
were as many Catholics as Protestants. I had never known Catholics
until I went down there. They suffered the same. It was the salvation of
me there, so untidy and so open; for the first time in my life I was free of
all this religion and Orangism. My parents left me alone; they gave up
the ghost of trying to control me. I was eight or nine years younger than
my next sister, Eileen (Dorothy, my favorite, was two years older), odd
man out, like an only child.[9]

Miseries of the political, social, and domestic scenes were compensated by the healing and instructive natural beauty of the countryside and the many unrestrained hours to wander the farm, fields, and woods.

The Trouble blew over. . . . My adolescence was spent in a magnificent
setting of lake, river, marsh, moor and hill, and I was free as Dan'l
Boone. I'm always grateful for this generous phase of my untidy life.[10]

Rural beauty nurtures Simon Green and Jonty, as it beneficently influences O'Dea Russel's childhood in Wall when, after his mother's drowning, the boy goes with his much loved governess to her family's farm. In "Narcissus unto Echo," these same experiences belong to Stephen, as they do to the narrators of other stories like "Myself and Some Ducks" ("The Turning Page") and "The Barrow."

Not that he had not joyed in the farm and its complex life: the strong sweet smell of the young red bullock with its great male's neck and head, its manly mastering of the drowsy cows and the swift, clean mating stroke and the surge of its great bulk much as a wave bruises a receptive, uncomplaining shore; the farther fields rich in their growth unto harvest, dressing their aloof beauty at the command of any kindly wind; roadside,

"I was eight or nine years younger than my next sister, Eileen (Dorothy, my favorite, was two years older), odd man out, like an only child." See endnote 9.
WEST FAMILY COLLECTION, PHOTOGRAPHER UNKNOWN.

The staff assembled with the Maxwells of Farnham House on the occasion of the landlord's wedding: Ellen West in the wheeled chair, West behind it, George West next to the child in the spotted coat. PHOTO BY VYVYAN POOLE STUDIO, DUBLIN, C. 1924. GIFT TO ASE BY PADDY MACK; SEE ENDNOTE 3.

"My adolescence was spent in a magnificent setting of lake, river, marsh, moor and hill and I was free as Dan'l Boone." See endnote 10. PHOTO BY JOHN M. EYLER, 1988.

Farnham House, Cavan. "There was a legend about Farnham. The lord in my time wasn't supposed to be heir, but his brother died suddenly, and his own son was killed in Egypt in the War. They said there's no two generations in succession would inherit the estate." See endnote 7. PHOTO BY JOHN M. EYLER, 1988.

Farnham's "battle-axe gate." Photo by John M. Eyler, 1988.

laneside, and rough stone wall graved with the crisp hieroglyph of moss; military fields of flax where small blue butterflies danced daylong as if the blooms had wearied of their stems and took the air for freedom: the tiny movements of the golden-crested wrens creeping like shuttles weaving into summer's tapestry the large impatience of the spring: love life and love laughter all warped into a thousand dainty patterns and every motif a hymn to the sun. . . . No summer since had known such magic, no evenset or start of dawn so clear and chill, no field more friendly ("Narcissus unto Echo," *River's End and Other Stories,* McDowell, Obolensky, 115–116).

The slow, moist feather-heat of her body was strangely moving to me and her patience and my touch on the smooth, warm eggs. Almost, I could sense the quickening movements, of the curled embryos within. Muttering, she settled herself over my hand and I could have wept for her faithful flame of life flickering through the nights and days of her long one-moon vigil.

My life and Daisy's: the twin flames of our lives flickering around the dusty doorsteps of night and day. . . .

I held my hand under Daisy for a long time till it too became moist and warm like the eggs, afraid to withdraw it and break the slow life-contact. . . ,

The year swung on . . . April into May: May with her hawthorn and cherry-blossom and thick nights of moon-brewed perfumes. April had lured blossom to the blackthorn, but May had far more alchemy and everywhere she touched a flower arose.

Each evening I shut up my ducks, and on fine ones I would sit on the wall overlooking the stream and sloping fields, hearing the many-footed dusk approach and stop—just beyond my sight . . . ("The Turning Page," *River's End*, 76, 81–82).

Farnham had a lovely park, with wonderful trees, and the woods went down to the lake.[11] *. . .The bird life in the twenties—tremendous. You could hardly see the sky for swallows and swifts and martins. The birdsong was terrific! In Wales now I counted about four swallows. . . . And the willow warblers and garden warblers came in, all the migratory population, rare birds. Some flew as far as down to Africa, to Nigeria; tremendous traffic. And the lakes had geese on them, strange ducks, some blown off course from America and Canada.*[12]

When turf time came I prayed through the dull school week for Saturday's weather to be fine, and when the free day came I would rise early and to avoid chores slip away softly across the pasture fields, through the templed beech wood, down the steep hill flank to the first lake; then I could look down on the busy heat-shimmering waste that was the great Rivary Bog, its husbandmen no larger than mice. . . . This craft of peat-getting was quite familiar to me, had I not mind-known it I would have remembered by blood and bone, each rhythmic gesture an ancient ritual act of kinship to the earth. Half dazed with content I watched the age-old movements—cut, sling, catch; cut, sling, catch—each block of moist blood-dark humus no larger nor smaller than another ("Song of the Barrow," *River's End*, 95).

The school house on the Farnham estate. "There was a teacher upstairs and one down. . . . I jumbled them all up to make the stories. I moved Rainey from Down." See endnote 13. PHOTO BY JOHN M. EYLER, 1988.

". . . Ever after if a bee mistook a February's half hour of false summer sun and crossed his path with droning flight he saw again the schoolhouse and its figurehead, Miss Ross." River's End, 1958, 8. PHOTO BY JOHN M. EYLER, 1988.

*The schoolhouse: Good old Master Ross. He had fifteen children of his
own, and they all lived there under that one roof, on eighteen shillings a
week, when he started. There was a teacher upstairs and one down. Miss
Hewitt was the second teacher. I jumbled them all up to make the stories.
I moved Rainey from Down. . . .* [13]

*Moyallon National School was a thriving establishment of eighty to
ninety pupils from two-year old infants to sixteen-year-old, sixth class
adolescents. When I was approaching two I used to join them at lunch-
time, dressed in petticoats, the girls fighting over me. I used to visit the
infant schoolroom mornings and afternoons, knocking on the door and
asking Miss Forbes for a kiss. She would cuddle me and send me home.
My presence was disruptive and one day the headmaster, Warmington,
threatened me with his cane, which made him my bête noire forever
more. In September 1912 I was finally sent to school in my new trousers
and refused to go. Miriam Hall, a servant we had was deputized to make
me, my mother being house-bound. I remember clinging to the netting
wire of the garden fence until my palms bled, Miriam tugging me legs.
Thus began eight years of fear and distrust. . . .*

*When I was ten, I went to my brother Harold's for a fortnight's
holiday and stayed for six months. He was teaching soldiers' children.
This was a blessed relief for, thinking back, I might have gone insane
with Warmington's pressures.* [14]

*Then I went to the Royal School in town; I got a scholarship. The
headmaster, Mr. Bain, whom I liked, went to California. Another man,
John Anderson, was the son of a night watchman — it's funny how snob-
bery affects people — at a school where my brother Harold went. Anderson
went to another school, a good school, in Dublin, and he was obviously
trying to shed his working class. Anderson got Bain's appointment, and
here I was in the school. I probably reminded him who he was, and he
didn't like me. Finally I brought my books home and told my mother,
"I'm not going back."* [15]

[Nan Connell] proudly disregarded [Thubby Knight] and went up the

"[Nan Connell] proudly disregarded [Thubby Knight] and went up the outside stone steps to eat her lunch with Miss Gibson. . . ." **The Ferret Fancier, 1963.** PHOTO BY JOHN M. EYLER, 1988.

outside stone steps to eat her lunch with Miss Gibson: they shared a thermos of tea. . . .

Stuffing the lunch packet up his jersey, Simon climbed into the armchair crotch of the big lime tree in a corner of the yard. . . . It was cool in the tree, almost chilly, the light dusky and green. . . .

He could look down on the hiving playground, the view like a map. He was level with the school-eaves and could see into the upper classroom where Miss Gibson and Nan Connell sat on a desk and sipped their tea: the sun-bright yard, the children talking, playing, squabbling, eating their lunches, their voices muted, a million unseen insects humming

"He could look down on the hiving playground . . . swallows slicing down the steep face of Drumbar Hill and sliding up over the school . . . Mrs. Rainey was hanging clothes on the line behind the playground. . . ." The Ferret Fancier. 1963. PHOTO BY JOHN M. EYLER, 1988.

round him in the tree, swallows slicing down the steep face of Drumbar Hill and sliding up over the school, the high swifts beating the bounds of the sky. . . (*The Ferret Fancier*, O'Brien, 10–11).

Mrs. Rainey was hanging clothes on the line behind the playground, her hair still in a plait, the old bleached-pink dressing gown roped round her narrow waist. She looked askance at the mobbing scholars, her mouth full of clothes pegs. . . .

George Edward Marcus Bastard Rainey: just as he smelled and tasted: chalk, ink, pencil-parings, stale breath off the swamps of his yellow false teeth, sweat, rank underclothes blended with a whiff of shaving soap and rancid face-flannel, cheesy towel and the sickly brilliantine that gummed his grey-dirty hair together from morn till night which he always scratched carefully with the point of a pencil or the end of a pen, digging the wax out of his big hairy-holed ears and rolling it into pickles between finger and thumb, turning his false teeth over

The school privies: they were a roomy rectangular building of brick divided equally by a single-bricked wall, at the end of the yard behind a moth-eaten privet hedge. Simon used to think that privet and privy went together. They had a shallow roof of corrugated iron and each compartment had a log seat with three holes in it over a dry drain, a roaring plague of flies feeding on the ordure every summer." The Ferret Fancier, 1963, 61. Photo by John M. Eyler, 1988.

inside his mouth and licking the bits off the backs of them (*The Ferret Fancier*, 9, 15).

The school privies: they were a roomy rectangular building of brick divided equally by a single-bricked wall, at the end of the yard behind a moth-eaten privet hedge. Simon used to think that privet and privy went together. They had a shallow roof of corrugated iron and each compartment had a long seat with three holes in it over a dry drain, a roaring plague of flies feeding on the ordure every summer.

Simon had been scared of the place in his early days, sooner to wet his pants than go alone into the tangy gloom, birds and branches scuffling the resounding iron overhead. . . . All the scholars knew that Mr. Rainey couldn't have been more mistrustful of hell's gate lodge than he was of the boys' privy and his concentration on that odorous house of ease trebled everyone's awareness of it (*The Ferret Fancier*, 61, 62).

*Then I went to a little country school in Gartbrattan to learn Irish, and
I had the best time of my life. We got half an hour for lunch, and we
organized "hare and hounds" on the hundred acres of bog right near the
school. The one who was 'it' would be given ten minutes and then he'd
start chasing, Miss Price standing on the steps ringing like hell. We were
covered in mud, half a mile away. Wonderful times.*[16]

"Except ye become . . . [as little children]" remains a pertinent West
theme. In 1956 he published a long poem by this title, inspired in all
probability by daughter Stephanie's pre-lingual awe at the rising moon,
an incident he described in conversation, though he did not at the time
mention the resultant poem.[17]

   . . . Except ye become—the Law:
   O child, are you this Law incarnate, do you fulfill the Law
   In all parts, have you become? Time wears on now to Christmas,
   Our annual image of becoming unto resurrection
   As the beast knew, 'tis said, crying Ah
   From awful reverend open throat across a stable wall:
   Michael's to Christ's Mass, the flowerless time,
   Earth's songless quiet time beneath the flowerfull
   Christmas skies; snow flowers on earth, white visitors;
   The kaleidoscope of frost . . .
   I am weeping, child, because I see no further than your finger
   That is the gnomon on the dial of my clouded ignorance. . . .

The clause alludes to Christ's insistence upon the changed life—
"Except ye be converted, and become as little children, ye shall not
enter into the kingdom of heaven" (Matthew 18). Such was the charge
to the disciples. For Nicodemus, it meant abandoning material priorities and being "born again" (John 3). Humility is requisite. Entrance to
the spiritual kingdom depends upon the seeking individual's childlike
willingness to be taught. Possession of such wisdom will inevitably seem
foolishness to onlookers and outsiders.

An important and recurrent character in West's rural Irish scene is the
local fool, with whom the narrator, even from childhood, sympathizes.

The English fool and the Irish amadaun come from a rich tradition that teaches the child-like fool's superior sensitivity to the spiritual reality, his paradoxical wisdom despite his innocence.

> 'Stephen? What is the Gaelic for summer?' . . .Miss Ross had read his mind and he blushed. . . . Being older by two years than any of them save Anne Stafford and being thrice as articulate, he knew he had more authority inside and out of school than had Miss Ross and he was aware she admitted this, implying he should help her and much as a monitor keep the larger unruly ones in hand (ll–13).

> . . . She frowned, unable to understand how such an arrogant boy could be so gentle and long-suffering for the fool whose slobbering mouth and deep, wide, wise-foolish eyes offended her and always smelling with his own sour smell and the odors of the dead things he carried jealously in his pockets. She shuddered, remembering the day she took a blackbird away from him. But for Stephen he might have attacked her, mouthing for his bird, calling it "Bawbee, bawbee" and saying Stephen would not marry her now for taking his bawbee away. She had flung it out of the window. Stephen had gone for it, returning it to Murray and himself holding the disgusting thing as if he loved it much as the fool.
>
> "It may be dead, miss," he had muttered, "but to Fooney its yellow beak and glossy feathers are beautiful" ("River's End," *River's End and Other Stories*, MacGibbon & Kee, 20).

Not only does the protagonist see with the fool's eyes the beauty in the dead bird; he must be proactive about his vision.

> *It's not enough just to see and comment on the shit and corruption: we must raise it up. There's a legend about Christ: He was passing a dead, rotting dog with his disciples. They tried to hurry him past. No, He said. Look. Look at its beautiful teeth.*[18]
>
> *Fooney, the fool, was a living character: son of a lunatic mother with a phobia about draughts and chills. A charming and gracious person—a sort of married Faversham who dressed herself up in furs all seasons and*

made Fooney wear three sweaters and a topcoat on a sultry summer day.
Her last attack drove her to the opposite and she was found wandering
raw-naked through the bog. Fooney had also a craving for clocks and
watches. He used to stare for hours at the big school clock and listen to
its tick. He was never in time and maybe he wanted to be time, like a
clock. His parents once employed a buck-toothed daily help who had
two ditch-begotten wains. She started to encourage Fooney and he asked
me the origins of his aroused feelings. Then she got him alone behind a
turf-clump and while Fooney could erect, he couldn't release and was so
enamoured by his pleasant sensations that eventually the girl got fright-
ened and had to yell for help. Fooney became very strong but there was
never any harm nor violence in him. Years later I saw 'Mice and Men in
London and realised I also had a fool.[19]

Fooney of "River's End," San Fairy Ann of *Towns*, the unnamed
inmate in the snow of "Narcissus unto Echo"—the fool remains for
West an evocative figure. He appears as well in Actaeon. In a fragment
of an alternative to version Q, Diana describes Angus MacGarran as "the
only person who really lives in and with the parish nature, with Nature,
were he aware of it, his senseless seeing a kind of purity." Everyone is
"carefully superstitious for his want of sense, as if the want were rich in
sense, *persona grata* with Kilsuan and the humblest peasant" "(Q-alt.,
358). Angus McGarran: "parish fool or parish saint. Child of God. God's
peeping tom" (R, 139; R disk, 117[20]). Initially frightened by his staring
at her, Diana defensively traps his reaching hand by cranking the car
window up on his fingers. How could she appreciate this strange being's
offering of flowers picked in the hedgerow? Angus is twenty-eight and
has missed the two earlier psychological stages of development usually
encountered, West believed,[21] at about fourteen and twenty-one. O'Dea
having taken on a godfatherly responsibility for him, Diana gradually
learns to cope with Angus's childlike unpredictabilities by distracting
him through his obsessions—with clocks, with St. Mongan's ancient well
on the rectory's land, with his grandfather's grave, and with his father's
imminent death from colon cancer.

Angus, Angus Og, daft Irish Eros, his words white birds, lord of the
shapeless stone and easter fool. Strange how foolishness is valid despite
all crafty cleverness. Christ, jester, jousting death and laughing all the
way to paradise, pain his password (R, 165; R disk,137)

. . . He owns everything, possesses nothing save clocks, lord of his
absent centre to the ringing seas. I suddenly see him as Ireland's bat-
tered folk-soul, as allegory for empty innocence in dangerous times,
ignoring explanation for any common fact. Briefly I envy him . . . (R,
256; R disk, 211).

Poet and preacher bear traditional proximity to the fool, and Christ,
the creative source of all knowing, is the associate of all three. In the F
version of The Lady Actaeon (titled Naked to Laughter), Diana explains
in a letter to a friend that Angus, also the name of the Celtic Krishna,
makes her think of Edmund (her dead, cretin brother), but

Dea sees him quite differently: as someone excused convention, as a
sort of crude Christ without worries about ways and means. God knows,
sometimes I see Angus as a sort of cross between Dea and Edmund—and
myself! He seems to be existing in the same territory where fools, saints,
and poets live. Angus asked me to marry him. He has taken to coming up
to the rectory at odd times, holding fantastic conversations with Mattie
from the kitchen door. He loves Dea, even if he does want to cuckold
him! Dea seems able to go with him into his witless fairyland (F, 401).

Upset from the beginning by her unexpected pregnancy, Diana tries
to visit a country herbalist for an abortion. Her maid, Ana, has gone
ahead to negotiate with a trade of chickens and has encountered Angus
en route. (Diana adopts an ironic, editorial plural.)

We hear a sardonic chuckle—it's only a pair of magpies: two for luck
or mirth or joy—good thing there aren't four. Ana expectorates for one
and looks hopefully about for the other two, still hankering to enjoy
the extortions of matrimony.

The cry again, wailing over the bog, an old gaelic boggart perhaps sinking in gurgling quickmud. These bogs are frozen dreams, dreams' graveyards, undying places locked in time which people burn for sala-mandrine warmth and for their fortunes in the shapes of fire.

Stap it!

That's Ana on a broomstick. We hurry along the taggly hedge, looking for a gap, not finding one and standing on the bank as Ana sounds again; Godsake, will ye stap it! Straining on tiptoe and dodging our sight through the twigs, we overbalance and fall against the ready thorns, lying on them, unable to go or get back until the wirey basketwork slowly sags and finally foals us on all fours on the marshy field that smacks with satisfaction when we hit it as Ana yells, half-crying now: Jaysis, Angus, will ye stap it! Git offa me (R 294; R disk, 241)!

Angus has a sometimes-threatening awareness of his own sexuality, being interested in the making of babies—at least as far as understanding that the family dog whelps and that Diana is also incubating offspring, having been "pupped." He also finds and treasures his ancestors' bones in the Kilsuan cemetery. He attacks the astonished gravedigger, who is opening the earth for the senior MacGarran's burial, and absconds with the skull of his grandfather. Angus comes to Ana's rectory kitchen with it, refusing to give it up even to O'Dea, and eventually he stores it among other curios in his bog-cave: poor Yorick's further ignominy.

Numerous experiences convinced West of the spiritual reality char-acters like Angus help him to portray. West was among the survivors when the influenza plague claimed more lives in Europe than the War had done, but he was laid up for a month. Such fever may have contrib-uted to certain of his extrasensory experiences; others seem to have had no such qualifying circumstance. He emerged from the flu, nevertheless, with perceptions he then wrote about in the unpublished piece called Deliriums, Dreams, and Realities.[22] The soul's temporary exodus from the physical body and the baptismal dreaming-back through all accumu-lated, temporal sensations were experiences that West also explored in "Narcissus unto Echo" and As Towns with Fire. O'Dea and his medical friend, Freeman, of Actaeon both have deeply affective, out-of-body experiences during their war service. Such experiences are integrated with other discoveries along the route to spiritual regeneration, to resurrection and Christ's conquering of death, the central mystery whose truth, West said, began to come home to him when he was in North America.

> . . . The mystery-myth-truth of Christianity? . . . I beat my brains against the four gospels. Then one morning I woke up with the idea of the spiral instead of the circle—cycles, yes, but on different planes and movement in two directions instead of one. This was worthwhile, I thought. It could take the pessimism out of Spengler and leave much of him intact. Goethe! a circle and gravity; a spiral and gravity plus levity. When planting some seeds for a friend I got the idea more strongly—roots delve while blossom climbs: matter—gravity; spirit—levity = the idea of the resurrection! I cursed the religionists for hiding it so long and so craftily [protagonist Stephen Muir is writing to Hollywood producer Mr. Rosen, trying to explain why he left America and the job offered to him] (Room without a Door, #1, 18).

Such resurrection is anticipated through the mystery of becoming child-like, fool-like.

> . . . I came to appreciate the Orpheus myth and the saying "Except ye can become as little children." In the world's long human history, not one man in ten million has ever been able to regain the mystery of true childhood and even a genius like Wordsworth could only attempt to describe the closed door. We have no intellectual concept for the word, un-born-ness (Room, 8).

Reaching seventeen, West took a job in a Cavan law office. The Casual Comedy draws extensively upon this period of legal training. After the late-childhood, psychological terrors from schoolmaster tyranny, military raids, and fevered dreams, this job helpfully warned him of a threat to his spirit and the potential in bourgeois respectability for cruelty and exploitation. The legal office sharpened his evolving judgment.

A story called The Half-Crown features a crucial incident from the long narrative and captures at least the jist of West's lived experience. Here is an upublished, first-person telling of a critical incident.

From seventeen to nineteen I worked in a lawyer's office and was supposed to start studying law in my own time. . . . I was a good clerk in that Anglo-Irish office. My employer said so. He had many Catholic nationalist clients. He was heir to the business, a long-established and wealthy one; and he had come to the office with a brilliant record as a student in England and in Dublin. He had very fixed ideas about caste and rated himself as a county gentleman as well as lawyer, something his wealth permitted him to do.

But I was happy in the office. It was crammed with black tin boxes bursting with parchment deeds folded like treasure maps; dusty records of finished cases all neatly tied with faded pink ribbon were stowed in every available space. Most of them were slow patient records of human troubles, for people seldom visit lawyers save when in some sort of a fix. . . .

At that time my life was clean, at least outwardly, and was not entirely thoughtless. For some reason I had started reading history for pleasure and my parents were pleased as they thought I was studying for the law. And I was reading the Bible for pleasure, too. I was not religious but neither was I irreligious. When my mother queried the Bible I said it held some good law, which was a fact because I had heard a barrister once quote Ecclesiastes to a judge.

Physically, I was slowly lengthening out; financially, I was just about holding my own. As usual, most of my spare daylight time was spent in the woods and on the lakes; in between I also spent a few hours with the girls. Looking back, I know that this period of calm growth presaged storm and some travail.

One afternoon an old country woman came into the office. She was nervous and worried and obviously poor. Poverty had not broken her dignity but the struggle with it had marked her face and form.

Her case was a very simple one concerning the writing of a letter to neighbours who were annoying her. She had a small farm with a little house, a cow, a few fowl, and a pig. She lived alone. I knew her environment well.

But to her, the case was important and she would not listen to anyone save the boss, so I took her into his office. The interview lasted no more than seven minutes and he led her out again and told me to collect five shillings. . . .

But I haven't five shillings, she whispered. . . .

My employer peered over her shoulder into the purse like a curious big bird. . . .

How much have you got there? he demanded in his Oxford accent.

She resented his curiosity but was powerless to protest. She had only half-a-crown and a few coppers and I knew she was ashamed to have so little money.

Take the half crown, Michael, he told me.

At first I did not think about it one way or another. Some of these country people are very shrewd and plead poverty although they might well have a thousand pounds in the bank.

But I wanted to get a few wee things in the town . . .

Har har har! the boss laughed, looking amusedly at me and dabbing his nose with a white silk handkerchief. Good Lawd, woman! You can't expect advice for less than that!

No, she muttered, looking at the purse. But I thought mebbie I could pay ye when I sold the calf?

No-no-no-not-at-all! He laughed loudly at the idea, looking at me and obviously expecting me to share the joke. . .

I did not smile because I felt something turning over in my stomach . . . and my eyes were beginning to see things they had never seen before. . . .

I made out the receipt and gave it to the woman. She thanked me, carefully folding the paper into an inch square and tucking it into a corner of the purse before she moved.

I watched her hands and I could name and number the hours and years of their labour. With her hands for a focus I could see the noble spinning of the seasons' weaving a star-sequined cloth for spring and a mist-grey robe for winter. My employer's head with all its great store

". . . Australia, tails: America, heads . . . I could not break my word to the coin." West's emigration photo by Moffett Studio, Portadown, c.1928. WEST FAMILY COLLECTION, PHOTOGRAPHER UNKNOWN, SEE ENDNOTE 23..

of legal facts meant less than nothing against the evidence in those old hands.

Watching the woman going out I saw her lips moving. She was still thinking dazedly, probably never before having met a person who would take a last coin. For a lawyer, the boss didn't know people at all. He could have trusted her with a hundred pounds. . . .

I jumped up . . . and ran after her. . . . I knew she would not accept charity from anyone. So I told a lie. I said the boss did not want the half-crown after all.

Agh, God save him! She said, looking at the bright coin on her palm. Do thank the decent man for me, will ye? . . .

Back in the office I let my eyes run over the shelves of old files and every file represented a fee. That was how lawyers made their money. It might be as good a way to make a living as any. . . . Maybe lawyers were necessary with all this property about and an honest lawyer could help people in times of trouble. But . . . I looked at my own hands and they were not soft lawyers' hands and my mind was not a lawyer's mind. Then my mind started working without any help, shaping and finishing thoughts before I saw them . . . thoughts I had never seen before.

It was an hour before closing time so I went in and asked the boss for permission to leave early. He agreed and I balanced the petty cash and started for the lakes.

Sitting on a big round stone . . . I began to work it out. . . . I could not go on allowing my parents to inject me with their fears of poverty and insecurity. Their only stem against poverty was to grab nicely and legally as many half-crowns as possible from people who put themselves in a position to own half-crowns.

They said, owe no man anything; never a lender or a borrower be; stare every man in the eyes; make hay; adversity flattereth no man.... purely economically, I had no case. . . . they were all bad law at bottom. As far as I could then see, everyone owed something at one time or another. . . . We were all debtors, owing our very existence to mothers who bore us and to fathers who begot us; to the earth for supporting us and feeding us with food and beauty . . .

I looked over the lake with its own unaging beauty that was much the same as when God had made it and that was a long long time before the first proud Roman coined his first legal phrase.

Standing up, I took a penny and spun it high in the air. . . .Australia, tails: America, heads. I spoke aloud as I caught the coin off the air. . . . It lay on my palm, heads uppermost. . . . I could not break my word to the coin (The Half-Crown).[23]

ENDNOTES

1   Questionnaire from Rhiwlas, 1963, 1.

2   *Vogue* (London), December 1969, 63–81.

3   The dairy apartment in Farnham in 1987 was occupied by Mrs. Mack and son Paddy. Paddy, too, grew up at Farnham, where his mother was the dairymaid; he reminisced about childhood play with West and generously contributed the large formal photograph of the Farnham staff.

4   ACW to Audrey Eyler, no date, received 2 December 1987.

5   ACW to John Boyd, 4 October 1962, British Broadcasting Company, Northern Ireland.

6   The name varies: Glennmore, Gleannmore, Rossmore.

7   ACW in taped interview with AE, July 1987.

8   ACW to AE, 17 May 1987.

9   ACW in taped interview with AE, July 1987.

10   Autobiographical statement, untitled, 1963.

11   ACW in taped interview with AE, July 1987.

12   ACW in taped interview with AE, June 1987.

13   ACW in taped interview with AE, July 1987.

14   ACW to AE, 2 December 1987.

15   ACW in taped interview with AE, July 1987.

16   ACW in taped interview with AE, July 1987.

17   Michael MacGrian, "Except Ye Become," *The Christian Community*, X, 11–12, November–December 1956, 150–154.

18   ACW to Maurice Leitch, c.October/November 1965.

19   ACW to Arnold Gingrich, 11 March 195?, *Esquire*.

20   Thanks to a Regency Grant from Pacific Lutheran University and the typing of Kay Whitford, the entire R version of The Lady Actaeon has been put on disk. The R is titled Ring Around Stone, purports to be by Mary Mongan Russel, and, according to the Artos address on the title-page, would have been completed after November 1975.

21   See my *Celtic, Christian, Socialist: The Novels of Anthony C. West* (Fairleigh Dickinson University Press, 1993).

22   Deliriums appears to be part one of two planned sections for "Confessions of a Hedonist." West returns often to the phrase "Except ye become," which, despite its King Jamesian sound, is not an exact transcription from *Mark* 10:15.

23   "The Half Crown," unpublished, but broadcast by the BBC, N.I., 1951; rewritten in 1952 as by "Michael MacGrian. C.A.M.West, Elmbank, Llandegfan."

CHAPTER FOUR

NEW YORK 1930: LOOKING FOR WALT WHITMAN

THE DETAILS MAY be dramatized, but the narrator's attitudes toward money and obligation in The Half-Crown are corroborated by autobiographical claims of its writer. West did, indeed, flip a coin and leave an evidently successful apprenticeship in the law office for an unsalaried, nomadic life in North America. In April 1930 nineteen-year-old West landed in New York, but he soon struck out for a wider look at the continent, not returning to the City until the autumn of 1931.[1] The North American experience, particularly his life in New York City, is examined in an 800-page part of the ur narrative called by the same title, drawn from Shelley's poem "The Flight of Love," that West later applied to some versions of The Lady Actaeon, Naked To Laughter. Simon Green of Corran has left the provincial village of The Ferret Fancier and is discovering equally oppressive conditions in New York. West's American experience is also explored in several published stories and novellas, which fit within the large pattern of the continuing ur narrative: "The Upper Room," The Moncrats (two versions), and Swineherd. West further explains this decision to emigrate:

Unlike most of my countrymen, I wasn't in America to make a fortune. I

87

*had the idea that America was even better than Walt Whitman's opinion
of it. . . .*[2]

"The Upper Room" in the *River's End* collection probably gives
an accurate presentation of this Irish immigrant's state of mind after
his initiation to New York. This "allegory on hell" reveals him as "no
saint," but as we saw in the law office incident, he does exhibit loyalty,
sympathy, and higher expectations than those possessed by the company
he describes in scenes of New York life. His American dream had been
geographical, one of "far distances and spating starshine, rivers leaping
to their oceans, avalanche, slow glacier, and sun-hot rock. . . ." (116). He
was young and fit; natural beauty was still a powerful lure. He had much
to learn; New York's distractions wouldn't seduce him long.

The nineteen-year-old West, as photographs and friends' accounts
confirm, was not tall, but he was athletic, unusually strong, and agile.
Among the careers he was considering was boxing. The theme of the
protagonist's surprising strength and agility recurs frequently enough
throughout West's fiction to suggest that the option was something tangible, not pure fantasy. Simon joins an Irish-American boxing club and is
regarded as a "natural fighter." At first aggressive boxing appeals to him;
then it becomes more interesting to be defensive, but trainer O'Dwyer
isn't happy about this change. Simon realizes the greed of his backers
and defects to local wrestlers for exercise, learning handy tricks and
holds. An injury to his thumb scares Simon into quitting. West's qualifying weight proved too great a disadvantage[3] and made him abandon
serious ambition about fighting. He has clearly weighed the risks: Jonty
explains to headmaster Boles in The Casual Comedy, who wants to
know Jonty's games, if he is to be admitted to his Dickensian school:

> I can row a boat, sir, an' I can run three or four mile without stopping.
>   We're a rugby school, Boles said, unimpressed. Can you box?
>   No, sir.
>   Fight? Fisticuffs?
>   Not much, sir, I don't like fighting, Jonty said.
>   You might get hurt—heh? Boles queried.

No, sir, not that...Jonty said.

What, then?

Wrestling 's better, sir, Jonty said. No one gets hurt, then (#1, circled 5, 239).

When he dedicated Naked to Laughter to friends Ormond and Irene Edwards in 1963, West claimed "All characters in this book, save one, are either fictitious, or else dead." By the exception, did he mean himself?[4] Did he mean Freya?[5] Naked's protagonist—Simon Green, son of Conor and Ellen—is poised between the adolescent stages depicted in the two published novels, The Ferret Fancier and The Native Moment. Naked To Laughter does not depend on a reader's knowledge of the other books about Simon Green, though responses may be enriched by such. M'Clatchie's office, for example, "is like Master Rainey's madhouse school—beef-floor standing for jangling playground" (104). Simon starts work in a meat-packing house run by Northern Irish Kennedys—brothers who have transported their Victorian, Orange values, religious and political, to New York. His vulnerability, implicit in the title and in Shelley's line, poignantly shows when he accepts some Italian co-workers' invitation to swim at a posh hotel. Not understanding protocol, assuming the maleness of the company from the exclusivity of the shower room, he appears naked at the pool's edge.[6]

> I felt as if I'd come at last to the further edge of time, all life's traditional meanings exhausted, the new year's door a cruel threatening threshold to a wilderness through which I'd stumble with ten million others, looking for dead hopes that could never live again, each man only able to be envious of the other's loneliness and I, naked to meaningless laughter, my parched mouth never without the big foot in it (45).

> I had to watch my first bright dream-drunk visions of the city changing, sinking into a kind of sickness, fear lurking round the corners, no longer beauty and the proud gestures of freedom; changing slowly into the copy of a criminal asylum, the citizens so-called sane acting out their various illusions of existence, the poor griping and the rich trading the

gripes for ease and profit, each one the other's deadly rival in a gal-
loping nightmare toward some perfected . . . hero, king of the ruins;
the strongest, cruelest one, the best conniver. . . (126).

Simon is capable of being affronted, but he remains slow to make
a decisive move. As he does in West's published novels, whose plots all
exhibit a picaresque quality, Naked's protagonist seems, morally, to float.
His big wrongs are sins of omission;[7] his inclination toward constructive
action is lethargic. Exactly what soul lesson Simon carries away from his
sexual relationship with the wealthy and older Freya Lethbridge, is not yet
clear to him, though the reader appreciates with him that he must move
on and that her world is philosophically, as well as materially, debilitating
to his creative, productive self. The relationship between Simon and Freya
raises again the underlying question of West's attitudes toward women.

Some feminist critics have been impatient to the point of cutting
West from Ulster's literary pantheon.[8] Their intolerance is regrettably
blind. Their indignation is understandable, but it is based on a limited
representation of the literary and social whole. The reality is much more
complex and more interesting than their dismissal implies. The ur reveals
West very early and over the years grappling with social implications and
applications of gender equality, probably as early as his New York experience with Freya, were she real or fictive. The historical settings for
his published fictions reflect with probable accuracy the attitudes and
vocabulary of their times. Although West's evolving feminism may never
have reached even the contemporary standards for political correctness,
the ur narrative's development attests to his courageous and liberated
thinking on this subject. Had The Lady Actaeon been published, West
might not have remained a closet-advocate of women's rights. Perhaps
he would have been propelled to marry the idea of gender-equality to his
social and artistic rhetoric.

Naturally enough, such pervasive change takes place gradually.
Early Actaeon characterizations still reflect much bigotry and country-
coarseness. He had been giving the matter attention, however, and his
study of it began effecting a discernible and positive direction. There are
hints in Towns Christopher's insensitive treatment of Andy Browne, with

Molly's proposal to Christopher, and Molly's impatience with expected rituals of courtship, but these aren't developed very far. It's at his crossing to the next world, after all, when MacMannan again confronts Andy Browne. In Actaeon the reader ultimately finds a presentation of women that is sympathetic, sophisticated, imminently transcendent of patriarchal Christianity's practice, and harmonious with the anthroposophical ideas of gender-equality, which West had first encountered in New York. Some Spring Valley students of Rudolf Steiner came on the discouraged West as he was considering a jump from a bridge. They persuaded him to visit their community; impressed by what he met there—although he never officially joined any religious group—he credited this rescue by Steiner's Christian teaching with the spiritual redirection of his life. It carried with it a change in his regard for women. Steiner's close friend Rosa Myraeder, a leader of the General Austrian Women's Movement in Vienna, contributed significantly to West's thinking about the equality of the male-female relationship.

> Myraeder seems to have covered all the angles, sociological, biological, psychological, and pneumatological; challenging dogmatic theology's interpretation of the Adam and Eve story, which, she said, was responsible for degrading women to the lowest level of sexual existence, sustaining fanaticism, blocking any real progress to human understanding of the male/female complex, and equipping male chauvinism with a pseudo-spiritual/religious prerogative. [9]

Early in Naked To Laughter Simon characterizes the reprehensible Loane as having the mind of a stud dog:

> He had begun with a half-wit fourteen-year-old. She died in the premature birth of the child.
>
> His relief majored all regret and his callous unconcern scared me a little until I was able to forgive him by putting myself in his place and was then afflicted by guilty dreams in which the harelipped girl kept blaming me for her agony, Loane sitting on the garden wall in his white coat and shouting for the neighbours to come and see (56).

A little later Simon observes that "Loane seemed only to be burking his own responsibility . . . his erotic commitments weren't necessarily evidence of individualism, since man seemed to share with all male animals the blind need to copulate. . . "(122). Simon's thinking about women is still woefully naive and selfish, as he goes on to observe that the difference between the blind needs of men and male animals is that "man had to shoulder responsibility for some kind of social or moral restraint since women never seemed to be out of heat, at least in mind, for one reason or another" (122).

But West shows Simon's progress. At art galleries on Saturdays and Sundays, Simon begins "to see some beauty in the female form beyond the sexual prejudice. My life in Corran," he says, "had only managed to teach me to imagine a woman with one specific activity in view." Such awareness may be the author's comment on himself; it may also remind the reader that the stories are intended to reflect Corran life, rather than to be the present West-lens of gender perception. Diana Hauley reveals the distance West moves, as she sympathizes with parishoner Elaine Fetherstonhaugh, "wish[ing] Dea could throw her at young Hawe," and "wonder[ing] what she'll make of the shreds of her life the old boy [her tyrannical father] has mangled:"

> Were law also social right he'd be in a home for looney patriarchs. She'll probably spinster alongside mother and then decay alone. Dea's hard, saying she has to do what she doesn't want to do until she decides to do something different. It's all right saying that in general but what can any particular church-mouse woman do in a man-directed world. If ever I creep out of my shell, it'll be as roaring feminist, even if I only blame the kettle for the pot. . . (R, 224, R disk, 187).

West notes the transformation in his own attitudes toward women as he reminisces about his love-life during the North American years:

> I never met any nice girls in the States, bar one. A Jewish girl asked me 'if I'd care to have sex with her'. We both had cold feet when we got on the bed. She had a lovely petite body with breasts as hard as apples. Bar

that, and one other girl, I never did enter in unto any girl, as they say in the Bible. I wasn't pure. I just never seemed to have the opportunity. The 'one other girl' finally initiated me. We just kept loving all night. I never was much of a masher.[10]

Then I fell in love and the woman took me through the gamut of emotional and physical experience, helping to cleanse me of the lingering sexual bigotry of my boyhood. But this broke the continuity I had established and, in the new light, my ideas and literary attempts appeared very abstract. I roamed again, but it was no longer possible for me to recapture that first old rapture of newness and movement, and I had to face up to the decision to go home, penny poor but perhaps pound wiser.[11]

The typical ur protagonist, as the young man, tends to be bluntly descriptive about female (and male) bodies; about sexual relationships he is neither salacious nor philandering, yet irresolute. The efforts of Actaeon manifest this evolving feminism, beginning with raw bigotry. A version of O'Dea's and Diana's story, probably the earliest (to judge by the clumsy plotting, the undeveloped characterizations, the unconvincing intellectual debate, and the cumbersome internal monologue given exclusively to O'Dea) concludes with a vengeful, church-fathers' view of diabolic woman. It shows in O'Dea as death makes a triple harvesting in a week of O'Dea's wife, his priestly superior (O'Dea is still a curate), and a parishoner. Plausibly distraught, but lacking the stylistic and cerebral sophistication that West will eventually impart to both characters, O'Dea rages on Diana's grave:

He spat out the dead flowers and ground them under his feet, catching up handfuls to rub them over his face.

Look! Look at her lying on the grave! Look at the bitch who followed me to thus eventually torture me! Look at her shameless legs lying apart, inviting me! This the body of accursed woman—this! This heap of putrid flesh!

He laughed with shrill and broken laughter, massaging himself until semen spattered over the grave. Then he turned away, cackling insanely. Blundering through the graves he tripped on a railing and fell heavily, knocking his head on a corner of a tombstone (197).[12]

The crack on the head precipitates a ghoulish vision of open graves replete with an olfactory detailing. Here, at the end of this early fragment, O'Dea argues inconclusively with a shadowy incarnation of himself.

In much later versions, West's now-female narrator, Diana, protests her pregnancy, but there's no inartistic flailing. West's later versions show an antithesis in sympathy and perspective, along with the artistic growth. She also masturbates, but the context is mature. She speaks directly about her body, but she does not demean it:

> I masturbate now and again, reluctantly, the result leaving me flat and depressed. This sexual need is really a kind of crutch, a variant of Pandora's old hope: no wonder they call it the poor man's supper, care momentarily thrown to the pantothenic winds, the brief connatus dying into sleep, the balm of poverty and distress: strange how the malthus-rich decry the proles' fecundity when they all think fux and fux more'n any labourer, the royals in the van. I'm growing democratic in my misery, sex the leveller, the want of it society's good (T, 361).

> My shapes are subtly changing, breasts footballs, sitting on my chest like those plump females in eastern stone; no appreciable pot as yet, just a small bulge, but all my clothes are too tight, waist disappearing, hams spreading—-39-39-39 and soon, I guess, 40-60-50. It is really extraordinary how the female body so ruthlessly adjusts itself, prepares for partuition: it's a fecund female body no longer mine, belonging to an anonymous stranger who grows and grows in wet womb-night. Pity we aren't oviparous—we could lay our eggs and hatch them in electric blankets. Dea says that sooner than later, they'll produce laboratory babies, humanoids, conditioned to work and fight, sexless mules: as a laboratory, I'm inefficient, no more than an egg on legs (Q alternate, 390).

It is helpful to notice a practical application of West's evolved attitude toward women. In a description of their Artos (a not-for-profit charity the

Wests and friends were developing) plan before it received that name, a concluding paragraph addresses gender-equality in the "West Project:" The group intends

> . . . sexual equality while respectful to the intrinsic differences in the sexes, and to the quality of their dual contribution to society. The women in the project will be quite free to decide how they, as women, may participate, relative to the sexless health of the whole.[13]

It is true that there is no truly sympathetic female among the Irish women in *All The King's Horses* (1981),[14] Poolbeg's reissued *River's End* with the North American stories removed and the new title story inserted. The contemporary reader also winces that West would use the name of his wife on the half-witted and victimized female in his title piece for this collection. If the historical context does not justify these features, one might wonder how much effect of acculturation a person is likely or able to remove. Perhaps no one can realize the pervasiveness of a prejudice until the fresh nose, coming in from the outside, catches the faint whiff of bias a soul has tried, in all earnestness, to eliminate. West was writing independently, without the steady help of institutional policy or consciousness-raising colleagues, in times and circumstances where most people were unsympathetic or still unaware. Even Olive, at least at one time, her independent employment and untraditional views of female domesticity notwithstanding, held with Woolf's Charles Tansley that "women can't write."[15]

It becomes steadily more apparent in the Actaeon that equality is an implicitly necessary condition for the ideal spiritual state West is promoting, although it does not dominate the other ideas he is trying to impart. Reflecting on his early views about women, West does recognize a transformation, and that evolutionary change will be steadily visible in the transcriptions from The Lady Actaeon here. His critical reception by some feminists in the eighties and nineties will be seen as an unfortunate cost to his staying West.

Financial worries seem beside the concerns of Actaeon's central characters, though West had them as he tried to support a big family.

Diana Hauley comes from wealthy parents; Dea, established in a mostly self-supporting rural parish, offers her the comforts of an ample rectory. Personally, West had and wanted very little. Money may not have been his priority, but a consciousness of a narrow budget does remain a life-long theme. It shows in the poverty of an early protagonist like Simon Green. In Naked To Laughter, Simon penuriously accounts for fifteen dollars: ten of which went for board and bed, $1.50 for laundry, $1.50 for outside meals, $.60 for fares, and $1.40 for all extras (591). He used others' discarded razor blades. West's bigger interest, however, consistently lies in a contrastive wealth in spirit. Material ambitions are not wrong, he argues, as he explores the North American continent that so many people had settled expressly for economic recovery, advancement, exploitation, or luck. Such interests, however, must not dominate. West narrates a series of experiences that teach Simon other values.

Cell with a View (appearing in Naked To Laughter, Room without a Door, and Shadows) is an unfinished episodic piece of the ur that uses a number of West's encounters on his trek between the Holland Tunnel and Lake Erie to illustrate these other priorities. Stephen Muir/ Simon Green strikes out for the open road. Stephen, unsurprisingly, finds himself broke and hungry after losing $35 learning to play poker in New York. Although he has had only four hamburgers and four coffees in ten days, the troubles and hostilities of other people still affect him so strongly as to diminish his appetite. Perceiving karmic ties to them, he is extremely responsive to Native Americans. Stephen possesses the extrasensory vision that West acknowledged as his own special gift— or affliction.[16] For example, Stephen takes a cue to part company with a fellow bum when the ghost-woman attending the fellow signals the drifter's implication in her death. Stephen "sees" this woman, as he sees the ancient encampments of Indians on the shores of the Great Lakes, as he had seen them along the Hudson and will see them later on the prairies. A couple of Indian women give him a lift to Titusville in their truck and let him sleep in their shed. They highlight the contemporary gap between the modern diaspora of Indians and the vital community Stephen sees recurrently in visions.

He hitches a ride to Buffalo with a couple of men who, under the

influence of the gin they are drinking, hit another car. They and Stephen
are arrested, but an Irish sergeant argues for Stephen's innocence and
he is released. In Erie, his Irish identity gets him the shelter of a cell in
the jail, where his sleep and appetite are so disturbed by the disorderly
company that he finally asks to be let out. This officer apologizes for the
rough night and gives Stephen fifty cents.

Gradually crossing the continent, West gathered materials for stories
that treated his experience of America.

> [In Swineherd] I tried to catch the great brooding (Indian) atmosphere of
> the prairies, where men moved like ants under the vast arc of sky. I'd love
> to go back to that farm where I worked so hard (3:45a.m. to 9:30p.m.) six
> days a week plus a half day on Sunday). Seventy years previous to 1930,
> the Indians were chasing buffalo there. [17]
>
> I couldn't come to terms with the Northwest and Canada, that
> great country and its vast expanses. I felt that the normal materialistic
> humans who were only there for the beer were resented by the land, most
> of them dragging their dry roots behind them like the characters in Knut
> Hamsun's novels, and importing their natal prejudices. [18]

> Roots in the earth, her hands, the fingers softly working like worms,
> roots there delving the darkness and up above the Plough, the sign for
> husbandmen; about the round summer's dancing foolfires, etching fit-
> fully the humpbacked contours of the barn, firebugs fairy meteorites,
> the cricket's endless filigree of sound: empty the homestead, no voices
> of children, no sacred laughter, no april tears: an old and ailing man
> drifting home on his own dreams, an aging barren woman maimed at
> birthstart by uncomeliness.
>
> She sighs, rising and carrying the spade and fork over to the barn,
> stacking them inside the door and standing in the opening, cool air
> tiding past her legs. . . ("The Monocrats", *River's End*, 186–187).

> Without directly experiencing it, Palliser would not have believed it to
> be possible that he could live closely alongside three adult people for
> months and never know an act of truly reciprocal companionship. . .

.And all around them surged the ripening reality of the monarch grain, their reason for being there at all; thousands of acres of it taking by day the irrevocable sun in a bluedust desert of sky and by night strong noah dews under the singing and apostolic stars: grain everywhere—barley, oats, and wheat but mostly the royal wheat leaping out of the black godbody of the earth (*Swineherd*, 19).[19]

[It was deja vue] in America, Ireland, and Canada—in Buffalo country in Canada, where I was. The farmer's son and I went to this place on Sunday to look for stone arrowheads. It was a horseshoe-shaped mound, an Indian center of some kind. And I had a strange experience.[20] . . .

I had extraordinary dreams. . . . It was like I was living in a haze, going through the motions as best I could. I dreamed—and now I can see it—my life as it has unfolded. . . . It was never new. Deja vue. . . . When I walked into that encampment or whatever it was . . . my legs wouldn't support me. Whatever they did there, those experiences were profound. . . . . From the Celts, B.C., to the Vatican archives, to Chartres, to the Welsh bard, they knew about it, but the Church headed off all knowledge like this. . . . It all began when Moses declared the I AM. That was utmost heresy. People had been quite content to be told to do their job. Then the ego men came, held on to power, became the leaders, and the mystery decayed.[21]

West moved on: from the wheat fields of Alberta, to the Pacific Northwest, to California, where he started in the screen-writing studios of Metro-Goldwyn-Mayer, to Arizona, to the oil fields of Texas, and back to the East.

I began to realise that a hobo's life hadn't much future. . . .

Returning to New York, I began to meet bohemians of various ilk who seemed to think I should have some ideas worth enlarging. . . . I had this strong, intimate, almost physical contact with nature. It has never left me, thank God. On the other side, the [transcendental] , in spite of myself and my self-fear of a puritanical childhood and religious bigotry, I couldn't help being drawn to Christian philosophy—some part of me

felt quite at home in it: a rather ironic development in such an appar-
ently materialistic society. American materialism had little or no effect on
me, ever—I still think it is less dangerous, more obvious, than the subtle,
pious materialism of Europe.[22]

His first job, apparently like his last one there, was running an
elevator in an apartment house. Later, taking one of Roosevelt's newly
created positions to help the depressed economy, he earned a wage
in Bloomingdale's fabric department. To make himself a persuasive
salesman, he spent free time at the art galleries. He studied styles and
fabrics at the Metropolitan. In the 42nd Street library he discovered that
Ireland was "the subject of countless books and comments in a dozen
languages . . . by people who thought that Ireland was an important
place:"

I began to read again, this time more critically. I started going to
museums and art galleries: at that time I think I knew the work and style
of nearly every known painter. But it was Rembrandt, and then Van
Gogh, who moved me most. New Worlds! I remember the first time I
heard Beethoven's Fifth, and I remember reading Bayard Taylor's trans-
lation of Goethe's Faust with great delight. I had to acknowledge the
increasing gap between what my mind was doing and what was in the
minds of my peasant-immigrant countrymen. I was lonely and alien. I
met several true mystics at this time, who helped me, although I couldn't
recognize the quality of their help at the time. Knowledge-wise, I didn't
have a clue, my mind near-as-damnit virgin like—with a couple of child-
hood exceptions—my body. I neither knew my own strength, nor my own
weaknesses.[23]

Although he had sent out a story at sixteen, West says he began to
write seriously in New York at age twenty-one.

I wrote on for a couple of years, working in jobs by day, writing by night
and on week-ends, living like a surly monk.[24]

In New York he completed The Life of Reilly, his first novel, which Little Brown tentatively accepted, then reconsidered for six months before refusing it. He said it never occurred to him to offer it to another publisher. He next wrote The Parish Pope. It also went unpublished and, like Reilly, was "lost."[25] What were they about? He wouldn't say, but if the rest of his practice serves evidence, it is likely that the materials of these novels were recycled and parts may even be intact under other titles from the ur text. The attitudes of fiction and testimony are consistent.

> *Most of my countrymen went to America to get a job. I went to America to be an individual, and I went to see America. My mother had read a lot of American history—Lincoln—who was her hero, Washington, and all that. She encouraged my reading. Anyway, I knew more about America than most of the Americans I worked with. It was a disappointing country, cruel yet magnificent.* [26]
>
> *I went to America . . . to find Walt Whitman. I didn't find him. . . . Walt was to be found in myself. . . . This was what Walt had been trying to say to me. . .* [27]

This was not my America, this hole-and-corner copbribing end of the sewer existence; this braggadoccio, this cave of bum-boys, tarts, small crooks. I could have found similar not ten miles from my home under the hills without the trouble of travelling abroad at all . . . no. ("The Upper Room," *River's End*, 116).

. . . My life had a rhythm: I worked till dawn, slept to eleven, and usually wandered about the town looking at people and things and spending the wet cold hours in museums in which I learned a great deal about America and the world ("The Upper Room," 113).

> *After five years, you could apply for American citizenship. I was running an elevator in an apartment house. Went to citizenship registration office, a shoddy, dusty building, counter along one end. A very long line of people submitting first papers was there. This fellow was sitting up there at the counter reading his paper, making all these*

people—immigrants—women and children, wait very humbly for him.
They all wanted to get into the great United States and not make any
commotion. I waited about half an hour. I went up to talk to the fellow
and said can you help me and he said "Take your place in the queue."
I said, "You'd better take it for me, because I'm not going to wait any
longer." So I never took out citizenship. I was disgusted with him, playing
with people's half-hopes and expectations.[28]

The depression I had left in America I met again in Ireland, but it
didn't worry me. It was the other things, the human ones—the chronic
depression of imagination—that worried me. Even my parents mistrusted
me, unable to understand that my detachment (which they took as feck-
lessness) was as much a way of life as any other. Within a few months I
was disillusioned and very lonely. But the natural beauty still was mine,
my vision of it sharpened and, besides, the girls were kind to me, I found.
But I couldn't write—I couldn't write a word, the resistance to creation
was almost a physical thing. Ireland is a fond, fierce, possessive mother.
Being Irish is also a kind of bad stepmother wish. And so, for a while, I
put writing away, living again on work and wits, like a gypsy sometimes,
and wandering—but this time taking in everything more consciously,
and even making notes.[29]

This period following his time in the States West has described in
Room without a Door. Stephen Muir addresses a twelve-page, single-
spaced letter to his former employer in Hollywood, explaining why he
will not accept the tempting offer to stay on and learn screen-writing.
West did sign on briefly at the MGM studios, but apart from the details of
such a job as Stephen describes, the decision to leave America was tied
up with a personal search important enough to merit West's keeping this
record of thought over it. Putting such a letter into a publishable novel
would, he knew, require drastic synthesis and cutting, but this ur version
preserved his self-analysis for later use.

Back home in Ireland in 1936, West worked briefly as general store
manager for Thomas Montgomery in Cavan, demonstrating that he
was "sober, trustworthy, and a keen business man with a sound knowledge of book-keeping and modern business methods." But then, Mr.

Montgomery writes, he left "to seek a larger outlet for his sterling capabilities. . . . It is with regret that I parted with him."[30]

Lucy Porter, widow of art historian Arthur Kingsley Porter, had taken a shine to West in bridge games in New York. Interested in Irish artists, and perhaps hoping this one would develop an attachment to a young woman, friend or relative, who also was visiting, she hosted him for a holiday at Glenveagh (the Porter estate eventually became Ireland's first national park).[31] Parts of this unusual visit West cast in a novella, one of a couple pieces he tentatively called Shadows. Whether Gloria and Stephen faithfully portray the rapport between West and Mrs. Porter's young guest, the unpublished story offers some important features of the teasing relationship between autobiography and fiction, as it shows further separation of the evolving writer from the evolving protagonist. It examines still another phase of the journey into socio-spiritual adulthood of West's protagonist, his Everypoet and Everyman.

The adolescent male whom West casts in the "River's End: and other fictions as Stephen, Conor, Michael, Adam, Mark, Jonathan, Simon, Adam, and as Christopher MacMannan, engages sympathy by his intelligence, his sensibility, and the sincerity of his quest, but when an assertive empathy rather than passive sympathy would prove the constructive, soul-and-society-advancing choice, he fails. Stephen thus anticipates the career and spiritual failure of Christopher MacMannan in As Towns with Fire (1968), and Shadows also helps to show ever more clearly how West uses, rather than confuses, autobiography and art:

Here the reader sees again the brilliant, spiritually evocative Irish landscape through the descriptive technique that becomes West's signature. The setting for Glencairn (Glenveagh) in primordial Donegal is inspiring. The castle — an "ostentatious keep in an awkward and unsuitable habitat under a fifty-inch rainfall," built in 1860 by "a Victorian tycoon of mediocre parentage and doubtful taste" — is a "pseudo-Norman stronghold in the bowels of most ancient Celtica," the birthplace of Columcille nearby. The story occasions a further sorting of some of West's ideas about christology, Christianity, karma, and individual freedom.

Shadows simultaneously offers an extended discussion of money, and the reader better understands West's own detachment from money's power. Beginning life at Moyallon and going through adolescence at Farnham had given West an extraordinary experience in watching lives that were advantaged by wealth. Materially, West's own lot was always meagre, but his refusal to care deeply about money was not the sour grapes of ignorance. Nor, as can be seen through his careful agricultural records, his success in military aviation, as well as through his store employer's testimony, was it a lack of practical and left-brain skills. Money—it was only the flip of a coin—had otherwise nothing to do with his emigration to America or with his departure from it. He can not, it is suggested by Shadows and Room without a Door, be tempted to seek money through marriage. It sadly confirms, too, the failure to recognize emotional and social equality of his female partner. All these values— regarding religion, nature, and material unattachment—are explored in Stephen's experience at Glencairn.

> Stephen sat on the wet balustrade of stone and did not wonder any more why Colm chose this land for birth, as indeed Finn the Fair foretold; no other land could birth a Colm half so ably, save perhaps Tibet: here Druid's light and shade still whispered of Saturnian mystery, each light-freckled peak a natural monument, each petrous shadow a druid gospel etched on stone, mute now and silent as the light was silent..... Quality, understanding, order: the three concepts came clearly and suddenly into his mind as if the stones had said. . . . He was grateful to the Americans for giving him this chance to see how landscape had shaped the man and had lifted the saint in Columcille and he knew now he could go, satisfied (Shadows, 11, 14).

On his first morning, Stephen rose at 6:00 to explore the lake and terrain.

> Climbing on, now too much aware of his own reactions for any pleasure in the exercise or view, he found no other word than trespass to suit his

mood; needless, heedless, unnecessary trespass, the rockscape muttering in sombre whispers: yours is the valley now but not the herculean hill.

On the top a great upland moor swept ruthlessly to a further crest, the silence now thick as tar, the burn a six-inch gully cut in the peat; the silence listened to something else, this god-twisted corner of Erin still a great ear tuned to the eternal vowels and consonants of planet and zodiacal star; where sighs as big as demi-gods still toiled with labour as gigantic as the ice which had tossed boulders like a frozen wave upon an ancient shingled shore.

Stubbornly, he followed the burn for some yards then stood, admitting the prying uselessness of it, knowing he could go on to the top of the next crest and find another crest beyond, and other crests beyond that. . . .

Sensing a movement at the top his sight flickered upward and he saw a great antlered stag peering down on him contemptuously, its forefeet planted on the rim. And down below, lonely on the strand, lay the little boat's ellipse, a frail and friendly manmade thing. . . (Shadows, 16, 17).

An ancient familiarity with Gloria — from another incarnation,[32] Stephen realizes — makes the few days they have together before her scheduled return to New York a strangely intimate time, but marriage is out of the question for him. When she proposes it, he says:

If Manitou prolongs time for our pleasures a thousand other miseries may also be lengthened.

Why do you say Manitou?

Because he is the deity under which we still meet and love.

Do you mean physical contact or love?

I mean love — how love, I don't know. We've never ceased to love each other. But don't ask me to take it apart? I'd sooner leave the blessed warming thing be. . . . I like most people but I love few — my inability......

This is also a mystery, Gloria, which the psychologists know little about an' religions have forgotten.....eros, philia, agape — the three faces of love? Agape embraces all three, philia holds eros, an' eros is stabled in Hollywood. . . . I'd have no compunction about existing on your money, provided I didn't drone exist. But . . . I'm far too unfinished to dispense

with the cold thrust of poverty—it prods me on and fuels me. Poverty
is not always an accident; it is sometimes a gift of grace. I just have to
keep moving to keep warm—can you see that? (Shadows, 80–81, 83)

Stephen gently turns down the arguments she poses with more talk
in this still-uncut draft (West has made marginal notes for future editing)
than any lover might be expected to endure. For purposes here, as was
probably true for West's purpose at that time, the exposition helps:

We are not only ourselves, Gloria. We're members of one another and
of a greater whole the health of which, ultimately, is our own health.
This modern mammary-gland sex business is the other end of the tremendous modern desire for freedom and new horizons. . . . [The] awful
loneliness of soul . . . stares out of [the eyes] of every child I see.....as if
saying, Is this all you've done in preparation for my coming?

   Oh yes, the child will be falsely answered, the shrugging self-
conscious excuses will be made, and the escapism taught—by bars of
chocolate or afternoons at the movies. Things like Oxford Groups and
Christian Science and the hundred other mole-hills will waste life;
laying it up in alien harbours for safety when it should be tracking the
unknown and hazardous seas of true and creative dream. . . . I think
many people wake up in the morning and shudder at what they see
and are scared to see—not wars nor pagan citadels—selves growing
unworthy of human dignity. . . . This is a queer way to tell a girl I love
her.......Darling, I do love you—enough to love and let go free.

   You're the queerest, maddest, nicest, sanest, irritatingist person I've
ever met, she said . . . her entire features soaked in misery. How can I
ever see the sun again?

   I may not see the sun again myself, he muttered . . .

   What'll you do?

   I don't know—bread on the waters! . . . I must get rid of this agnosti-
cism and I must find meaning—egoity—in myself. If I fail I'll see no
meaning in anything and then I may do anything.

   He picked up a pebble and fillipped it high into the air over the
drop at their feet. That may be me, he smiled, suddenly frightened as

he watched the pebble swiftly answering gravity's awful call (Shadows, 91–93).

The author's autobiographical chronology indicates the important divergence between West himself and that evolving protagonist who so much of the time would seem to merge in identity.[33] Stephen's philosophy obstructs the reader's empathy.

> . . . His loneliness now [was] similar to chronic indigestion round his heart and just as tangibly disturbing. But he knew, with a little patience, that soon it would blend into all his other indigestions, enriching them and making a whole and tolerable major discomfort of all that he had now worn for years (Shadows, 98).

Indigestion is a short-sighted analogy for all this character's self-awareness, and such failure is repeatedly West's point. The lines Stephen remembers from poet George Herbert's "Grief" acquire a condemning irony by the time this life-walk reaches *Towns* and Christopher MacMannan's compromised end:

> O who will give me tears? Come, all ye springs,
> Dwell in my head and eyes; come clouds and rain . . .
> A narrow cupboard for my griefs and doubts,
> Which want provision in the midst of all.

Drawing upon his prodigious memory to evoke the autobiographical experience and translating through his keen descriptive powers the landscape that harbors the spiritual forces affecting humanity, West anticipates *As Towns with Fire*, where the implications of Stephen's choice are explored and West marks even more significant distance between himself and his evolving protagonist. Stephen's understanding is lopsided; it neglects empathetic action. While individualism must be nurtured, such insulation of the self has hurtful consequence. One may not, despite blind Milton's consolation, merely stand and wait in order to serve. Time precipitates change. People are moved along. An individual

must embrace obligation to others or egoism becomes derailed by egotism. Egotistically focused ("aesthetic-philia usurping the function of
the moral-agape"[34]), the quest turns into a self-indulgent, irresponsible
drifting.

Indigestion is Stephen's myopic, egotistical analogy for the emotion
he feels.[35] By the time Stephen has become Christopher,[36] he does follow
the trajectory of the pebble. Christopher, West has said, was "an igno-
minious failure."[37] He was a failure, yes, but that is not to say he was, in
West's view of the "star-wide eye of time," a finality.[38] His soul's progress
will become measurable in his next incarnation (and its potential taken
up again in the next fiction of this ur protagonist's chronology).

Stephen's and Christopher's Hamlet-question was obviously important to West; his notebooks show that he pursued it with zeal far beyond
that he gives his adolescent male characters. With his poet-protagonist
Diana Hauley, West goes at it with hammer and tongue-tongs. In the
life, as in the art, there is no escaping the matter: Diana's monologue
is a steady interrogation. How can the questor know whether action or
inaction is appropriate?[39] Can even the self-aware, individualistic artist be
mistaken? Is not spiritual wisdom doomed to appear foolish in a material
context? What is mutual between the self and the other? What permits
rapport between the one and the many?

> I didn't try to have any villains at all: I tried to make engrained and
> traditional thought-forms and habits the composite villain. The Lady
> couldn't leave her prejudices and live and so she went for a dolorosa
> walk down and down and down into the country and finished up beside
> a tinker's fire, finding there an awful bestial but real humanity, all
> prejudice spent. The Minister was a tryer but caught up in the mystical
> reaches of his own mind: a sort of Hamlet who has the right ideas but
> always put his foot in it—and so . . . unnecessary incompatibility: the
> lady couldn't forget her past and the Minister the future, each of them
> betraying and disregarding the present. (Two major soul illnesses of
> modern times). Also, I hinted all the deep race prejudices, the high
> and low nationalisms—all of which are bloody, anyway. I tried hard
> to project all these characters as, I suppose, a playwright projects his

characters on a stage—that might be a key. I tried to say that birth,
breeding, cold intellectuality, empty tribal and racial attitudes, etc., will
never lead us to the door of heaven .[40]

West probes such questions at all social levels in Actaeon. When he
is through with Diana and O'Dea, he addresses the disinherited tinkers.
In Denis (Dinnie) Dempsey West has created so strong a character, in
fact, that Dinnie threatens to demand his own book. Had West lived
long enough, he might well have capitulated. He adopts a heightened
rhetoric to present him:

> O a vulpine stoneage man this Dempsey under his barren vine, his
> brutality of indifference lurking behind the pious banality of his shrewd
> commercial smile, his t'ank ye sur and god bless ye m'am no different
> to a banker's limpid handfast or managerial dismissal of a redundant
> man; his guile his goad and bit, obsequiousness a sham, his hail and
> well-met an estimation of potential benefit and very like his diplomatic
> dog called Torry that can steal turnips from a field while Delia whines
> a drop of milk for an ailing child and Dempsey marks a roost of bush-
> perched chickens; humility a disguise for arrogance, innocence and
> ignorance, real or pretended, a cover for vicious spleen—in all, so like
> his brother humans that were he not a homeless tinker smelling of
> smoke and poverty, he would be a kind of common man.[41]

Finding one's way is no simple course for any human. One forever
must be accommodating the serendipitous without abandoning the purpose, separating picaresque from quest. But neither is such a modern
pilgrim's progress entirely without guidance or finally without hope.
This progress shows as Stephen, emerging out of West's own Glenveagh
experience, becomes Christopher and the identities of character and
creator unambiguously diverge. None the less symbolic, cautionary,
and poignant for West, Christopher MacMannan in dying in his plane's
crash becomes emphatically fictional. Despite all the promise in his
nature and despite his own laudable expectation, his irresolution and
self-absorption exact their price. He has been too casual about others'

deep feelings. Christopher, the wannabe artist of the fiction, must settle for karmic hope at the auspicious age of thirty-three. His only committed efforts at poems he had foolishly made a bonfire in Belfast. Now he has fatally neglected to stow his parachute. Anthony C. West, in contrast, had more than half his life yet to live; moreover, whatever sympathy he may have felt with Christopher's serendipitous approach and with his neglect of responsibility, the thousands of pages West left, published and unpublished, are at their philosophic least, a monument to action. They bespeak, however, with that relentless effort, an artful reiteration of the soul-search. Had the war left a more conventional mark on West's cosmological views, he might have received wider welcome on the established literary scene.

Although he never became well-known, he has been hailed with those fiction writers like Joyce and Beckett, who commanded and demanded great reach from their readers. Beckett, Thomas, Lawrence, and Saroyan among his contemporaries struck appreciative chords with West, too. As much as he admired the talents of these modernists, he did not share modern cynicism, especially after his R.A.F. participation in the international destruction. It is not that West is either maudlin or sentimental. As a matter of fact he is often sardonically funny, e.g. as he depicts Simon carrying his eel, Ophion, in a tin can around Dublin in *The Native Moment,* or as he deplores a character like schoolmaster Rainey of *The Ferret Fancier* for his exploitation of others and dirty habits. Humor again plausibly and strategically builds with disgust in judgments where MacMannan ought to turn a scrutinous gaze on himself.

> One afternoon he heard a woman's voice singing *Charmaine* in the front room the other side of his partition wall. . . . Her husband was an army sergeant and MacMannan has only to see him once, with Kipling's help, to keep him for a stark mnemonic for war and British Empires: an old sweat straight out of fourteen-eighteen, with a stupid waxed moustache on a long simian upper lip, full wet arrogant sensual mouth, blue-black jowls and chin, shoulders braced back almost to deformity: a man, not himself, but a précis of all the King's Regulations. It was an outrage to create and condition such a being, automaton smelling of shaving-soap

and boot polish, all balls and bellow like Dempsey's shorthorn bull.

Mrs. Dunt was a pretty little woman, very nervous shy and child-like, with butterfat skin, tiny ineffectual hands, deep-blue long-lashed innocent eyes and glossy black abundant hair and . . . [with her cheap and cutting perfume] her comings and goings left behind a kind of diaphanous image of herself that always seemed on heat.

Her buck sergeant left for work every morning at twenty past eight, after blowing reveille on his nose for five minutes between hawks and cannonades of coughs. He returned after five, retreating left-right left-right up the stupid stairs, halting one-two at his door, knocking sharply one-two-three, provoking a flurry inside, the door opening with scraps of hysterical laughter.

He marched inside to a mumble of talk, a chair creaked and then the grunts of a man bending over his boots. The boots dropped dead on the floor and dishes chinked, Dunt's resonant voice coming sometimes loudly and imputative.

Silence for the meal. The dishes were cleared and Dunt relaxed on the squeaky bed which soon squeaked a second time as Mrs. Dunt came aboard with giggles.

Laughs, chuckles, protest and squeals, mumbled pleadings, modest protestations, the old bed groaning like a Cutty Sark in a horse latitude, a head, shoulder or backside sometimes thudding against the partition wall and jingling the flowery wares on MacMannon's wash-stand. The laughter became a constant soprano protest interrupted by moaned denials, the heavings and squeakings increasing slowly to a climax that, hearing it for the first time, scared MacMannan since it sounded like a straight case of ravishment. Finally, after a long silence thrice as disturbing as the rutty preparations, the woman subsided into a grati-tude of groans and tears, Dunt's gruff voice obviously trying to comfort and calm and then becoming impatiently sharp and barrack-square angry, the whole affair ending on the sharp note of a smack and a small yell of protest, thereafter a thick sulky silence grudgingly returning to normal movements and conversation, Mrs. Dunt breaking into one of her airy songs.

The first evening it was interesting, invoking, almost unconsciously,

MacMannan's own lust. But futher overhearings disturbed him, and finally bored and sickened him. He felt like hammering on the wall at the right moment, spoiling Dunt's aim (*As Towns with Fire*, Knopf, 209–211).

In Actaeon, with undeniable humor, West presents Diana's taking on the formidable job of educating a local girl for service as her personal maid:

> He found me or dumped on me a maid or a learner-chatelaine or, rather, appointed me keeper of a non-maid, one Ana Eager whom the boys call Eager Ana. I'm supposed to civilize her and explain the difference between high wide and handsome and the narrow path called strait, a via doloroso about which I'm not too sure myself. Her full name is Anatha which she says her mother discovered in the bible.
>
> I'm not exactly cordon bleu myself but what I'm liable to spoil, Ana can incinerate. So far, I daren't ask anyone in to a meal, not that I want to. Dea eats what's going, the sort of person who only eats to stay alive and not t'other way about, unlike the numerous gourmands and gourmets I've known. When I complain he has no idea of the depths of Ana's repertoire, he says: Be patient. She has a fine head. Help her and she'll learn, good habits are just as catching as bad ones. Find her some decent clothes, make her belong. . . (R, 115–116).[42]

Literally and metaphorically, my Ana is *laide*, if not quite *belle*. Where e'er she walks, she drags her lure. Her eyes are large and grey, calm innocent and secure, her skin grey, her hair a reddish brown, her hips and udders sway as she works and as she works she hums and sings: let him go or tarry, sink or schwim—her untiring theme as she bangs and breaks her way along the days.

Brickbats, her boiled eggs, her scrambles glue, the frieds rubber omelets, her toasts pure carbon which Dea calls the original philosopher's stone. I do fergit t'time, m'am. Don't be stein' it if it's not up t'scratch. Chops, cinders—I forgot. T'cat. Steak, saddle-leather long time on range. T'cat. Cat fares well but looks unhealthy.

Going and tarrying, she dreams daylong of saintly parsons, waking
in wanting nights and driving a tank along the landing to the bathroom
where mortal storms ensue as she wrestles with the bidet, an innovation
that fascinates her, mishandling the faucets and scalding her intimates
(P, 101).

. . . I found her a bra and we got out the sewing machine and with
much kibbling inserted gussets and lengthened the straps, until she can
get one the proper size. To consolidate the improvements, I supplied
a green sweater and girdle to balance the bra, throwing in a tweed skirt
and a pair of nylons: my goodness and guinness—Miss Ana Eager, still
eager but not so.

Eager Ana. She nodded to herself in the mirror, I behind her: four
of us, three two or one through a looking glass. O who is fair? She says
sadly: Pity t'face's not so good. Me teet's all bad. I tell her we'll have
them repaired. Lord, m'am, I hate oul dintists!

Who said that clothes maketh not the woman. On her improved
looks she could take her place in the county pews in church. Dea is
delighted, saying that she may now begin saying no and meaning it:
can any woman ever say that and mean it?

Can you not say no and mean it? I ask her. Shure, I can, me laedy.
They jus' don't heed. Are you not always risking a baby? I know, me
laedy, but it hasn't happened yet.

. . . What would you do with a baby?

I'd have t'get rid of it, I suppose, m'am. Me ister was fillt an' she did.

How?

There's an oul woman beyant Annan Bog, M'am (P, 103–104).

West strategically lets humor build both sympathy for and judgment of
the protagonist: Seeing so much, so accurately, this studied soul from
Simon to Christopher to Diana and O'Dea ought to see just a little more.

In the late thirties the threat of international war was increasing.
He served competently in the Royal Air Force, but war eventually made
West a pacifist.

*Even in 1936 . . . I dreaded the bruited war, hoping it would not come.
By this time I had read a lot about the first world war, talking to many
men who had served in it. . . . [43] [War had] left me with a vivid memory
of many maimed and wounded men walking about in 'wounded blue'
tunics, there being several nearby manor houses requisitioned as hospi-
tals.[44]*

Will Mytton was the name of the sore-faced soldier. I remember that
because of the funeral. This man had an armless friend called Devon
whom Mytton called Dev and I remember that because of Dev and
De Valera, the name then of a terrible rebel. Devon didn't come from
Devon but from the middle of England. He had worked on a farm.
Mytton used to light his cigarettes, even help him pee. . . . They told
. . . about their battles in No Man's Land, saying how stupid they had
been when they had a chance to be made prisoners before they were
wounded. It was the same big shell that wounded them both and killed
five of their companions. Devon's arms were so shattered to the elbows
that the doctor had had to saw them off, leaving him two short stumps.
Because Mytton was so slow and hard to understand, Dev did most of
the talking and was quite cheerful notwithstanding the lack of arms. He
expected to get a good pension and new mechanical arms and hands.
Many times Mytton tried to disagree with things Dev said but usually
gave up. My mother said he was the better educated man. Dev had
only been a farm labourer. I wondered how he could work on a farm
now. He couldn't even manage a horse. Privately, he told my mother
that Mytton had family trouble as well, that he was also wounded in
the privates and that his wife had gone off with another husband (*As
Towns with Fire*, Blackstaff, 33).

*I never did wholly accept the stated reasons for the war although . . .
agreeing that the nazi confrontation was right, if all too late. . . .*
    *Ignorance, they say, is no excuse in law, but had I known more at
the time . . . how the Four Freedoms would be shelved . . . But then, the
bombs I helped to drop were, relatively, just as destructive, the victims not
bothering to ask their tonnage and method of ignition. Nostra culpa. . . .*

On actual operations, I made no friends. I had companions, comrades and fabulated camaraderie. . . . I was helping to kill . . . contradicting in myself all the notions and half-notions, opinions and experiences I had accumulated about living and dying ("The After Vacancy," 72, 78).

West's political views were socialistic and unmilitant. In 1980 he voted for the Plaid

as a constructive and democratic way to voice Welsh opinions and complaints, rather than leaving it to some Free Wales Army. I never wanted to see an exclusive Israeli-type nationalism and would like to see a flourishing truly bi-lingual cultural nationalism built on a sound economic base, malice to none: one that would take care of all citizens instead of using and exploiting them.[45]

At home his parents had misunderstood his resistance to settling down conventionally in Cavan. The owner of Farnham gave him permission to live nine months at Killykeen, where he retreated and wrote what appears to be the intensely autobiographical "Myself and a Rabbit."[46]

The cottage had been built some hundred years before as a shooting-fishing-cum-pleasure lodge, and was still kept in excellent repair. The local landowner for whom my father worked at the time allowed me to live in it, free of charge. On principle, I was not easy about accepting favours from people like hereditary landowners because I did not agree with them. . . . I never felt really happy on those big Irish estates, either as the son of an employee or even as a guest. Too much underpaid labour has gone into the making of these places and the religious politico-racial complexities of the times augmented the serfdom of the miserable Anglo-Irish workmen. . . .

All the ominous cloud of disapproval of my parents because of my refusal to get what they called a good position was only disturbing when I was unable to write. Everyone seemed to agree with my family that I was a ready well-favoured young fellow slowly drifting into some unnameable mode of life . . .

That my mother failed to understand me was most discouraging. She had inoculated me with this itch . . . for she directed my reading and taught me all the nature lore I knew, and many times pointed out the beauty of an evening shaft of sunlight over grey-green rainswept fields. Her Fords, Luthers, Carnegies, MacDonalds, Dickenses, and Lawrences were praiseworthy examples of self-faith and initiative, although she did bunch together her artists, theologians, and industrial opportun-ists with catholic generosity. But she tacitly denied me the right to try. Living on one's wits and black coffee was a grave offence against her Victorian code (872–873).

Was the disappointed lover cited in this admittedly autobiographical rabbit story the one he said he had met at Lucy Porter's, the "Gloria" of Shadows, this American who "had a soft voice and full warm lips," whom he "might have married had not time and distance lied to us?" Threatened by war, impatient with Ireland's repressive attitude toward art, misunderstood at home, and resisting the ties of marriage, West, in his late twenties, abandoned Killykeen and wandered all over Ireland, trying to write. He went back to Kildare, an area that he remembered well from the time his older brother, teaching there in a military school, came to his rescue and invited him to stay with him for at least six weeks, school at home having become so threatening. He explored Kerry and wrote about it in both Room without a Door and the novel called *Wall*.

I lived in Kildare, near the Curragh; when I came back from America, in Kerry, in Dingle, and all around there, and in Donegal. You get the wind and the storms coming in off the Atlantic, and then the sun comes out again. It's wonderful. They should be kept sacred, those places; Donegal the same, a faery place.[47]

In the spring and summer, West caught eels, for profit, living on the land like a gypsy, like an Iron Age Celt.

I've fished for eels in Cavan. There was a closed season the first six months of the year. You had to have a Fisheries Board license, and you

*weren't supposed to fish for them between sundown and sunup, the
time when they fed. We worked five thousand yards of line—a thousand
hooks, and at night. We never caught many the week around full moon.
The wild, dark dirty night was the best. We exported to London. Local
consumption was nil.* [48]

"I like streams, Magnus—watch 'em all day. My hands in 'em, my
feet. . . . ."

"Come an . . .! Wha' d'ye want t'sell eels in Duddlin for, anyways?"

"Not my idea. Devlin an' Lucey think Dublin needs eels an' elected
me because I've cosmopolitan experience. We're stuck with a whole
half-ton of eels an' the London prices won't pay the carriage now with
all the cheap continental fish coming in for the Cockneys" (*The Native
Moment,* 5).

He made another significant move in 1938—to London, which was
on edge, "the newspapers . . . watching how, when and where Herr Hitler's next cat might jump, while always trying to be careful not to offend
the horrible little man." As he continues (in "The After Vacancy"),

*London was a wonderful place where no one worried about your soul if
they hadn't seen you at church. It had more hope, idealism and imagination per square yard than l960's London, plus TV and the Pill, has per
square mile.*

　　*I got to know quite a few young artists, poets and writers; I met a
few older established men of letters and though they had plenty of advice
to offer me about how to go about writing, not any of them was writing
the masterpiece they claimed to know how to compose and not one of
them offered to find me a small job that would keep me writer-alive. . .
.The young unknowns were . . .hungry fighters all, misering their ideas
and unwilling to discuss them for fear of diluting their potency, all of
them living in a kind of creative bud-burst without the post-war flippant,
cynical hedonism while still enjoying existence to the full. It was a brief
time of innocently good creative expectancy that was, did we but know it,
already doomed* (72).

In these years as a single young writer, West enjoyed a few contacts with established literary people. Returning from New York he had met Sean O'Casey on the ship; in London he met James Stephens.

I didn't know many well-known writers—I knew a lot of triers, hungry-fighters generally in the artistic world—painters and the like. They were all broke, all living on sort of one meal a day, and living on their dreams. It was a fine place in many ways; somehow there was a beautiful sort of creative feeling in London then which I can't feel now. . . . I had several long talks with O'Casey on the boat coming back from America. He was . . . at the production of "Within The Gates." He was a nice man . . . quite committed to the Communist kind of thought, which even then in my inexperience, I thought a pity. I thought he should be an artist first, which he was, and a great word-spinner in his own right, instead of hitching a star to any fabricated political ism or philosophy. He was quite dogmatic in many ways but not patronizing.[49]

Hearing from Dr. MacDonald, a literary Scotsman he had met the previous autumn, . . . that James Stephens, the Irish poet, lived in London, MacMannan got himself invited to a cocktail soiree in Stephens' house.

The oddly bourgeois living-room was packed with young, middling and old men and women, the whole a kind of tipsy round-about with Stephens at the centre. He sat on a big hassock in the middle of the room, very like a leprechaun, a glass in his hand and talking away to whatever front or rear happened to be near him: a very small man with a noble head. He had written and published books when MacMannan was trying to bite milk from Kilainey's acrid dug. No parishman, from Landlord down to Vincent de Paul Tommy-John-Joe-Micko Flannigan had ever mentioned his name, when a generation of Americans were falling over it. Nor, for that matter, the name of any poet since safe ass-creeping Tom Moore hung up the harp on Tara's non-existent walls.

Knowing no one, MacMannan found a seat on a settee in a corner and stayed there. . . . He forgot about the party and stared helplessly at the gulf between his own life and Stephens's, suffering all over again the ignorant, unsupported blindness of his own adolescence and first maturity with all its witless, uninstructed, bleak betrayals of innocence and first small decent faiths.

AE's protégé, talking, talking, talking to people who could only guzzle his liquor to help them admire themselves: drinking stage-Irishman sad as a graveyard yew. Stephens looked across the room into MacMannan's eyes and slowly nodded in racial agreement—a kind of sad appositional recognition that burned like a beam of clear light through the haze of witless chatter and shallow sociability (*As Towns with Fire*, Knopf, 104–105).

It's impossible to credit any particulars in this literary contact, but West began to publish in England. "The Scythe" had appeared in *Ireland Today* in 1937. Now *John O' London's Weekly* offered him nine guineas for the rights to "Farewell To A Kid" in November '39.50 His play called "The Window" was taken up by a small theater near Marble Arch. West had spent the summer of 1939 on the Channel Island of Sark, working, he says, on a novel he had started when he returned from North America. Which part of the ur was this? Room without a Door? Wall? Perhaps The Lady Actaeon? He had found himself back in London in September, with his writing put on hold when Chamberlain declared war. Earning Red Cross certification in First Aid on 12 January 1939, West drove ambulance in the Air Raid Patrol for a year. On 15 January 1940, he married.

MacMannan was buying a cup of tea in the ARP canteen when Nan Berry, a Red Cross nurse, came in with a leggy pretty girl who was introduced as Molly Chester. The fine grey eyes, oval face, light-brown hair, shaped lips, even teeth, the walk gestures, the bodily balance all challenged him with dreamlike familiarity. They sat at the same table and Nan rattled on about this and that, the Molly girl saying little, MacMannan nothing at all since he was concentrating on his elusive memory of her or of the face and figure of some woman he had seen unknowingly half-remembered in a street. It was only when they got up and walked away from him that he finally remembered.

He asked Nan Berry about her friend. . . . She said that Molly Chester also remembered the day she had smiled at MacMannan and that their meeting was not accidental. She had recognised him again in a group photograph that Berry had shown her. She was twenty-one. Her mother had died some years previously, when she was at a boarding school with Berry. She disliked her father's second wife and had trained as a secretary and was now supporting herself working for a small chemical firm that was fulfilling war contracts, and so she was in a reserved occupation.

She has her own little flat near Regent's Park, she is a virgin and she thinks you're wonderful. . . .

Although Berry seemed more than willing to act as go-between, MacMannan discouraged her. He knew the next move was his and knew, were it positive, that his life might take a sudden and unexpected turning . . . (As Towns with Fire, Knopf, 141–142).

ENDNOTES

1   Autobiographical statement. sent to Gartenberg, [1976?], ACW Interviews.

2   ACW to Gail Leeson, MacGibbon & Kee, 28 April 1963.

3   Ormond Edwards, taped interview with Audrey Eyler, 1989.

4   Incidents have been published as separate stories (for example, "The Sick Deer;" see bibliography of published works in the appendix), a pattern typical of the snipping, borrowing, and recasting within West's papers, but most of West's North American experience is explored through this unpublished work and in Room without a Door.

5   In a letter to Timothy O'Keeffe, West puzzles over Schaffner's incredulity toward Freya Lethbridge in Naked to Laughter. West calls her "one of the most 'real' people in the whole MS" (21 November 1964).

6   The incident is described on pages 84–87.

7   This Little Pig, an unpublished short story, offers an unusual counter to this pattern, even though the protagonist, Michael, is only fourteen. Penny Bum Curran lays a plan to marry Bob the Bike Kenny by seducing Michael. Bob never sleeps with her, but she claims that her child is his, forcing him to marry her. He suicides. She gets his farm and his name, calling the baby Robert Michael. Michael is apparently responsible for the child, but he escapes all but the new sense of consequence for the small action of an individual. Revised as The Pig and the Poke.

8   Michael Bromley, "The Quiet Revival of Anthony West," in the *Belfast Telegraph*, Wednesday, 20 March 1985, p. 14 notes his absence in "Images," as does John Kilfeather in the *Irish Times*, Saturday, 20 April 1985, "Somewhere Up in the Clouds Above," Weekend section, 5. See Patricia Craig's introduction to her anthology of Ulster writing, *The Rattle of the North*, Blackstaff, 1992.

9   She helped edit the *Dokumants der Frauen*, the first journal in Austria devoted to women's point of view, and published *Kritik der Weiblichkeit* (1908), ACW to AE , 23 November 1986.

10 ACW to Dorothy O'Connor, November 1958.

11 ACW to DO'C. 28 November 1958.

12 Actaeon fragments, "Earliest?" section marked "Chapter 10," with note in top margin: "Prologue. This is the cosmic dream of man . . . " 176–201.

13 ACW, description of "West Project," 18 April 1972, box 8, Documents.

14 I haven't changed my mind on this claim since reviewing the book for the *Irish Literary Supplement*, Spring 1982, 12.

15 ACW to Obolensky-McDowell, 7 May 1957.

16 The intensely autobiographical beginning of Room without a Door (#2,7) includes this comment in Stephen's explanation for leaving the California film studio: "Four years ago at Christmas Time, this time, in New York, my light went very dark while also I discovered that I had definite pre-knowledge of death concerning two normally healthy workmates who died suddenly."

17 ACW to Ted Hickey, 3 August 1977. "The Monocrats" in *River's End* is a parallel story.

18 ACW to AE, 23 November 1986.

19 *The Evergreen Review*, II, 8 (Spring 1959), 16–21, 202–237.

20 West wrote *Swineherd* to distill the unusual experiences on the plains of Canada.
    These distance feelings were renewed when I visited Newgrange and similar so-called druid sites in Ireland and Wales, and now I still resent the loss of spirit over the six thousand years between then and now, not to mention the shambles of Protestant and Roman Catholic history in past and contemporary Ireland. ACW to AE, 23 November 1986.

21 ACW in taped interview with AE, June 1986.

22 ACW to Gail Leeson at MacGibbon & Kee, 28 April 1963.

23 ACW to GL.

24 ACW to GL.

25 ACW in taped interview with AE, June 1986.

26 ACW in taped interview with AE, June 1986.

27 ACW to GL.

28 ACW in taped interview with AE, July 1987.

29 ACW to GL.

30   Thomas M. Montgomery to All Whom It May Concern, 3 Aug 1938, Personal.

31   I am grateful to Ciaran O'Keeffe of the Office of Public Works, Letterkenny, for information on Glenveagh. See "Glenveagh Castle" by William Gallagher, a publication of the Office of Public Works (1993), for the Porters' role in Glenveagh's history.

32   In Room without a Door Stephen is provided with a spiritual genealogy as well as a physical one. He had previously incarnated as a "Red Indian squaw, violated and killed by European settlers. A male member of the Albegenses sect burned at the stake for heresy. A Celtic John-Christian slain by Norsemen. A Jew in Roman service in Palestine at the time of Christ, tortured and killed in Rome for accepting Christianity. A Greek female of Eleusis. A priest in Druid times at Corran, his home. An Egyptian, twice, male and female. . . . . .A Chaldean. . . . . .An early Celt. A Persian. . . . . . .An Indian. . . ." #1, 4–5.

33   "John Montague seemed to think that I was attempting [West probably refers to *Rebel to Judgment*] to write up a kind of autobiography: no. no. no. . . . one *Sons & Lovers* per century is sufficient. But then, who can say what permutations of soul arise when one takes a pen in hand?" ACW to John Boyd, 4 October 1962.

34   Erosion, 3–4.

35   "[Stephen's] loneliness now [was] similar to chronic indigestion round his heart and just as tangibly disturbing. But he knew, with a little patience, that soon it would blend into all his other indigestions, enriching them and making a whole and tolerable major discomfort of all that he had now worn for years (98)."

36   See the discussion of this evolution in *Celtic, Christian, Socialist* as West's four published novels reveal it.

37   "General Comment," 1 June 1969, Notes to *Towns*.

38   Erosion, 8.

39   Only Christ, he says, could have complete awareness, have "no unconsciousness." Men must not lose sight of the individual for the community (wood for the tree), for that would be totalitarianism in action; nor vice versa (tree for the wood); for that would be a form of egotistic fragmentation and anarchy: men need community to be men and community needs men. Erosion, 5.

40   ACW to JS, [4 February 1958].

41   Thieving, brutal Dinnie ultimately takes to his heels in the darkness, bolstering his courage with alcohol and boasting a panoply of roles, as West dramatizes his resilience (R, 648–651; R disk, 538–541).

42   The R version has been entered on a computer disk by Kay Whitford, thanks to a Regency Grant from Pacific Lutheran University. The scrolled page number for this reference is 97.

43   ACW to Gail Leeson, 28 April 1963.

44   ACW to GL.

45 ACW to Mr. Thomas, 9 April 1980, Children's Education.

46 This story appeared in *The Bell*, XI, 4, 860–872, in January 1946; when Devin
    Garrity noted that fact, anthologizing it in *44 Irish Short Stories*, 1955, he did not
    mention that only the last four of the original thirteen pages appear in his collec-
    tion. Did West or another do the cutting?

47 ACW, interview with AE, June 1987.

48 ACW, Account of Irish rural customs, 5, Autobiographical, box 1.

49 ACW to Meirion Edwards, BBC-Wales interview, 29 April 1970.

50 Terence O'Reilly (pseud.) May, Vol 11, 5, 43–47; West mentions stories—
    plural—taken by *John O' London*, but I have located no more than this cited
    one about the goat, which is excerpted from The Casual Comedy part of the ur:
    20 Nov 1939, *John O' London's Weekly* to ACW, offering 9 guineas for first British
    serial rights to "Farewell To a Kid."

Chapter Five

LONDON 1940: GESTURES OF DEFIANCE

I . . . married in 1940: perhaps, as much as anything else, as a gesture of defiance.[1]

Was West referring to the inauspicious context of the war, which jeopardized all efforts toward conjunction and settlement? Was it that, as Molly in *Towns* eventually did to Christopher, Olive proposed to him? West married Olive Mary Burr, an English girl, a highly trained secretary like Molly, whose academic competencies included English literature and French. He met her through friends at sessions on Anthroposophy. He had been interested in Rudolf Steiner's humane teachings since, at twenty-one,[2] he encountered them in America; Olive had learned about Anthroposophy in France. Both were sympathetic with the efforts in England to start a school. They went to a civil registrar for their marriage; years later they observed a second wedding ceremony in a Christian Community service. He had wisely found a partner who also appreciated his writing.

We were a good match. She is more intellectual, more practical.
. . . Wife or no wife, she is a hard critic. She said . . . firstly, a book must be readable.[3]

Olive was dedicated to his art, critically astute, independent, unsentimental, and patient. They became a loyal pair. It's impossible to fault his judgment on this matter of their suitability. The ship of marriage groaned ominously in some bad weather—no surprise—but it was oak. From the start, she honored the precedence claimed by her husband's muse, and shared his allegiance to spiritual priorities.

Olive became a formal member of the Steiner-influenced Christian Community. Although he officially joined neither the Anthroposophists nor the Christian Community, West participated in programs of the Community and maintained an aggressive interest in the socialist, Christian, anthroposophical studies for the rest of his life.

> *You might call me a lay Anthropop but as a writer I claim to be free, malice to none. In describing the attitudes and foibles of my contemporaries I'm describing my Self; peeling the onion, hoping that I have enough artistry to make my contributions palatable (I say a prayer whenever I begin a new opus, that I won't be led to do much harm to Christ and to Steiner).*[4]

Many of his letters are devoted to anthroposophical study and his fiction probes some of its ideas.[5] West occasionally published in bulletins of the Christian Community, a group founded by German Lutheran seminarians who organized between the Wars and sought Steiner's counsel. Poised sympathetically between the two groups, West explained the "Anthropops" as the more philosophically inclined, the more theoretical, and the CC as the more practical and social. Hence he could speak of people's being temperamentally more suited to one or the other, or a friend could say to him that an article was "too anthroposophical for the Christian Community journal."[6]

Although he loved to follow world politics from the outside, he appears to have had little patience with the internal schisms and administrative quarrels of any party or institution. He and Olive tried a move to Ireland, living in Belfast and its environs, both working for the Navy Army Air Force Institutes until Olive's first pregnancy forced her to stop; meanwhile West ran deliveries and checked stock to guard against

Olive Burr, visa photo for au pair *service in France, 1937.*
WEST FAMILY COLLECTION, PHOTOGRAPHER UNKNOWN.

internal pilfering. The account of MacMannan's experience with this "kind of para-military supply organization" may explain as much as West knew about his own employment's short tenure, although the reader of the novel infers from her coinciding visit that the revengeful jealousy of Christopher's former lover lay behind the loss of the position.

Without any warning MacMannan was dismissed from his job and within a day was unemployed, no reason given nor any accusation made although, a few days before, he had been earmarked for promotion and warned that he might have to move into new territory but with a salary increase.

He knew he had never made any major practical mistakes and very few minor ones and had never discussed his attitude to the war with any colleague, nor never attempted to saddle his Rosinante to charge local and provincial windmills. . . . . All he could think of was that, for some reason, he was now seen as a poor security risk, an alarming suspicion in a land where muffled totalitarianism, now overlaid by wartime bureaucracy, had been in existence since Carson had recruited his drum-valiants to defend the fords of holy Ulster (*As Towns with Fire*, Knopf, 241).

My Belfast history? Wartime, blackout: misty cobbled streets with the air-raid bombs and children screaming in the dusk. Had a room in gasworks area, the smell constant as the sweetness of death and rotting flesh. . . .
No work, Olive carrying Michael and trying to earn two pound a week for us while coping with morning sickness. January, cold, drizzle-and-smog. We used to go up the hills weekends.....felt nothing, all feeling beaten and spent; hatred too, and fear—not suffering, no. Can any cornered animal suffer? How can anyone suffer when bare survival of integrity means so much?[7]

He may have felt "beaten and spent," but the experience became useful material for his art. Their general experience in Northern Ireland informs *As Towns with Fire*, especially the American edition by Knopf in 1970. In the same letter West describes, for example, the Belfast incident that he transplants in *Towns* to Crewe (Blackstaff, 409–410):

. . . Was firewatching in Belfast before I went into the bloody airworks. Standing one summer evening at the side door of Woolworths with several crafty 'colleagues'. Three Americans were wheezing a little girl in a shop doorway. My companions said she was 14. Her mother was waiting down at the end of the street. She was asking a pound apiece. The yanks wanted a package deal, three goes for two quid. Finally she consented. First one went while the second opened his fly. Then second went and the third produced his cock and stroked it. My companions told me they would now all be poxed. The girl went down to her mother and

"In a dumb way I was fighting for world peace. I had not volunteered to destroy Germany." West standing in back row, third from left. Cirkut photo perhaps by W. A. Rumble, The Watch House, Overy Staithe. Photographer untraceable. PHOTO THANKS TO GEORGE WOOLSEY, K. DUNMIRE.

West in Royal Air Force uniform. WEST FAMILY COLLECTION, PHOTOGRAPHER UNKNOWN.

handed over the dough and got told off for dropping the price. Mother
had several daughters operating.[8]

When Michael John was born, 24 August 1941, they were living in
33 King Street, Bangor.[9] In order to support his family and to fight the
Nazis, the would-be-pacifist decided to join the Royal Air Force. When
her husband left, Olive soon decided to return to London.

> *. . . I made a wrong move. I should have waited, should have had faith,*
> *in the Greek sense of the word pistis. But I was afraid and so, to get out*
> *of the war, I got into the war, conditioning myself not to think. It was a*
> *mistake. I should have waited (If the child is worth bearing, it is worth*
> *gestating). But the 'law' says that one can only know truth after the*
> *error's commission. . . . The uniform was a disguise; physically, I was*
> *anonymous, a number, and yet valued as a potential instrument..*[10]

West was sent to South Africa for military training, a place that
extended as well his literary resources.

> Meg Rutherford was her name, a South African not long in England
> and now working for a London paper. . . .He picked her brains about
> South Africa, a country to which he had once thought about going.
> She gave him a depressing picture that wasn't new to him: Paddy Reilly
> with black skin and mealie-patch in lieu of a white skin and spud-patch
> (*As Towns with Fire*, Blackstaff, 121–122).

> *It was an extraordinary time. I had extraordinary dreams. I wasn't half*
> *here. It was like I was living in a haze, going through motions as best I*
> *could. I dreamed—and now I can see it—my life as it has unfolded. My*
> *life seems . . . it was never new. Deja vue. All the time.*[11]
>   *After a couple years' training, half of which were spent in waiting, in*
> *which I saw more of the world and of South Africa in particular (one of*
> *the saddest countries it has ever been my lot to experience), I was finally*
> *posted to a Pathfinder squadron, the one Guy Gibson started, and was*

commissioned as a navigator-bomber cum meteorological air observer, on two-man Mosquito aircraft.[12]

After a silence, Brice said: It's still a mystery to me why you're in this at all.

I told you once, I'm a poor man in need of a job, MacMannan said.

Ireland couldn't give you a living?

No, unless I consented to bury myself like the fellow with the coin in the Gospels. And now, I'm buried anyway. I'm on the wrong track, but if I leave it, I may not be strong enough to find a way through the jungle on either side. On the other hand, despite its population, Ireland has given me everything I have.

You may go too hard on yourself?

Better that than punishing strangers! (*As Towns with Fire*, Blackstaff, 493)

Creatively, artistically, I wasn't strong enough to withstand it all, to objectify it. Other artists seemed able to do this—Dublin was full of British runaways—Hitler's Harriers, the wits called them. I had no contact with them—their escapism seemed just as totalitarian as anything else. . . . Am I my brother's keeper? . . . In retrospect, it was a peculiar state of mind. I was becoming naked; watching all clothing platitude, opinion, and attitude falling away from me. All those personal impressions and intuitions, of that time, haven't much external value. The process of becoming naked went on and on until I was naked, numb, and dumb: standing in the storm's quiet eye.

. . . By a series of fortunate 'accidents' [West did not believe that any events in life were accidental[13]*] I was given one of the finest pilots in the service. (Poor pilots, like poor navigators, got the chop too easily.) I had no emotional-creative contact with my pilot at all. It seems strange, considering all our mutual hazards, that he could have been someone in an office whom I saw every day, and that was all.*[14]

I navigated best as I could, only incidentally for myself, mainly for my pilot since I didn't want to kill him by a mistake of mine. He couldn't

understand me but, nevertheless, he was a magnificent Mosquito pilot
and Mozzies are hard kites to manage, betimes. All right, I would think
for him, too: try to think the thoughts he couldn't think or didn't want to
think. I had no friends—only this inarticulate and dangerous association
with my pilot.[15]

Faithful to their singular wartime intimacy, though never really close, they maintained a Christmas correspondence afterward. In 1975 pilot Wilfred Yeadell returned to their old base at Woodhall Spa—"to see if there was anything left of the old days." He reported that Tattershall Thorpe, the little village, had been submerged in a large mall, and the Fergy (Ferguson Fawcitt Arms pub) and the Mucky Duck (the Black Swan in Coningsby) were now "all formica and chrome." Locals had no interest in the history of the old airfield. It had almost disappeared in grass and bushes.[16] The selectivity of his memory surprised him, he said. Tattershall Castle dominates the landscape, but Yeadell had no recollection of it.

627 Officers mess is still complete, gutted and about four inches deep in chicken manure all over, but the buildings are still there. Took me back a bit, I can tell you, as we walked through that entrance way from the road. It was a bit difficult to try to describe my feelings to the others; the youngsters would have no doubt laughed anyway, so I just wallowed in nostalgia on my own. The old sleeping quarters have gone; a couple of big houses and a chicken farm have taken over. . . .

Our last port of call was Woodhall Spa and on to your cottage. This had hardly changed at all, although I could not find the pathway through the woods from the aerodrome fence to the road that we used to use. The cottage and the pathway to it across the fields was [sic] just as I remembered it. . . .17

While West was in Africa, Olive stayed for just a short time in Ireland before returning to London, from which she and Michael were evacuated to Rochedale in Lancastershire. In 1944 West joined Squadron 627 and the laborer's cottage—with mattresses on the floor, one table, and no electricity—next to the airbase in Lincolnshire became the contrastively idyllic home cited by Yeadell and described in *Towns*.

> Two big rooms down, one a tiled kitchen with a pump over the jawtub and the other a large sitting-room; three bedrooms upstairs; some old kitchen chairs, a table and one single iron bed; a comfortable dry closet in the back garden (*As Towns with Fire*, Blackstaff, 441).

> *I was lost: Couldn't afford to wonder what it was all about. I had joined up to help eradicate Nazism. . . . In a dumb way I was fighting for world-peace. I had not volunteered to destroy Germany. . . . I had the spring but it was very remote—used to lie awake in the nissenhut and listen to the nightingales—wonderful birds. I had no answers—scared to make any. I clung to the squadron comradeship which was very real.*[18]

MacMannan packed his kit, watching his hands. They were quite steady and still clean: the wounds they might have caused might also have been deep, sore, but bloodless. And yet there was a glimmer of the hunt's excitement in him, a blind going into limbo and no longer sure of anything, like the mystics when they faced chaos and heaven's wild winds, themselves their own masters, guides and light. . . .

Greater love hath no man to murder for his friends: the evening sun a phoenix dying again in lovely whorls of cirrus, darkness already garnered by the east. They all packed into the Black Maria and it started rolling to the flights across the aerodrome. The short journey was like a stage on an initiation, all the neophytes expectant of the dark psychopomp, staunching their nervousness and putting witty phrases in the mouth of their suspicious fortune.

They located B Bertie standing like a big dragon-fly on its delicate-seeming undercarriage and clambered up the little ladder, settling themselves as one of the attendant acolytes closed the outer hatch and sealed them off from the known world . . .

They were given the green light by the control caravan. It was exactly 1816.30 hours. Seaton eased his throttles forward and the speed gathered, the engines taking on a rhythmic triumphant beat, the exhaust stubs beginning to glow white and blue and yellow like furious flowers, the runway lights running together into a solid streak. Airborne: up undercarriage and a slow shallow turn to port. MacMannan switched on the Gee and watched the strong healthy blips moving across the screen. With it, until it faded and the Germans jammed it, he could take an exact fix every minute if necessary and find the illusive winds to the nearest degree and knot.

He changed from outer tanks to main and switched off the navigation lights, logging it and telling Seaton to climb as near the operational height of 15,000 feet as possible as they had a good ten minutes in hand before setting course. It made wind-finding easier, rather than climbing out on track through many wind levels. Very soon the lighted runway was no more than an inch long, the land below fading into darkness and sleep. . . .

Although the land was still quiet, dark and dead below, at 20:15 hours he told Seaton they were over the target area, asking him to orbit. Seaton was doubtful, unable to see any sign of life and then they heard the raid controller making radio contact with the Flare Force Lancasters and with Noakes, the Marker Leader, and saw the primary blind markers flowering far below, followed by a fairy row of flares that turned night into a bright-moon day. . . .

The brilliant white photo-flashes stabbed into the darkness as each Lancaster released its load, the cameras synchronised with the impacts. Each crew had to bring back a film of its prowess and flak or no flak the bomb-aimers had to hold their aircraft steady on the aiming point or else risk wild deliveries and serious reprimands. . . .

The gathering fires reddened the clouds of smoke and dust as Lancaster after Lancaster went in and dropped, the entire target area now a single erupting burning mass like a volcanic crater. MacMannan was sweating although the temperature outside was minus ten degree centigrade. The searchlights coned a tiny silver bomber. It looked pathetic and defenceless, hardly seeming to move. Then it suddenly disappeared in an exploding mass. MacMannan watched for parachutes but saw none: six men, six young men.

Another Lancaster went up…Christ, they're getting hammered,

Seaton said. Let's get t'hell out of here?

Course 282 degrees, MacMannan said. It's straight out over Texel. There'll be defended areas to starboard.

They saw the faint outline of the Zuider Zee on port, Texel ahead. Over the sea Seaton put the Mosquito into a shallow dive and roared home (*As Towns with Fire*, Knopf, 382–387).

Leave came again and MacMannan went to the cottage. Mrs. Basings had had it scrubbed from top to bottom and it was fresh as a new board. There was just sufficient furniture and a double hairmattress on the floor for their bed. Molly could make a few curtains. She had the big cot and bedding for the twins. It all seemed right, bone-bare clean essentials and with the exception of the sacred parlour not much different to how he had lived at home. He ordered coal for the old rat-trap kitchen range and bought a primus stove and dug, cleaned and manured the garden and put in some late greens; clipped the overgrown privet hedge and barrowed lovely white quartz gravel from a pit behind the farmhouse. The soil was almost pure sand and when he went down a foot, it was entirely golden sand. He made a sandpit for the twins and opened a refuse pit behind the privy.

Molly arrived in the middle of the week and was so delighted that she wept a little. It was better than Buckingham Palace (*As Towns with Fire*, Blackstaff, 445).[19]

It promised to be a good leave . . . although he almost dreaded the contact . . . the children shy, seeing him as a quarter stranger. . . . their innocence of war and its ways an eerie frustrating thing that denied the use of words to explain his brief appearances between absences. O Christ in Ballymena, how could he maintain himself as their father in this their most formative blotting-paper age without tainting their imitative faculty with the dead dog excuse that they might also run amok, if and when their own majority met with hard challenge and apparently hopeless frustration. The war-makers never seemed to think of this, branding all fathers in sons' eyes as licensed gunmen while parsons praised corpsed heroes into graves. (*As Towns with Fire*, Blackstaff, 373)

I had a white duck when I was in the Air Force. Michael and Mary killed it. We used to take her for a bath in the evening to the nearest pond. She was a marvelous pet. Very intelligent. She'd follow us, quacking loudly if we walked too quickly.[20]

What did you do to Jane? he asked them.

They didn't answer.

I'm not going to punish you, he assured. I only want to know so I might do something to help her.

We were playing...Conall whispered.

We were playing, Gwyon agreed, nodding.

. . . .

He wandered over the fields, ashamed to let Molly see him crying. When he returned, Jane was no better. . . . a little while later the duck made a sudden quack and died, the bright-eyed head falling over the edge of the box and so close to her he was that he felt the death's exquisite pang like a snapped string: the broken cord or shattered chord, her little note of music silent. (*As Towns With Fire*, Blackstaff, 558)

I didn't think. I obeyed orders. I didn't think because I had to exist, although I knew I was helping to destroy that other Germany of Goethe, Schiller, Herder, Fichte: the Germany the Prussian had begun to destroy more than a century before, helped on [by] my British chauvinism and autocracy: Hohenzollern princelings made Roman emperors. . . .

Olive had a big belly, her sleepy child moving in her. The child was born to me, yelling healthily. V day came and the squadron comradeship fell apart, all the boys measuring themselves for civvy suits. I'd lost Jane, I'd lost the comradeship, nothing seemed to have much meaning. The new baby.......Maybe, I sometimes thought, it would have been better had I not come back—death was quick in Mozzies: but I knew that death was never quick—that, long or short, it had its own time. But it would have been nice to have been able to tell the duck that the war was over......[21]

West's father, George West, died in September of 1942; West's second child, Mary, was born in December. It had been in the summer of that same year, back in Ireland, that Sean O'Faolain boldly celebrated "Myself and Some Ducks" in *The Bell*. O'Faolain was exuberant: "We have never printed anything more original, fresh, and beautiful in concept and style. . . . We must hold our breaths in the presence of one of the most tremblingly sensitive imaginations that has yet ventured into . . . Irish life"[22] Although the conclusion of "Myself and Some Ducks" was aborted by the censors,[23] O'Faolain eventually ran two more of West's stories. He was still enthused after the War, and West retained an appreciation for O'Faolain's help, but O'Faolain grew impatient with West's prolixity: ". . . In the name of God almighty when are you going to give birth to a nice wee mouse without any more knots in his tail than is necessary, . . . SMALL ENOUGH FOR AN EDITOR TO PRINT?"[24]

> *Sean O'Faolain gave me a leg up there. I was writing my own thing;*
> *I belonged to a nonschool, hammered out my own philosophy. I had*
> *no formal education. I was breaking through—had broken through in*
> *1939—then the War came. The war took fifteen years of my life.*[25]

Three months on, February 23, West's mother, Ellen Clements West, died and was buried next to George in Saint Gobhan's churchyard, Seagoe, diocese of Dromore, near Portadown.

> His mother, dead: hot heart still, blood stagnant, cold, body dressed in a box, nature taking over the empty vessel and beginning to reduce it to dust; no longer the active being when meadow, grove and stream and earth and every common claimed her. He chanted to the empty bleak aerodrome what he could remember of the Ode as a kind of epicede, feeling an addition to his existing self-loneliness (*As Towns with Fire*, Blackstaff, 439).

The Wests' third child, Bronwen, was born late in 1944.

> The twins were restless. He got up and went to them. They were awake, almost as if they knew, lying there in the darkness, their eyes black holes in their almost invisible faces. He kissed them, asking them to be good

because Molly was making a brother or sister for them.

Will it be like us? Conall asked.

Yes, up to a point, he said. But it will also be like itself.

Has it come out of Molly yet? Gwyon asked.

No, not yet, he said. But it's on its way. Try and go to sleep.

The pains started near dawn and increased with the light. Mac-Mannan wanted to get the midwife but Molly delayed him, saying there was no need to pull the woman out of bed and then make her wait, maybe for a couple of hours. But Molly misjudged her labour and when MacMannan wanted to phone the midwife, she begged him not to leave her. Helplessly, he watched her, terrified by his own incompetence. She tossed the bedclothes aside, arching her knees and throwing her entire will into the down-bearing, groaning in her throat like an animal. Spellbound, he watched the great sexual rent distending and saw the dark crown of the child's head. It forced slowly through, waited and came on again. He had never seen anything so immediately inevitable in his life and now worried about the child, his concern for it a pure instinct. Molly made a vast effort and the head came cleanly, followed by the oiled body like a wet fish slipping through a hand and there was the immediate promethean cry of triumph or of fear or loss or gain—he didn't know, a new being lying there in the cradle of Molly's thighs (As Towns with Fire, Blackstaff, 467).[26]

The war continued. As West marked for the bombers in raids on Hamburg, Dresden, and Oslo, as well as on strategic installations up and down the European coast, his mother's spirit was his frequent companion.

We had some . . . uncanny experiences together: my mother, who had died in 1944, had become more 'real' than the dangers, and many a time my hardheaded pilot never realised that there were three souls in the cockpit, not two.[27]

He was demobilized on Midsummer's Day, 1946.

I remember on that longest day of the year getting up and going out into
the dawn. It was lovely. I stood thinking. I didn't get the chop, and there
were all those fellows I knew who didn't come back.[28]

Christopher MacMannan, like West, agrees to make an unrequired
meteorological flight over Ireland when his official term of duty in the
RAF is over, but for Christopher it is fatal. West survived the dangerous
flying assignments.

Trying again after the war with his promising new voice in *The Bell*,
O'Faolain ran "Myself and a Rabbit," again under West's pseudonym
"Michael MacGrian." This time West escaped censorship. In 1946, he
also received the encouragement of a Rockefeller Atlantic Award. In the
spring of this year Jocelyn was born. With four children now, West took
up the cottage-farming, which Christopher MacMannan loves and does
so successfully.

After demob, I helped organize an adult education centre which planned
to challenge increasing state-ism and nationalization of . . . thinking
[1947]. It was good fun and honest work, but it failed for lack of funds
and post-war apathy.[29]

Albrighton, near Shrewsbury, where West raised vegetables, pigs,
and chickens that were locally marketed, was the first among numerous
socialist experiments the family joined. Besides its productive gardens
and barns, it offered a conference center, largely for Anthropsophists and
Christian Community members, and its leaders intended also to train
Christian Community priests. Although it wasn't making it financially
when the Wests eventually left,[30] this experiment was successful enough
while it lasted not to discourage them from trying to establish its like
many times in decades ahead. The Albrighton experience introduces, in
fact, a pattern of hope, successes, and failures that would dominate West's
entire life; the process was to repeat itself at least six times. This pattern,
moreover, parallels in certain ways and informs the course of his literary
career. He encountered at Albrighton members of an anthroposophical

group from Essex who had struggled and disbanded, but its patron was eager to revitalize it.

With organic farming ideals shaped by theories owing much to Goethe, West became deeply interested in Ardleigh Park and was trusting where he soon learned not to be. This Colchester project initiated its management on Anthroposophy's "bio-dynamic" principles in October 1950. Intending to give Ardleigh Park at least two years, the Wests had moved from Albrighton, but problems soon developed between him and the financier, Winifred Elin, making him file a "Report on leaving Ardleigh" on 26 June 1951. Elin's early letter might have held some clues to what lay ahead, for after mapping out the garden and field-plantings, describing all the procedures she had already undertaken for procuring livestock and composting crops, and agreeing "to his propositions, i.e., Tony West—£4 per week plus cottage, Olive & children—lunch & tea daily," she proposed to separate the newly employed couple. He and three children would live in the cottage, and Olive, the new baby, and children home on holiday (at the time Michael and Mary were staying with Olive's mother, Ruby) were to live with her in the manor. What could she have been thinking? Olive says she found herself being pressured into a domestic servitude that was not part of the original plan. West gradually concluded that, whether she was devious or deluded, Winifred Elin was toying with people and with Anthroposophy, that she was ignorant and defensive about organic farming, irresponsible about the budget, and that she was sanctimoniously inconsistent about the use to be made of her home.

> For some reason you accused ___ of bringing in dark forces! Now, this is the worst kind of anthroposophical witch-hunting. Winifred, you would have to convince me that you really could see into the astral world before I'd listen to any dark force story. Why not say to ___ that you didn't want him after all? Then, apparently X incarnated dark forces! Lord save me, but we all have very dark forces! That's one reason why we're on earth at all. . . . .
>
> One thing X let fall, and apparently it shook her considerably, coming from you an Anthroposophist. It shook me rigid, especially after

*all the fairly deep anthroposophical conversations we had had. During
the suggestion that some young woman who had an illegitimate child
should come here, chiefly because she was a good type and a good worker
and quite nice, you blatantly laid down the law that no illegitimate
would ever live in Ardleigh Park. Now, how by all that's wonderful do
you synchronize that statement with all that Steiner has ever said about
birth, death, and reincarnation? Any wonder why I say that I'm not really
convinced in your Anthroposophy?*[31]

After charting her basic managerial departures from the plan he
thought they had agreed to follow, he listed numerous little examples,
saddening or maddening, of her negligence or defiance. Driven to a
specificity that made him uncomfortable—he felt obligated to demon-
strate that the contract-breaking, of which she was now accusing him,
was "by no means entirely one-sided"—he included this account:

*In May 1950 [before assuming occupancy], at your request, I put in an
acre of wheat, which you wanted to have ground up for bread. When I
returned in October I found said wheat converted into a cat's lavatory.
Peasant as I am, I hold that wheat is still a very noble grain.*

    *As if I had mislead you, you told me that you had thought we
could see the milk of one cow, after the official telling you directly in
the cowhouse that you could not. You said that you would never . . .
[have had] the dairy [done] up had you known. Now, I know that you
always wanted that old dairy done up because you were fond of it (a good
enough reason in itself, by the way) but why try to make a case out of it.
And incidentally, how could you sell milk from one cow when said milk
was going to two households and a calf?*

    *I asked you to spray the wheat and rye with 501. Three weeks later I
asked you again. . . . You have never touched 501 to this day. . . . Surely,
as a conscientious BD [Bio-Dynamic] enthusiast, this would be one of
the first and last jobs you would do? On issues like this I just can't get
excited any more about your desire for a BD farm. As a member of the
Experimental Circle I fully expected you to work closely with me in these
things. Really, I can't help feeling that it's all a sort of hobby with you*

*and that it all becomes a bit of a bore when it threatens to disturb the
tenor of your existence.*

*I still think . . . you . . . see the place as it was in its heyday, thirty
years ago. It will hurt you to hear that Ardleigh Park is a mild laughing
stock with most of the neighbors but they figure that the Elin sisters have
plenty of money and that's the way they want to spend it. I don't mind
a tinker's dam what the neighbours think as I don't think in their terms
at all. You're trying to live in the two camps, and one of the camps is
dead and the other is not born; so therefore you're not living anywhere, in
reality.*[32]

In this same "Report on Leaving," West told her he was going to
Wales, thanks to an offer in May of a house. He had no job prospect and
no funds. He would return her present of cash (£120) as soon as he could
borrow or earn the money.

An idealism that West never discarded motivated his adoption of the
Ardleigh project. At the same time that he became increasingly canny
about implicating people beyond his family in the dreams, he repeatedly
risked and encountered disappointment in such ventures. Almost immediately after the Ardleigh failure he went to Westmoreland with a similar
purpose, this time at least taking the precaution of testing it alone before
moving the family to the estate of the shoe-manufacturing Somervelles.

*I chose Ardleigh . . . because I knew the place and its people and
problems, turning down the prospect of two materially better jobs. . . . I
figured that even at the end of two years the Ardleigh soil and finances
would not be yet rich enough to carry a large and growing family, whose
demands on all counts would increase rapidly with the years. During
the two years I saw no great hope of any substantial cash return, but was
quite prepared to slog on. . . . After the two years, I would be forced to put
some of my idealism in my pocket and concentrate on providing for my
family. . . . I had hoped to work into other pioneer jobs on other farms,
using Ardleigh as a sound reference. . . You see, I believe in BD, and in
its place in this crack-pot civilization of ours. . . . Apart from actual BD*

procedures: as you know I have certain ideas and convictions regarding the social side of Anthroposophy, but these I had no wish at any time to foist on Ardleigh Park.[33]

Reflecting on such experience when he was seventy-six, West explained,

I went to farming for a few years, working on derelict places and trying to revive them. There was an intimate personal symbolism in all this. I worked for and with folk, many of whom had made fortunes out of the war. They had money but little hope, little faith. I had faith and they seemed to live on it. Farming had always been a second nature; I didn't have to think about it: listen to a farm, and it tells you what it needs.[34]

West simultaneously anchored his agricultural idealism with detailed accounting.

When I was helping on derelict farms I always insisted on a good, tight bookkeeping system, finding usually that the farm's disorders were duplicated in the books or, lacking books, in the mind of the farmer. At the same time, I never barrened the farm just to produce a tidy ledger.[35]

He worked in the garden . . . for the relief it gave him. Molly was surprised at his skill. Some folk are born with spoons in their mouths, he said. I was born with this, instead. He held up the spade. Culture's first instrument and maybe, even, the final one, when all these swashers have buckled themselves out of existence (As Towns with Fire, Blackstaff, 452).

Not every agricultural recommendation appears to have been sound by present standards. He probably would agree now to revise a note like this: "Insulate greenhouse heaters with an asbestos box and pack with sand or cinders."[36] His life-long crusades to control pests organically, to recycle waste, and to revitalize land, however, strike any contemporary reader as visionary. In a job application he submitted in 1959, when he was approaching fifty, West described his agricultural expertise as

> *more than semi-skilled in the associated crafts, including management*
> *and maintenance of machinery: also knowledge of accounts, records,*
> *costing, etc. [with] hobby interests . . . in land-reclamation, grass produc-*
> *tion, and pedigree animals.*[37]

A collection of carbons for essays[38] called *Farmer's Boy* is the primary evidence of West's formal agricultural writing, though his expertise
in the subject is apparent throughout his fiction and correspondence,
and a couple of these publications themselves have turned up. In this
Farmer's Boy series of roughly a half-dozen pieces running about 1500
words each, the narrator is a hired man who gradually gains the boss's
confidence as he increases the vitality of the farm. He describes the boss
in the first of these exemplary (not necessarily contiguous) paragaphs:

> Although he is not a suspicious man he can't seem to get over the habit
> of doubting a workman's conscientiousness. I don't blame him, and I'll
> just have to re-educate him by example because, if unchecked, I feel his
> mental attitude when matched against the powerful proletariat would
> precipitate the danger of land nationalization which few of us want but
> into which the less discerning of us could be talked.
>
> If I want a smoke and a breather when the boss is about, I take it.
> His absence or presence doesn't make me work any more or any less.
> I give him his rank—his capital is involved, not mine. But if he ever
> contemplates something which seems to me to be daft, I'll pull him
> up much as he would pull me up under similar circumstances. So far
> the score is about even.
>
> He says I coddle the animals too much, and I tell him a nervous beast
> is often a poor doer. Some conscious kindliness to soil and animal often
> offsets a little of farming's inevitable brutality and violence.
>
> Maybe it's because of my peasant blood that I seem to have more
> instinctive respect for the soil than many a 'titled' farmer, although I
> know I'd be much more comfortable were I more callous. Rich brown
> soil running off the plough still thrills me more than a thousand acres of

ripening Canadian wheat curtseying to the sun. Somehow, I still believe that the earth is the Lord's and the fullness thereof and that we're all farmers' boys working for bosses that are not yet born.

These articles are a striking form for West, and they may help to explain some of the editorial disappointment in his sales. The "Farmer's Boy" essays present the voice of a cheerful, eccentric, forceful expert. Here West can be as idiosyncratically assertive as Carlyle's Teufelsdröckh. The record shows that although some editors and reviewers were flatly dismissive of West's didacticism, of his plots' unhurried length, or of his Romantic intensity, as many admired his talent and regretted that he simply wasn't right for their particular markets.[39]

From *River's End* in 1958 to *As Towns with Fire* ten years later, West usually received appreciative press notices, though some reviewers ignored or failed to probe the substance of his thought. Some reviewers admitted difficulty: "The reader will . . . not mind the work [of reading the book several times]" or "It may look like the standard blockbuster, but it is harder going. . . ."[40] A few openly resented the presence of idea and argument, preferring what West called "all this present concentration on the psychopathic and quasi-abnormal."[41] Opposite responses to this idiosyncratic prose can both be understood: A shrewd editor can say the " . . .incredibly long discussions [are] just not acceptable; [they are] . . . extraneous to the novel itself.[42] And an equally wise reviewer can argue that calling them extraneous is like calling the hell-fire sermons irrelevant in Joyce's *Portrait* because Stephen Dedalus is more attracted by the flesh.[43] The magnitude and depth of West's knowledge and vision did make it challenging to absorb, and editors, while recognizing his genius, were naturally frustrated in trying to direct it to commercial purposes. "I am amazed and astonished at your knowledge of mythology and of ancient and alien civilizations. . . . My criticism is not either of your ability as a writer, or your knowledge as a man, but simply that . . . you have done something that just does not work out."[44]

West knew he had to integrate with the "thin edge of the wedge" the philosophical substance with the whole novel, but it was difficult to make this material unobtrusive. When he started to polish a piece from the ur for publication, he was likely to begin with pieces in which the characters articulate the ideas explicitly. Through much revising he gradually subdued the message to character. Weighty exposition and a preachy tone[45] may nevertheless protrude and compromise artistic effect. The discussion in the Lincoln Cathedral between Brice and Christopher of *As Towns with Fire* remains a mild, published example of this tendency. (Possibly, in defense of their conversation, it could be said that the context of war justifies talk that would otherwise seem more natural from podium or pulpit.) Unpublished and unpolished typescripts include much stronger examples. Some early samples from his fictions read like Menippean satire, pure ideas being equipped with legs and tonsils.

Such discourse runs concurrently with the intensely poetic descriptions that also mark West's style. West's American colleague Jack Curtis diplomatically put a finger on this feature when he called *The Native Moment* a "slugger as well as a poem." [46] While some readers excused high lyricism or ecstasy—along with bombast—in the context of adolescent themes and sensibilities, others dismissed both rhetorical extremes as nineteenth-century.[47]

Readers' tolerances varied, but neither the emotional intensity nor the spiritualized analysis appealed widely enough to a literary market weaned on Hemingway and maturing with Norman Mailer.[48] By the second half of the century, many people were no longer trying to integrate the fragments of their own inexplicable existence and became increasingly dismissive of anyone who still did. Having given up on a cosmic whole, such readers satisfied themselves with clever arrangements of the bits and pieces. Apart from artistic principles and taste, West confronted a twentieth-century intolerance of the pulpit. God, after all, was dead. American culture at mid-century was obviously very interested in adolescence, and editors initially were excited to see West talking about it better than most, but James Dean and Elvis Presley were not making soul-journeys like Simon Green's.

There was also that problem of authorial freshness. He was, it was true, ultimately exploring and developing a soul's progress, but he feared he would appear simply repetitious when Obolensky decided to put out *Moment* and *Rebel* separately but so close together, and *Ferret* was shortly picked up by Simon and Schuster. He would have liked seeing at least the later two offered under one cover, but resigned himself to waiting for the future to explain his situation.[49]

Although art-full, West's high-flying rhetoric is not exactly artifice. Reading his letters and having experienced his conversation, one also begins to realize the naturalness for him of this autodidact's discourse. Unlike most people, he didn't require a boost from accident, intimacy, or alcohol; even the subjects of conventional small talk—the weather, pets, sensory objects—were likely to be caught-up, elevated, and integrated into the cosmic whirring of his remarkable thought. In its presence, people might be fascinated, intimidated, or repelled, but they certainly noticed. Mere notice of the fiction, however, could not guarantee sales, and understanding of West's views and strategies required more than being caught up by stylistic force or manner.

There continued to be occasional grumbling about his vivid descriptions of sex and violence. He had met censorship in putting his ducks in their row for *The Bell* in 1942, and *The Ferret Fancier* in 1963 was also put under wraps in Ireland. His fiction's realism could offend a fastidious reader, just as his religiosity could annoy a modern sophisticate. West sought the criticism of Owen Barfield, prominent literary man and one of the few Anthroposophists he knew, however distantly, whose combined spiritual and literary interests ranged compatibly with his own.[50] When Barfield in 1957 published *Saving the Appearances*, West read it and wrote to him, and when *River's End and Other Stories* appeared, West was glad to receive Barfield's reciprocal evaluation. Admitting that he didn't read much contemporary fiction to compare, Barfield praised West's special gift for "toughness and delicacy" but suggested that West had crossed the line between "coarseness and smut." West acknowledged that he was "inclined to use a shout where a whisper would be quite sufficient," but he defended himself:

> *Those of us, the have-nots, who have perforce crawled on our bellies*
> *in slime must somehow describe this slime because it is also life and,*
> *indeed, by current standards, ninety parts of modern life. Your sensitive*
> *and subtle mind would, of course, react against an "Upper Room" type*

of story. I tried to do this tale in the third person but could never get the
necessary sing. I had to describe it in the first person, as first-hand experi-
ence. . . . I was only 20 and didn't have a clue and had to experience
these things as they came, to endure, tolerate, or enjoy them. Were I to
concentrate on the qualitative positives, I'd only ever try to write an odd
poem.[51]

In the agricultural articles, a genre between fiction and practical
exposition, West found a remarkably congenial and affective venue.
Here he was unlikely to raise Owen Barfield's sort of objection to his
prose; here he could effectively address at least the ecological part of the
anthroposophical vision.

I can continue to gain tolerable personal satisfaction by the soil itself and
very often the boss pulls my leg on my preoccupation. But I contend
that if we can get somewhere near the right soil according to its type,
using fair virgin earth as a prototype, we can continue to grow good
crops, weather notwithstanding.

    Too many men on and off the land, including the pundits, seem to
have eyes only for the end-products in terms of quantity and cash and
they only more or less indifferently fulfill the prior care and cultiva-
tion as expensive and often troublesome means to that end. . . . Like
many another man on the land, the boss is a mixture of traditionalist
and modernist with a gap between and this gap often worries him. . . .
The spring before last he insisted on giving the eight acre home field
a dose of five tons of limestone to the acre while muttering the rhyme
about lime starving the [soil?] every time he saw the spreader at work.
This field had a low ph content and was badly infected with wild pansy,
daisy, crowfoot, and sorrel although its natural drainage seemed efficient,
and being a home field it got, as usual, more than its share of muck.
But for all the weight of calcium, the expensive clovers have not come
on well and the crowfoot is like rhubarb. It is just about the clover's
opposite, reversing the latter's virtues. I tried to tell the boss that five or
twenty-five tons of lime to the acre would not get at the basic causes
for this acidity. . . .[52]

By the later versions of Actaeon, the increasingly exemplary Rector O'Dea Russell hopes to establish a model agriculturally based community to care especially for emotionally disturbed adolescents, this theme poignantly of interest to both Wests, especially in the last decades of their lives. Through Artos, the charity the Wests helped to organize and direct, they aimed, in an agricultural context, to assist young people suffering from mental and emotional trouble.

West's agricultural writing drafts hold another important interest for this study, as they show West drawing directly on autobiographical data—thus, at a very practical level of artistic purpose, staying West. As with his literary fictions, he might create, transpose, and modify situations or characters, but he could be simultaneously faithful to personal experience. For example, the hired man responds to his boss's question, "Why don't you make a stab for yourself [at owning a farm]?"

Lack of capital plus a large family.

What would you like to do if you had the money?

Build up a co-operative farm. I know a few people who think the way I do.

No bosses?

The work's the boss.

That's the hardest employer you can find?

Maybe—but perhaps the fairest and least complicated. . . .

What'd you do in the war—farming?

Air Force.

Flying?

Yes.

Pilot?

No—office-boy! Navigator!

Don't suppose they gave you a decent rank?

I got a commission—the Air Force in its need was fairly democratic.

Time and again I was offered places, but knew enough by now that I couldn't deal with folk who put more value on static 'safe' capital than on progress. I sold a few articles on agricultural topics. By this time I was

becoming experience-constipated, kidding myself that I was staying alive,
while guilty for betraying the writer in me.

He need not have been apologetic about these original experiments
for agricultural readers. Like the Pollexfens, who as Yeats said of these
ancestors, gave a tongue to the sea-cliffs, West could give merds and
muck-shovelers eloquent voice. "The Boss" and the "I" are appropriate
foils for each other, the employer offering the narrator occasions for
agricultural sermons about redemptive schemes. Technological strategies, folk cures, vegetable and animal lore—a library of farm information
piles up with this thin but strong narrative ploy. The audience expects
information and opinion rather than diversion and is doubly rewarded.

Reflecting on his experience at Albrighton fifteen years later, West
said

We never did manage to tame Albrighton. I think there is a kind of
karma in these old properties that were once so well-loved and cared for:
then they were neglected and I think the elemental beings became bitter
and angry, and one has to placate them again.[53]

While still members of the Steiner-influenced group at Albrighton,
the Wests had their second son and fifth baby, Jeremy, and their sixth,
son Christopher, who came in 1949. In this period *The Bell* printed one
more in the rural series about a young male's socio-sexual awakening,
"Myself and a Birth,"[54] still under the name Michael MacGrian. Features
of this old mill story, elaborated and reworked, appear later in "Narcissus
unto Echo."[55] Again, memories of the farm life of the magically beautiful
Irish countryside are the sources to which West turns. In the years at
Albrighton, those immediately following the war, West was writing, and
he was gaining important, communal farming experience, but he wanted
artistic confidence and direction. He offered the BBC a poetic play,
which they found "too long." Was it part of 600-page "Apple Tree" that
he later reworked as "The Mowin' Man"? Other efforts at plays—from television script proposals to closet dramas—show that West did not abandon
the genre after the war interrupted production of "The Window", but

none in the file approaches his best fiction.

Similarly, he continued to write poems—although he did not call them that.[56] Half a dozen poems appeared under the MacGrian pseudonym before June 1953, beginning with "Two Sonnets: January, February" in *Rann*, 4, Spring, 1957.

> *I'm not a poet. I'm a scribbler, a storyteller. I wrote a couple of plays but they weren't produced. One, "The Window", about the Troubles, was going to be put on in London, but the War put an end to that. . . . I've little or no knowledge of the mechanics of poetry and have to leave that side of it to the poets themselves. As prose-writer . . . I'm more concerned with the validity of the Platonic idea. And I think that, in the end, the real poet will say far more than his prose contemporary since, relative to the poet's own content, the disciplines involved seem to expect that the poet be more exact.*[57]

West's files contain about a hundred poems, unsurprisingly often about nature, and he published a handful of them in small magazines. He tells an editor that writing poems helps him "escape from incarnating hard human facts."[58] West makes Christopher MacMannan a fledgling and ultimately unsuccessful poet (*Towns*); he presents Diana Hauley of Actaeon as a successful one. Critics of West's fiction have repeatedly commented on its poetic quality, even if they have been disparaging about such lush prose in the postwar twentieth or twenty-first centuries. Hardly a writer matches him for lexical variety and precision,[59] and he commands the poet-painter's descriptive response to rural life and landscape.

ENDNOTES

   1   ACW to Gail Leeson, MacGibbon & Kee.

   2   ACW to Dr. Engel(?), 18 February 1963. Health.

   3   ACW to Timothy O'Keefe, 27 Dec 1964. Here West also comments that Olive
       generally agreed with it [Naked to Laughter, the unpublished novel about
       Simon's life in America], as she had agreed with *Ferret*, and not about many.

   4   ACW to Audrey Eyler, 20 November 1987.

   5   These books and lectures are among Rudolf Steiner's works that have been
       helpful to my understanding of West's thinking: *Christianity as Mystical Fact*,
       (New York and London: G. P. Putnam's Sons, 1914); *Discussions with Teachers*
       (London: Rudolf Steiner Press, 1967); *The Education of the Child in the Light
       of Anthroposophy* (London: Rudolf Steiner Press, 1965); *The Nature of Anthro-
       posophy* (New York: Rudolf Steiner Publications, 1964); *Woman and Society*
       (Lecture at Hamburg, 17 November 1906. London: Rudolf Steiner Press, 1985).

   6   ACW to Bronwen, nd [c.1979], Letters from Children; OW[?] to ACW from
       Drayton House, Stourbridge, 28 October 1976, Box 1, Aid to Friends.

   7   ACW to Roy McFadden, 16 March 1963, BBC.

   8   ACW to Roy McFadden.

   9   Olive confirmed these details of their life in Northern Ireland in a telephone
       conversation, 25 February 1995.

  10   ACW, taped interview, 1987. See also autobiographical statement written in 1963
       and edited by Olive, Biog. I, II, III.

  11   ACW, taped interview, 1987.

  12   ACW to Gail Leeson, MacGibbon & Kee, 28 April 1963.

  13   *There is no such thing as a human 'accident,' Arno: all apparent accidents are
       means to ends and if people neglect the ends, that's their own business, but the ends
       are still there*, ACW to Arno Karlen, 15 May 1962.

  14   ACW to GL.

  15   ACW, "The unreality of war:" War notes for *Towns* in Notebooks, Criticism.

  16   Yeadell's son M. H. Yeadell reports yet another change. Parts of the old base
       have been rescued by the Thorp Camp Preservation Society and turned into a
       museum. Veterans of 627 hold annual reunions, a sixtieth's celebration being
       planned for 2003. MHY to AE, 13 March 2002.

  17   He enclosed a slide. Wilfred Yeadell to ACW from Leigh-on-Sea, Essex, 18
       December 1976, Box 3, Letters. I have emended the punctuation and spelling
       where necessary for clarity.

  18   ACW, "The unreality of war . . ." in Notes for*Towns*, Notebooks/Criticism.

  19   See Yeadell's note about the cottage, above.

  20   ACW, annotated transcript of interview with AE, July/December 1987.

  21   ACW, "The unreality of war . . ." in Notes for*Towns*, Notebooks/Criticism.

22 *The Bell*, 1942, Vol. 4, No. 4, 253–4.

23 As John Boyd (?) told West in an undated letter, though he regarded him as "our most vigorous writer and our most poetic prose writer," West's stories were unsafe: they were likely to be thought "too sexy or pagan."

24 The date, 21 II 1948, may be mistyped. Boyd's saved letters date from 1960–1974; the mentioned ten-page carbon does not appear among them.

25 ACW to AE, interview, 3 July 1986.

26 It was Jocelyn, his third daughter, not Bronwen, whom West delivered alone, but the experience served him well for the writing of *Towns* in the nineteen-sixties.

27 ACW to GL.

28A CW, taped interview with AE, 1986.

29 ACW to GL.

30 Olive West, in taped interview with AE, July 1989.

31 ACW to Winifred Elin, "Report on leaving Ardleigh," 26 June 1951.

32 ACW to WE.

33 ACW to WE.

34 ACW to GL.

35 ACW to TO'K, 17 March [1961].

36 Box 26, Agricultural Notes: Scrapbook.

37 ACW to M. Athrope of Exeter, 17 September 1959.

38 Article No. 2, by "John Whitfield" is marked "Accepted 28 July 55" with a letter from J.Hammond of *Country Fair*, London, attached; I have been unable to confirm that the drafts cited here were published. Most bear the pseudonym "Michael MacGrian"; one by "Tom Whitfield" also has "Conroy Carter" crossed out. These agricultural pieces are especially difficult to trace, as West did not seem to want to talk about them even as much as he would talk about his literary productions; he apparently kept no list of them, and he published them under pseudonyms. The reader is referred to the Chronology for those agricultural publications I have been able to confirm.

39 See, for examples, Robert Hogan, "Old Boys, Young Bucks, and New Women: The Contemporary Irish Short Story," in *The Irish Short Story*, ed. James F. Kilroy, 169–215, Boston: G. K .Hall, 1984; Michael Bromley, "The Quiet Revival of Anthony West," *Belfast Telegraph*, 20 March 1985; letters: Bernard Farbar, Berkley Publishing Corporation (101 5th Avenue, New York) to John Schaffner, 8 August 1960; Susan Jacobson to John Schaffner, 11 November 1969.

40 John Berthelsen, "An Irish West Rises As Novelist," Sacramento, 10 April 1970; Michael Bromley, "The Quiet Revival of Anthony West," *Belfast Telegraph*, 20 March 1985, 14.

41 ACW to W. Bittner, [Autumn, 1970].

42 Warren Eyster to ACW, [early August 1959], Obolensky.

43   WB to ACW, 14 November 70.

44   WE to ACW.

45   West is guilty of sounding "preachery," as he says to TO'K, January [1960], but not pompous or pretentious.

46   Jack Curtis to ACW, 7 November 1966.

47   ". . . His style and subjects are sometimes dismissed by the hip—the fake knowing, the fake superior—as old-fashioned." Arno Karlen, "Surviving Ireland," *The Nation*, 3 May 1965.

48   As Storm Jameson says on the dust-jacket for Knopf's *Towns*, "Mr. West has a powerful and original talent which sweeps him to the opposite pole from the Hemingway-and-washing-up-water of much contemporary writing."

49   ACW to Ivan Obolensky, 31 August 1962.

50   Barfield's law firm (Royds and Barfield) later became the solicitors for the charity the Wests and eight friends formed, the Artos Agricultural and Housing Association, of which West was the honorary (unpaid) secretary. Olive West, interview with AE, July, 1989.

51   ACW to Owen Barfield, Elmbank, [October 1958].

52   "Farmer's Boy," #2. Jack Curtis to ACW, 7 November 1966.

53   ACW to Baroness Uslar, 25 May 64.

54   XIII, 4, 47–57.

55   Early in my work on West and before I learned of the anthroposophical influence upon his writing, I wrote an article about these two stories: "The Old Made New Again: Imagery in Two Stories by Anthony C. West," *Eire-Ireland*, Fall 1985, 52–64.

56   ACW to AE, 2 December 1987.

57   ACW to Ms.Rogers, 2 March 1970, Biog\Aid to Friends.

58   ACW to Ivan Obolensky, 7 May 1961.

59   Robert Hogan ridicules West for using words readers do not know. West does use some words that defy even the *Oxford English Dictionary*, but hundreds of his unusual choices suit so well they give great pleasure as they educate. "Old Boys, Young Bucks, and New Women: The Contemporary Irish Short Story," in *The Irish Short Story*, ed. James F. Kilroy, 169–215. Boston: G. K. Hall, 1984.

CHAPTER SIX

1950 ELMBANK: HALFWAY TO MOTHER IRELAND

HALF-CENTURY, THE YEAR daughter Brigid was born, found the Wests still at Albrighton. They soon left this experimental community for Colchester's Ardleigh Park, but within six disappointing months were ready to make still another important and this time, gratifying, change. Independent of any socialist community, the Wests were offered residence at "Elmbank," a place in Llandegfan, North Wales, which they agreed to look after for its American owner, Basil Jones, a Welshman who had comfortably made his home in California. Because Jones's wife did not wish to live in Wales, he could not occupy his property himself and was glad to have West caring for it.

> We migrated to Wales in 1951, sort of half-way to Mother Ireland, and again into the middle of a post-war depressed area. . . . It was a good house in the middle of a field, a perfect place for a writer. We lived like primitives. The kids were happy enough — best time of their lives. We used to take them to the seaside, walking like cows, the two youngest in a pram. We couldn't afford a bus. [1]

West at Elmbank, Llangdefan, 1957. WEST FAMILY COLLECTION, PHOTOGRAPHER
UNKNOWN.

A sketch called Jacky Boy gives a first-person account of a lighter
aspect of domestic life at Elm Bank. A rescued jackdaw joined the family's pets, normally cats and dogs, and "remained a slovenly thief, a trick-
ster, and joker with an extremely perverted sense of humour." Jacky
never could be managed:

> He could tear the daily paper into neat strips before anyone had seen it;
> he once stole a pound note, ruined several packets of cigarettes, pinched
> toddler Stephen's sweets out of the child's hand. He did not store his
> finds, he just flew out the door with a wanton laugh and dropped them
> in the long grass.

A local merchant was not amused when the bird followed West to the
market one busy day, painted a customer with excrement, and toppled
cocoa tins and bottles. When the bird began to resent the baby's sleep
and squawk on her chest every time she dozed off in her pram, Jacky out-
stayed his welcome. Fortunately a lonely elderly couple was persuaded
to adopt him for, the narrator confesses, "It was beyond my moral power

to destroy the bird and beyond physical power to control him."[2]

The children were young, and though they were desperately poor, now many of them remember very happy times at Elmbank. There the Wests continued to hope that by living narrowly they would some day live communally and co-operatively on the land in the post-war economy. The hope frequently expressed in his letters of making enough by his pen to meet their needs probably was not quite as preposterous as it might now seem. Yet West could not or would not do the short, slick piece for the commercial interests of publishers.

At least in the beginning he was naive about publishing procedures. When his first novel, The Life of Reilly, had received an encouraging response, then a six-month delay and silence, and ultimately a rejection from Little Brown, he says it never occurred to him to send it to anyone else. He discredited his own effort and tossed the returned manuscript aside. He said he lost it and had no other copy.[3] Similarly he had dismissed and lost The Parish Pope, the other long fiction he said he wrote in New York. Yet more than a beginner's ignorance has to lie behind his actions by mid-century.

After undertaking his American quest, going through certain transcendental experiences there, and being introduced there to anthroposophical thought, West credited spiritual reality with increased importance. The collapse of the Wests' dreams for Albrighton, Ardleigh, and other communal projects did not diminish this larger commitment. After each he felt he had learned appropriate lessons to be better prepared for the next effort. One must cast his bread upon the waters; he must not look back having once set his hand to the plough; he must not be anxious but must consider the lilies. . . . These images in the Scriptures convey the attitude he practiced. If, as he did believe, art and the writer became a conduit for a creative force beyond them both, the imperative for the artist—besides studying the craft—was to repress the obstructing ego. Possessiveness about his manuscripts, worrying about their safe journey when larger "Luciferic" forces were looking after and directing them anyway, would be presumptuous. West's horrifying experiences in the war had not led to despair; they had deepened his spiritual urgency.

*All I ever hoped to do was, eventually, to make a quiet steady living by
writing, not to write for a living (I'm hopeless at that) save incidentally.
I quite consciously set myself a target based on the labouring wage for
a 70/80 hour week. In my opinion, no reasonable artist has any fiat to
value his work as a commodity and he should never ask for more than
basic needs. His real pay seems to be in the form of creative satisfaction.
And had I, for instance, netted a sum like 20,000 bucks, I would have
had to pray and monk hard that it wouldn't slow me and produce the
same sort of effect as poverty, from the opposite side. I'm 49 this year, 7
X 7, and it seems I had to wait until my overabundant vitality died down
a bit before I could come to terms with myself, or else remain a frustrated
dilettante. Other men have had their plain or fancy muses, mine is
Mistress Poverty and my ass is sore with her goad. [4]*

As usual, his spiritual ideal emerges in a complex binding of equally
strong, farmer-practicality. As writing never produced enough money
for the Wests to live on, they depended on Olive's income. She originally showed, according to her headmaster at Pitman's College, "considerable literary ability," having "gained some distinction in advance
English examinations."[5] She read her husband's drafts critically, but put
her energy into practical ventures to generate a small but more reliable
income. She claims never to have enjoyed a maternal and domestic
role.[6] Throughout the following decades she added to her business
training experience in real estate, a handcrafts shop, a cafe, and a natural
foods market. West sometimes took on odd labouring jobs to supplement her wages or cooked in the cafe. In Anglesey, in 1952, housing
secured but income desperately needed, he tried a factory job at Saunders Roe building boats, but besides finding work on the line oppressive,
he became very ill and was unable to work at all for weeks.

*We were poor. We were on the dole for three years. I worked a short time
at Saunders Roe, my one industrial experience. Terrible. Then I started to
write a little. Had to get the War out of my system.*

Another daughter, Miriam Margaret, was born in the summer of

The West family at Elmbank, Llangdefan, c. 1955: (Standing, l-r) Mary, Michael, Bronwen, Jocelyn; Olive, ACW holding Stephanie, Jeremy; (front, l-r) Christopher, Miriam, Bridgid. WEST FAMILY COLLECTION, PHOTOGRAPHER UNKNOWN.

1953. He published some poems: "Fable " in *Rann*, 16, Summer; "Four Prayers" and "Like a Flame that Burns Quietly," in *Rann*, 17, Autumn. "On Killing a Sheep" was included in *Irish Writing*, #25, 16–19, 72, under Michael MacGrian.[7] Another poem, "Spring Song" appeared in *Rann*, 18, and "Love Song," was in issue number 20. Stephanie Ellen, the Wests' ninth child, was born in September the following year. For nearly ten years after the War, West said, he found writing difficult and sporadic; then, in the middle of this decade of the nineteen-fifties, he reached a point in his spiritual and artistic development that he described as "breaking through."[8]

By 1955 West was writing relentlessly—at night when the house was quiet. Daughter Mary recalls from Elmbank the sound of his fast, two-finger-typing coming through the darkness and the morning sound of the starlings imitating the clicking of the keys. Poverty continued to hound them—his daughters groan at the recollection of the improvised school clothing; nevertheless he and his children remember the Elmbank

years with affection. The list he retained of manuscript-mailings confirms these years were actually very productive ones; furthermore, they
included the new attention of an American audience. Devin Garrity
had in the last year included "Myself and a Rabbit" in *44 Irish Short
Stories*. With great enthusiasm about "Narcissus unto Echo," *Esquire*
began publishing the string of his stories: "The Turning Page" appeared
in December. "River's End" and "Not Isaac" appeared in the March
and September issues, respectively, 1957. He began to think he might
depend upon a modest income from writing after all. The notebook
record of submitted manuscripts he kept from September 1956 to July
1959 indicates titles, destinations, replies, rejections, and other pertinent
correspondence with publishers—nearly a hundred titles. At the end of
this prodigious list of stories and novels is another list, "To Do:" Fix road,
fix walls, fix greenhouse, fix yard, fix roofs, painting, and slate. During
the day he was also caring for Miriam and Stephanie, still at home.
Their scribblings, turning up on his typed pages, evidence the multiple
responsibilities of their father's attention.

> However, we survived. It cost me four years to pick up all the threads I
> had let go in 1939. It was a struggle. I was rich in experience and poor
> in skill, in the craft. Around 1955 I began to break through. . . . Esquire,
> the American magazine recognized me, taking six of my stories in a row.

Correspondence out of Wales charts his rising expectations, letters
and telegrams that began with notice from *Esquire* in 1956.[9] When West
sent *Esquire* "River's End," editor Arnold Gingrich was ecstatic. This
story, "the best he had seen in twenty-three years of publishing," sur-
passed Hemingway's. He promised it would be advertised and featured
with unprecedented care.[10] This new man, West, became the subject
of more than one publishers' lunch, and Gingrich made his stories
the object of eager exchange among his associates and friends—David
McDowell of Random House, Bernard Geis of Prentice-Hall, Merrill
Pollack of Simon & Schuster, A. L. Hart of Macmillan, and others.
    Within months, *Esquire* had added "Not Isaac," "Gun-Play," and
"Song of The Barrow"—totaling a half-dozen—and Gingrich and his

A. C. West with pipe, c. 1956. WEST FAMILY COLLECTION, PHOTOGRAPHER UNKNOWN.

staff were predicting West's glorious future.[11] New York's major publishers were in line to enlist him for longer work. Would he like to expand "River's End?" Did West already have a novel to offer? Prentice-Hall was "tremendously interested in this brilliant new writer," but Geis would have to be content in second position, Gingrich told his friend of more than twenty-five years; McDowell, who had just left Random House, had been in queue first and was hoping to make West a feature in the company he was now establishing with a newcomer to the business, Ivan Obolensky. West hadn't decided yet and was under no official obligation, but McDowell had already offered to print a collection of stories. Meanwhile, Hart had also written that Macmillan would be interested if West's present options didn't work out. Simon and Schuster, at Merrill Pollack's initiative, were eventually able to publish *The Ferret Fancier* (1962), and Robert Gottlieb of Alfred A. Knopf did an edition of *As Towns with Fire* (1970), but those events anticipate the chronology of this moment by four novels.

Paramount Pictures called to congratulate *Esquire* on the 1957 March issue and appeared to be considering "River's End." West readily imagined the story as art-film, "Miss Ross with God in her right hand and a lingam in her left, Anne Stafford breaking through the soil like Disney's shoots, Turley a wind-tossed withered bloom—all drifting through the river of Stephen's mind: beauty, humanity, lust, violence, death, and resurrection with the snake-charm of the river broken. . . ."[12] Although Paramount never called back, Benoit of Montreal did, and put down $300 with a promise of $1200 more by filming time the following spring. Agents called, offering to manage his burgeoning career for the usual ten per cent. It seems clear, and the *Esquire* stories still justify their perception, that in these early months of the relationship, West's editors thought they were observing a new star. Furthermore, the letters suggest that Gingrich, Pollack, Arno Karlen of Curtis, Gottlieb, and McDowell, especially, personally enjoyed their contact with West, genuinely wished him success, and initially went extra miles to match their publishing needs with his production.

Four novels eventually saw publication in the decade between 1959 and 1969; in addition to *Ferret* and *Towns* there were *The Native Moment* (1959) and *Rebel to Judgment* (1962). Each has appeared in more than one edition, two of them in three; they have been published in the States, in England, and in Ireland—North and South. *River's End and Other Stories* and *Native Moment* saw translation in Europe. The $1500 check—a big one in 1956—for the story "River's End" was the largest payment West was ever to receive for a manuscript, and it is no surprise that his hopes were fueled by it, by the $500 for each of the other five stories, and by the extraordinary attention of these *Esquire* years.[13] Having found, apparently, the bird (ducks?) that laid golden eggs, would the author not nurture it at all cost? Why, then, did West stop writing short stories and risk sending the magazines longer ones, which he must have known they could not print?

The answer is complicated. There functioned among the parties a remarkable mixture of courteous obligation and independent savvy, naiveté and cynicism, artistic integrity and commercial drive, undaunted faith and farmer-practicality. West had, indeed, astonishing impact; the rejection notes from *Harper's, Playboy, Atlantic,* and others are full of the "I always love to read a West story, but it's too long for us" messages. His decision to turn away from short stories was deliberate, and it was not done capriciously: his editor originally encouraged it.[14]

These New York editors were busy people, reading hundreds of manuscripts, meeting thousands of deadlines, and above all trying to sell millions of books. They had little time to linger over last night's star-spectacle. As their relationship with West grew, under acts of gods, daemons, and plain ordinary mortals, newness of the commodity naturally wore off, the surprise of his style of course dissipated, and West's glowing brilliance began to seem to some a nostalgic confinement to vignettes of male adolescence; without success, his agent urged him to move away from the topic. He protested that he was trying

> . . .to work out an angle of the adolescent complex (shambles) which men
> in space won't cure and to . . . imply that the coming generation is being
> spiritually crucified and distorted, and their decisions must be equally
> distorted and irresponsible when they have to assume power in life and
> politics. I'm not married to the adolescent theme . . . I'm just trying to
> work through it.[15]

He also was not being merely autobiographical, as some charged,[16] but selecting things from his own and others' lives to see some

> light in this terrible problem of adolescence and teen-age-ism. . . . What
> do you do with the bastards once you have nursed them—ask them to be
> good small rats and find themselves a pair of glands like old Mar[i]lyn's?
> Take it up to the limit of soul and stop short at the spiritual interpreta-
> tion? Tell them to be good taxpaying mountaineers and musclemen like
> HRH the Duke de Edinburgh? Life still a game of football and Water-
> loos still to be won at Etons? Shit for that, says I.[17]

Now, seeing his larger, evolving narrative practice, it is possible to understand both continuity and differentiation in his many efforts to address one stage and then another of the soul's development. The first push to extend the length of his fiction came from Obolensky who, while offering to publish *River's End and Other Stories* (1959), was eager for a novel. West had tried long fiction, but his experience had not made him confident about it. Now, in 1957, he had a couple long manuscripts he had been tinkering with. Yes, Obolensky and McDowell could see them. In November 1956 he had sent them a longer short story tentatively called "The Lady Actaeon." Obolensky was impressed. Give up the short stories, he insisted. You're a novel man. Shouldn't I keep some stories going for bread and butter? he worried. No. They'll get you nowhere (though they had gotten him somewhere, as West later pointed out, and at that time he was willing to go on producing them). As novels were long and expensive in time and money, he doubted to Obolensky that he could afford their luxury. We'll take care of you. You must write novels, was the message West, incredulous at his fortune, heard. Ivan seemed insistent. So West started "letting go the strings of [his] mind which had up till then been held short. . . ."[18] There was no turning back.

That September, when Obolensky met him in Shrewsbury, he still seemed all enthusiasm for his Irish novelist in Wales. The *River's End* stories were collected. He was very taken with "The Lady Actaeon," urged a few, specific changes, and left West with the amazed sense that he had been providentially claimed by a wealthy, idealistic patron who actually empathized. In addition, McDowell had recommended a trustworthy, informed New York agent, John Schaffner. They would all cooperate in West's roseate future. West felt assured by Obolensky's sympathy over his uncertain income, his offer of personal sponsorship (the Shrewsbury arrangement was oral, so details can't be documented, but he did follow with a letter asking that Ivan's offer of a 'blind' loan be a $1000-advance against his story "No Fatted Calf"[19]) that would insure West's time to write, so he would not have to rely on the magazine market.

More persuasive to West than all his charm and talk, Obolensky had, himself, written a very compelling novel, *Rogue's March*. His publisher's "strong feeling for the Red Indian consciousness and spirit" was

proximate to West's own feeling for the Indian and for the Celt. Here
was a precocious, "powerful thinker and delineator of man," a "hard-
hitting, iconoclastic," prophetic "expose[r] of casuistic and Machiavel-
lian politics" with a "bardic quality of invocation." Obolensky explained
that, there being in most British writers (he made the Irish no exception)
a resistance to the unfamiliar, a preference for rock-polishing rather than
rock-hunting, West would be an unfamiliar fare to American markets.
Expectation would be offended, he warned, but as truth and strength
would triumph, West should not be discouraged.

West took Obolensky, he says, as a fighting, idealistic publisher. He
went home from the Shrewsbury encounter with the impression that he
had secured a place with a firm who would trust his potential and work
closely with him. He liked the fact that the firm itself was a struggling,
bold, underdog venture. The group was new, small, intimate. It was
difficult to separate the personal from the professional gestures of kindness and confidence, but to do that seemed at the moment unnecessary
and, moreover, the fusion was part of its appeal.[20] Bring copies of your
stories, Obolensky had said in his note from Hyde Park anticipating
their interview, to refresh his "atrocious" memory: September turned
into October before any money arrived. When it came, it was another
$500 check from McDowell, the rest of West's advance against royalties
on *River's End and Other Stories*, following the initial April payment
of $500. David said Ivan would send word very soon about "his own
personal arrangement" with him. There is no record that it ever came.

West's discussion of his poverty (the problem never went away) is
controlled. The tone is urgent, yes, but declarative, even detached, never
self-pitying, and often relieved by humor, as he usually makes his claims
for the family rather than himself as sufferer. As it turns out, this early
letter is typical of his address to the theme, directly or allusively, in hundreds of letters he was to exchange with his agent and numerous editors
over the next three decades: His destiny has so far led him to writing;
his alternative is farming, that other truly creative branch of human
endeavor. Getting established in either activity requires "wolf" money he
does not possess. He will not compromise his art or his theme. Must he
quit? He is only trying to see his destiny, malice to none. He is grateful

for whatever advances or royalties can be sent, and sorry to be a nuisance.

After the September meeting in Shrewsbury, there appears to have been no further word from Obolensky for nearly two months. In a gracious letter of 22 November 1957, West implied his doubts about this extraordinary relationship with his publisher, gave the discreet reminder, and bid to regain his sense of autonomy. The letter appears to have crossed in the mail with Obolensky's Christmas greeting and [$500]. A thank-you in a subsequent letter for "an enclosure" suggests that $500 more may have followed it in January. These payments are recorded as advances, however, and there seems to be no mention of what West understood would be Obolensky's temporary and dependable patronage.[21] Obolensky's late-January (24, 1958) response to that West letter [16 January] assumed a blithe, not-to-worry tone, as he apologized for his silence due to heavy editorial responsibilities, anticipated his April trip to London, and admonished West in the meanwhile to "polish, polish, polish" for his imminently brilliant career. He signed, perhaps with careful ambiguity, as West's "poor old editor."

In Obolensky's defense, it could be said that his new author's circumstances must have been a congenital puzzle to him,[22] as the problems of the poor were to nineteenth-century Parliamentarians. The evidence of conversations held and fantasized between them recalls major Victorian debate. In this draft to Obolensky (24 July 1959), West lets fly at other implications:

> And you finally managed to hit the thumb on the head when you said on the phone that you thought my family was too large. It was just as large as when we talked in Shrewsbury? . . . From the coldly materialistic and empirical viewpoint with its Malthusian twist, you are perfectly right. But if you prefer that viewpoint, then you must stop thinking about Atlantis and reincarnation.

In another draft for the same letter (23 July), West is more explicit, but no more likely to have been persuaded by Ivan Obolensky, John Schaffner,[23] or anyone else who challenged the size of his family:

*. . . That was (forgive me) a very bourgeois remark which shocked me,
coming from you. It made me quite hopeless that you would ever know
my dual personality. Families are karmic things. . . . I know, I in-know,
that it is directly due to my large family and not at all to a naive writer's
ambition or to economics that you are publishing a manuscript of mine
in November. No, Ivan, I can't let you make remarks like that out of the
karmic context.*

The 24 July version continues:

*Big family, yes, but not any more expensive than were I a single drinking
man gargling a quid a day, although I'd probably be praised for that
activity and clapped on the back as one of de boys. . . . One by one my
kids will jump the nest and . . . leave me quiet with the satisfaction that I
helped give them a body again. Richness is relative.*

Had the Wests been Roman Catholic, would his editors have shaken
their heads knowingly and said nothing? A Protestant with a religious
explanation for so impractical a circumstance received no court.

David McDowell had already been stunned at the discovery that
West possessed no carbon copies of the manuscripts floating around
New York offices from *Esquire*.[24] He had never in all his editing days
encountered such a situation. West apologized more than once, and
explained lamely that he always made such a mess with copies. Cor-
recting carbons may well have seemed a nuisance to him, but some
twenty-thousand, fairly well-typed pages of his carbons kept thereafter,
cast doubt that correction-messiness was the chief obstacle: other reasons probably lay behind West's neglect of carbons in these years. No
small reservation would have been the double expense in paper. One
manuscript in the file is typed on meat paper he procured from the
local butcher. All the extra pages in the children's discarded school notebooks are filled by their father. The backs and margins of second-class
mail are full and filed. He had to be very frugal; he was poor and prolific. The words flowed easily, and he knew he would improve only by
writing more of them. Secondly, in regarding many of his manuscripts

as unfinished sketches, mere potentials for books or stories sliced from
the ur text, he very likely did have them in some related form within the
accruing narrative. Most important of all, he resisted personal attachment to his creations.[25] In light of his economic necessity, his prolixity,
and his commitment, such valuing of his words as their duplication and
filing could seem all the more a spiritually obstructive vanity. On the
back of McDowell's incredulous note, West has penciled, "If you had
as little regard for most of the mss. I sent out you'd have written them
on T. paper with a burnt stick and posted them in the china bowl." His
explanations to McDowell seem to reflect at once Narcissus turning away
from his jeopardizing image toward Echo, West unpossessively casting
his bread on the waters according to Ecclesiastes and the servant from
the New Testament parable, investing rather than hiding the talent.
Again,the incident underscores egoistic (as opposed to egotistic) nuances
of staying West.

Shortly after sending the long Actaeon manuscript off to New York,
West had strong second thoughts about it and immediately asked Obolensky to waste no editorial time with it himself, but to rush it back.
He repeated his request several times. There was neither action nor
response. Meanwhile West drafted *The Native Moment* and sent it on
before Christmas. No one acknowledged receipt of that one either. The
long silences of his publishers and agents were as disturbing to West as
any feature of his relationship with them. He was contrastively prompt,
faithful, imaginative, and prolific about his own letters. Not that he consciously presumed upon their time: he acknowledged their being occupied. He deserved better than he received, however, as Warren Eyster
and John Schaffner both told him later, especially over the Actaeon
manuscripts.[26] Periodically throughout that winter, West requested and
expected the return of the long and of the original, short versions.

He felt bad to disappoint them, and he desperately needed the
money, but he would never sell his soul. He sent manuscripts he knew
were unready, because he genuinely wanted editorial direction from
these experts who had paid him high compliments and advanced him
money in evidence of their expectation (he had no way of measuring the
competition for his editors' time):

*I asked you . . . not to spend too much creative time close-editing . . .
[saying] that a few general directions would be sufficient for me and that
I'd change and rewrite within 400 pages, then let you have a MS fit to
edit.*[27]

Though he would attempt to make requested editorial cuts, he was
as likely to return an even longer version.

Sent Esquire *a long-short story a fortnight ago . . . but it's probably too
long and too unslick and too avant garde. I know I'm failing to write to
any specific magazine's requirements, but it's part of my evolution under
pressure....I dunno. There's such a hell of a lot yet I just don't damnwell
know. I'm [broken]-through, in a new land, but it's all so strange and
I'm so gauche, no one will believe me. Reverend sirs, I've sinned: sinned
by not keeping carbon copies, by trying to write against mounting debts,
by trying to play off my rapid-growing pressures against the essentially
slower rhythms and by expecting the gulf would not widen; by over
writing, by trying to getasmuchintothelastlineasIcould because the
following week might silence me. I've sinned by trying to write the holy
history of man into a novel....yea, mea culpa. . . . I don't pad, Warren
Eyster. Don't have to—too much to say, too much to draw on. I over-
crowd and get off the lane into the dear bogs, and this is as bad as
padding and leaves a similar taste in a reader's eye.*[28]

He said he was hampered on the other end of the process by this
usual feeling:

*I've always got to be careful about my personal reactions to any finished
opus for soon as I finish it, it dies on me and I've no more interest in it
than in an old [stick].*[29]

In light of the ur, with its many rewritings of Actaeon, that lack of interest
must be regarded as short-term.

The Wests' California landlord died and Elmbank had to be sold.
West looked without success for another position in estate management,

and he continued to write. Prospective employers were more than once put off at the idea of having nine resident children. He finally included this paragraph in one application:

> We have nine children in all, six girls, three boys. I know by experience that the size of the family usually puts an otherwise interested employer off and therefore, I'll try to say something about them. The eldest boy, Michael aged 18, may not be concerned, as he wants to do a two-year catering course here [Anglesey]. Mary, the eldest girl, aged 16, is a fair hand with horses and can drive tractors, etc., and has a keen interest in the land, and she would, I believe, be able to get a reasonable reference from the people with whom she works on a farm during holidays and week-ends. She is still at the grammar school here, finishing her GCE. All the children are self-reliant, country-bred and raised; the youngest is five and also school-going. They are all well-mannered and obedient. (No TV, and movies few and far between).

Responses were so discouraging that they even considered emigration to Australia.[30] Fifteen years later he reported little change in their financial picture, and they had never moved farther than England.

> I have never paid any Income Tax since the war, a condition due in part to a large family and in part, to a low income. . . . I have not had any income from writing for over four or five years [c.1973–1977]; and never have at any time earned an income from writing that was tax-liable. And I never had continuing royalties from any source.[31]

By the end of the year his poverty was exacerbated because the film plan had dissolved with Benoit, affecting his financial plan by $1200, and his family was about to be evicted.

West had promptly begun a revision of The Lady Actaeon with Ivan's original suggestions in his head, but the characters had minds of their own, and his conception for this novel was, as is now apparent, the most complex and sophisticated thing West ever attempted: it gradually focused his own intellectual and artistic development, presenting the adult evolutionary efforts of his ur protagonist. Instead of a thirty-page alteration to 150, the manuscript expanded to 1500 pages, and McDowell and Obolensky were, as he could anticipate, dismayed. (West knew, however, they need not seem stymied: Obolensky had told him how McDowell had originally helped him cut the *Rogue* from 1500 to a manageable 600 for Random House.[32]) According to Eyster, their newly added editor, the firm decided partly because of West's straits to publish *The Native Moment*, which needed proportionately little changing, while they waited for West to cut Actaeon to an affordable size. But no one communicated these decisions and circumstances to West for months. Then suddenly, in the spring, 1959, Eyster announced a tight publication schedule for *Moment* and told West to rush his alterations within three weeks on the copy Ivan would carry with him to London in April. The right hand, however, seems to have had no idea what the left was doing.

Eyster was apparently as surprised as anyone that Obolensky had arrived in England without any manuscripts—carrying neither *Moment* nor Actaeon. In an undated letter that spring of 1959, West described to his agent the circumstances of this meeting:

> There I was in London, broke, living on the charity of friends, looking for a [job-cum-house], feeling responsible to McD&O for their past help, plus [being eager about] a novel to be rewritten. . . I tried to explain it was useless talking to me about rewrites, that I was finally in a cleft stick. Obviously, Ivan didn't have an idea about my fix, and obviously he didn't want to have. He put the blame for the delay on Actaeon on me because of length. I declined to pin him down to specific statements or to remind him that he could have sent it back to me the previous November . . . No point. We had just no human contact at all and I had the awful sensation I was talking to a body of abstractions that was so deeply committed in other ways that it was quite useless trying to say anything to it. The sheer unconscious cruelty in the whole thing scared me. Ivan still talked big about my great potentialities, about the stuff of mind he had, about what was going to be done. . . . As impersonally as I could, I tried to make him see that, financially, as a writer I was finished, pro tem, or

maybe for ever. . . . No, he couldn't help me financially. Okay, that was
that, at least. I said I would have to get a paid job. He said, yes, get a
job (while still thinking about a rewritten Moment, although I had told
him I couldn't rewrite, as I was fixed in London with friends in a small
flat, minus paper and books). He gave me ten pounds to feed the wolf,
in such a naive way I was quite amazed. The boy had little or no contact
with realities at all. . . . It was like a Chekhov short story. Ten pounds
was neither here nor there: the point that I was ostensibly a committed
and potential writer and he was my publisher holding a bundle of MSS
seemed quite irrelevant. . . . I was little more than a bum on the touch.

McDowell soon left for Crown, dropping contact with Obolensky, and the office was re-organized. In sending on $54 that Ivan had owed West through an accounting discrepancy, Schaffner reported that Ivan's comptroller had received a penal sentence.[33] Warren Eyster later wrote West an explanation of some of the firm's debilitating circumstances.[34] The social sympathies between publisher and author, however, regardless of their business arrangement, could hardly have been more disparate than those between Obolensky and West. Their reunion in Ivan's suite at the London Ritz, where Ivan, heir of the Astors and of Russian royalty, apparently would live for weeks at a time, epitomized it for the writer, who had dyed his old shirts black for the interview to hide their wear. Money was tight, Ivan said. The firm was struggling to grow, Ivan said, yet he displayed no signs of the difficulty that would be recognizable to any penurious Yankee or Irish peasant. West knew real poverty and was unpersuaded. "Here was the Ritz and jet-flying. Were I developing a young firm I'd sail on a cargo boat and live in a garret," he protested to Schaffner.[35]

The plan finally emerging from their discussion was specific, clear, and potentially redeeming, as West understood it: Ivan would send all the manuscripts immediately. West would provide at once the alterations on *Moment* and rewrite Actaeon by the end of August. Ivan would advance him $1000 on sales of *Moment* to secure the summer months for writing. Copy for *The Native Moment* arrived, and West discharged his obligation within the stipulated time. Still no Actaeon and no word from Ivan. By 23 July, much of West's precious summer writing time reserved for that manuscript had passed. He sent Ivan an impassioned, long letter. Why the delays after the promises?

Obolensky never really answered the question. He acted surprised, as his conscience was "absolutely clear;" told West to keep his criticisms professional rather than personal; concentrated on West's failures to follow his original advice about Actaeon, and promised again that West's golden hour was at hand.[36]

West's letter is not unkind but it is very direct, and it reaches its most emotional heights when West addresses not his own desperate need — emigration by this time seeming his only alternative — but Ivan's apparent betrayal of what West saw as Ivan's artistic vision. He explained to Schaffner, "I was actually . . . sad to discover in Ivan these same awful intolerances, . . . the things which the author of *Rogue's* [March] had panned so well." One draft of the original letter had charged Ivan: "Come down out of that publisher's tycoonery with its bats and dead jackdaws and write five more *Rogue's Marches*. Yes, bigod, the Indian episode".[37]

It would be gratifying to report that everyone at Obolensky company, confronting the situation more honestly and sympathetically, resolved to improve it and did. A letter four years later from Ivan to West guilelessly inquired whether the writer might have a big new novel for his spring list. Then Ivan, like Schultz's Lucy back again with her football, told West "Keep your fingers crossed. There is something in the wind that may be very good for you." What? He refused to say because good luck could be destroyed by premature disclosure. He hoped things had gotten better for West. He expected to see him soon and would call "if something happens that is quite exciting."[38] This seems to have been Ivan's last letter to him. West, however sadly, discharged his money-advances from *Moment, Rebel,* and *River's End and Other Stories,* and separated himself from Obolensky, who himself took up another career.[39]

Until now, no part of Actaeon has seen the light of publication, though it had once been accepted by MacGibbon & Kee. Nearly two decades after the separation, West writes David McDowell, without telling him that he speaks of the old Actaeon in new guise,

This present thing I'm at—I call it the Shapeless Stone at the moment,
may come off. It'll be a direct comment on the state of 'christian' Ireland,
as in the Fifties, through an English woman's eyes, for a change.[40]

Obviously, the story of the Actaeon manuscript did not end with
West's first publishing company. Its importance for him only expanded:
in fact, it is arguably his most important accomplishment.

The effusiveness of his early editors and their profession of confidence in West would have turned the head of most people who take
up the pen. One trait Anthony C. West never did reflect, however,
was artistic vanity. There was no room for egotism in the world-view
he adopted. His many children were a part of the destiny he wouldn't
dream of egotistically protesting. Providing for them was another part
of the responsibility. Luxury certainly did not matter, but an unselfish
carefulness about resources—physical and intellectual—did. He avoided
display, crowds, parades, and pretension of any kind. His responses to
fan letters and compliments were always modest, respectful, genuinely
appreciative.

Now, in the late fifties and nearly fifty himself, West was hopeful that
these sophisticated, big-city, highly experienced, American professionals
were accurate enough in their declaration of his genius and their predic-
tion of his illustrious career to bring him a small, steady freedom to write.
He was father of nine, and broke. If something financially secure and
literarily wonderful were going to happen, it might very helpfully begin.
This American start with short stories was auspicious, most promising.
His *Esquire* editors on the whole had behaved generously,[41] Gingrich
guiding him toward respected firms, steering West carefully away from
untrustworthy agents; arranging a sustaining advance for him. He had
come to a practical rescue with the initial "C" when the other Anthony
West asserted his prior claim on the name, with that chilling possibility
that the stories had been succeeding on the strength of his well-established identity. Anthony Cathcart West was trying to "stay West."

In a retrospective light it seems especially unjust that West's sally
into commercial publishing was with so unusual a team. It appeared
to answer his dream: an idealistic venture that would compete boldly,

creatively within the publishing establishment; an apparently generous, aristocratic, visionary, artistic backer who talked and wrote like a soul-mate; an experienced, knowledgeable editor who seemed to offer the critical judgment and direction West knew he needed and felt ready to accept. It is sadly ironic that he encountered at this start "bad practices, broken promises, and general inefficiency."[42]

His earlier success with the small journals—*Irish Writing, Ireland Today, Rann,* and *The Bell*—had been encouraging. West's literary models had been orthodox, Shakespeare, and, in translation, Goethe; the Romantic poets; he acquainted himself with contemporaries like Yeats and Lawrence and Thomas. Yet he knew he was outside the main-stream of modern experimentation with fiction. Joyce amused but never moved him. To West Joyce was technically superb, a clever, city writer in touch with pavements, but not with Irish earth. Virginia Woolf he found "frighteningly refined for [his] coarse peasant bowels."[43] He knew he was not in the mainstream, but he also knew that joining it would be, for him, disaster. He had to obey "bourgeois formalities," as debts "breached his defenses, let in the wolf" (he didn't even mind it at the door, he said, but he didn't want it sleeping on the bed[44]), and "offended his fastidious daemon." His first responsibility, he insisted, was to that daemon, "big as a bus."[45] He never really wanted to be published in magazines, he admitted; he never wanted to be a "literary hyena"; he never wanted to "cock the walk." He just wanted "to lift up a common stone and say with utmost conviction, this is also God."[46]

West's maverick self-education and independence distinguished as well as damned him, and he was aware of both the advantages and the perils. His pleas to his editors for guidance have to be understood as something other than a diplomatic modesty. He recognizes an uneven-ness in his work and explains it is the result of carelessness when eco-nomic pressure forces speed, at base a failure to attain smooth synthesis of experience, a human as well as artistic failure.[47] What he meant by that, as the ur explicates, is a more subtle soul development than most people have ever thought to look for in themselves.

The practical part of his plan was simultaneously to put out enough that 10% succeeded, enough to bring in $500 every three months. "I've

always held to the naive attitude," he explained, "that if a man has something valid to say and says it well, then it will be an economic proposition."[48] That there is a positive and predictable correlation among subject
value, quality of presentation, and sales may seem a preciously naive
attitude to persons acquainted with the history of literature and publishing. Even West could hardly have said the same thing by the end of
his career. The eminent successes that began with *The Bell* and were
affirmed with *Esquire* were followed by too many disappointments. The
sheer "bad luck," as other people—not West—would describe it, that
attended his publishing career is sobering. Apart from his troubles with
censorship, registered manuscripts disappeared in the transatlantic mails;
uncopied ones vanished in editorial offices; more than six times editors
changed companies in the middle of his productions; companies reorganized and transferred him; some never paid him for work accepted;
his most promising publisher drowned before his accepted novel could
appear; half-a-dozen times novels were scheduled for publication and
dropped, one of them advertised and excerpted before being canceled
for lack of funds; his first and last publishers went bankrupt.

The pattern of disappointment after acceptance in his publishing
resembles the starts and dissolutions of his communal farming ventures.
Add these to the strains of world war, exile, social isolation, poverty, and
domestic life with eleven children, and one might wryly observe that the
whole should have driven this writer at least to drink. But West didn't
drink either. "Losing oneself" he regarded as an unpleasant sensation.[49]
"Let me be conscious" prays Christopher MacMannan, as his plane
goes down. The sober indomitable questing of Anthony C. West's mind
and spirit is extraordinary. It continues to offer the most important key
to the complexities of his publishing history, as well as to his fictions
themselves.

This quest—with its bridging of extremes, the temptations of the
ego to Narcissus, the tedious journey of the Mariner—can be further
understood in light of West's special rapport with his family. Why did
the Wests have so many children, whom they seemed unable to afford?
Olive's comments are doubly surprising: They intended three. There
was no pill; they refused to use a sheath; rhythm didn't work well, but

if they hadn't been careful, they'd have had more. Abortion was out of the question. Neither of them was "good with children." She felt she shouldn't have had any, not being domestic.[50] His cheerful reference to his partner's professional and domestic balancing act may reflect both that imperception feminists have lamented as traditionally male and at the same time a peculiar truth:

> My wife is English and is 39 and very fit. She has top qualifications in secretarial work, also French, and has first-hand catering and business experience, having established and run a pier cafe in Beaumaris for four years and also a handcraft shop which her sister [Olive's single mother, Ruby, for years was known to the children and to others as Olive's older sister] is now managing. She finds that with the clothes-washer, etc., (most of the children helping out with chores and ironing), she has ample spare time and likes something to do and others to meet outside the home.[51]

An unusual objectivity characterized the Wests' attitude toward their children. The possessiveness typical of so many parents seems markedly absent and symbolized by the West children's respectful address to them by first names. His spiritual-philosophical stance on child-production (discounting any traditional wisdom about a male's biological detachment from children's gestation and delivery) helps an onlooker understand. He and Olive recognized their children as pre-existing and reincarnated souls who had chosen the Wests for re-entering the world. While he took this office of conduit very seriously, he may have been diffident about "parenting" in the current use of this term. Some resentful memories expressed by his younger daughters make it at least sadly ironic that the brilliant in-seer of adolescent development in *The Ferret Fancier* should have insensitively created lasting hurt among some of his own progeny. Perhaps he was earlier more understanding of his sons than of his daughters. Perhaps, however, the experience with daughters gradually helped to enlighten him (by the time of his sympathetic, late characterizations of Diana Hauley, West's daughters were adults.) He consciously offered empathy to his boys. Here he writes a school official with more than stated "sympathy" about one son:

> *Personally, I can't help but have some (hidden) sympathy for him, as I*
> *went through a shocking couple of years of pressure and impotence when*
> *his age, while outside of school I could count the crows and see the grass*
> *growing.*[52]

To her school teacher regarding a daughter's truancy from gym class, he writes at least with sympathy:

> *to explain that our apparent laissez-faire attitude stemmed not from*
> *approval of her flouting authority (usually an unwise as well as morally*
> *dubious exercise), but from delight at her general interest and enthu-*
> *siasm at _____ — the first time she has ever enjoyed being at school; so we*
> *were reluctant to make any move which might have lessened her welcome*
> *contentment.*[53]

Naturally, West does not appear to have thought himself insensitive to either his boys or his girls. He did not look at them "through the rosy spectacles of family egotism," but at them as "potential individual[s]."[54] He responded to teachers' letters about the children's progress,[55] not hesitating to defend the children when their behavior seemed justified and to challenge the teacher's action when it seemed unwise. A teacher had detained thirteen-year-old daughter Miriam after school, causing her to miss the bus and therefore to walk home in the dark, seven miles along a lonely road. Discreetly refraining from telling his daughter the contents of his letter, West reminded the teacher she'd have put herself and the school in "an invidious position if . . . something went wrong." He assured this teacher,

> *I am not trying to tell you your job, but would ask you to admit that I'm*
> *not entirely inexperienced in child management and direction, and that*
> *I've always been concerned with this long slow process that eventually*
> *culminates in the emergence of the reasonable adult citizen.*

He had explained that

As parents, sympathetic to a teacher's daily difficulties, we have always tried to keep open the essential liaison with the teacher . . .

and, furthermore, requested that she not

give [his daughter] these archaic, Tom-Brown lines: give a constructive reasonable task that suits the offense.[56]

West's comments about children—his own or others' ("In families like mine, children come and go, and I cannot help observing them")—do show an individualized understanding and sympathy, but they may also address a wider consequence than the child's feelings of the moment. His daughters recall a time the children were rescuing a baby rabbit from the cat, and their father swooped in on them, delivering the rabbit back to the cat, and roaring at all of them, "That was the cat's! That's Weasel's dinner!"[57]

For neighbors he requested from his doctor a preparation that had cured his own child's bed-wetting:

This little girl . . . is a charming child, but her parents are ordinary work-people and haven't got any ideas, and they were going to get some sort of electrical equipment to attach to the bed so that a bell would ring when the urine started to flow. My God![58]

Verifying the identities and procedures for the received prescription, he tells the pharmacist that the child's "parents haven't a clue," but "in a large family like mine, one is faced with small contacts with other children . . . and one can't help noticing the evolving of the new generations."[59]

West recognized nine senses, including with the standard five senses movement, balance, and speech. Beyond these were "higher" ones of reason, concept-recognition, and subtle perceptions that distinguish the mature human being.[60] He advised his niece that it could take a long time for [her young son] to "come into" his limbs, and he recommended crocheting, hand games, and playing scales on the recorder.[61] He did take children seriously: "They are tomorrow's citizens, in spite of television and cold materialism."[62] These eleven, special, independent souls chose to come down through him, he believed, and would make their own karmic journeys with what help he could give them.

A neighbor who lived across the road from the Wests when he was an adolescent in Rhiwlas, moved with his family to England. Nineteen years later, father of adolescents himself, he stumbled on West's work in the library, remembered him, and appreciatively wrote him that he found *As Towns with Fire*. It came back to him that West had talked with him once about war, and West had said something like "We've advanced technically but we haven't come to terms yet with ourselves as human beings; a Bronze-age Celt could not have killed five or twenty-thousand people in a Christian air-raid." He continued to thank West for the attention he had paid a child, regretting only that he had been too young for "real" grownup conversation. Since then he has not met anyone "half as interesting." He adds, "Talented people are often arrogant, too, but you were never that. My remembrance of you is of a very *human* person indeed . . ."[63]

West's letter to his first grandchild[64] characteristically presents his sympathies with young souls (he was at the time himself father of a three-year-old):

Llanberis,
North Wales.
8 August 1967.

My dear Sarah:
    Welcome.
    I was delighted to hear of your safe arrival, apparently belated altho' I suspect that your mother got her dates wrong while you quietly obeyed your star. Anyway, you are here and I hope to see you soon. You have come again into a rather difficult world, I'm afraid, but doubt- less you have come equipped to cope. You are in for a busy time—you

have to learn again a whole world's ways, starting at scratch: walking,
talking a new language, learning to think, growing and suiting your-
self to the ways of human beings. Your name, Sarah, is a very ancient
one, at least 4000 years old, and it means 'princess'. And you are born
under the sign of Leo which means that you will have a big brave
heart, and women with big hearts are good things. You are my first
grandchild and that makes me a little sad, too, since I must be growing
old and getting nearer the door through which you have so lately
entered, altho', to tell you no lie, I still don't feel all that much older
than you are and, certainly, I am not nearly so wise.

You will not be able to read this yet but when your parents read
it, you will feel my love for you through their feelings and hearts and
minds.

Again, welcome and God's good going to you.

Affectionately yours,
Tony

West held that the force by which an artist creates belongs also to the
ideas of reincarnation, of resurrection, of perpetuated life, and thereby of
spiritual continuity.[65] This idea, on which he meditated every day,[66] lies at
the heart of "Narcissus unto Echo," one of the *Esquire* stories (1956) and
regarded by West as his most successful published statement.[67] Destiny
for him, therefore, is never enemy, always friend.

Souls may come into this life with a heavy destiny before them and they
are unable for one reason or another to change the negatives into posi-
tives and so, apparently succumb. But somewhere along the line there
is a complex of great or small circumstance which, if used in a positive
manner [gives] the entire life . . . a new and creative turn. If it seems to
have put more on our plate than we can eat in this life, it is because we
have ruined our own digestions." [68]

Here is the spirit Geis had sensed when Arnold Gingrich had
shown him the first manuscript. He shrewdly wanted to "harness" for

commercial fiction the "same promotional horses" that made best sellers of inspirational works.[69]

West's many children needed support; Elmbank lost, he needed to find an affordable large house; Olive's income alone couldn't maintain them; he wasn't receiving the money he needed, and the experience with Obolensky had been difficult, but at the end of the fifties, West had reason to be hopeful about his writing future. Six stories had come out in *Esquire*, the last, "Gun-play," appearing in 1960. *River's End and Other Stories* had been published by McDowell, Obolensky in New York (1958), and *The Native Moment* in 1959. The title story of the collection, "River's End," had been *Esquire*'s most celebrated. On faith, then, into another decade, the Wests scrimped along.

ENDNOTES

1   ACW in interview with Audrey Eyler, 6 July 1986.

2   West told me about Jacky, as he told me about the stag at Glenveagh, although he never mentioned his having written about either one.

3   Whether parts of Reilly appear in subsequent novels or stories, West did not say.

4   ACW to Ivan Obolensky, Warren Eyster, David McDowell, [mid-August, 1959].

5   Roland Fry to Whom It May Concern re: Olive Burr, 15 October 1937, Personal.

6   Notes on untaped interview with Olive West by AE, 6 July 1986.

7   "Not Isaac," a third-person revision of this story, came out in *Esquire* in 1956 and he subsequently collected it in both *River's End* and *All the King's Horses*.

8   ACW to Eileen ___, an anthroposophist, 19 October [1958?] *Some two years or so ago I sort of broke through and slowly discovered the cumulative increase of my own powers, malice to none, and believe me, this is no mean thing for a person like myself, straw-behind-ears an' a'. . . . But, I also have the cumulative background of 26 years of Steiner and, DV, in maybe seven books or so I may move through into real adult consciousness in the light of etheric Christianity, all the old nagging Luciferic Christianity riddled out and the etheric residue harvested, the tares laid away. Luciferic christianity (small c) really only goes far as the Cross and cannot journey into risen-ness and true egoity.*

9   See West's correspondence in box 1, with Gingrich, Obolensky, and Schaffner.

10   Arnold Gingrich to ACW, 9 July 1956.

11   See "Piques in Darien: Anthony C. West and his New York Publishers," *Eire-Ireland*, Fall, 1992.

12   ACW to Arnold Gingrich, 11 March 1956.

13 *Esquire* published "Narcissus unto Echo" (March) and "The Turning Page" (December) in 1956; "River's End" (March) and "Not Isaac" (September) in 1957; "Song of the Barrow" (July) in 1958; and "Gun-Play" (September) in 1960.

14 *Trying to make some income by writing, he began aiming for magazines with short stories. His success with* Esquire *encouraged him, but Ivan said he should aim to publish novels instead. Eventually, in spite of Ivan's withdrawal of support for the switch, he comes to agree that long fiction is his medium* (ACW to John Schaffner, [June or July] 1959).

15 ACW to JS, 18 August 1962.

16 ACW to JS, 15 May 1962.

17 ACW to JS, 29 March 1962.

18 ACW to JS, [June or July] 1959.

19 ACW to IO, 22 November 1957. West reviews the circumstances for Schaffner in a letter of 15 December 1961.

20 ACW to JS, 15 December 1961.

21 Schaffner reports that Obolensky was vague about his financial transaction with West when Schaffner objected to his fusion of personal and business relationships. JS to ACW, 11 December 1961.

22 Schaffner concludes it is hopeless that Ivan could understand people who had to work for a living (JS to ACW, 11 December 1961).

23 Schaffner was West's agent from 1958 through the sixties.

24 DMD to ACW, 3 October 1957. West had apologized to McDowell for not keeping carbons, 8 April 1957.

25 His own library of his publications is incomplete, and he offered no bibliography of his works among his papers.

26 ACW to John Schaffner, 15 December 1961; Schaffner to ACW, 25 August 1966. Warren Eyster to ACW, May 1960. This letter turned up in another box of West's papers that came to light when Olive moved, after my original sorting of the papers and after the writing of "Piques in Darien."

27 ACW to IO, 24 July 59.

28 ACW to IO, Warren Eyster, David McDowell, [mid-August, 1959.

29 ACW to Obolensky, Eyster, McDowell, [mid-August, 1959]. He also notes ". . . *The only thing that didn't die entirely on me was that Echo/Narcissus story. And in this context, I've no writer-pride at all.*"

30 ACW to Chief Migration Officer, Australia House, nd. [1959?] ACW Interviews. (They also considered Brazil: ACW to B. Consulate, 1 November 1958, and Iraq c. 12 March? [1960]. ACW to JS. Ten years later they talked of emigrating to Portugal: ACW to Paddy Swift, 10 May 1969), Biog.\Aid to Friends. The Wests had relatives in Australia, as Ellen West's sister Maria (the inspiration for the red-headed aunt in "Narcissus unto Echo") had emigrated and reared children there.

She died 18 August 1974. Her daughter, Doreen Binding, records her mother's name as McClements. West's own sister, Eileen, emigrated to Australia after her mother died and never retained contact with the family. From an inquiry by ACW to his sister Dorothy in 25 March 1977 (postcard) it appears that Harold West's son, Patrick, also went to Australia.

31 ACW to Dept. of Health and Social Security, 26 January 1977, Bank.

32 Ivan Obolensky to ACW, 7 May 1957.

33 JS to ACW, 10 May 1962.

34 Warren Eyster to ACW, May 1960. It and a letter from Schaffner to Obolensky, 23 March 1962, further justify West's perceptions of his treatment, although they show it to have been part of a larger pattern and not a behavior bestowed particularly upon West.

35 ACW to JS, undated letter [spring 1959].

36 IO to ACW, 7 Aug 1959.

37 ACW to IO, 23 July 1959, draft.

38 IO to ACW, 27 February 1962.

39 ACW acknowledges receipt of news that Obolensky has joined Middendorf, Colgate & Co., New York Stock Exchange, in a letter to Ivan, 27 January 1970, when he writes to retrieve the rights to *River's End*.

40 ACW to DMcD, [c. 7 January 1977].

41 Perhaps *Esquire* was "really rattl[ing] its own dice." W. Eyster to ACW, nd [early August 1959], Obolensky.

42 John Schaffner to Ivan Obolensky, May 1960; copied to ACW.

43 ACW to O, 7 May 1957.

44 So West's friend Ormond Edwards told me in a London interview, January 1989.

45 Draft to O, 23 July 1959.

46 ACW to Mr. Smith at Obolensky, 6 May 1958.

47 ACW to John Schaffner, [28] November 1958.

48 ACW to JS.

49 ACW to JS, 4 February 1958.

50 Notes from an untaped interview with Olive West by AE, 6 July 1986.

51 ACW to M.Athorpe of Exeter, 17 September 1959, ACW Interviews.

52 ACW to Mr. Pardoe, 12 Jan 1965, Children's Education.

53 ACW to Mr. Machin, 26 January 1978.

54 ACW to Mr.Pardoe, 9 January 1963.

55 ACW to David Jones, 22 Nov 1970, Children's Education.

56 ACW to Miss R, 11 November 1965, Children's Education.

57 Mary and other daughters, in taped interview with AE, July 1987.

58 ACW to Dr. Krause, 22 February 1961, Health.

59 ACW to Weleda, 11 February 1961.

60 ACW to TW, 13 July 1980, Siblings, Ir. Rel.
61 ACW to MD, 13 July 1980.
62 ACW to R. Krause, 22 February 1961, Health.
63 Peter Green to ACW, 11 February 1984.
64 ACW to Sarah Gill, 8 August 1967, Letters from / to Children. My thanks to Jocelyn West Gill, Sarah's mother.
65 To McDowell & Obolensky, 7 May 1957.
66 ACW to Edward Blishen, 29 March 1963.
67 Notes for ACW's letter to Uslar, 27 November 1964. Uslar.
68 To Obolensky, 6 May 1958.
69 Gingrich quotes from Geis's letter in his own letter to West of 6 March 1957.

CHAPTER SEVEN

1960 MAELFA: ON A GREEN HILL

DESPITE IVAN OBOLENSKY'S SILENCES, the decade began auspiciously for West's publishing with new editions of his first two books. In 1961 a London edition of *River's End* by MacGibbon & Kee bore West's expansion and plot changes in "The Monocrats," and Hillman-McFadden (Bartholomew House in New York) produced a paperback edition of *The Native Moment*. "All the King's Horses" was issued in the *Transatlantic Review*, London, in December. *The Colorado Quarterly* published "The Fairy Midwife."[1] Roy McFadden (February 24, 1961) reviewed *The Native Moment* for BBC Ulster, insisting that West was a poet who in Simon Green has "the emphasis and intimacy of William Blake's world. Like Blake, instead of abstractions, he sees the bulk of actual things: people and pubs, lakes and eels, potatoes and children." McFadden praised *The Native Moment* for being "boldly and wordily about untidy and unmeasured Life with an old-fashioned capital L." "Myself and a Rabbit" was included in *Irish Stories and Tales*, New York, by Washington Square Press. In 1962 "Looking for Bridie" came out in the winter issue of *Audience*, in Cambridge, Massachusetts, and his poem "As Queen Bees Soar" in another American journal, *The Second Coming*. Fischer Verlag of Germany brought out an edition of *River's End*.[2] There were Italian and

German editions of the earlier *Native Moment*, Ernst Geisenheyner having become his European agent. His editor from MacGibbon & Kee, Timothy O'Keeffe, gave him Irish empathy as well as a critical ear. Throughout the sixties the financial anxiety and disappointments were repeatedly countered by artistic successes—or is it the other way around?

Five of his novels and novellas came out in the sixties; he was encouraged to expect paperbacks of *Ferret* and *Rebel.* But *Playboy*'s new fiction editor turned down his predecessor's plan to condense and print *Rebel to Judgment*, and New York publishers declined a cooperative effort with MacGibbon & Kee to put out Naked to Laughter. European sales never did match hopes; translators faced consequential problems with his style: "The Upper Room" appeared in Germany as, alas, "Over the Garage."[3] In March 1965 the problem of confused identity surfaced again when the *Buffalo Evening News* reviewed his work under the other Anthony's photograph.[4] In April 1965 he wrote to his bank manager: "I can't help feeling fairly confident. . . . Last year I made a fair bit of money, surprising myself"; then he described 1966 as "disastrous."

Armed for the new decade with an expectancy that was both genuine and necessarily assumed, West made appeals through letters to publisher, bank, and tax official, seeking whatever small adjustments could help and seemed fair. The money problems persisted and staying West remained his challenge. The Wests were still trying to re-establish themselves in a house. On April 24, 1959, they had moved into "Bryn Afon," a rental in Penmon. Olive and Ruby, her mother, were running a handcrafts shop and café in Beaumaris. For a while Olive was managing the food business, and Ruby maintained the other sales. Then new restaurants in town began to affect the café's trade; needed repairs on the building had to be deferred. Olive took a secretarial job in a hospital. West continued to write and to look for a post as an estate manager. In March 1961, the owner wishing to retire in the house, they received notice that they would have to vacate Bryn Afon by May.

Olive turned up a ten-room structure in Rhiwlas for £250. Her husband was elated for her and for them all. Twenty-five years later there was still pride in his voice over her success in finding Maelfa. This place required renovation, but they were undaunted. They began negotiating

A. C. West in cravat, early 1960s? WEST FAMILY COLLECTION, PHOTOGRAPHER UNKNOWN.

The Wests with their first nine in 1960 at Alberlleiniog: (back row, l-r) Bronwen, Olive, West, Michael, Mary; (front, l-r) Jeremy, Christopher, Brigid, (Carlo, the Labrador retriever) Stephanie, Miriam, Jocelyn. WEST FAMILY COLLECTION, PHOTOGRAPHER UNKNOWN.

for a bank loan and a builder. The following letter must have resembled no other this realtor ever received:

> *Dear Mr. Roberts,*
>
> *We went to Rhiwlas on Sunday afternoon—myself with the intention to measure the house. Then I got nervous that the plans I'd produce mightn't pass, and cause further delay. (My wife's finding out if the Building Society has any plans.) From what you said that the plans needn't be professional, I thought it would be safer, perhaps, to try and approach a local Saro draughtsman and see if he could help. Then I thought there might be a local lad in your office who wouldn't be averse to earning the nominal fee whatever it should be, in the circumstances. Maybe you'd be kind enough to let me know. . . .*
>
> *So, we went up to the jerusalem hills instead. It was a fine day, and my oh my, the view was not of this world. Surely there must be a native son with talent for paint or ink? If you ever hear of any man who thinks he might say something, let me know, and I'll have a look at him. I've never found anyone yet myself. . . . There should be a singer for these hills—modern, progressive, and hopeful—writer, poet, or playwright, malice to none.*
>
> *Thank you for sending us the application form.*[5]

Mr. Roberts didn't try to match his correspondent with his reply. He wrote one sentence to the effect he was pleased they liked the district, and if he learned of someone with something to say, he'd certainly let West know.[6] They secured a loan and contracted to have at least lights and plumbing completed by June. Maelfa became their home for five years, the last two children, Katherine Sarah Antonia and Simon Gwyon, arriving there in 1961 and 1964, respectively.

The Wests tried repeatedly to establish a charitable farm and community. In the sixties they borrowed in order to have property of their own to sell, eventually to benefit this philanthropic plan. With the loan they acquired a couple acres of land in Wales, Gwynfryn, which they intended to subdivide and sell as individual building lots. By adopting this tax-free plan with a small group of friends from Albrighton days,

The last two Wests, Katherine and Simon, with their parents. Llanberis, 1971.
WEST FAMILY COLLECTION, PHOTOGRAPHER UNKNOWN.

they hoped to get started. But the market was slow (it was 1981 before all the lots were gone). Struggling with debts, they managed to sell Maelfa in the mid-sixties for considerably more than it had cost them and purchased a less expensive dwelling, Bryn Goleu, in the town of Llanberis, where Olive ran another café. In 1966, the Wests moved into Bryn Goleu, where they lived for the rest of the decade, West writing now in a house-trailer parked at the bottom of the yard.

In rural North Wales, service from his bank had been impressively personal, one sympathetic and literature-reading official even putting his own money into West's account to hold off the penalties of overdraft.[7] With reason, West grew frustrated to see such personality diminishing in the system as people like his manager, Mr. Ellis, retired. The new management treated variances categorically, and he naturally resented any imputation from the bureaucracy that his intentions were fraudulent. This later protest typifies his responses to warnings about insufficient funding.

My naiveté in the whole matter was genuine. I am not a grabbing citizen
and official forms of all kinds scare the wits out of me. . . .

    I volunteered for the RAF in 1940 and finally served in 627 low-
level Pathfinder Squadron as Navigator and Meteorological Observer,
commissioned and honourably demobbed in 1946 with a gratuity of £75.
We have reared a large family of eleven, all of whom are responsible law-
abiding citizens, with very little State help.

    Our present income is now £30, OAP [pension] plus one Family
Allowance, plus an increasing bank overdraft.

    I sincerely hope you may be able to help me in this.[8]

Mr. Ellis could no longer run interference.[9] By mid-decade the
oldest three West children were independent—Michael had taken a
catering course and gone eventually to South Africa; Mary had studied to
become a nurse in London; Bronwen "with her big heart," as her father
observed, had taken a job temporarily in a Steiner school in Bristol.
Jocelyn and Jeremy could find holiday jobs in hotels up the coast,[10] but
Christopher, Brigid, Miriam, Stephanie, and toddlers Kathy and Simon,
remained at home. There were still plenty of mouths to feed, and poverty
continued to dog him.

In 1961 West was fifty-one years old, strong, working hard, still
bringing children onto the planet, and still feeling hopeful about the
contribution he might make through his art. A close friend from New
York had died of cancer,[11] but he enjoyed some other strong friend-
ships that had begun after the War: at Albrighton with Ormond and
Irene Edwards, with Olive's school-friend Gerda and her husband, Rex
Massey[12], and, for a brief time in Wales, with Beryl and Peter Grwffyd.[13]
In the sixties he was also supported artistically, emotionally, and intellectually by several remarkable correspondences. Late in the nineteen fifties
West had received an appreciative letter from a reader in Custer, South
Dakota. Dorothy O'Connor was a prescient American of unusual heritage: a Chinese-Norwegian who grew up close to the Lakota. She was
an eager, lonely, deeply reflective, university-educated reader, occupied
with management of a motel during the tourist season, with obligations
to husband and family, including the schedule of a daughter in her late

teens. Dorothy became his devoted reader and epistolary friend. The correspondents met only once, for a day in London museums when Dorothy and her sister, Marilou, took a European trip. West dedicated the Simon & Schuster edition of *The Ferret Fancier* to her in 1963. Two years later, at 42, she died of cancer. Dorothy gave West practical help—posting clippings, notices of publications, and reviews—and she provided a female perspective on shared interests, especially literary, psychic, and spiritual ones. While there is no grossly obvious application of Dorothy's traits to his characters, her reported dreams, he said, did help him create the dreams for Actaeon's Diana, and he seems to have clarified his ideas as he talked about them to Dorothy in the letters.

The new life in Eire prompts Diana Hauley to keep her journal,[14] in which she confesses she feels like a rootless cutting, ambivalent about the motives for her marriage to this Church of Ireland clergyman. Until probably the mid-seventies, West struggled with a third-person omniscient narrating for her story, and the ending consistently continues with the third-person report of her death. Readers are given more of Diana's thought by version D, but not until version I (the only one with a date on it, 1977) does he make the first-person switch that helps him effectively present and develop her candor and intellect, her acute poetic sensitivity, her ironic wit, and her sensuality, all of which build to within a few hours of her death (its circumstances, reconstructed by her surviving child, then appear in a post-script).

> Truth to tell, I wanted out, change, new views, different horizons; bored with life and people, fed up with watching others vying to say bright important things with false faces, mounter-uppers and putter-downers, pretending to serve—to help themselves, measuring others' shoes to see if their own feet might fit. I was gripped by a cold increasing fear of life and my own impotence to find a straw of truth in a dangerous haystack of needles: life-change in more ways than one, my life a nursery of worn-out toys: walking in darkness, my head a box of matches that I strike for momentary light—brief intervals that die to dense the darkness.
>
> With agoraphobic feelings nigh panic, I watched the misty shore of Wales recede like the pulling of a tooth, wondering as pan to fire,

whither and for what, until the consummation happened on the boat. Too shy to warn him I was virgin, I was terrified until the end ignored the means, discomfortable resentment canceled by sensation I never knew was there (R, 5; R disk, 6).

I told him that never having met any male with sufficient intellectual nous, I had refused marriage and its known complications. He accepted this with such final understanding that, to remove his possible conclusion of unnatural frigidity, not that at that time this mattered one way or t'other, I impulsively mentioned Allessandre DeVigne, the smarmy so-called papal count and one of my mother's mystical parasites who, disturbing my sexual awakening, had hyptonized me at fifteen to prove, ostensibly to discover, if I were Pericles' mistress in new disguise, my mother, going through her Grecian phase in lieu of an earlier Egyptian, swallowing every word of it, while I was left with years of vague athenian dreams, my life hardly one thing or another.

He asked me more about DeVigne, then said, scaring me, that he sounded very like one Magnus Hugh O'Neill, a man he had known in Dublin before the war, who had claimed descent from the royal Hugh, the one who had turned roof-lead into bullets to fight Elizabeth. His O'Neill had claimed a stint as a Tibetan monk and had had a scheme to start a church for rich old ladies of both sexes: an atavistic clairvoyant enthralled by the psychopathic lie who thought that by hypnosis he could reproduce the ancient temple sleep, his guinea-pigs providing him with knowledge of creation; climbing over the wall because he lacked both will and patience to look for his own door . . .

I asked if this were possible: oh yes, he said, each man is all of living history. This gave me pause and I changed the subject. My walls are too high, my room doorless and I prefer it so.

But, sex here and there, everywhere in fact as winds blow, I ask myself if I'm going to use this good man as file to blunt or sharpen my protracted frustrations. Perhaps I want a personal guru like mother, someone who knows or claims to know more'n Canterbury, Whitehall and stock-exchange if, one for t'other, these three are any different. And I don't yet know how I'll share a hitherto well-worn life, share autonomy, establish mutual reciprocity, if that's not tautology. Old maids are prone

to metaphorical cats, have in-grown ways and habits and I can't expect
to be immune. I'm nothing like a wife as yet. I'm a broken bride with
spinster mind intact (R, 6–7; R disk, 7–8).

Diana wants peace. She resists the mold that marriage imposes upon
women; she doesn't want to be "the half of another"(R,8), but she is
astonished at the force of her own passion, never before experienced for
any man or woman. Her husband's physical interest, much to her worry,
seems not to match, though he is dutiful, patient, and strangely prescient
about her intellectual responses. In the A version of Actaeon, probably
a very early (and incomplete) one, O'Dea tries to talk explicitly about
marriage. Diana has been thinking that marriage doesn't seem to mean
very much to him, but he counters frankly that were it so, he wouldn't
have married at all—that perhaps he sees even more in it than she does?
She objects: the way he carries the concept of marriage makes her feel
as though she's sharing their bed with the Eternal Feminine, and she
admits to being jealous. O'Dea replies,

> But that's only another name for a man's soul? You can't blame me for
> sleeping with my own soul—wouldn't be much of a husband without
> it? I could just as soon blame you for consorting with your own soul,
> the Eternal Male (A, 109–110)?

O'Dea persists—with no intention of being difficult—in his peculiar
reserve. Diana realizes that he will never give himself to pure indulgence
in sex; he concedes that he wouldn't think of submitting entirely to its
dictation, but asks her not to put more weight on the fact than it can
sustain:

> If we're going to lift sex out of its marriage context, we mightn't have
> married at all? Most naïve marriages founder on this fact: sexual delight
> never promises to sustain itself at its initial intensity. While, on the other
> hand . . . if the overall marriage union progresses into understanding
> intimacy, sex pleasures themselves become part of the total embrace
> (A, 110).

They continue to talk about guilt complexes over sex, Diana raising St. Paul's familiar counsel. O'Dea tells her the apparent connection between celibacy and religion is much more complicated and derives not from Biblical authority but from

> the decadent gnostic emasculation. . . . . The virginal forces of women had always been esoterically employed in the cults. . . . The Bible is not at all a prissy document; its spades are always spades. It never avoided the normal sexual act—it avoided the misuse of sex . . . All this holy distaste of sex is a very modern fabrication. In ancient times sexual union was really a well-defined ritual act effected under certain constellations (A, 111–112).

A conclusion like the Virgin Birth, furthermore, reflects other misunderstanding of esoteric fact, Christ showing in the Temptation in the Wilderness his rejection of the miraculous. Mary of Matthew was a Temple dancer. "To be born of a virgin," O'Dea explains in another version, is "an esoteric statement, [having] nothing to do at all with physical partuition" (D, 694).

O'Dea is a religious diplomat. Diana is cynical about the clergy, who "taught how to fool God while killing His creations." Her irony, even flippancy, gives West a way to present logical quarrels with traditional accounts: Human alienation, she says, is the result of the Fall—"put upon us all by old Jehovah when he sacked his gardener over an apple" (R, 11; R disk, 12). But even if she can distance herself from guilt over conventional beliefs, has she "sinned", she wonders, by sacrificing her poet's freedom? She insists that her art is not negotiable, that her inner artist's self remains virgin. Why does O'Dea—a cleric—find her—a religious rebel—attractive? The conscious lure, at least, lies in the fact that O'Dea, like the great Romantics, believes poets still have contact with the spiritual source (R, 19; R disk, 18).

West tries boldly to integrate O'Dea and Diana's physical intimacy and candor with the couple's theological, theosophical investigation. In an early version of the honeymoon a conversation has been going on while O'Dea is in the tub and Diana is sitting on the lid of the toilet.

They joke about bulls and horns as he towels himself, their passion rising. He carries her to their bed. Passion spent, he resumes his explanation, "I've been thinking about Mithra." Diana—and the reader—are amazed. "Sex releases me," he excuses himself, and—undaunted—goes on:

> Pure Mithraism had a profound conception of the highest God . . . Mithra was not originally regarded as a god. He was originally a sort of substitute for the excarnate Christ—the Cosmic Champion or Ormuzd, representing the totality of the powers behind evolution. The bull escaped and ran beserk. Mithras captured it with the help of his dog and killed it. This is a prefiguration of the Michaelic act—the time of the moon's separation from the earth which Genesis quotes.
>
> Was Mithras a real being, then?
>
> Yes and no. I'd say he did live on earth at some time but in the sense of an overshadowing of a highly developed soul, as Krishna did actually live on earth but in the eastern conception of inspiration rather than a complete incarnation. This was the only way the great gnostics could see the Christ, which was the meaning for the very definite Christian creeds. Even as Saul, Paul couldn't take it. Mithraism had the seven degree initiation which the Church fathers also recognized. Nathaniel, who'd transcended guile, was a fifth degree Mithras man. So was the apostle Bartholomew. He was able to recognize Christ as the incarnate Ormuzd, much as the Magi recognized the Matthew Jesus as the incarnated Zoroaster. The tragedy of the Hebraic complex was the same as that of the other old cults which held on to the Messianic expectation as long as they could in spite of their decreasing spiritual consciousness. The Hiberno-Druid was one of the few who knew what had happened. Columcille is proof of that. He should really be our patron. He should really be the patron of the British Isles. The great Julian the Apostate was the last Mithraic priest-king. He set out for Persia—why? History doesn't know why.
>
> Darling, you're quite extraordinary. . . . Making love to me with ancient history!
>
> Mithraism and sex go very well together, he chuckled, kissing her (Q-fragment, 178–179).

Diana and the reader might well be skeptical, women evidently
having been excluded from Mithraic initiation, if for no other reason.
But such exposition is further integrated with the imagery underlying
the conception for the novel, helping West reveal and bridge the limits
that past and future preoccupations impose on Diana and O'Dea, respectively. On their last day in Kerry they pass a boy leading a beautiful black
bull to stud.

> Dea gets out to look for a natural necessarium as a young man comes
> along with a lovely black bull, a new leather halter with bright brass
> buckles and links on the noble head, the rich yeasty bullsmell reminding
> me of Hauley. Natural enough, I suppose—these rural invocations
> asking me to relive a half-lived life, right or left foot forward, the years
> between childhood and now, abstractions—approximations of existence.
> I wonder how many lives within a life is one expected to live: doubt-
> less, Dea would answer as many lives as days, day by day, ignoring the
> accumulating years, his past never threatening his present. He's fortunate
> to be so equanimous. My past—a kind of hereditary illness potential to
> new disease, the future liable to be sick before it wants to happen. Per-
> haps, with time, he'll give me some of his interior optimism for health.
>
> He says the bull and boy hello, asking the breed.
>
> Welsh black, the boy says, the bull drawing him on, the hind hooves
> pivoting round the point of tenderness in its ichorous nose. His father's
> the champeen of Wales!
>
> Dea smiled, asking: What's he doing here?
>
> He's after the girls, the boy says, smiling, throwing a loud look all
> over me.
>
> Boy, bull, and Dea go up the road with slow chuff of leathern hooves,
> leaving me the white-thorn's wan scent. My life's a biography of scents
> tastes and random sounds—a ring of countless keys that can suddenly
> unlock forgotten doors to time-buried rooms, tombs, tumuli and sep-
> ulchres where petrified memories linger lifelessly, ugly and benign,
> a-waiting my own eventual decease (R, 74–75; R disk, 62–63).

Further links are forged as West makes Kerry the ancestral home of

O'Dea's dead mother, whose heirloom emerald ring Diana is wearing. Sean O'Sullivan, an old blind seanchai, welcomes their visit, remembers O'Dea's family, and honors them with a tale of the prehistoric invaders who first brought the bulls to the island. The mithraic association recurs in the flashback to Diana's childhood when her volatile father shot the beautiful young bull that trampled the rose-garden.

> The red shorthorn bull came charging across the lawns, into the sunken garden and the mazy trellis round the rosary with sounds of crunching matchboxes, the anxious men in hasty chase with ropes and sticks, hoping to remove the beast before it was noticed. Father saw it from the study window and came out, loading a shotgun. I knew he saw the bull as concentrated symbol of frustration, scape-thing responsible for his loneliness and loss of wife, my distant mother now consorting with her gurus whom he called damned babus, in hope of better way to heaven. He aimed the gun a few feet from the bull's left ear and I hardly heard the shot. It tossed its great head in wild gesture of unbelief, sank to its knees and rolled over, the broken trellis tangled with climbing roses roped lustrally over it. The half-dozen men, shocked acolytes, watched, their brains refusing the evidence of sight, as he broke the gun, the spent cases jumping behind him, turned and walked back to the house. Thereafter, year after year, I feared his kindness, locking my room at night until the day at the butts he cried aim to death and took the arrow in the throat by standing in the way, leaving me little but a heap of feudal yesterdays and insolvency, along with his scale model of Hastings: had Harold had him for commander the decision might have been reversed, the Saxon line entire for a thousand years and England that much richer (R, 76–77; R disk, 64–65).

Significantly, Diana's death is ultimately occasioned by a black bullock in the dark road.

Through such imagery, ancient practices are evoked in contemporary applications and West is able to assert continuities and disruptions in what he perceives as the cosmic design, especially Ireland's place in it. The job was huge and difficult, while the potential tantalized. There

remain volumes of his study-notes in addition to the thousands of pages
of the twenty-some tellings of the story itself. West defends its scope to
Schaffner:

> *The whole thing has come through as a sort of modern Faust now. I've*
> *dug deep, maybe too deep, but I had to find the bedrock. . . . Actaeon is*
> *long and complex, I know, but all the complexities could be cut and the*
> *whole thing brought into line with Ivan's original assessment, to which I*
> *stuck tightly all through. . . . Actaeon needs a hell of a lot of work on it*
> *but basically, it should all be there in the rough and should lend itself*
> *to a fusing of all the themes and threads into a compact and artistic*
> *whole.*[15]

He appears to believe that these esoteric ideas, at first fully explicated, can become so integrated, so implicit in the materials of his tale,
that with the fortuitous working of time for the acceptance of them by his
audience, he'll be able to reduce the volume and his readers will infer
the whole. West will then have made his destined spiritual and aesthetic
contribution.

Among the Q fragments lies a pertinent transcription from Goethe's
Faust, Part II, Act 2:

Mephistopheles:
　　No more. That privilege I gladly waive, of hearing about tyrant
versus slave.
　　Those struggles bore me: scarce is riot done,
　　When lo, the blockheads start another one.
　　And none can see he is the dupe and game
　　Of Asmodeus, who inspires the flame.
　　They fight, they say, dear freedom's cause to save;
　　But, seen more clearly, slave is fighting slave.

Mortal vision is presently obscured. The Lady Actaeon's

*'gen' is based on the fundamental Manichaean realities which will be
there when churches and states as we know them have faded and which
will eventually enlighten the dark places in science.*[16]

Now the esoteric origins of Christian truth make explanation necessary, and he finds it always a challenge to avoid telling when he well
knows that art should be showing.

*All this straight esoteric stuff doesn't make an artform on its own and
would only confuse itself and all the other issues in the mind of a reader.
I only tried to put the solar system in a pail.*[17]

On the other hand, he exercised the faith of a believer that truth,
being implicit, will appear and obtain, belief complementing his artistic
impulses.

The early responses of his editors *had* been very encouraging, and
the reader, looking over the record and aware of the life-long commitment West held to this novel—a tale he had been tinkering with for
nearly twenty years and would continue to rewrite for the next thirty—
can imagine just how gratifying Obolensky's first interest must have
been. West never abandoned his conviction:

If I concentrated Actaeon, it could be the strongest thing I'll ever do. [18]

The correspondence with Dorothy O'Connor glosses many of the
ideas of his Actaeon effort, although without his novel's text, she must
have followed his associative leaping with difficulty. Certain of the tale's
themes appear: the supremacy of *Corinthian* love, the relations between
matter and spirit, the problem of suffering, the obstruction created by
Freudian psychology and sexuality, spiritual evolution, the differences
between male and female knowing, the help available through understanding myth, history, and geography. This long letter, typical with
single-spacing and little paragraphing, offers a dense collage of them:

8 July 58

Dear Dorothy O'Connor,

Thank you very much for your encouraging letter with the poem
[Delmore Schwartz, "Starlight Like Intuition Pierced the Twelve"]. I
was glad to have them since I'm in a trough and maybe you'll hoist
me out again on the ropes of your fresh mind. The poem—no: strange
how many moderns can still only 'atuit' Christ in the Gnostic mode—
wisdom, beauty, power, but minus love. We've had wisdom beauty
power, still have it.....what's happening? Atom bombs? No love. . . .

James Joyce: Odyssey, you'll probably only get intellectually, much
as religionists get the seven journeys of St. Paul. May sound strange
but I don't know what place Joyce has. I've always suspected he had
a strong church-guilt complex and now his brother in a recent book
vindicates me. I know many people think the sun shines in Joyce's
underpants: one has to be careful about him. The powerful invocative
intellectuality and imagery, the supreme ease of language—but then,
somehow, he only found things to dirty on them. If you could imagine
Joyce as in his church, he could say all these things in the opposite
way, under the name of God. I think he was a blindman. Lawrence:
He was, I think, a true worldman. He wrote against the awful Anglo-
Saxon prissiness and prudery, broke down false barriers. Had he known
more he could not have done that, just as Delmore Schwartz would
have written differently and no less well had he known more. Lawrence
will we read when Joyce is a literary curio. Anyway, we'll see.....Law-
rence did try to see artistically-physiologically. Eckhart, Tauler—the
medieval church mystics—Lawrence somehow belonged there. Pity the
modern mind can't get to know these older men's idea-processes. Their
terminology is so quaint, nowadays. But they knew a lot—more'n we
do, in many ways. Don't brood—think, unravel.....

What I don't think we can afford to refuse to see, to bear witness
to, are the two faces of sex: often we love in spite of as well as because
of sex—sex, the popular great unknown! It's a hell of a problem. Men
as men know damn all about it. Women probably know more if they
could know what they know...I dunno. I mean, I don't know how to

*rationalize the Freudian pansexualism on close intellectual terms: one
can only describe mating, pregnancy, etc. biological surface processes.
Most modern light entertainment has disguised subliminal sex-
advertisement; most books, and all our funny stories, I suppose. We are
actually conditioned to think sexually, erotically....about what? Half
the world sitting on a one-minute merrygoround. Not that I'm trying
to go back, but our great grandparents, by and large, had as much sex
activity as we have but they didn't 'image' it so much, somehow. I think
maybe Goethe's Faust might answer it, could one get right behind it.
Goethe was certainly no prude.*

*I suppose, in one sense, a stone, for instance, has perfect, sleeping
'form'. But it can only be a stone. But then, I've come to our mutual
problems by a twisting different route and if I talk out of context it will
confuse and even annoy. You have yours now? You have just as much
on your plate as you can eat. I don't say this although I can agree with
it.........Life is not what you have, what you are: it always is what you
haven't, and what you are not: always the unseen bit that's over: maybe
even tomorrow's jam could poison us today were we to have it? I think
your complete maturation would increase expectancy utterly beyond
any intellectual finite recognition: why should the negative aspect be
the ruling one? No earthly reason why it should? Three loves—eros,
philia, agape: eros more or less what we have; philia, love of wisdom,
perhaps, and agape the totality of unpossessive creative world-love,
egotism all transmuted—your complete maturation perhaps? Christ
asked Peter three times: Love me? The traditional translations and
interpretations don't show any understanding for this scene. Between
eros and agape there is suffering. I didn't put it there: seems to be a
law: anyway, you'll know yourself that the few things worthwhile which
any of us have, have been bought by sweat and unhappiness. But
damnit, I can't put a life philosophy in a short letter, so please don't
judge me too hardly. I'm trying to work some of these things out in this
present novel—hell of a job. Maybe I'm only going into the labyrinth
without a sufficiently long and strong thread, minus Ariadne. If you
read the Greek myths (Celtic ones too jumbled altho' just as valid)
from the view of soul attitudes, maybe you could see more clearly your*

*'complete maturation'. Maybe.....Anyway, Zeus still roams free over
your Black Hills.*

*Must ask you for any clear-cut sayings. Couldn't plagiarize. Your
dream-life: I don't know but you could be one of the 'new' people, the
'new consciousness' people who are coming into the world increasingly.
You do not sound at all like a 'moony' person since your thoughts
are so definite and clean-cut, and because your blood is so powerfully mixed.[19] The esotericists state that from now on there will be a
profound, if very gradual, change in consciousness in many people
which will lead into the 'art-form' world and whom it will be difficult
to mislead with all this modern hocus-pocus. I don't dream much —
only sometimes. Sometimes I weep with utter sadness: very occasionally I laugh: once I was enjoying something in a way I had not been
able to do since I was a child and Olive woke me up, thinking I was
smothering; was I mad. In your sleeping you go through the 'gate' into
the soul world, so-called. It is around us all the time but our modern
consciousness does not permit us to know it: without 'conscious'
introduction (initiation) were we to see, we'd go nuts. We must do
everything consciously, under the lordship of the Ego: in pre-ego times,
before around 400 B. C., sleeping and waking dream was a normal
way to live, dreams more and more intense the further you go back.
The psychologists admit a soul or unconscious existence (charge one
money to peep into it!). Our modern consciousness has evolved out
of the dreamy clairvoyant state, that other evolution which Darwin
missed). Our brain and body are merely a dense reflecting apparatus,
in one sense, on which the soul plays. Dreams, normally, are half-free
or partially free soul experiences only partially reflected on the body
and consequently, usually distorted. As such, they don't mean much in
themselves, one way or another. They are only very partially 'imaginations' in, say, the sense of Coleridge. He had them but took drugs to
expedite them and got lost. Coleridge was a great personality with
many germinal ideas and intuitions, which he was not able to fulfill.
Space and time usually change in dream, too. But one cannot 'read'
a person from prepared general theories and graphs, a la the psycho-
analysts. Each person is individual and different, and brings different*

'history' into life, conditioned by birth, environment, associations—
each person a whole world in his own right.

You are very like my Lady Actaeon in this damned book—imagine
me trying to write about a woman, something I swore I'd never do. But
then most women try to write like men. In this context your letter was
very helpful—you present me with a conscious intelligent woman, two
feet on earth . . . with a profound 'secondary' existence in sleep which,
in actual fact, rather contradicts her, shall I say, day to day, grave-the-
end intellectualism (no criticism implied—I know little more'n you
do).

It is strange, too: Black Hills—Snowdonia. Here, a very ancient
mystery centre, the elements and the rocks still 'remember.' Snowdon,
the highest one, over 3500 feet—was, 10,000 years ago for many
centuries, a mystery centre and yearly, knobble-kneed climbers who
come only for the bare danger-thrill, fall and get killed and damaged.
Snowdon still doesn't like their attitude! Your Black Hills—5000 miles
away, another Snowdon: old post-Atlantean centre coming down into
decadent Sioux times: don't under-rate your environment: it aids for
to dream, which the semi-disincarnate Sioux knew well. It's close to
the Zeus world, still; the old sky-gods—O not so unreal as might be
thought. But again, all this is brutally out of context, so don't take
my say-so too literally; take it artistically, if you will. No, death will
resound your music far better than the dream.

But tell me dreams, externalize them in daylight: dream....?
God you are sister to my Lady Actaeon—all the answers but without
reasons for them. Ordinary life with its hosts of clever men who merely
rehash the past according to their own whimsical limitations will never
provide answers for people like you. We live still in the rubble of Babel.
But tell me some dreams?

I'll end here. I still don't know how River's End is faring in your
USA.

Today is warm and sultry. June was March-mild and wet; farmers
all behind with the hay and the meadows growing on into seed. They
try to work as their forefathers worked while working much less. They
have no joyance in work any more, it's all a slavery: they have lost the

earth now. Calvin taught them to despise it, the ole bastard. Yes, the
psychos would have a word for me, also. But I know more'n they do,
thank God. They can't scare me.

    Thank you again for your good letter and please forgive this untidy
one. God bless, Tony

Dorothy supplied a series of her recurrent dreams, vivid and haunting, thoughtfully and modestly recounted. Diana's "doorless room" is linked to one of them; her dream also seems to be the source for the title of Room Without a Door. The F Actaeon includes an adaptation of another of Dorothy's dreams in which Diana freely dances, resenting Dea's restraint:

> With oneir[omanic] guile she is running away, seeing herself going shadowly and silently through the mazy gorse until she walks slowly along a shore of shining sand which glitters like crushed glass. She is barefooted, the sand soft and warm, the sea on her right a bluebag blue, diamond dusted where slow waves fray. She wants to dance, each gesture to be an unsaid word.....
>
>   Mumble, mumble......
>
>   Yes, yes.....she mutters impatiently.
>
>   O'Dea's voice is calling. She turns back, seeing her line of footprints like question-marks, asking each yard where it is going. I'm going shopping for sins—so there! she answers them.
>
>   Mumble, mumble......
>
>   Is that all? she whispers, frowning. Shaking her head, she starts to dance, naked save for a long silk scarf of lemon-scented green that wings about her shoulders. She takes wide floating strides, bending over and touching the sand with the tips of her fingers, first left hand, then right (F, 46).

Here is the dream Dorothy had described on 15 July [1958], her "very nicest recurring one" that "defies relating more than the others because the feeling is so deeply intense":

My music [plays] of course and I'm walking and dancing (mostly dancing) along a beach of glitter sand. The sea is very rough but there's no roar and I always note this. The air—well everything about me—has this radiant brightness. I'm naked except for something like chiffon on my shoulders and arms. It feels very lovely and it floats out as I dance. I actually promise myself that I'll wear just this forever and ever. Then I always think two things: first that people will think that I'll catch cold; second, that they might think it's indecent. Then this feeling of complete happiness and carelessness surges over me. But more than that this feeling of complete freedom and it's the loveliest thing I've ever experienced. Can't explain. Nothing happens except I dance and dance along this endless beach. At times through this long dream I think it's a pity that there aren't people to watch me because I dance more beautifully than anyone can possibly imagine: and it really is [beautiful?]. But I don't really care. Goes on and on and my free feeling continues throughout.

This is the dream from which I always wake crying, and so sad I feel I could die (a cliché but that's exactly the way I feel). Years ago I used to go stumbling into my parents' bedroom with: "Daddy, I had a dream" and "Shush-h-h-h come over to this side and get into bed." It never helped. Later, needless to say, I would wake my husband but sleepy comforting words and "Now, now" shoulder pats proved wholly inadequate, too. I must hasten to say tho' it's not *their* fault. It's me. I guess that despair makes me seek a tenderness or gentleness that greatly surpasses anything that one person can ever give to another (that's expecting too much—you see?) Hell, I don't know what I *really* want. But now I've learned to lie very quiet and listen. But I never hear much.

West wrote a long response to her the next week, appreciative of these candid images. His letter also gives further insight about the Actaeon characters and ideas he is developing.

Thank you for your good letter with the dreams. I'm tired and written out now but I'll see what I can say. The dreams are fine. The

*dancing one lovely and clean. I know about flying ones—I jump and
then soar! Believe it or not, when trying to 'invent' a dream for the
Lady Actaeon, I made a 'cave' one by the sea. Yours is much fuller and
better of course, and the cave symbol is a very old one in men's minds
and not necessarily a sexual one at all.*

*I wouldn't attempt to rationalize them myself, altho' the psychos
would. The long and complex one about cave and tree is of course a
true dream: a variant of a sort of archetypal experience; in line with
the old meeting with the Sphinx, and the 'Noon-Day' or Mid-Day
woman, or the Celtic Watcher by the Ford (which latter I've also used
in Actaeon). These people always ask questions. The Greeks met this
woman as Demeter, the Great Mother. One asks oneself what one
is doing about life—usually one can't answer and is remorseful and
embarrassed: one should really know! in some ways, I suppose, it's an
Ego's reaction against basic totalitarian preconceptions and ready-
made judgments of life by others, and by oneself: we always keep on
judging, judging, judging.......'They' are unable to assess one's innocence or guilt: 'they' know one may only really do that oneself. Don't
please underestimate the fact that our attainment of egoity has been
a long and hazardous travail: in ancient times Ego could only be
mentioned within the Mystery Cults. The Ego, the I Am, the Unknown
God, Christ—all synonymous: Moses and the I Am—first time in history an initiate leader was permitted to speak of the I Am outside the
cult. One reason why Christ was killed: He was the Unknown God, the
Archetypal Ego. He spoke ego-ly in the marketplace and offended the
Temple boys. And, oddly enough, the ego, as we have it, even now, is
still empty—your three-cornered cupboard! It could be said that every
human ego is, potentially, a Grail Chalice: or, the opposite! Even
today, most of us are more or less egotists, not egoists. People don't like
egoity—makes 'em itchy: measures their own behind-ness. The fullness
of egohood is the direct knowledge of God.*

*. . .The sensations of floating and dancing are soul experience:
the soul does actually launch itself on the wide sleep-sea. The ancient
Greek dance was a 'copy' of planetary and stellar movements. I'd say
that the veil (for want of better words) between the physical and soul is,*

in your case, more diaphanous than most: this can also be uncomfortable and cause you to be sensitive and tender. But you can't expect any human being to appreciate as deeply as you might feel, how you feel. It's unfair to expect such: a Van Gogh—the poor bastard could only paint and paint his terrible tenderness and vision; no one listened, no one even paid him, except his brother.

Also, another point: unless dream is consciously willed and sought for, sleep should be dark and dreamless: many are an immediate result of temporary bodily discomfort—too hot, etc. (I have fierce ones sometimes with slavering animals—own sordid and unregenerate soul-forces coming out for a look-see.) But daily conscious life's the thing—any interference with it by dream or by outside pressures is an imposition. The charitable mastery of one's own ego-consciousness in waking life is our work: the true seer doesn't 'go over' to wander about—he goes with a double-firmness of egoity and rigidly controls himself at all times.

I'm not 'panning' your dreams. I'm only suggesting that you try to keep your day and dream worlds quite separate: you can't afford to float in a kitchen with a kettle of boiling water in your hand. But you can take it as correct that you can't start 'over there': you must start from the here and now.

There are actual places on the earth's face where imaginations come easier. David knew very well why he wanted Jerusalem to be at Jerusalem—against all so-called (modern) economic justification. A clever modern city-builder would choose a far more accessible site. S. T. Coleridge: Try to get a decent biography. He had real clues about the reality of thinking—his term imagination didn't mean what is commonly said to be imagination. There is a fine American edition out with the first of his notebooks.

I enclose a short evening meditation by Rudolf Steiner, the Austrian esotericist and philosopher, the grand-daddy of them all. If you like, say it over before sleep with as much concentration as you can muster.

One of the good mystic formulae is that a person should try to make grateful peace with his own life, past and present existence; there is no one to be blamed save oneself, and one should not even

blame oneself: what's done is done. I tried to present a little of this in
"Narcissus [unto Echo]". The soul-subconscious is very wise and seeks
its own happiness and/or sorrow for its own enrichment. The Buddhist
and Chinese conceptions try to aim at nonattachment; fair enough, I
suppose, but a coldish approach for Western man; much like—devil
take the endmost: he who craves life will lose it—that's the opposite:
self is best served when the neighbour is served best.

Leaving the churchism-cum-Grahamism approach out of it, the
gospels are full of sound and living advice. Have you ever really tried
to read St. John? My basic sources are actually very few although
I've poked about here and there. I know now fairly well when a writer
or a poet has something suitable to say to this day and age; a lot of
well-received stuff I read is just plain bowel-wind coming up instead of
going down, plus whiskey thinking—rehash of buried other-men ideas.
But then, we all think out of the ideas of others. I had a good idea for
a movie scenario once and wrote Charlie Chaplin in Switzerland. His
secretary replied: Mr. Chaplin never uses any ideas but his own......
Charlie must carry his own special air about in bottles. Why, when we
eat a potato we also consume the farmer's spiritual energy. This sort
of closed egotistical thinking would make us all into mental Kentucky
hill-billies goin'down to the well with a muzzle-loader.......[0]

Two other extended correspondences were prominent in the sixties. The writers contrasted dramatically to Dorothy O'Connor, but
all three offered riches of personal encouragement and stimulation to
West's mind: Christine Countess of Longford reviewed *The Ferret Fancier*
with great enthusiasm, and West's note of appreciation started a long
exchange; Charles Davy, who edited *The Observer* in London, privately
shared West's interest in and knowledge about anthroposophical topics.
West obviously valued them all, especially two of the three directly for
his work on Actaeon. The esoteric density of typical paragraphs to Davy
opens occasionally to the uninitiated but persistent reader to show the
same ideas as are embedded in West's fiction:

. . . Percept: pure percept:

*Christ the Pure Percept? The eternal impermanence of the
etheric? . . .*

*Spirit and matter: the return to pure Manichean conception? What
is matter save temporarily static spirit? (the cold fertilized egg on the shelf
awaiting the mother bird's warmth to begin a new cycle of life?) Artistically, a stone often tells me much when I fondle it in frost or summer and
put my lips on it, my friend and brother at a few removes, the darling
child of a high hierarchy: matter? A lump of terrible patient peace that
can innocently become a killing club in a man's violent hand. . . .*

*Matter, spirit, and atoms: In the Spiritual Hierarchy cycle Steiner
mentioned several things about the Gita, in the context with the enthrall-
ment of matter, which I always had a kind of hunch about. The atom
bombers mechanically, amorally, disenthrall the elementals (forces);
release but without redemption. We must redeem the elohistic stone?
We must be Christ to it, eventually: or else.....I'm interested in thinking
(emancipation) personally and . . . because I want to try to put something of it over in a book in lieu of this worked out psychological
he-said, she-said business with the loud or lewd help of mere personal
fantasy. . . .*[21]

*. . . We haven't yet come to terms with sexual phenomena, haven't
yet got a grip on human love! (I tried to work at this aspect in poor old
TOWNS—it runs all through the book, but the critics, still involved
with the copulative act and all the fancy superstructure of theory built
thereon, have no awareness. . . .) Science is now investigating the sexual
'machine,' inspired by Ahrimanic power-hope, with experiments anon
similar to the merely physical heart transplant business, plus all the
associated merely physical 'rejuvenators' that will enable men of eighty
to copulate like hot young boys. You're going to get it, whether you like it
or not. Ergo, with what can it be creatively and constructively opposed?
We have no occult physiology. This modern wave of sexual freedom
and uninhibition risks terrible decadence but as we are it seems that it
must be gone through with. If it were merely a matter of the eventual
overcoming of 'biologic man', it would be easier, but sexual passion
(lust-cum-affection or non-affection) is more than biological in the usual*

meaning of the word. It has Life connections and is concerned with
incarnation, that is, with the spiritual worlds. If education is going to
license the luciferic enjoyment for the ahrimanic satisfaction, where are
we? Morality (the emergent human faculty): immorality: amorality. It is
one hell of a problem—is, I think, the problem. Asceticism is no answer
and if there is no individual moral responsibility, with the help of the
Pill, then freedom degenerates into animal license. . . .

Reincarnation-wise, the healing may depend on the incarnation
rhythm, souls, male and female, eventually understanding their physical
experiences and so...may take another 500 years. . . . It's up to us to try
and understand the evolution of eroticism relative to ego-consciousness.
Were we able to become conscious of the ego, we could cope.[22]

West was deeply interested in ideas espoused by the third-century Persian prophet Mani that had fused with Gnostic teachings of the early Christian era. Mani, taking some of his inspiration from Zoroaster, Buddha, and Jesus, described a spiritual struggle between light and dark forces, presently mingled with good and evil, but eventually bound for separate existences. The individual soul encounters these forces in the journey through life and death, recognizing through mind and accruing wisdom the liberating truth. Reincarnation, lying at the heart of West's Christian thinking, was central among Mani's doctrines that were revitalized in the late nineteenth century by the discovery of Manichaeism's long-lost scriptures. West's comments to Davy suggest he had no interest in ascetic aspects of the Manichaean legacy, but West did regard its teaching of karmic development through successive lives, the familiar Christian concept of resurrection, as the viable spiritual counterpart of Darwinian physical evolution. He was therefore interested in the history of Gnostic groups like the Albigenses, who were persecuted for Manichaeism in wars that led eventually to the medieval Inquisition under Pope Gregory IX in 1233. Through the history of the Church he made his way around to the history of Ireland.

Through certain Manichaean and Gnostic views, West found disparate and conflicting details of the Gospel narratives seemed instead to cohere. He recognized the presence of much ritual coding in Biblical texts, seeing John as a particularly important esoteric record. A ritual suicide by a king, for an instance, could (as Dea explains to Diana)

> keep the door open for the tribe. . . . This is also one of the facets of the Crucifixion—it is expedient one man should die for the race. . . . Poor Judas offered himself but he wasn't big enough. Golden Bough Frazer had no idea. With the coming end of this duality-thinking a work like *The Golden Bough* will be a sort of curious literary monument to twentieth-century man's insensitivity, together with most of the nineteenth-century theology and Bible criticism. One may only hope and pray that the end of this duality period is not too violent. . . . We also have all the ingredients for a total peace if only we could oust the ruling spirit of fear . . . the parent of violence (Q fragment, 34).

He registers progress in what may be an impossible task of making theological and religious argument engaging as a part of character, and he hopes thus to be persuasive through narrative. These forms may seem inherently resistant to each other, but West makes valiant efforts. His letters to O'Connor and Davy allude often to his study of writers like Goethe, Coleridge, and Lawrence, artists who, he thought, held spiritual clues. In the Q version of Actaeon he approaches esoteric readings of the Scriptures through the artistry of Gerard Manley Hopkins, poet-priest. He has Diana challenge O'Dea, "You accuse Hopkins of treason to his muse?"

> No, he says, I'm trying to understand the man, may he rest in peace.
> Where, then, do you think he went wrong?
> I wouldn't use the word wrong, myself. Misguided, perhaps?
> All things counter, original, spare, strange . . . I quote.
> Yes. Scared of his own vision, he adopted a ready-made one and shut his dare-gale skylark in a cage. . . . As priest, Hopkins had only theoretical christianity, like most of his colleagues. The kind to which you, for instance, object—churchism that merely repeats the same things to each generation. He ran away from himself, mistrusting the potentiality of his own insights.

But isn't all christianity an assumption of various theories? A kind
of wilful, if well-intentioned, delusion?

. . . Then he tells me that Hopkins, for instance, didn't know that
there were two Jesus children, the royal Matthean one, born early
January 1 BC, and the priestly one, born Christmas, 1 BC, the Baptist
as expected prophet in between, born on the first of June, 1 BC, both
the Jesus children with parents called Mary and Joseph, belonging to
the same royal Davidic clan that had been kept alive by hook and crook
for a thousand years. He claims that Rome 's known this altho' it's supposed to be a common heresy, that many of the great painters knew it.

Four parents, two children, and one Christ?

Yes, it's what the gospels say. The royal child, the brilliant one, dies
around the age of twelve, at the shewing in the temple, giving himself by
act of spiritual substitution to the priestly one, the composite personality
living on until the actual incarnation on the 6th January 31 BC. The
Lucan child is the origin of the legends about the divine fool because
his nature was total love (423–424).

They move on to other mysteries. Diana raises practical questions
and objections, as O'Dea gives West a pulpit for parry: What about Judas?
Why did Christ submit, even welcome such an awful death, when he
might have avoided it? The tomb business? Easter? Resurrection? The
magi and the star? Was Jesus an Essene? It is hard to sustain. Hopkins
and poetic vision can be a wedge, but West is forced to abandon the poet
in order to advance the material he wishes to explicate; furthermore,
West grows tired of the "he-said-she-said" impediment, even within a
first-person informality where he has dropped the cumbersome quotation marks.

Their debates give West occasion to explore controversial topics
of doctrine and ritual like celebration of the Eucharist. Word gets out
through the servants that O'Dea observes Communion in his private
meditation every morning, a practice objectionably Roman to some of
his parishoners.

. . . Except in general, I've never specifically queried any of his churchly rituals, nor he my poems.

A celebrant's only a bridge, he says. One never celebrates for oneself alone.

For what, then?

He sidesteps this by saying that the problem of the eucharist is complicated and still contentious. Dissatisfied, I press him, and he says there should be seven sacraments, his church only allowing for two, its communion only sacrament in name.

Back to Rome?

Oh, no—just a deeper look at the on-going christian mystery.

Mystery—eating the pagan god—magical transformation of bread and wine?

Why object? Most folk accept the nuclear equation—the unblessed release of pure force latent in all matter.

Atomism may be necessary?

Yes and no, relative to existing morality and only as pure science, not applied.

They're here and we'll have to live with them?

We can't live with them without the moral antidote and the citizen, unaware that chaos underlies all creation, has no answer, lacking the spiritual vision of their inherent destructiveness. Nor, indeed, can world-economics afford their exploitation for minority profit.

Isn't this the age-old attitude to any innovation?

No, luddism has nothing to do with it. Nuclear science isn't wheel, horsecollar or steam engine. It provides a quite unmanageable cumulative pollution of which the merely physical effects are the least dangerous. Intensive nuclear development will link with and increase the earth's own radioactivity and create even more terrible problems. The churches have no answer because they've rejected the pauline trichotomy and sooner than later they'll have to stand up and be counted or else agree to proclaim the anti-trinity of force, change and matter which science has already established in most minds.

Is this why you celebrate every morning?

Perhaps...

I begin to feel sorry for him, he is so serious and self-convinced. I know by now he sees christian evolution as a continuous process despite the various backslides and aberrations and his devotion of years to the problem makes me nervous, when matched with my scrappy, tentative knowledge. But I'm also curious on behalf of my own. To keep my iron in his fire, I suggest:

Science will eventually straighten everything out?

Pure science could but applied science is now the creature of the multi-national profiteer, the groundling majority only capable of ritual protest.

His eucharist—con tran or no-substantiation?

A true mass, it seems, must have four parts or movements—message, offertory, transubstantiation and communion; is an action, a spiritual symphony with beginning middle and end, an apodo[sistic?] state-ment, angels on pins notwithstanding and his anglian eucharist has only two movements, transubstantiation denied or avoided by legalistic equivocation.

But why try to revive a dying habit?

Transubstantiation has to do with the redemption of matter, with respect to Mrs Eddy. Reversing Einstein's famous formula, the latent force in love can also move mountains.

Love?

It's the growth element in creation, all else eventually disappearing.

Along with humanity?

As we think we know humanity.

Humanity may eventually starve itself and blow the earth up?

Even so, the sufficient number will remain.

Sheep and goats—gomorrah tomorrow?

There's a long-term equation involved. It's one of man's functions to destroy the earth but in such a way that it lasts him as long as he needs it. The earth's dying anyway, all the time and man has no fiat either to hasten or delay.

What price your freedom?

Freedom's our challenge which we're free to accept or ignore and the quite immediate future will put increasing strain on our powers of decision, many people opting for a cain-quiet existence by accepting totalitarian dictation. It's already happening in elementary ways.

Who or what's going to lead a constructive reaction?

They'll be thinkers, neither protesters nor political roustabouts.

Would you remain in the church if the reformation were reversed?

Probably not, if nothing new appeared. A legalistic fusion of two failing monopolies doesn't guarantee spiritual solvency. Rome would have to renounce the bulk of her expediential dogmas, the protestant getting rid of the restrictive puritan ingredient.

He claims that the reformation case was established solely on the new testament while unaware or else disregarding the fact that a mass was in being for over three hundred years before the new testament canon was settled; that sacramental usage goes back beyond hebrewism, via the Archpriest Melchizedek as mysterious representative of what could be called spiritual duration. And then the protestant error was compounded by theologians who materialistically investigated the bible and christianity, losing all trace of the spiritual Christ in the process and demoting him to the status of a moslem prophet.

Why? Why insist on the existence of invisible imponderables that may so easily descend into a body of new superstitions? I protest defensively, not without heat, not knowing if I defend my early belief or later non-belief.

Sooner than later, there'll have to be a total audit of our vague beliefs and cosy attitudes, relative to thriving scientific dogma, or else accept that the ape is, indeed, our Adam.

I ask if he has ever talked to colleagues like this.

A few, he says, including roman catholics who have less far to go than their protestant counterparts but who are powerless to move because they've nowhere to go, once they challenge the Vatican.

I say nothing will ever change Rome's monolithic ways...

Don't bet on it. World-wide worsening socio-economic conditions could demand a more constructive answer than the pious homily and a young and progressive clear-sighted pope might do wonders.

He'd never be elected?

Never is a long time...

I let it go. Whatever I might say, he'll have his answer and, whatever the answer, I'll come out the same door as I went in and I'm not really concerned, nor can such intangibilities really move me—altho' his expositions can! Or move me, perhaps, only inasmuch as their practical application might threaten my not-unreasonable, quite neutral attitude to existence. . . (R, 182–186; R disk 150–153).

Diana, being more immediately interested in the relationship between O'Dea's religion and his sexual response toward her, leads him to questions about Christ's sexuality:

I make bold to ask: Can you prove that Christ ever existed?
    On the intellectual level, no. On the pneumatological [spiritual], yes.
    The philosophical?
    Philosophy can make out a case for God or no god, but not for Christ, otherwise there wouldn't be an argument. When one reads the christian philosophers, one finds they could only introduce Christ as subjective belief, not as philosophic fact.
    Same for the churches?
    In the main...
    I give up and try to get him to talk about sex.
    He says it's dynamite, the lusty man never stopping to think that sex happens to him . . .
    Did your Christ have a sex life?
    He didn't have to have one.
    Repression—sublation?
    Sublation's the better word, in the sense of resolution to a higher unity but not subjective denial or repression which is the way of the pharisee.
    Asceticism?
    No, asceticism's something else. Why should I or anyone presume, from purely subjective motives, to punish the elohistic body by wilfully cultivating psychosomatic imbalance, whatever the profane or sacred intention?

Many do just that—all the time?

Yes, many deny one obsession in order to enjoy another one (R, 64; R disk, 54).

Diana remains ambivalent in her feelings on most religious subjects. She finds the idea of reincarnation repugnant(R, 208), but she concedes that Christianity remains a harmless check on the machinations of the hoi polloi. O'Dea responds that Marx said something similar.

Migod, the polyglot confusions: Dea's bible, Jews gita, Christian Koran —the sheer complexity of belief and still they talk of unity among believers: tough patriarchs, judges, prophets, kings, high priests and low, exiles, remnants, lost tribes, returns and then that final one proofed by past failures, nationless, landless, throneless, neglected, rejected, denied, scorned, distrusted, the butt of every human ill and old brutality, betrayed by friends and only one small woman brave enough to look for him: cave-born magi-man nurtured on defeat and, evenso, the dream as strong until that final refutation before a civil servant's civil question: what's truth in lieu of law and order (R, 276; R disk, 227)?

The couple adopts remarkably separate roles in the parish. Diana is no conventional rector's wife, nor does O'Dea—to give him his due— expect her to be. The church services bore her; she prefers to take walks during Evensong. She is frankly amazed that O'Dea has married her on such trust of her spiritual qualifications, full as she is of religious doubts and dismissals. He seems to know, even to anticipate her responses on theological subjects, and never chides her for apostasy. This gentle toler-ance becomes his most saving feature. Neither Diana nor the reader can write him off as arrogant prig or complete egg-head.

Eventually West tries yet another method, more plausible, for brief covering of volumes of theological and historical argument, traditional and esoteric; at the same time he gestures politically in making Kilsuan's Roman Catholic priest, Father O'Connor, the most sympathetic com-pany around for Dea.[23] The Church of Ireland rector invites the priest for dinner, and Diana summarizes in her diary their good time discovering

their sympatico. She provides short analyses of the abstractions and con-
troversies that also interest her. This device makes the wade through
metaphysical discussion about as engaging as could be possible for the
uninitiated.

As with Dea, O'Connor seems to have a similar sense of disillusion-
ment with his church and makes the old difference between court and
church of Rome, saying that every time the vatican tried to benefit itself
in common politics it had to compromise with its apostolic mission.
Like Dea and with more cause, he disagrees with elements of vatican
hegemonic absolutism while still accepting involvement, matching
personal integrity against establishment casuistry that's all too well
designed to cancel individual criticism. If you can't stand the sweat,
say I, get out of the sauna...

Both of them are well up on the history of the church, mentioning
personalities and events that happened centuries ago as if they belonged
to last week: ultramontanism versus gallicanism, popes good bad and
indifferent, Innocent III and the false donations, pagan confrontations
in lieu of christian understandings—Boniface and the destruction of
Florence and Dante, Clement's mishandling of big Henry Tudor and
the stupidity of Elizabeth's excommunication, Aquinas, his enlighten-
ment and death, Dea startling O'Connor by saying that Aquinas was
probably the last Hohenstaufen and heir to the dynasty after Conradin
and the unexplained involvement of Valois with the saint's murder
which Dante apparently hinted; church and state and church or state
and Dante's old warning about mixing oil and water; reformation and
counter-reformation; inquisitions, persecutions, tortures, greed and
power, incorrigible Irish religiosity both sides of the Boyne; Aristotle,
Augustus, Tertullian, Pelagius, Erigena, Columbanus—names and
names of old dead men whose living mark remains in heavy time and
human attitude. I wonder what they all would think about our present
christian convolutions and our fine new ways to destroy each other—no
longer for soul-sake, for money: mercenaries for mammon: an old pope
I believe banned crossbows and against that 'tis said a monk invented
barbed wire and some cleric the modern bullet: from stone via arrow,

bullet, bomb, blockbuster to atom bomb, heigh-ho, and now some
pretty gases that kill you where you stand, sit, sleep or fornicate: lovers
of the world unite in death... I wish I had a tape-recorder.

Both these decent men belong to an organization that has let more
blood than two world wars in name of prince of peace. O'Connor seems
to think that the declaration of infallibility was a retrogressive step and
ill-advised, making me wonder how claimed infallibility could possibly
be advised by anyone lower than god. Dea disagrees, saying it could
work both ways, that it could empower a young and progressive pope
to bring the church into the modern world by purging the Vatican's
backlog of legalistic medieval attitudes and dogmas, and outmoded
dualism. Ireland and the faith and possible disestablishment...migod.
[Celui qui] mange du pape en meurt...think I.

They discuss Chartres and its platonic and aristotelian savants, cis-
tercian and dominican, O'Connor very interested in the place, mentioning the black virgin, the mysterious Nephthys one, Dea saying it
was a pagan-christian shrine with origins in unchronicled time, before
the british isles were islands; Compostela, Marco Polo, the Khans and
Columbus, the Arab aristotelians in Spain, the horrors of Albi inspired
by a pope named Innocent of all things. They're like two cricket enthusiasts discussing old test matches. . . . I store up questions for Dea until
my head spins and I leave them for bed.

Dea asks O'Connor for help in some scheme whereby the two communities might work together without trespassing on each other's beliefs
(R, 361–363; R disk, 296–299).

Like Diana, most fiction readers will be exhausted by the combined
intensity and abstraction, and relieved when she puts down her pen for
a hot soak in the tub and a retreat to sleep. When she returns to these
topics later, however, after the priest's visit, the reader also has had time
to reflect and is ready to resume the questioning. O'Dea invites her to
look at the charts he has made and the reading notes he has kept about
them. She at first is dismissive, but she reconsiders. Here then is yet
another way West tries to impart the historical, ontological, and theological matters he is eager to have the reader understand:

Nevertheless, drying a rainy afternoon, I looked at his notes—books
and books of notes numbered and crossreferenced like a miser's ledger,
the obvious hours of meticulous concentration rather frightening to a
ragbag mind like mine: kings, high-priests, calendars, starmaps, solar
lunar planetary times, babylonian roman temple times, along with
comments by a score of authorities ancient and modern, all differing
on the dates of nativity and crucifixion.

   . . . He seems to have the whole business down in writing, cross-
checked against the gospels. Nevertheless much remains—the actual
meaning of things like the baptism, immaculate conception, transfigura-
tion etc etc etc; miracles arrest trial crucifixion and then that resurrection—the stickler when knowledge has to become faith again: full stop.

   Altho' I'm reasonably convinced that a man called Jesus of Nazareth
or Jesus of Bethlehem surnamed Christ—the Christ a title and not a
name at all, really did exist and probably said and did the things attrib-
uted to him that put him in the doghouse because as Dea says he hadn't
gone through the schools and was seen as a charlatan, was murdered
by the romans at the instigation of the temple jews who, like the Tories
and Hitler, preferred appeasement in an itchy land, putting poor Pilate
in a dilemma by facing him with a royal Jew of lineage longer than his
own divine god-emperor. Letting Jesus go would have been more than
his job was worth for the wheels of the establishment can grind like
god's, exceeding small. And, as usual, the murder settled nothing, made
a martyr and started a new faith that eventually crept into the world's
corners, built churches and cathedrals, swayed dynasties, caused bitter
wars and genocides like Albi, burned heretics, tortured spies, spawned
a thousand sects from we-free-kirks-to- kamachatka—all proclaiming
their notions of truth but never once answering Pilate's question altho'
Christ said that knowing truth was freedom. . . .

   And here am I with little faith in faith or faith in truth outside the
rising of the sun—I with three thousand million others (R, 367–368;
R disk, 301–302).

Occasionally, West has Diana write some poetic lines that are to
be read as evidence of her craft, but he wisely keeps them unpolished

musings, often notes or virtual lists. The following lines, for example, are prompted by her efforts to understand O'Dea's more tolerant, less cynical views on twentieth-century war-mongering:

I can't make excuse for history, even if I knew what history is, more than:
        A politician's brainstorm
        A general's battle plan
        From Caesar's wars to Battle of Berlin;
        A Churchill's yen to play Lloyd George-and-Marlboro
        A Hitler's poisoned dreams
        A Franco's Spanish Main
        A Stalin's paranoia
        A Roosevelt's monomania
        A kaiser's love of harmless soldier games
        A czar's purblind recalcitrance
        And Genghis Khan
        Attila and Napoleon
        Cromwell and conquistadores
        Conquests and inquisitions
        Racks and iron marys
        Thumbscrews and rubber truncheons
        Electrified genitals
        Brutalities and rapes.
        History is mincemeat,
        Wars murders woundings dyings
        Is autocracy democracy
        Egalitarianism
        Marxism Leninism
        Churchism carrotocracy
        Corruption capitalism nihilism
        World poverty and starvation
        Exploitation and earthquakes
        Its evils living on long
        After its goods are buried.
        History is money

And profitable persecutions
Is any man's opinion
From Philistines
To these old gaelic ructions.
Is bigotry and disgrace.
I'll make a history of ploughmen, shoemakers and servants,
Soldiers and sweated labourers,
Of common men who died and suffering anonymous mothers,
For tramps and tinkers, pickpockets and pimps,
For all the millions history has killed
Frightened burned bombed . . .
(R, 266; R disk, 325)

As Diana's poem-making deserves evidence, O'Dea's formal
preaching requires equal showing. His allegiance to Christ requires
christological explication; his theology is full of studied and defended
unorthodoxies; his practical ministry in the parish emanates unsurprisingly from I Corinthians 13 and from Mark 12:31: humble neighborly
charity without pietism. The F version provides a five-minute sample
from one of his sermons,

I'm not asking you to be good and pious; to wear religion like a Sunday
coat. Sunday is only one day in seven. Make all days Sundays. Help
one another, understand one another, keep from judging one another,
share troubles charitably. Money cannot buy morality—a name's
honour depends on the owner's creative action. Microscopes cannot
find morality nor can formulae fix it. It would be better to walk nakedly
and without water into the Sahara Desert than to attempt to enter a
scientific paradise without morality. And what is this morality? It is a
state of balance—Christ's temperance: a state of gentleness, kindness,
forgivingness. It has but two laws—not ten or twenty. Love of God and
love of neighbour. These loves stand together and without one another
each one is quite meaningless. And what is love? It is life. We have
moved through creations of Wisdom and of Power in the far past. We
live now in a time of generating love. In the far future when we wish

to say "I live," we shall say instead, with more conviction, "I love." We walk as sleepers through an age of contradiction but do not be frightened or confused. Everything we think we see is but a dream with all the irrational complications of the dream. The life-love solution is simple and concise, once greed and love of power are removed (F, 402).

How, Diana wants to know, does he describe the world-state toward which he urges his parishoners, and how does he embody his own objectives?

>...You want egalitarianism?
>
>No, I want compassionate recognition of inequality.
>
>Tolerant socialism?
>
>Yes, genuine socialism, not totalitarian socio-economic theories — a three-tiered state: fraternity in economics, equality in law, liberty in culture (R345, R disk 283).

West makes O'Dea's own economic fortunes inconspicuously secure. He has inherited wealth, but has put it into a trust that will support his vision for a co-operative farm comprising the Kilsuan estate and neighboring lands. He lives on the stipend from the Church and never uses income for himself. He prefers to walk or ride his bicycle around the parish wherever possible. Diana's Bentley embarrasses him. O'Dea remains self-effacing and undemanding in other ways as well. Diana regularly gives him credit for his integrity, for not pushing domestic roles, ascetic disciplines, or his personal, intellectual tenets upon her. His refusal to impose upon her with what she thought would be normal sexual needs, however, becomes an increasing source of mystery and frustration, and she finds his inexhaustible patience "scary." His views are happily unconventional, yet, Diana winces, "gift-horses have sharp teeth like Ridinghood's grandmother" (R354): O'Dea won't discuss anything in a personal way.

>When I give tongue to my objections and criticisms of the present state of women as inferior sexual objects, he always listens attentively,

as he always listens to me attentively, agreeing with much that I may say, admitting that over centuries, man has taken advantage of woman because of her feminal qualities and responsibilities, exploiting and abusing her natural abilities—his liberal non-resistance driving me almost hysterical so I tend to drive all my nails below the wood and bruise my thumb at the same time. He said once that male and female will have to renounce partisanship and agree to look for the androgynous concept, that logical and legalistic argument can only destroy itself and leave the problem in worse state than before: he says he wants human liberation—not manhood or woman-hood: human-hood—handing me his Christ as the androgynous prototype which immediately makes me think that history's packed with male priests, premiers, popes—bar one, apparently—prelates pontiffs patriarchs and curates, not a female to be seen, any that are mentioned usually smuggled in by the servant's entrance...

He insists that Freud's free expression of the natural instinctual being over-simplifies and risks return to the authority of mere instinct in sexual matters through which mankind has labouriously passed, sexual behaviour in itself contributing little or nothing to the sum of constructive human relationships, one human advised to use another merely to assuage biological appetite and thus confusing the crying demand for better communication between folk, irrespective of sex or race. I follow of course in general but in particular I need answer for the now, a start made now on reformation since charity's supposed to begin at home, and better solution than this un-free condition (R, 355–356; R disk, 290–291).

The early Davy letters coincide with the central years of the O'Connor ones. Two capable minds and alert sensibilities, unknown to each other, approach through the same friend at the same time some of the same mysteries, but with education and acculturation that radically differ. West accommodates them both, respectfully, forthrightly, affectionately, and puts to use the enormous advantages both contacts offer to his spiritual quest. Her death ended the letters to Dorothy in half-a-dozen years; with Davy the rich exchange on shared intellectual and spiritual interests continued more than twenty years before it was cut off by both correspondents' failing health.

Overall, this correspondence has helped me a great deal, in that I am made to realise that I dare not try to include specific statement in a would-be novel . . . I often see the hour-glass as my symbol. I'm in the bottom half and trying to climb into the top one, but the trickle of sand (time and movement) keeps blinding me and I'll only be able to see clearly when the sand is exhausted, or when the glass is upended, bottom becoming top, if one can avoid being smothered in the ensuing 'land-slide.'[24]

West steadily depended upon his epistolary friends, giving, soliciting, absorbing and synthesizing. With fewer exchanges but no less loyalty, West also in these years corresponded with Christine Countess of Longford, aristocratic, unpretentious, beneficent, charming. These three markedly different correspondences also illustrate West's verbal flexibility, his courteous payment of social deference, and his tenacity about staying West.

Letter-writing supported his quest mid-decade during discouragement like that over Naked to Laughter's acceptance and then rejection, a sale that would have been "a big check [but was instead a] . . . check on my confidence, which is always a weak thing . . ."[25] He had indicated similar extremity of his situation to Dorothy in 1959, when the New York editors were often silent, housing was tentative, and he had no money.

No word yet, from anyone. This morning, per registered post, I had a nice surprise: a Notice to Quit these premises before and not after the end of February. And, in the same post, I had a letter from my unfortunate bank-manager which informed me my overdraught was at its limit again. So, at this moment, I'm more'n broke—I'm way behind scratch. Creepers....but, fantastically, my writing goes on and on and in an odd way takes heat from the worry but when I have to come out, I'll be so naked I'll be scared. I've written Schaffner today. His reply will either sink me or swim me and if it's sink, I may stay down this time. As I said

to Schaffner, I may be suffering from temporary jinx-itis or else plain
unvarnished immaturity. I'm a very late developer, anyway. It is really
quite fantastic—I could be on the side of the road, broke, friendless,
hungry and a debtor with a family of nine, all at the merry age of 48.
Maybe I haven't suffered enough, maybe my nose has to be rubbed off in
the shit—I don't know. This bloody bureaucracy is killing us all. I know
more about real farming than any man in this country. That's not a
boast, believe me. I can see the corn growing. I could take a tractor to bits
and put it together again blindfolded; build a [barn]...oh, God.

I may not be allowed to do anything this life. If I didn't have the
conviction of reincarnation, I'd go crackers. I must have been a long-
haired bastard in past lives. People like me (and like you) have seen it all.
We are born again. We painfully discover that civilization is on the same
merrygoround as when we left. We don't wholly believe in big business,
better bombs, beautiful aeroplanes: we know just that much too much for
churchism and communism and claptrap: all we have is the bare sexual
instinct plus a host of disappointments and a gaggle of preconceptions
which civilization doesn't let us sort out. No use blaming anyone. If we
knew more in charity, we could do more, charity to all.[26]

In its early excitement about his publishing, the Obolensky firm
had pointed out West's need for someone to handle his contracts, to
sort and sell his productions. David McDowell had recommended John
Schaffner to be his agent. The cache of letters, exchanged between
Schaffner and West, grants a third and highly detailed understanding of
West's expectations, effects, financial need, and professional, publishing
difficulties during the sixties. The stack of West's manuscripts had been
passed on to Schaffner by the *Esquire* editors, who had been caught by
"River's End" and "Not Isaac," now in print, and who had encouraged
West to send on anything he had to show. *Esquire* had chosen from the
stack and published six stories. McDowell had anthologized those and
others, and Obolensky, meanwhile, had pushed him toward longer fiction.

To Schaffner and the editors among whom the pieces had been
widely passed around, it must have seemed as if a painter had mounted

an exhibit merely by opening the studio: sketches; cartoons for novels; dramatically, realistically rendered scenes; then, pure philosophical discussion with no action at all. Schaffner, who was equally direct with praise and criticism, called this section "two hundred pages of boredom": fragments of what seemed straight, undeveloped autobiographical exposition. Characterizations without plots. Plots without characterizations. Few of the pieces were fully crafted short stories like the *Esquire* gems, although some parts scintillated. Other pieces were completely unformed. There were "little pieces . . . sharp and concise and unadorned," then an "adumbration of words," a sort of "literary auto-intoxication."

Schaffner had been incredulous, baffled, irritated, yet still impressed enough by the eccentric brilliance of his new assigment to retain him. The criticism he leveled at the material in front of him was, understandably, severe. West's being in medias res was not perceptible to an outsider; West left it to his death to reveal his method. Furthermore, although West could see much of the road behind and before him, even he could not see his creative route's full course. He felt as though he had a "young head on old shoulders." West's reply to Schaffner's initial assessment of this pile of typescripts is an illuminating document.

> Now what you call my modesty is not a virtue; it's a tight and realistic assessment of my own lacks and shortcomings as a human being, but that's between me and God, and by hard experience I've proved that every time I move too far away from it, I get lost; and losing oneself is an unpleasant sensation . . . and on the other side, all I may dream and think must come down and squeeze through the rusty needle-eye that's my small and human self. . . . It is my failure, so far, to attain a smooth synthesis of experience and is as much a human failure as an artistic one. I may have to die first! [27]

Yet West could anticipate the outlines of the journey. By the end of the fifties, he had at least sketchy versions of the whole ur structure before him: the substance for the four novels which were eventually published, plus Naked to Laughter about New York; the Embryon cluster about his wandering in the western United States; Room without a Door about his itinerant life in Ireland before the War but after America; O'Dea's childhood in Wall; major sections of what became The Casual Comedy, and even The Lady Actaeon—the last three setting the protagonist in the widest possible context of Ireland's spiritual and geophysical history. The parts of the ur that did see publication may well have been most of the typescripts West says he destroyed when he moved. However, enough pieces and versions sit yet among the papers to connect them. *The Native Moment's* place of origin is apparent in contiguous parts of *Room*, and it is now possible to see both the method and the chronological pattern in early versions of those sections of the ur that directly became *Rebel*. (He did save some revisions that did not make the publication deadline or were not used by Obolensky. Visible, too, are some fragments and their places of extraction for *Ferret* and *Towns*.[28]) The ur even posits those "what-if . . ." tangents, like A Son for Éiru, imagining Simon Green-Stephen Muir's life if he had married Vuya, successfully worked the land, and produced more bourgeois daughters like their good-hearted but unadventuresome mother.

West admits to Schaffner the autobiographical source for some of the pieces, although he minimizes such inspiration for others; furthermore, he explains the "ragged edges" of a story called Epigon in Taurus as the "too obvious" evidence of his having "prized it free" from a longer work. Alluding to his editors' earlier astonishment at his having kept no copies of manuscripts sent to them, he began his review of Schaffner's criticisms with a claim about re-creating manuscripts that makes even more sense now than it could have made to West's agent.

> *Now, page by page, I'll run over your letter, regarding your mentions on the various MSS (some of which I can hardly recall. Yes, I will keep copies now. I have all the rough notes....wasn't scared of losing them. I could have recreated them, maybe in a better form).*[29]

John Schaffner's response, including the long silence, becomes a prototype of West's ultimately wide experience with editors, agents, and publishers. First, Schaffner waited four months before he answered at all. Then he apologized for not answering the "several good letters" of this writer "of great originality . . . and promise . . . wide range of talent . . . genuine poetic ability . . . [with] remarkable feeling both for character and for place." Then he said, equivocally, he was "seriously rather excited." Schaffner endorsed Obolensky's advice to go on with the novels, and he discouraged West from thinking that popular magazines would be interested.

About these magazines, from *Harper's Bazaar* to *Playboy*, Schaffner was right. That world-pervading commercial spirit West was deploring would preclude it. Still, West believed that if the writing were good enough, it would not be refused, and despite his preference to do long pieces, income from accepted short stories would help. When Ivan had persuaded him he would be sustained in his primary effort by these powerful, visionary, literary men, West had inferred that they were as committed to benefiting the commonweal as he. Trusting their schooled expertise and many contacts, he hoped they would perfect his skills and direct his address.

West's sense of his literary fecundity seems realistic. Conventional "writer's block" is never part of his vocabulary; usually he explains his difficulty as a need for philosophical, spiritual maturation in himself. He pleads the continuing need for personal study and wise, critical editing. He would offer his creativity—enough people in the know had praised his originality and talent by this time to make him trust in the potential of his gifts—and he would promise his indefatigable effort. He would work like a frontiersman. Fifteen writing hours a day suited him, he said. The family (nine children at this time, not all of them still at home, though two more were yet to arrive) had been managing to live on eleven dollars per person per month in those lean fifties after the War. He didn't need much now, he said, but their free housing had disappeared with Jones's death, and their income had to be at least dependable to free his concentration. As he expresses it to Schaffner,

> If you can scold, steer, and praise while I keep getting the stuff out.........
> believe me, I'm only starting.[30]

West thanks Schaffner for taking up his appeal for frankness and offering him nine mostly chastizing pages:

> *The painstaking letter has moved me very much. I know well your time is money, too, and it is gratifying to find a professional like yourself with an honesty of idealism who can make patience and real interest for stuff that is rough and uncouth in spite of any inherent potentialities. . . . Just keep hauling me back, kicking my backside, telling me without a tooth what you think good and what you think lousy.*
>
> > *Don't please ever be surprised at a wadge of solid gaucherie—it's just plain ignorance, or an ignorant inclusion of a half-way valid thought. With the exception of a few modern poets and the M&O publications which they so kindly sent me, I've read little or nothing for years concerning modern imaginative fiction. I've been looking at nature in a sort of Goethean way and reading philosophy and theology for grist and for pleasure. I'm not intellectual and I'm not clever and you will find, all over my so-called MSS, unfrozen and undigested and indigestable lumps of foreign matter for the disposal of which I would be most grateful.* [31]

Schaffner deplores the "hideous or vulgar word derived, he thinks, from psychological or educational jargon" like "intuit" and "ideology," and terms that seem to him a "meaningless series," though he recognizes that they are important to West: words like "sonic," "tonic," and "yonic." He condemns the the "over-lushness," the "over-writing," the "literary embroidery." West responds,

> *I suppose I can't use words which have endured changed associations, but I do feel and see them, sometimes, in their pristine meaning or half-meaning.* [32]

Self-educated, West developed his literary language from Shakespeare, the King James Bible, the Romantic poets, and his very good ear for the Irish English. [33] It is no surprise that his antique or peculiarly faithful, root use of words annoyed his agent; Schaffner had no reason to recognize the vocabulary of religious esotericists or of historians of first-century Christianity. It helps a reader now, however, to recognize all that West was doing. West admits to Schaffner that

> *Words are my strength and they're also my hazard. They'll float or drown me. . . . I know it's dangerous for a writer to risk falling in love with his tools: start kicking soon as you smell it.*

He moves to a further level in his explanation of "unspatial imagination," which most readers would be unable to gauge without added information.

> *I know well enough that the unspatial imagination is one thing and the true art-form of it is another: I know I must obey the rules—but I only know a few between once upon a time and happily ever after; that's why I'm so grateful for your living interest. M&O and yourself, between you, know all the rules.*

West often provides in these uncut, thoroughly explicated ur tellings, such a concept as he is explaining it to himself. In the way a teacher prepares far beyond materials that would ever fit the hour or address the level of the students, he feels compelled somewhere to present the matter at this depth or in this detail. Later he will reduce it, consolidate it, or merely just allude to it. Eventually, he probably will not even mention the concept or object at all, but its full-formed prior existence in his own thought is essential, he believes, as it will give the presentation unobtrusive substance.

Schaffner's original conclusions after his reading of approximately twenty West typescripts evoke sympathy. No wonder he did not find West's explanation entirely penetrable, but the archive confirms that West was not, as one editor glibly described it to Schaffner, merely "opening the lid on fancy's box."[34] When he charged West with vanity, indolence, or sloppy effort, Schaffner could not have been farther from the truth. The reader can appreciate now why West had been so "indiscriminate" as to forward obviously unfinished work. The impression of casualness, even carelessness, about his typescripts, was especially created among his New York publishers when West failed in those early days to keep carbon copies of the pieces he mailed away. It's apparent now that he retained the cumulative ur. He expected his editor or his agent to say, as Ivan had done, "This has possibility. Do X and Y to it." An incident could be reconstructed (he had probably done it numerous times already)from the cumulative ur if his papers were lost in the mail, but he did hate to lose editors' particular criticisms. Why else wait for that specific Actaeon from Ivan? Obolensky had both encouraged him to write novels and said West added too much; Eyster accused him of padding. He also risked slicing off too little.

> I was asking editors to cut across their policies by accepting my 'life-slices' since I happen to see life in slices, without beginning and without end; no harm in that, by and large, but there is harm if I fail to accomplish a due and valid art compression and concentration.[35]

Nor would Schaffner necessarily have perceived that West's slices had karmic continuity. Many pieces remained "slices," subservient to larger patterns, a condition understandable now to one seeing the whole. No pride or pretension kept West from showing undeveloped sketches. He expected to work more on them. It had upset him when Obolensky published *Rebel* and *Moment* before he felt they were finished. West was so prolific and so unpossessive of his words that, especially at this stage, he saw himself as the producer of eggs the group might teach him how to gild, rather than as their mature golden goose. Another part of West's reason for sending such an array lay, of course, in its being that metaphoric casting of his bread upon the waters (Ecclesiastes 11:1). Sending things that were unfinished and even unformed compounded the original impression of carelessness, but this practice, too, had a basis in his cosmic, evolutionary view.

Then there was his financial plan. To Schaffner he explains he had

> sent—flung, thrown—out stories that were no better than abortions or premature births. I had to. Ivan Obolensky knows this. I know too damned well that it would be better to write one perfect tale than ten

*fliers but, naively, I just went on the superstition of a ten percent return,
to wit, $500 every three months.*[36]

At one level he is referring to Obolensky's forcing his desperate
action by failing to come through with funds West understood were
promised. But he had also justified it artistically: in writing millions of
words, he would have to learn something about writing them better.

Magazine publication hadn't been important to him, he had said,
although he had "manag[ed] to tumble the bull six times" in aiming at
Esquire. (Schaffner had warned him he was "too original" and "too frank
and earthy," besides being too long for the magazines.) He wasn't even
pleased himself with some of the pieces New York had liked.

*Significantly for me, some of the better things I've done, apparently, were
done as incidentals. That's ironic. The things I manage to write out of the
corner of my eye have always been accepted by people like you.*[37]

Inexperience so far had led him, however, to trust these professionals
to recognize and select what was good, maybe marketable, and to supply
criticism for improving the rest.

Despite his acknowledgment of progress, West held throughout his
life the motivating consciousness that he was mapping a vast territory,
and that his own life was not going to be long enough to finish the
trip. The morning he died he reiterated that awareness of long soul-
development he had expressed to Schaffner thirty years before, and had
always accepted as a karmic insufficiency. He rolled a fresh sheet onto
the platen, typing "I am so slow, slow, slow, slow." The colossal territory
he was charting was old and once, he believed, it was better understood. It was like America, itself prehistoric and in those so-called "Dark
Ages" known perhaps to Nordic mariners, druidic masters, and scholars
intent on studying the magnetism of the earth,[38] but as new scientific
paradigms had created new priorities, even geographically tangible realities had become shadowy in folks' understanding, to say nothing about
the spiritual ones. Tim O'Keeffe's encouragement at the turn to the
sixties reinforced the expectations articulated by Obolensky. West was

doing something no one else could do, addressing topics no one else was approaching, and the writer muttered in reply it took some sort of man to drive the sun-chariot.[39]

We begin to see what moved this explorer, what made him stay West. He had little interest in being famous. Although he felt honored by acceptance in Aosdana, conventional literary establishment was not to him a self-validating attainment. He was no religious proselytizer, collecting soul-scalps. Nor was ordinary, ego-driven machismo a significant force. The child's sexual experience may have been precocious, but the evidence of West's adult relationships with women—attractive as Christopher MacMannan seems to have been to them—gives no sign of his having measured his worth by sexual encounters, and no correspondence has revealed an unrequited passion for a Maud being spun into poetic gold. The record of the typescripts does show, however, that nothing distracted him very long from his spiritual exploration, from his spiritual quest. He was a seer, as resolutely as Coleridge's mariner, reporting what he saw. He sailed on his hope of making a personal, karmic advance and a social contribution through the development of his writing craft. Periodically he added to, or copied out, or re-cast swatches from the ur log. After all, it took money to float expeditions; even modest mariners had to eat. His repeated use of nautical imagery becomes increasingly poignant.

> I am truly sorry to have to accost you again—and do please forgive my lack of faith, but this small ship, riding as it is before the wind under bare poles, soon loses buoyancy by niggling worries over meeting ends. . . . While everything seems potential and prosperous, the actualities, even if temporary, are . . . embarrassing. The 'mate' gets into bad humour, the 'crew' is surly, and the holds stink of shifting doubts, while Columbus can only whisper out of a dry throat—On, on, Eldorado; but the chandlers frown and scratch their heads.[40]

Humor rescued him, and it showed again in a whimsical poem that grew from the same circumstances. Whether he ever sent it to Obolensky is not clear.

October the sixteenth: moon two days from full, the Menai Straits a
tongue of silver in the blue mouth of the hills.

   Voice from de tomb whoo whoo.

   O be my valetudinarian

   I watch and pray

   Where is Actaeon that all swains?

      Deadsea scribble

      Messiah of de doghouse

      And Lady Actaeon, twice commended

      Long short story not

      My countree 'tis of thee

      Liberty, frat et eternitee

      An' ole black Joe Stephen

      The home sweet home

      Poor Olive has taken a job to fox the wolf

      Wolf whelping – me fosterling

      Nipples raw.

      And no real MacKee yet

      Says grinning Gibbon: no Schaffner:

      No Germany: no nothin'; no joke.

      By whitewaters of Wales weeping

      on toilet

      looking at blank paper

      damn shame to waste it

      sybil it

      open door

      see what the draught says

      O god of eenie & meenie

      Moe and hallelujah

      Sister Anne

      Ah don't want no obo

Furlined sandstorms
An don't want t'walkabout

Time time time
Voices whispering
Time time time
Time is terrible
A bomb going tick-tock

Just tell me if you can't
Find her
There'll be no moaning
At the bar.

West pressed ahead with what he had to do: sending out his work to editors would test two possibilities, whether the times were right with informed people — editors and publishers, his indices — ready to listen, or whether he had developed his artistry enough yet to reach them. When West's publishing successes are recalled, natural hopes do not seem improportionate. How many writers receive "best ever" responses from their editors? It had happened to him more than once, and Schaffner had told him he had been paid far above the usual rate for his victory with *Esquire*. The remarkable feature of these experiences is that they did not turn his head. They merely intensified his self-discipline and concentrated his method.

In August of 1961 Obolensky said he was planning to publish a little book, Gold into Straw,[41] to hold West's good name in the forefront for the next big novel. Then suddenly, in October, he was signing a contract with West's agent for another title and rushing West's emendations by 30 November to publish *Rebel to Judgment* in 1962. About *Rebel*, West had this comment for John Boyd of Northern Ireland's BBC:

> *I tried to pack a lot into it; and to get a dig at landlordism, the first curse*
> *of Ireland. . . . I can't help matching what was in the back of my mind*
> *with what they [reviewers] say. . . . I only wanted to say that violence,*

prejudice and lust pay lousy human dividends which we, as Irishmen,
know all too well.[42]

West had meanwhile finished another novel, like *Rebel* in its featuring of aspects of a young rural boy's growing into sexual maturity and
social-spiritual responsibility. He persuaded Obolensky that it would
compete with *Rebel*, however, unless the two were to appear under one
cover.[43] Obolensky agreed to release it and *The Ferret Fancier* secured
West's reputation as a novelist. The book was published in 1963 by
Simon and Schuster in New York and by MacGibbon & Kee in London.

It was also like others among his books and stories in that it bore a
problematic title. West often proposed phrases from Shakespeare — for
this one, "At Fortune's Alms" from Lear, when Merrill Pollack feared
Americans would find ferrets distasteful. The alliteration plus the softening with "fancier" helped, although it was not an American sort of
word either.[44] *The Ferret Fancier*, nevertheless, was hailed as a minor
masterpiece and enjoyed success in the States and in England. On the
English edition of *Ferret*, which became West's preferred version, West
appreciated Timothy O'Keeffe's insight and literary judgment. Working
with him in the early sixties was one of West's happiest professional memories. He continued to consult him long after O'Keeffe had left the company. He came to feel that O'Keeffe, partly in being a fellow Irishman
among the Sassenacs, possessed at least another set of prejudices for
reading West's work. If O'Keeffe couldn't see whatever it was that West
was intending in a manuscript, West accepted the fault as his own. As an
editor, he was generous in spirit; at the same time he was upfront with
his criticism, writing, e.g, about some draft ". . . It's obviously got virtues
and howling great faults." "There are good and valuable things in it but,
overall, I'd count it one of your failures. . . ."[45] His personal notes are usually short, candid, and often wittily acerbic, prompting in West's replies
a brothers-of-the-oul-sod informality, even stronger than that normally
evoked by his literary correspondents from Ireland:

Apart from the flu, I'm in good nick, despite the pressures, and sweating
out the Ostrich *[To Hide An Ostrich was a working title for* Towns*], my*

*behind bare to the fierce elements and a lookout on the road in case the
bailiffs . . .*[46]

*I'll give him [an editor soliciting biographical data] whatever gen he
needs but I'm getting a little more cautious in my old age. Before I've
made no bones of myself but it seems that the more these intellectuals
know, the less they're interested and much more interested when you're
dead and if you wiped the ass with the right hand or the left or both.*[47]

*Thank you again for all your kindness and great patience. Please try and
think that I'm not striking an attitude. I'm not. Nor have I any jokers
save the usual oul one in me underpants.*[48]

It was conventional enough to opt for the familiar matriotic image to
explain to O'Keeffe his ambivalence about returning to live in Ireland.

*Let's hear from you. I'm trying to make up my mind about Ireland. I'm
almost scared of the Old Woman, now, unsure if her fondness for me still
lasts. It'd be terrible if she scorned me.*[49]

His letters often, however, include a referencing of women that is
at best common-crude, now politically unacceptable, diminishing to
them at any time. It appears especially when he is writing his to countrymen—to Irish males. West slips from mere informality to coarseness,
easily adopting images that aim to be ingratiating—wink, wink, nudge,
nudge—to other men by demeaning women.

It'd be grand if Rebel *stuck. If there's interest, make what kind of a deal
you can. Like USA, if they stick a pair of toots on the cover . . .*[50]

I know these oul Irish heifers, too.[51]

*Eddy the Ready [Rebel to Judgment] was nothing like the lush dame on
the jacket, believe me. She was a withered oul besom in reality, God help
her . . .*

Apart from West's artistic editing of the expression, this patois was probably unremarkable to the recipients. It was so prevalent that it has taken generations to produce cultural sensitivity to the problem. There is no reason to suppose, for instance, that West was surprised in 1954 by the closing of a note received from the *Manchester Guardian* encouraging West's daughter to apply for work there because they "liked them voluptuous," if the girls were "also good."[52] Yet the contrast in his style evoked by a gender-specified or culturally-located audience would probably make West himself pause, were he confronted with its cumulative impression.

Parallel to this tone adopted for other males, an ingratiating courtliness often marks his addresses to women. It was not unusual for his generation; the inferred condescension may have been unregistered by its deliverer. These greetings are typical: "Gail Leeson, ma'm:" or "My dear Jill Weldon.[53]

> *Regards to Mrs. O'Keeffe and the family. I'd love sometime to see that daughter of yours, just to cheer me up. Mine eye has followed beauty all my days . . .*[54]

Diana Hauley's characterization becomes all the more intriguing, for when West started on her he probably did find the task very uncomfortable. As he had said to Dorothy O'Connor, "Imagine me trying to write about a woman, something I swore I'd never do. . . ." As Diana begins to speak for herself in Actaeon versions of the seventies and eighties, her creation has to have become an instructive exercise in gender understanding for her author.

In the sixties and seventies West received several radio airings of both his talking and his writing. John Boyd and Maurice Leitch gave him some appreciative publicity in Northern Ireland with *The Native Moment*, a poem called "Fable," which West said his children had judged with approving laughter,[55] "A Sweet Mouse-Trotting Cup," and "Not Isaac."[56] They also did some short interviews.[57] Both they and he were always concerned about West's giving offense to their audience on matters religious and sexual. Not surprisingly, too, West's stories were inclined to be too long for their standard twenty-to-thirty-minute slot. But neither interviewer could gauge the greatest impediment to West's delivery of other work they hoped to receive from him. While it had implications for length, it had nothing to do with his vernacular.

Leitch had offered West an autobiographical assignment for Ulster's BBC, a "Return Journey," with extremely liberal parameters and a full year in which to complete it, following a summer trip to Ireland in 1965. As West was doing something similar for the American *Holiday* magazine, had another agreement to write a piece for *The Golden Blade* in England, and was also writing *As Towns with Fire*, which dealt in part with Ireland, the combination seemed to him internally reciprocal and the deadlines possible; moreover, he was excited about doing the research. Optimistically, he signed on. He was to discover it was not the kind of writing he could provide, even about Ireland. No one imagined a travel brochure or an historical essay: he had no quarrel or misunderstanding about genre. The editors did, however, expect conventional organization, a smooth representation of place, something lightly personalized, and avoidance of the deeply scholarly or the controversial.

West worked on this problem of the Irish spiritual inheritance—he seemed unable to define it otherwise, to separate its parts or to find any smaller subject worthy of investigation—for all three editors, but only through fiction does he approach a close-to-satisfactory control of this leviathan. Arno Karlen for *Holiday*, Maurice Leitch for the BBC, and Charles Davy for *The Golden Blade*[58] all waited for concise, publishable essays. West's thicket of facts and insights understandably becomes a commercial editor's despair; only Teufelsdröckh's editor would have taken it in stride.

West had turned down Karlen's invitation to do something on North Wales, when he read samples Karlen sent him from *Holiday*.

If I were to attempt an article about Anglesey on say, Pritchett's model for Greece, it would be quite insipid and boring, since everything in Anglesey lies in the realm of Imagination and has to be kind of resurrected: and the amount of research entailed is considerable, in any effort to pick some meat off the dry bones.[59]

When Karlen suggested Ireland as subject instead, West was interested:

> *While my effort would . . . be an attempt to measure the change between*
> *1930 and 1960, I can't say how the whole thing would actually reach its*
> *final form. But I should be able to give you a long and organic piece that*
> *would lend itself to professional cutting/editing. I'd have to take a look at*
> *the records in Dublin to firm my facts. . . .*
>
> *The exercise might well begin a fresh line of country for me, in which*
> *I might use my chaotic experience to practical advantage, while fulfilling*
> *the 'law' that one should try honestly to be fresh and creative.*[60]

Karlen had personally impressed him, and with good reason. His letters, his copy-editing commentary on *Rebel to Judgment* (Karlen was then freelancing for Obolensky), and his own fiction reflected a spirituality that resonated for West from the start. West assumed he was talking to a man of forty and was flabbergasted to learn Karlen was half his own age. When he told West he was Jewish, West found that heritage as significant as he had Dorothy's Asian-Scandinavian blood and Native American context.[61] West spoke to Arno with a fatherly urgency about the spiritual features of their writing. He grew excited about Karlen's proposal.[62] The ancient "participation," a spiritual perceptiveness, which he believed once pervaded all human culture on the planet, had longer been evident in Ireland where spiritual realities had been longer protected. He would travel to Ireland for this *Holiday* assignment.

The intellectual and spiritual quest that the ur narrative represents receives an explicit treatment in these essays West tried in the mid-sixties to prepare for audiences in three different countries. The "Dear Arno" essay (there seem to be four extant versions) offers an objective statement of his research into his cultural-spiritual identity.[63] This essay may be as central to understanding the drive behind his creative work as *A Vision* is to Yeats's achievement. Here he offers a definition of self and country that synthesizes his academic and esoteric studies.

The first conventional assumption West challenges is nationalism. It is not that West like Whistler chooses not to be born in Lowell, but he does refuse to be bound by an ungenerous, petty concept of nation.

Pearse may have sounded good, he says, with his appeal to national blood, but the concept of nationhood in Ireland was no older than Jonathan Swift's humanitarian defense of those whom England was exploiting, Swift's general dislike of the Irish quite apart. Ireland's organization was

> *a loose connection of tribal, dynastic territories lightly held together by, firstly, the pagan cult and later, by the christian cult; the latter, itself, existing for centuries in two antagonistic forms, Celtic Christianity and Roman Christianity ("Amadan In Tir na nOg," 11).*

West's second challenge is directed at the evolution of consciousness, a theme readers of his novels immediately find familiar. While he admits a *"terminus a qua* of about 10,000 B.C." he is more interested in another way of looking at human development—"man-time." A new-born child

> *has just completed one epoch of existence and is beginning on another. Or, according to some embryologists, it has just completed or recapitulated many epochs. But, qualitatively, its time is colossal. Time . . . is also action, is becoming—in potentia and in actu. It's like an iceberg and if we insist on swearing on the seen ten per cent while losing sight of the buried ninety, the natural melt may make a liar of us, turning us turtle ("Revenant in Tir na nOg," 10).*

Aquinas, he says, had tried to create a smooth synthesis between two kinds of awareness—the old, participative consciousness of people that dominated cultures before about the fifth century A.D. and the modern one.

> *It was the Greek who gave to Europe the old vision in modern shape, Israel working in parallel alongside, moving away from participation into on-looking and increasing speculative experiment. . . . In Ireland, the participative dream went on, quite undisturbed ("Revenant in Tir na nOg," 16).*

It went on, West explains, until Roman Christianity began to impose itself on the Celtic version.

> *. . . It isn't fair for latter-day rationalists to claim that the exponents of Christianity in Ireland allowed a kind of cunning graft to occur between the pagan participative wisdom of the Iro-Celt and the new corpus of imported faith in the fourth and following centuries. I think the Iro and Cymric accepted christianity on the basis of existing wisdom, producing the gentle and heroic Grail christianity which was of quite different quality to the Constantine variety, and there is sufficient evidence extant to prove that, for a long time, a definite difference of opinion, if not actual hostility, existed between the two forms. Constantine christianity supported the hypothesis of Predestination, whereas the Celtic conception maintained the basic Indo-Aryan fact of reincarnation, which the former failed to understand, vis-a-vis the slow establishment of the doctrine of the Incarnation. I suppose it could be said that the specific opposition was contained in the two words, Jesuology and Christology—the worldly Peterine and the cosmic Johannine conceptions. These problems have never been solved . . . ("Revenant in Tir na nOg," 23).*

The Christ problem is his third inquiry with the implications for church teaching and individual spiritual awareness evident in Actaeon's discussions, and the fourth is the connection of all these things to Ireland.

> *I want to straighten out and see through what has been said about Ireland—all this turgid, emotional, solipsistic thinking, self-pity, ethnic hypochondria, washed down by Liffeys of guinness and dirged by suffering Anglo-Irish music-hall songs. What is this Ireland, her genesis, her coming into being and subsequent uneasy existence ("Revenant in Tir na nOg," 35)?*

He was persuaded that Ireland's links with Christianity predated Patrick (who probably went to Ireland, West thought, to learn Saturnian mysteries rather than to make converts). He steadily regarded the reports of conquerors and suppressors with suspicion, as he did the analyses of scholars who were dismissive of legends, myths, and tales.[64] He views his country's history with a comparative sympathy afforded by long exile and much reading.

> The Celtic-trace, Gaelic and pre-Gaelic, is now practically a pious fancy and the Irish brogue itself is due, probably, more to the Elizabethan accent as to anything else. . . .In the ten centuries between say, 840 and 1840, the population increased from a very small figure to around eight million, due to heavy immigration from Europe, and from England, Wales, and Scotland, under planter policies that acquired the best land and pushed the Celtic and Anglo-Celtic minorities west of the Shannon. Celtic Christianity and its hierogrammatic use of Gaelic [were] slowly suppressed by Rome and Anglo-Norman and finally extirpated by Tudor, Stuart, and the following Cromwellian and Williamite plantations, innocent Celticism tragically confused with suspicion to rebellion against church and state. The indigenous Gael [was] quite unable to keep up with the rapid changes in European politics and religion ("Revenant in Tir na nOg," 35).

West mentions to American writer Jack Curtis that

> for the past two years I've been trying to work on three projects . . . a novel based slightly on my RAF experiences, along with . . . an article on Ireland for Holiday, also a commission for the BBC, N. Ireland, to do a kind of revenant's sketch on Ireland. I've the use of the Bangor University Library here and have done what probably amounts to a degree course in Irish and Anglo-Irish history and I may have even cracked the Iro-Celtic problem . . .[65]

Here lay the chief impediment to his meeting of commercial editors' expectations. His topic had mushroomed on him. He said he didn't "know how to explain it without leaving behind the common historical-religious-political-psychological approach and going right into the

straight pneumatological account." Of course he knew that would not
be acceptable for magazines. "Most people don't like the digging to be
too deep." He knew he was "unable to toss off the clever comment with
a bottle of stout in the other hand." At the end of the decade, Leitch at
the BBC of NI was still waiting for his script, prodding only most gently
and stressing the assignment's great latitude. [66]

What had happened? West had often written to the newspapers
to register his citizen's conscience. His papers include an ample file
of such sallies on current topics, among them the rise of new China,
employment practices in a hydro-electric scheme for Llanberis, ecological effects of a dam on the Nile, noise-pollution by Gatwick airport,
preservation of the Roundhouse in Chalk Farm, the mysteries about
St. Patrick, and prejudicial language. While his attitude can readily be
deduced from his statements, the outlines of the situation are often intelligible only to someone who already knows the issues, yet he could be
incisive and brief:

> *19 August 1971*
> *The Guardian, Manchester*
>
> *Sir:*
>
> > *Must army marksmen in Ulster shoot to kill? Might they not try*
> > *to wound and arrest alleged terrorists? After all, intelligence-wise, dead*
> > *men are very silent.*
> > *Yours very truly,*

The essays contracted by Arno, Leitch, and Davy had been attrac-
tively pertinent to his most important commitment. When he tried to
draw together his vast reading on Irish pre-history, archeology, Christian tradition, and esotericism, however, the subject became gargantuan
and, for commercial standards, uncontainable. These editors could not
use the pieces that he finally sent. [67] Despite the force with which he
might deliver his ideas, West fought hard against calcification of his
thought; he tried to preserve a teachable attitude. Their cosmic scope,
his extensive information, plus his increasing sense of insight, fortified

by his resistance to "hardening off in his ideas," as he put it, made these
expanding articles contrast strongly to his assigned letter to an editor.

> *Poor Ireland and the bright belles of Bunratty. I fail to see much sign of*
> *Minstrel Boy romance, with all due respect to Dr. Tom Moore, much as I*
> *fail to see romance in, say, the fratricide of the American Civil War, or for*
> *that matter in any bloody war ("Revenant in Tir na nOg," 38).*

> *I'm not decrying nor denying this fierce heart-love that most Irishmen*
> *seem to have for their birth-place, if not for their country. It's very real:*
> *being born in Ireland is being born with a cross on one's back and*
> *although we may curse it, let no foreigner try to remove it. . . ("Revenant*
> *in Tir na nOg," 41).*

Even for the third expository piece on Ireland, for the uncommer-
cial, more academic and anthroposophical standard of Charles Davy's
Golden Blade, West found it impossible to produce a tight, decipherable
essay on Celtica. Davy wrote him that he was "starting plenty of hares . .
. but they are dashing off in all directions." He found West's draft "like a
research programme . . . [offering] many questions, not many answers."[68]
These assignments were related, all-encompassing, a puzzle West could
not abandon. They had fired his enthusiasm. He made several visits to
Ireland in the last fifteen years of his life—for the republishing of *The*
Ferret Fancier by O'Brien Press, for his admission to the Irish academy
of artists, Aosdana, for the chance to see his ailing sister, Dorothy—but
all especially to collect information integral to these essays. He hoped
to return to live in Ireland, but his health broke, and he was confined
to a flat in London. He and his prospective editors eventually gave up
on publishable articles, but he continued to plow the richness of his
research into the ur.

The story emerging through the documents of this decade reveals
West at what may have been the hardest time. Although his biography
could be made to sound like a collaboration by Thomas Hardy and
Mahatma Gandhi, the middle to late years of the sixties were indis-
putably grim. The depth of his research and the implications of his

discovery formed just one part of the difficulty, significant as that part was. The period illustrates with paradigmatic vividness several of his writing dilemmas: the enduring contest between his wolf and his muse; the cost of isolation for inspiration; the tension between exercised faith and candid doubt; between honest confession and scrupled reserve; and perhaps most ironically, between justified expectation and repeated disappointment.

Like Actaeon, Naked To Laughter in 1966 sat rejected after numerous reworkings. Merrill Pollack of Simon and Schuster had eagerly read it, hoping to follow *The Ferret Fancier*, a "gem of literary control," with "Simon Green . . . wide-eyed and innocent in the new land." He wrote Schaffner three single-spaced pages about his disappointment in discovering that West's "delineation of character and place, episode and vignette, was not going to end; on the contrary, it was the essential structuring of the book." The 800 pages about Simon's poverty and his desire to escape New York he thought lacked any other motivation. Although Pollack realized that Simon by the end "is moving from youth to authentic manhood," he did not appreciate that West was exploring another discreet phase of adolescent development. Naked to Laughter is not *The Ferret Fancier* retold or a mere documenting of Simon Green's hopes to travel. Pollack is entirely convincing when he says he has experienced "anguish" over the situation. He regarded West as "one of few writers of genuine writing talent" that he had seen for a long while, knew his poverty, and "hate[d] like bloody hell to lose Tony West" now.[69] Had it been just a matter of reducing the number of episodes, West would gratefully have accepted pruning, but Pollack—wisely enough for his market—couldn't see a profit in this novel.

West said three more major works were in his head—"all 'there' if I can get to them"—a novel on Wales (The Jewel in the Snout ?), one on Ireland during the Troubles (The Casual Comedy), and a "play-novel [The Mowin' Man?] with music against all the unnecessary stupidities in this our present world."[70] As *Towns with Fire* was also being born.

In 1966 another purchase under mortgage was being renovated for the family. West had taken a laboring job to meet expenses and supervise the reconstruction at another house in Llanberis; that restrained the wolf but cost him writing hours and energy. It wasn't that the Wests saw no money at all, or that they were hopelessly impractical. They held unusual priorities. In 1965 he told Charles Davy of their socialistic dream, hoping Davy could recommend interested and capable participants:

> *Recently, my wife speculated and borrowed money to buy a smallholding which was later sold at £500 gross profit, less two acres with a valuable road frontage for which we have full planning permission to build 14 bungalows. This is in desirable Anglesey. There is a latent profit of £1000 per bungalow, with lot. If we do it as individuals, we'll be heavily taxed on profits. On the other hand, there's something like £14,000 which could go towards a farm of some sort, or some sort of associated crafts/ mal-adjusted children establishment. I wrote the new Threefolders some time ago. They think and the Charity Commissioners think that a chari- table trust can be formed on this broad basis; or that a private limited company could be formed. We would have to borrow on the first house to exploit the building. But what we want is some sort of way by which we can help to do something creative, using the 14 lots, plus if necessary the value of this house which is put at £2750. One must legitimately defeat the claw of the incometaxers. I, personally, claim to know as much about BD methods as the next one, and I'm not psychologically/sociologically deficient. Is there any way in your experience; are there any people avail- able; to help start something. I wouldn't stop writing. I can earn some money and could possibly earn quite a lot. I know there's an element of professional jealousy even among associated Anthro. ventures, but— malice to none, malice to none. I have a keen young builder who has taken to Steiner who'd be willing to throw in his lot and skills and act as instructor. . . .Is there any way of bringing a few Mahomets together with a mountain or two? This is very vaguely general, I know, but please think it over.[71]*

At mid-decade West was also finally writing his way through his war experience. *As Towns with Fire* came out with MacGibbon and Kee in 1968, Alfred P. Knopf following with an American edition in 1970. With the exceptions of two reviews (unfortunately prominent, if not very penetrating, ones[72]) *Towns* was well-received. It was his longest book and the last of West's novels to see publication; the ur protagonist had made it only to an auspicious thirty-three. Anthony C. West had forty-five years to go. Dorothy O'Connor had died in November 1965; West wrote later that during her treatments for cancer he'd "never had such brave letters from anyone in my life."[73] Her memory obviously continued to encourage him, and he was bolstered by the studies he shared through letters with Charles Davy. Finally, there were those repeatedly cheering notes from Christine Countess of Longford. She had taken his *Ferret's* side in her review for the *Irish Times*, and West precipitated the nourishing shower of her effervescence by his appreciative letter. She had offered him friendship with her literary admiration. She also provided an informed and honoring contact with "mother" Irelnd.

ENDNOTES

1   IX, 3, 253–261.

2   From 1960 to 1984 West maintained contact with Continental, especially German, publishers, but translations never proved very successful. See Box 2, Geisenheyner & Crone.

3   Ormond Edwards, interview, June 1989; see also OE to AE, 15 August 1991.

4   *Buffalo Evening News*, 13 March 1965. See also ACW to John Schaffner, 1 May, 1965.

5   ACW to G.L. Roberts, 19 September 1960, Real Estate.

6   GLR to ACW, 3 October 1960, Real Estate.

7   Bank to ACW, 31 January 1963, "A cheque for £50 has been presented...against your private account."

8   ACW to Douglas Jay, MP, 2 April 1979, Bank.

9   *River's End and Other Stories*, London edition, was dedicated "To my Bank Manager."

10 ACW to Mr. Ellis, 11 July 196[8?], Biography I–III, Domestic.

11 Was this friend made into Stephen's correspondent in Room without a Door?

12 Dedicatees of *Rebel to Judgment*, Ivan Obolensky, 1962.

13 Peter was a poet and local teacher whose talent impressed him. West introduced him to Cecil Day Lewis at Chatto & Windus, who printed Peter's first book. His many letters to West, primarily about his own poetry, were filed with West's original papers now in the Linen Hall Library. Garth and Mona Hatherly, dedicatees

of the London edition of *The Ferret Fancier*, were CC friends in Wales, farmers who practiced Bio-Dynamic techniques. They later were participants in the project at the Baroness Uslar's Paradise House.

14 An early Q fragment makes the diary a record of many years, begun when Diana's friend Jocasta gives her a lockable, green, pigskin-bound, monogrammed volume with clip-in pages, promising to make it an annual present (box 16, pica page).

15 ACW to John Schaffner, 26 November 58.

16 ACW to David McDowell, 28 November 1958.

17 ACW to JS?, 23 July 1959.

18 ACW to McD & Obolensky, 28 November 1958.

19 Dorothy's grandfather was a Chinese orphan adopted by sea-captain Edward O'Day, and brought to Nebraska. He took the name of the captain and his ship (Boston Maritime and Gloucester Museums have wooden model and photographs), where he had served as cabin boy, Edward Day Cohota. He married a Norwegian, her name probably Halstrom, shortened to Hall, when her family moved to Minneapolis and then to Valentine, Nebraska. Their son Henry and wife, Lucy Krauss (Dorothy's father and mother), homesteaded in Chadron. Eventually they ran a small store and restaurant in Parmelee on the Rosebud Reservation bordering Nebraska and South Dakota. Selling supplies to the residents, Dorothy's parents reciprocally purchased their beadwork and painting. The family later donated the Henry Krauss Collection to the museum in Pierre. Dorothy's brother was made an honorary member of the tribe. It is easy to understand West's appreciation of Dorothy's cultural inheritance. I am indebted to Dorothy's sister, Marilou Cooper, for this information, 4 November 1995.

20 ACW to Dorothy O'Connor, c.22 July 1958.

21 ACW to Charles Davy, 4 December 1962.

22 ACW to CD, 8 December 1968.

23 West said of Actaeon: *I was fond of this bit of Irish beef and it is the honest-to-god truth, so help me: I mean in the light of a review of Emerald Isle conditions.*

24 ACW to CD, 21 February 1963.

25 ACW to Jack Curtis, 17 August 1966.

26 ACW to DO'C, c. 22 January 1959.

27 ACW to JS, [4 February 1958].

28 West made me a present of a typescript of *As Towns with Fire*, which includes some sections raided from the very early ur, and even the published versions of the novel are not identical. The Knopf edition, for example, includes an account of Christopher's weeks of camping in the Mournes between his enlistment and his reporting for training in the RAF.

29 ACW to JS, [4 February 1958].

30 ACW to JS, [4 February 1958].

31   ACW to JS, [1958]

32   ACW to JS, [4 February 1958].

33   A clipping from *The Sunday Press*, 17 February 1963, indicates West's interest in James J. Walsh's recognition of the Elizabethan traces in Irish pronunciation: *The World's Debt to Irish* (Boston: Stratford Co. Publishers, 1926). Notes and Sources: Clippings, Box 18.

34   JS to ACW, 21 December 1958.

35   ACW to JS, [4 February 1958].

36   ACW to JS.

37   ACW to JS.

38   Eleanor Merry, whom West read with a judicious skepticism, describes these scholars in *The Flaming Door* (London: Rider & Co., 1936), chapter 9.

39   Timothy O'Keeffe to ACW, 8 February 1960; ACW to TO'K, 10 February 1960.

40   ACW to Ivan Obolensky, 22 November 1957.

41   IO to ACW, 2 August 1961. West used this title on more than one piece. Here Ivan may refer to a section of the ur also called The Haymaking, or it may have been West's heavily symbolic interpretation of the Rumpelstiltskin tale.

42   ACW to John Boyd, 7 September, 15 September 1962, BBC.

43   ACW to IO, 18 August 1962.

44   ACW to TO'K, 27 December 1964.

45   TO'K to ACW, 2 December 1980; 12 January 1972.

46   ACW to TO'K, 19 February 1965.

47   ACW to TO'K, (Rhiwlas) Sunday night [1964?].

48   ACW to TO'K, 8 November 1[9]62.

49   ACW to TO'K, 22 June 1964.

50   ACW to TO'K, 2 April 1965.

51   ACW to Maurice Leitch, 8 December 1965.

52   L. P. Scott to ACW, 25 October 1954.

53   ACW to Gail Leeson (MacGibbon & Kee), 28 April 1963.

54   ACW to TO'K, 1 October 1981.

55   D.L.Ross to ACW, 10 March 1961 for 27 March broadcast in "Spring Voices."

56   David Gower to ACW, 19 April 1977, BBC. Date of broadcast not set. West was asked to resume his pseudonym, Michael MacGrian. ACW to John Scotney, 31 March 1977.

57   Radio Ulster scheduled him for two hours of interview again for Samhain, 31 October 1983. See contract with Judith Elliott, BBC.

58   Davy, editor of the *London Observer*, pursued his Anthroposophical publication under the name Charles Waterman. West uses the name John Waterman for the spiritual teacher in Room without a Door.

59   ACW to Arno Karlen, 15 May 1962.

60 ACW to AK 16 March 1965. He did publish a piece on Llanberis in the
    Caernarvon & Denbigh Herald, 15 May 1970, under the pseudonym "Trefwr." A
    typescript is filed under "Causes."
61 ACW to AK, 13 April 1963.
62 ACW to AK, 26 July 1965.
63 ACW to AK, 16 March 1965. West tried to rein himself in by adopting the "Dear
    Arno" approach of a letter, but apparently to little avail. He was afraid of selling
    his soul. The four versions vary in length and it is not obvious that any is finished.
    "The Tree and the Stone: lacks pages 37, 38 and ends at 55. A coda on Breifne
    follows, begins with page 17, and continues with pages 2–13. "Revenant in Tir-
    na-nOg" runs through page 46. The coda is again begun at 17 and runs through
    27. Two other versions bear the same title "To Wrestle Shadows or Amadan In
    Tir na nOg;" one is 66 pages long and the other stops at 48. Neither includes the
    separate coda on Breifne. "Dear Arno," Box 9. The correspondence with Arno
    Karlen runs only through 1965. On February 26 Karlen notes that West still has
    an assignment on the record for Anglesey Island, but offers the Irish substitute.
    West's last letter about it dates 26 July 1965.
64 Letters to Adam Bittleton, 3 November 1965, and Anabelle ___. 26 February
    1969, summarize many of his arguments on the subject. See the Charles Davy
    correspondence.
65 ACW to J. Curtis, 17 August 1966.
66 Maurice Leitch to ACW, July 1970.
67 ML to ACW, 1 December 1970.
68 CD to ACW, 12 August 1973.
69 Merrill Pollack to John Schaffner, 14 December 1964.
70 ACW to J. Curtis, 17 August 1966.
71 ACW to CD, 21 February 1965.
72 See ACW's last letter to Christine Countess of Longford, next chapter.
73 ACW to JS, 5 September 1966.

Chapter Eight

1970
WALES AGAIN

Names in the correspondence between Christine Countess of
Longford, and Cathcart Anthony Muir West had been a leitmotif from
its start, as this "lady sweet and kind" in generous admiration of his work,
granted him the familiarity of calling her by her first one. He had begun
the personal exchange with his thank-you:

Maelfa, Rhiwlas, Bangor, North Wales
13 March 1963

Dear Miss Longford:
  MacGibbon & Kee sent me on your review of the Ferret, in the
Irish Times. *While there seems to be convention that writers should
accept critics' kicks and kisses in silence, on the other boot why
shouldn't one write a person thankfully for a great favour. Thank
you very much. Until I saw the* Observer *notice last Sunday, I was
becoming despondent about ever being able to penetrate the hard
shell of intellectualism that seems to be growing over the minds of the
clerisy: not that I can blame anyone beyond myself, but having to face
up to a sense of failure isn't a joyous occupation, in that perhaps one's*

approach to life and the description of it is mis-timed and invalid.
Goodness, this awful business of having to have a kind of blind faith.

I'd been looking at the problem of adolescence and, trying to make
sympathy stand for understanding, and perhaps wastefully, I did three
short books on it, all related and parallel. . . .

As I've said to Timothy O'Keeffe of MacGibbon & Kee, a kind
and insighted review always makes me sad, guilty, in that I know I've
missed many of the precious minutiae that, more'n anything else,
govern one's totality of reaction to life. One just can't be too careful
and I've never yet been able to afford the luxury of being slow. You
set me a bit high when you said the book was written for truth, not
commerce: true enough but mainly because I'm not much of a hand
at writing any other way altho' inclined to put me big fut in it: and
I don't disclaim the labourer's right to some hire, if only because
publishers are businessmen without much ambition to be art-patrons,
although Timothy O'Keeffe, god save him, has helped and encouraged
me in kind and in cash.

If this note offends and breaks rules, please forgive me, and
please don't feel that you should acknowledge it. Living up here in
the foothills of Snowdonia, I've few contacts and little opportunity to
cross check against existing literary thrusts. It's not a bad place, here,
although Calvin's oul ghost still stands between the people and the
reality of modern loneliness. This time of year especially I often have a
strong urge to up and over the sea and find me a roof and four walls in
a quiet corner of Ireland, getting away from this creeping bureaucracy
and the dry husks of materialism, but I suppose I'd only run into the
same things in Ireland. Rhiwlas means green hill—Gaelic glas. The
locality is a cross between Kerry and Donegal; Snowdon itself was a
kind of Celtic Jerusalem the time of the old hill-cults. It is painters'
country but needs a new Turner to catch the swift and arrogant play
of colours. May's the best time, angel-time, the air a sweetness: stone
walls, heather, horizons and the singing voices of the women in a
tongue the Roman heard, the children not understanding you . . .
Thank you again. Sincerely,

20 Herbert Street
Dublin 2
March 19, 1963

Dear Mr. West,

Thank you a thousand times for your letter. As you may have gathered, I am madly enthusiastic about your work. I haven't read your other books, but I would take Sean O'Faolain's word if I would take anyone's. This one reached me late, as the Irish Times *got my address wrong (and the same thing happened to your letter). I hadn't read the English papers, knew nothing about you, read it 'without putting it down' and discovered a new planet; then I banged out a notice which would have been much better if I hadn't done it so quickly. When I read the book again later, I found it better than ever. I hope it won't disappoint you if I say I'm not quite a professional critic. I've a habit of refusing to read books I don't like, and the decent* Irish Times *allows me to send them back. (I won't tell you whose I sent back last week). I don't belong to any intellectualist gang. But I like to think I'm the general public, or the novel-reading public, and I can't believe that the public will feel less enthusiastic about you than I do. As I have never been a boy, and my memories of female adolescence are next to nothing, you must be pretty good to have interested me so much. I am really grateful to you for the pleasure you've given me.*

I'm all in favour of Wales, especially North Wales, as a refuge for artists. But I'm sufficiently mad about Ireland to hope you'll come back some day. It wouldn't solve your problems, but it would be good for us. You know there are mountains here too. Anyway you are right to keep away from 'contacts', and it would be cheek on my part to advise a man who has all those children, as well as all that talent. I'm looking forward to the next book.

With thanks again
Yours sincerely,
Christine Longford (Christine Countess of Longford, to be exact, but that doesn't matter)

When he was in Ireland the summer of 1965, interviewed and enter-
tained by John Boyd and Maurice Leitch for BBC, Belfast,[1] West paid
the countess a call. His thank-you to her described his trip.

Rhiwlas, . . . 21st July 1965

Dear Lady Longford:
    *. . . I've read with a tangle of impressions, new and old , and now
must try and sort them out, DV. I'll send you a copy of the edited BBC
script, if you'd care to see it. . . . Don't know what I said. . . . We had
spent an entire afternoon in a Belfast pub, meeting folk and talking—
this Irish ability to talk! I met some liberal RCs in Dungannon who
were much more aware than most of the Prods. There's this 'new tolerance'—don't know how deep it is. I'd like to help deepen it. Overall,
I may have gained some valuable impressions which will do more for
the book I'm working on than for the* Holiday *article. It was lonely to
realise how much one has drawn away from the jangle and pound-
chasing consciousness: the loneliness of the long-distance writer!*
    *Seems that I'm 'seen' as an Ulster writer, now! (Probably due to
your good notice of the* Ferret, *as much as anything else.) The Ferret
is banned in Eire, although I believe some progressive parish priests
have read it with appreciation. I've read John McGahern's The Dark:
agreed with it in general, if not always in particular: it's banned too,
apparently. Pity.*
    *The lakes are still secret and beautiful—presences, still. There's a
young man Gough in Cavan who has clues. He has a pub in the Main
Street. He has a bronze-age spearhead on the wall. If you're ever in
Cavan, try and encourage him, please: a good modern citizen, I'd say.
Generally, I feel, Ireland's in the modern melting-pot . . .*
    Thank you for your kindness. Godbless,
    Anthony C. West

Gate Theatre, Dublin 1, July 24, 1965

Dear Mr. West,
    Thank you so much for your letter. I'm sure you registered well on

the BBC, and I'd certainly love to see the script, only it's a nuisance for
you to pack up and post things. I'm glad to hear there are some decent
people in Dungannon, in spite of the Old Orange Flute, and I'll look
out for Mr. Gough in Cavan. Yes, use them all in the next book. . . .
How right you are to stay out of London and the job-chasing jungle.
(You said 'jangle,' but I really mean jungle, I must make it clear owing
to bad typing). You may be a world-figure sooner than you think, and I
may live to see it. You are my latest enthusiasm.

 I'm ashamed to say I haven't yet read The Dark, *though it has*
been pressed on me from all directions. But without reading it, I could
be sure it was wrong to ban it. It's in good company anyway, with the
Ferret *and* Plato.

 Good luck and thanks again from Christine Longford
  [Under the signature, this postscript:] Christine Longford.
  Address me how you like, my Christian name is what matters.
  It distinguishes me from my sister-in-law, who has written a
  best-seller about Queen Victoria.

There follows a gap of more than two years. The next letter is the
countess's (though she refers to one of his that is missing here), and
her formal paragraphs have disappeared. She has further increased her
sociability by replacing many of the expected flags between independent
clauses with commas. Names remain a theme.

20 Herbert St, Dublin 2, Jan 1, '67

Dear Anthony C. (what a nuisance you have to insist on the C.
because of the other man, whom I don't read), thank you so much for
your letter. I suppose I ought to congratulate you, and I do really, but
£800 doesn't go far these days, it looks mean, they might have made it
a thousand. Still it's better than nothing. Of course I'm quite sick that
the English are doing what your own country ought to do. It's getting
easy for them, they only have to look at our banned list. I suppose
you're right, you must go on being Free Irish, like the Free French in
the war and the Wild Geese before that. . . . A young nephew of mine,

Tristram Powell, (son of Anthony who does so well with his novels),
turned up one day to do a feature for the BBC about the McGahern
country, and had a great time around Boyle and Loch Key. Why
wouldn't they take some pictures of you and your country? It would be
interesting, and now you have all the stuff about Clones and so on.
No, I'm sure you won't write a Bunratty article. I wonder if you've seen
those coloured postcards of hideous girls playing harps, you probably
have, but I'll send you one all the same, it will amuse your family. I've
heard Kinvara is almost worse, it was started as an overflow castle, just
as good and something cheaper, not for banquets so much as teas, and
now it has enormous banquets at staggering prices for the American
film-magnates and rich English who hunt with the Galway Blazers.
Talking of Clones, there's rather an emphasis on that country lately,
a man called Eugene McCabe has been writing plays. Also Paddy
Kavanagh's Tarry Flynn *was turned into a play and done in the new*
Abbey, and it really made a good show. But poor Paddy looked like
a corpse, let out of hospital on parole for the first night, very sad. Be
glad you're well and strong and so young, though you think you're not,
you've plenty of time in front of you. Yes, the squeeze is awful, — and
moving house is almost the worst thing that can happen to anyone.
At least you know now that some people know how good you are. I
spent some time explaining to somebody that you were not the son of
Rebecca West and H. G., and that you were not a Catholic writer, so
let's be sure that this year there will be no more need for explanations.
Happy New Year and thanks again from
    [She signs] Christine Longford.

In the fall of 1968 (the letter missing) he apparently wrote to tell her
about the imminent publication of *As Towns with Fire*. She responded
from Herbert Street on the 24th of October:

Dear Anthony, (if I may call you so, sir. You know what my name is,
but I don't expect you to call me by it if you find it painful, as I'm so
much older than you are), thank you very much for your letter. I'm
looking forward to AS TOWNS WITH FIRE more than I can say. I

won't be doing my amateur criticism of it this time, but I've already alerted my friends by talking about it . . . and I'm delighted to hear David Marcus has some of it for the Irish Press. *He's doing wonders for that paper: I think he's the only bit of good news from Dublin, where everybody's hating each other more than usual about religion and politics and the arts and business and so on. . . . the reason . . . simply SLUMP, lack of money, which you understand very well. I'll be interested to read what you say about that war, and about the North. It was odd, I had the idea of going to Derry a week or two before this last trouble blew up. I thought it was my duty, as it was the only ancient city of Ireland I didn't know and I wanted to admire the architecture. It's certainly beautiful, but I got the impression of fearful hatreds, the Siege seemed to be going on still. I hope you've slammed all politicians hard.*

Llanberis, 27 October 1968

Dear Christine Longford:

Thank you very much for your kind letter.

(To explain: I've always given people their rank, inherited or won. It makes life a little easier. And from the little I know, you and your late husband, god rest his soul, have done more than most to vindicate your inheritance within our envious Irish environment, and had there been and were there more like you, there might be less tied chauvinism and more free patriotism.)

What you say about Dublin seems strange and rather sad: why should there be so much in-grown backbiting? It's not money—it's something else: there's tremendous natural vitality in Ireland which doesn't seem to be able to fend for itself. Maybe there's too much drink and talk: it's a philosophic impossibility to have production and simultaneous contemplation/talk about it. (God made the heavens and earth and thought about it, afterwards.)

I was sorry to hear that you were no longer reviewing, but it may be for the best for, did you not take to Towns, you might have been awkwardly placed. The book wasn't mentioned in today's Observer *and* Sunday Times, *which could be rather ominous, especially as the literary water fairly spates under the daily bridges, and a new book, even were it word-of-god, can be forgotten within a fortnight. For the sake of Timothy O'Keeffe, at least, I sincerely hope the* Observer *will mention* Towns *next week, altho' goodness knows what will be said, as the book may seem to be surfacely rather naive and I suppose one has to put up with the merely psychological dissection that tends to stuff existence into the present, transient theories, with the doubtful help of all the usual, age-old sexual implications. It may be that both church and state, both sides of the Sea, will object to one's attempt to see the Irish 'problem' in deeper perspective: our wise old witch, our fairy godmother who, as Pandora, grants hope but lets one poke through life for scraps of truth and goodness....*

Roan-red coats of bracken now adorn the flanks of these old Eurasian hills, last golden butterflies light the ever-angry gorse, swallows long gone, birch-trees dressed overall in sovereign coats and yet....I see Ireland, not Wales, myself still a guideless youth staring at the untouchable beauty with a kind of holy fear—awe, a better word. My TV.

Thank you for talking Towns *to your friends. I hope it won't entirely disappoint. All good wishes, Sincerely,*

He followed this letter within six months with another:

Bryn Goleu, Llanberis, 4 Mar 1969

Dear Christine Longford:

Greetings and good wishes.

At the risk of the accusation of name-dropping, I would like to dedicate the American edition of TOWNS *to you, as a small recompense for your generous interest, if you're able to accept the gesture, as such.*

I have cut and polished and tied better together, taking out two sex-scenes. Knopf is publishing it and they say they intend to make a splash with it this year sometime.

February fill-dyke, first with snow—and then with snow, again, this year. It's a late spring.

There is some talk of my being asked to spend a year at Berkeley University, California. It would mean a time-loss, yes, at my age, but I might save some dollars to help me keep going. What could I say to young fictioneers except work, you blighters, and sweat...

Please let me know?

Godbless,

Tony

[PS] Altho' I'm no good at articles, VOGUE contacted me as a result of TOWNS and I'm doing (or have done) a thing for them. I have a nice relationship with the Lit. Editor, an American girl, who had read the FERRET in the States. (Me an' Vogue..!)

20 Herbert Street, Dublin 2, March 8, '69

Dear Tony,

I'm absolutely delighted of course, charmed and flattered by your kindness, it's fame for myself and not a bit of trouble with this addressed envelope and all. Only one thing: I do still like to call myself a writer, (though I hardly write anything), so I like to be called Christine Longford without additions. Or if it does any good in America, say Christine Countess of Longford. You see what it is, personal vanity and prejudice, I dislike the word 'dowager'. Some women in my situation say you use it only when you have children—but I don't know if that's strictly correct. Anyway give me Christine L. or Christine Countess of L.

It's splendid about the American edition. I hope you haven't cut too much. I thought you were going to put more in. The Northern aspect of it should go like wildfire this year, as it's in the news. That sounds heartless, but you know what I mean. Nobody else has gone so deeply into the 'region', then Ireland, Europe and the world as you have. By the way, what a bore the Irish Times is nowadays. I can't bear

to look at any more photographs of O'Neill. Also I keep on sending
back terrible books I can't read. But I manage to remain friends with
people who work in the office, and with equally decent people who
work for the Press. I'll even read VOGUE if you write for it.

   Yes, why not go to Berkeley, California? At least you wouldn't be
snowed up as on Snowdon, it would be a nice change, you deserve it.
Beware of becoming a television personality in America, you could do
that too and be very rich. But I really believe you could save dollars,
and not get taken over. Good luck, and many thanks again
   from
   Christine.

Bryn Goleu, Llanberis, [no date; early May 1969]

My dear Lady Longford:
   Greetings and good wishes.
   I write in case you may be able to suggest a lead.
   We've been looking at our 'future' here, against potential income
and despite all the educational grants, etc., and that this is a rural
area and still fairly backward, the cost of living (and living quietly at
that) eats up everything before one gets it. The American advance on
TOWNS cleared us, but if we go on as we are, we'll slip back again,
and then the solid worry builds up anew.
   I have made some preliminary enquiries about Southern Portugal
in the hope that one might be able to live there simply with the people.
We could clear around £2000 on the sale of this house. I, personally,
crave warmth: spring here has been wet, windy and cold and one has
to battle against the weather. On the other hand, Portugal is far away
and one could get stuck there with a family. I've written Paddy Smith,
an Irishman who lives there, asking him to let me have some local
information, if he will.
   Then, the other day, I saw that Eire is giving artists full tax con-
cessions—the first country in the world to do so! (There'll probably be
a stampede of the big money-spinners in TV and 'instant' literature!)

*Could one get a place to rent or to buy in southern Eire—Waterford,
Wexford, or Youghal? Do you know of anyone who might consent to
help a not unreasonable Irish writer by not charging him through the
nose? (Anyway, if and when I do this Welsh novel, I'll have to move, or
risk stones in my glasshouse!)*

*If you can think of anything, or if you have any suggestions,
please do let me know.*

Always sincerely,

20 Herbert Street, Dublin 2 May 15, '69

Dear Tony,

Yes, do, DO come back to Ireland. But I don't know a thing about
the Deep South now, except that it's over-run with tourist traffic and
oil. And I don't know anyone who has houses to spare, or anyone who
isn't hard up. Still, I may get an idea. I'll keep my eyes and ears open.

You know the objections of course better than I do, mostly about
schools. I know one family who emigrated from the Twenty-six Counties to the Six only for the sake of a school, and I was ashamed I
couldn't defeat their arguments. But the loss on social services would
be offset by your saving on income tax. And the children would learn
Irish quicker than Portuguese—or would they?

Why not start looking around the country you know? I mean, just
this side of the Border, Cavan or Monaghan. It's not so sunny, but
really the south isn't either. It can snow in Cork, the quays in Waterford can be icy, the east wind in Wexford is fearful. Yes, Youghal used
to be nice, but since it was tatted up for a film and Claude Cockburn
lives there, it must be much changed. I don't know him, do you know
anyone who does? My only idea is to find someone with local connex-
ions anywhere, and no I can't think of a soul. This is no use at all and
I'll have to stop, but I'll certainly go on thinking about it, you've set me
a problem. I may write in a different vein quite soon. Just wait.

Christine

Llanberis, Monday, 29ᵗʰ September 69, Michaelmas.

Dear Christine Longford:

    Greetings and good wishes.

    The Welsh Arts Council sent me particulars of what it calls a Fellowship at their Gregynog (Newtown) centre, asking for applications from artists for a four-to-six-month stint there for a £1000, plus expenses. . . . If they contact you, please try and praise me a little without sinning your soul? Personally, I doubt if I'd get my small toe inside the door as, doubtless, there will be quite a few 'clever' fellows after it, but the £1000 would let me get this present opus finished without worry. . . .

    Did you see Koestler's article in yesterday's Observer? *It made me hopping mad in a depressed way. Koestler has finally discovered some of the results of the 'Fall of Man'. God, these elementary profundities all based on 19ᵗʰ century hypotheses with their built-in contradictions, left hand never knowing what the right one is scratching. The modern form of old Augustine's universal human, plus Averroes. Felt like writing to tell Koestler to read Aquinas, who did try to see the individual. But what would be the use...? 'If science could find a way to make us immune against suggestibility...' Another new brainwash and a souped-up Malthusiasm. Say a prayer for me to help me get this present thing finished and I may answer some of these arrogant bastards.*

    I hope you are very well?

    Godbless,

When the decade turned, West was still in touch with the kindly Countess.

20 Herbert Street, Dublin 2, May 12, '70

    Dear Tony

    (My name, by the way, is Christine, if you could bring yourself to use it, but if it embarrasses you, at my advanced age, I can hardly insist). Thank you so much for your letter, and my goodness, for a

beautiful card at Easter, still on my mantelpiece. This is going to be
full of apologies, and a few excuses. Knopf did send me a handsome
copy of TOWNS, and I never thanked them for it, I know I should
have. Another confession: I lent my English copy to someone who was
hard up, (I shouldn't have done that either), and I haven't been able
to compare the two versions—I think the word is to 'collate' them, so
I'm not sure how much more you have put in. Anyway I looked for my
wellknown favourite passages, and found they were still the same, and
I do think it is a good and unique book, I needn't say so again.

More excuses, and don't laugh. I didn't have the flu, but all my
friends did and felt like death, and I felt like death without it. I've
never been so cold or so cross as this last winter, and I had dentist
trouble and sprained my ankle. And the Gate has been shut up: first
for re-decoration, when our good kind government promised us a lot
of money, then dry rot was discovered, and the Corporation told us to
take the roof off, which of course we didn't. And THEN our rulers quite
lately said they would pay for it, and put us down for £68,000 in the
new budget, which looked pretty good to me. And now the man who
did that has got the sack for gun-running. (You know, the man who
seemed so decent, and let artists off income-tax). So everything has
been put off again, with civil servants and lawyers and architects and
engineers all proposing to have meetings and not having them. This, I
admit, is a small thing, compared with the present state of the nation,
which is perfectly fearful. Dublin is Hell at present, with the political
mess-up, and you know all about the North and I needn't tell you. As
you say, to Hell with racial, religious, and political exclusiveness. It's
much more important that you are writing books, and the notices of
TOWNS have been good. Thank you again for my lovely free copy,
and I won't let it out of my hands, or at least out of my flat. It's not
even in a bookcase now, but put away in a cupboard. I've had a lot of
books pinched off me lately—but you can see I have a bad attack of
persecution-mania, and I'd better stop. More apologies, and this time
for bad typing as well, and heaps of thanks and best wishes

from Christine.
Bryn Goleu, Llanberis, North Wales. 14 May 1970.

Annwyl Christine, by my dear lady I meant just that, in the sense of the song: I know a lady sweet and kind. And you are not old. The once and only time I met you I thought that here is a woman with the heart of a young girl. So there.

You seem to have endured the same kind of winter that I did — haven't known one so long and cold, and I keep swearing — never again. But I think it's not only the weather, it's also the awful state of the world and the whole psychic atmosphere so that even our sleep is disturbed. But I'm glad you're well and still fighting.

I hope the Gate survives all these arguments. It has nothing to do with transient politics and is a creative part of Dublin.

This gun-running business is almost comical and I hope it doesn't turn tragic. On the surface it looks so Irish and adolescent. I'd think that Lynch is more worried about an influx of wild weapons, than about the North and South. He is like a man trying to ride half a dozen wild horses in a very small circus ring, John Bull, as ever, the ring-master. The Dail is really in the Bank of Ireland, an advisory service in Maynooth. These few yearning hotheads seem so blind to the international realities.

In the context, I happened to see in a friend's house Conor C O'Brien's 'Casement'. I don't know what O'Brien intended. It was all so remotely nostalgic. Poor Casement — a weak, idealistic, humane, essentially decent and vain human-being...and it's all so long ago. I was more interested in that awful person, F.E. Smith, the vicious in-fighter, hungry for position; and Carson...all small men praising their own egotisms but dancing to anonymous tunes. May God save us all from such 'leaders'. . . .

On that trip to Ireland, when you talked to me, I found all the essential 'basics' unchanged, unreformed, unrenovated. (I must do that b. BBC thing and I'll have to go back — this time with the bit in my teeth.) When I think of it, if the Irish Radio wanted my talk (sic) that was on the BBC here[2], I can put them in touch. I am, afterall, a kind of Irishman....still. . . .

I must do a novel on the Trouble. I have a whole tight scheme for it, somewhere — beginning, middle and end: catastasis and then catharsis, all old Ireland's loveliness thrown in for good measure. Apart from heart and energy, it's always time/money and research — the collection of the actual accomplished facts; and I'm 60 this year, as well, and have to finish this present thing. Not to mention the May and my annual desire to wander and just to soak up the new year's anguished beauty.

In Ireland that time I saw a tinker woman in a float, driving a smart pony. A child on her arm and bright yellow hair down her back and tied with a green ribbon. She was bold, brazen — strong, sunburned and arrogant...it's possible I'd have made a better tinker than a writer. These intellectuals are so carping and unkind. Recently I met several nice people in London and they all seemed so lax — charming and yet, so anxiously frustrated. Many of them seem to be going to mediums instead of psycho-analysts, plus the odd whiff of 'pot', in case Lucifer might open a door for them. I'm not critical. It just depresses me.

I'm sending you copies of the US TOWNS' reviews, in case you'd like to see them. If you don't want to keep them, please send 'em back in the enclosed envelope — all fairly major reviews and all good, bar two; and I can quite understand why I drive Lask and Schott up their respective walls, since I threaten to remove the sand in which their heads are buried.

It was good to hear from you. Please take care of yourself.

(The US TOWNS has less sex, plus the Mourne part, I think. Otherwise it's much the same, and is, I think, the better book.)

20 Herbert Street, Dublin 2, May 17, 1970

Dear Tony, thank you so much for sending me these, all GOOD, except for the two. Lask is much nastier than Schott, I don't think Schott would put anyone off buying the book, as he gives it heaps of space and the heading is good. Jack Curtis, whoever he is, is a decent man. And thanks for your letter too, and the cutting from the Guardian which I hadn't seen, — not to mention the envelope, most considerate. I'll certainly do anything I can for your BBC talk, if I come across anyone sympathetic in Radio Telefis Eireann. They're in an awful mess at present, and cutting down everything for current news items, economy and internal disagreements. No doubt in the world you're an Irishman, if anyone is. Only yesterday I met a Belfast woman who told me she had been interviewing a Belfast man who wanted a job: she asked him what was his nationality, and he answered quite simply 'I don't know', and he didn't.

> *Ever so many thanks again and best wishes*
> *from*
> *Christine.*

One more letter from the countess remains in the file:

81 Ailesbury Rd, Dublin 4, 12/2/73

Dear Tony,

You must think it shocking that I haven't written before to thank you for a most beautiful Christmas present. But I have an excuse — perhaps too many excuses. Observe I've changed my address from Herbert Street to Ailesbury Rd, considered a much grander address in Dublin but I don't like it so well myself. That was before Christmas and the move was a torment, as I have an awful lot of books, I mean a splendid number of books, and I don't know how many have been stolen or lost, (but yours, I'm glad to say, are quite safe and in the best bookcase). Before I was 'settled' I gave up the struggle and escaped to a comfortable hospital at Lucan which is a disguised looney-bin for drunks and melancholics, and I claim no credit for belonging to the second category. There I spent Christmas and was given turkey in bed, but refused to pull crackers or wear paper hats, which was a black mark against me and I've only just been let out and seen your lovely plaque for the first time. How extremely kind you are to me. It was in fact broken clean in two pieces, but not irreparably and I'm not superstitious, and now I've recovered my spirits and health and strength. I'm capable of climbing ladders and hanging pictures and mending much more difficult things.

Enough of my own troubles and I'm much more interested in you and your work, and looking forward to the next book. Thank you a thousand times, and excuse this paper, which was all I could find . . . Do come back to Dublin one day, won't you?
  Christine L.

His thoughts were regularly in Ireland, for West continued—even to the morning of his death—to revise the two Ireland-set works that stretch autobiographically between them from his physical infancy throughout his intellectual and artistic development. Both experienced aborted publications, yet in them West employs his most persuasive, mature narrative strategies; integrates the Irish materials through setting, plot, characterizations, and imagery; shares the findings of his lifelong quest, and reflects upon the vicissitudes of the search. The evolution of these novels becomes in itself a monument of achievement.

Narrative is West's forte. As he explained to O'Keeffe, "Once I get the first explanatory-exploratory part . . . done, the rest will run and I'll settle down to me 30 pages a day."[3] Intellectually and spiritually, he lived outside—beyond—the apocalyptic pattern of the traditional Romantics. He was fond of using a modified ellipsis to suggest continuation, not omission. Three dots (unspaced) in his letters and his typescripts rarely sufficed; usually he employed seven. The convenient or arbitrary endings of narrative are technically difficult enough to manage—but philosophically he dismisses finality. As art is an avenue to spiritual reality, his term "slices of life" bears only slight sympathy with Naturalism's critical term: the Kilsuan talk, for example, reverberates authentically, as West has a wonderful ear for dialect and an eye for details of peasant life and character. The implications of the raw realism, however, are transcendent, not deterministic.

The history of the Actaeon novel offers keys to West's artistic aims and strategies, to his spiritual discovery, to his ideals and limits, to his puzzling behavior that can alternately seem incredibly naive, artistically heroic, profoundly and poignantly trusting, and "foolish [as he says] like a fox." Actaeon is more than an incidental slice of the ur narrative; it is its culmination, artistically as well as chronologically and spiritually. The novel

probes the question of Ireland's place in a spiritual context, as The Casual
Comedy attempts the question temporally and politically. The Glenmore setting (West's Yoknapatawpha) for The Casual Comedy eventually
becomes Ballysuan, the River Kilsuan (Kilcoll in early versions) parish in
Actaeon. It includes a Protestant church built by one Chauncey, Earl of
Glenmore, who in the middle of the seventeenth century reconstructed
the Pagett-Jones estate dating from the Ulster Settlement; by 1650 he had
added the church and most of Ballyouley. Chauncey lived profitably and
shrewdly for eighty years; then came the Battle of the Boyne. West surveys quickly the subsequent tenures of five earls, elaborating on the earl
in residence during the Great Famine, father of The Casual Comedy's
present one, who rebuilt the manor (a room for every week in the year
and a window for every day) and along with other structures, erected a
neo-gothic church and rectory, the latter with "fifteen rooms, stables and
farmery on seventy acres of good glebe land" (The Casual Comedy #2,
Circled 6, p.10). This rectory becomes the setting for Actaeon. Ferris,
the coachman of the Comedy, becomes the Russels' chauffeur; no other
characters' names seem to be carried over, but West moves forcefully
onward with his argument in this geophysical context.

By late versions of Actaeon, West has realized an effective solution
to a problem that nags him through other works and earlier versions—
the intellectual loneliness of his narrator. The adult mentor to the adolescent has been his usual device, but there has been always a risk of
something stilted, a danger of condescension or authoritarianism, and
the tutoring adult must give way to the maturing mind of the child,
so the tutor's demise is predictable. Paul Noble initiates young Simon
Green in a wiser reading of the Old Testament stories before he dies;
Paul Noble's prototype appears in Two Men and Two Folktales (the
date of this typescript, 1953), a short story whose technical awkwardness
suggests West had been experiencing the problems with this device even
earlier. Sean O'Sullivan, Sean Rua, and Master Molloy are crucial mentors for O'Dea Russel of Wall and Jonty of The Casual Comedy; John
Waterman spends vital hours instructing Stephen Muir in Irish history
and mythology before Stephen's own fatal crash on the Dublin road
from Kerry (Room without a Door); John Stone meets the same tutorial

need for Christopher MacMannan in *As Towns with Fire*. Through such figures West has been able to evoke particular modes familiar enough to readers of Irish literature, modes of preliterate cultures for handing on information—the bardic, seanchai, and memory vision or fís; these figures also evoke Ireland known through heroes and saints. But he does not stop there. Ireland of the "dark ages" and Ireland of early cultural migrations both interest him, as do the Irelands of mysterious archeological evidence and of Roman church accounts. West's study of these sources was extensive.

The Glenmore/Kilsuan setting, the area of ancient Breifne, included Cavan, where West had spent his years from eleven to nineteen. He thought it to have been one of the last centres of the esoteric, participative, Celtic Christianity, and had ties therefore with the ancient mystery centres.[4] He was convinced that a Celtic gnosis, which predated the imposition of Roman missionizing of Ireland, absorbed a knowledge of the Crucifixion, and linked Gaelic culture back to the Noah-Manu wisdom of some proto-Celtic group of the earliest migrations after the last Ice Age. Ireland had become Europe's teacher when the Greco-Roman-Mediterranean complex was in ruins. That role ended of course after the Anglo-Norman crusade and the Romanizing of the Celtic Church. He thought censorship and subversion of the Christ-complex began at the Crucifixion and that by 400 AD records had been pretty thoroughly fixed or destroyed, though a Celtic gnosis was longest preserved in Ireland. The Norman destruction of York and Armagh he thought of a piece with the genocide of the Albigenses and the probable but never proved murder of Aquinas—parts of an effort to obliterate a Dionysian half of spiritual forces that the Christ, through Jesus, had united. All his roads led to Rome as the transmogrifyer of a beneficence that once flourished in Holy Ireland. The correspondence with Charles Davy offers the best exposition of this aspect of his quest and its progress;[5] The Lady Actaeon and The Casual Comedy are its fictional results.

His quest culminates in his best versions of Diana's and O'Dea's dialogue, the whole defining and describing his staying West. The novel reveals the scope of West's vision; it illustrates his talent and helps to explain his zeal while it demonstrates his astonishing prolixity. The more than twenty versions show his experimentation with different narrators, different structural modes, different conditions for and resolutions to the plot. Probably because of its organic, Protean quality, the novel's being so deeply the manifestation of West's own ever-evolving intellectual, spiritual, and artistic perceptions, he found it difficult to conclude.

West's protagonists usually carry so much freight with their combined world-views, their serendipitous approach to sexual conjunction, their burgeoning artistic talent, and their religious inquiry that some readers have been no more successful than this neighbor who wrote cheerfully to him about *Towns*, "It didn't leave me cliff-hanging. And I just skipped the war part and the long political discussions." Then she turned the writing over to her spouse, who shared some of MacMannan's feelings about the military experience. He praised West's powers of observation but objected to the hero's "utter sexual conceit," which to him seemed to conflict with his intellectual snobbishness. "I admired your hero in many other ways but he was too withdrawn from humanity." Precisely. This man got the message but not West's point. His wife supposed there was a point, but she wanted only thrills without spills or reflection.[6]

In Actaeon West distributes the intellectual and artistic load, making his leading characterizations more plausible. He divides his central persona, giving the interest in religious history and Celtic archeology to O'Dea and the aesthetic, poetic brilliance to Diana. In part, it is a familiar Romantic pairing of artist and priest—as Bronte, for example, explores so thoughtfully in *Jane Eyre*. The interests complement each other, as they spring from the same root, Blake's holy Creative Imagination; liabilities attend extremes in either role. West's exploration of female psychology and sexuality is unique for him with Actaeon. Whereas the women of his published fiction—e.g. the landlord's wife of *Rebel to Judgment*, who stands remote, beautiful, and intimidating as a garden-goddess or Molly, "earth-mother opposite of MacMannan's ungrounded self"[7]—receive peripheral treatment and serve narrow roles, Actaeon moves her front and central. Her characterization becomes brave and complex. West even provides authenticity and drama enough for the neighbors, though they would surely be offended by his descriptive realism of a digital rape.

West's artistic growth, measured by his control of O'Dea's and

Diana's minds, is remarkable to watch during the decades that this story develops. He retains the basic events and plot, while the argument and cerebration grow increasingly sophisticated. One structural complication, introduced as early as the thirties to West's developing schema, is a lesbian relationship between Diana and her friend Jocasta. West reflects considerable ambivalence about this device, rejecting it wholly in some early expansions of the friendship, in other versions considering its potential for a menage á trois at the rectory, giving Jo another, male interest, or taking her out altogether. In an early fragment,[8] which shows as well that O'Dea, not Diana, had the poet's role at this time, O'Dea Russell's internal monologue permits the reader's acquaintance with a range of obstacles(both tangible and abstract)to this marriage he is suddenly planning to make.

The contrasts among the versions show the huge growth of West's characterizing art as well as his increasing appreciation of the feminist perspective. There is nothing subtle or appealing about this voice, perhaps the earliest, of O'Dea:

> We shall meet soon again, never fear. I'm hooked, m'am. Goodbye, softly and sincerely, and tell your friend what I said concerning her status as lover: Tell her I feel the deep hurt of my possession of you and that, when your elastic hymen snaps, I'll think a prayer for her. . . (Garden Party, 27).

This mostly first-person (part of it seems to be a dialogue between O'Dea and his soul-spirit) version by Russell is clumsy and immature. "Concerning her status as a lover?" "A snapping elastic hymen, m'am?" The descriptive West may be anticipated, however, in the third-person conclusion of this same fragment:

> She walked out of the desk into the sunlight and turned to wave to him, her form suddenly transfigured. The avenue swung to the left, rising steeply, her figure thrown against the ascent, her gait more slow. The sunlight boiled around her as she climbed until she shone—a blot in the blinding reflection from the castle windows. Her friend was

standing under the port-cochere, waiting, walking out slowly to meet her (Garden Party, 29).

As early as the thirties and forties (to judge by typewriting evidence and quotation marks, along with textual references to World Wars and Nazism), West is making Diana and Dea conduct the theological and religious debates central to his purpose. His approach, however, later grows demonstrably more sophisticated and egalitarian. Here is O'Dea in the G version, intentionally kind, perhaps, but condescending:

> "Di, my sweet, you're lost," he said kindly, shaking his head at her. "Philosophy never clarified, philosophically, the fact of Christianity. Not its job."
>
> "Well . . . ." she muttered helplessly, "maybe you're right."
>
> "I am right," he said coolly. "Far as I've gone. I'm not just expressing personal opinions for the sake of hearing myself and, anyway, you did want to know the run of my mind."
>
> "But, Dea," she said urgently . . . "I know the church? You'll never get recognition for these unorthodox ideas!"
>
> She was genuinely protesting now. He was pulling down all her own plans for their future (G, 27–29).

Later characterizations spare the reader such small spirits in the dialogue—or monologue. In the early presentations O'Dea is dogmatic and almost bullying. Diana is conventional in her doubts. In later ones, however, his disagreements with his wife do not challenge her abilities or diminish her. West seems to have absorbed the idea of an equal relationship between men and women necessary to his wider argument. O'Dea's characterization becomes free of this bludgeoning ego and Diana becomes carefully agnostic rather than ignorant.

Jo assumes varying responsibilities, West's artistic needs evolving as he deals with prejudices—society's and, perhaps, some of his own. For a while she occasions Diana's story by being the recipient of her narrative through dense letters, but these give way to the diary. Then "Joko" is made to visit Diana during Diana's pregnancy and extend the long philosophical discussions with O'Dea. She permits West to consider the menage á trois and to reject it quickly because of the unconventional change the characterization has taken. O'Dea is no prude, but his attitudes toward sexuality have distanced and distinguished him from both women.

Jo bears a prominent role in the longest, most detailed (E) version of The Lady Actaeon (698–699A), affording both revelatory letters and, when she comes to visit the Irish rectory, much dramatizing of the diary's internal debates. Jocasta Sollas-Hutton has inherited her family's estate. The place holds no attraction for her, and she offers it to O'Dea for his utopian schemes to shelter handicapped children and establish a self-sufficient farm. Before her delivery, they do not wish to upset Diana with O'Dea's proposal to move to Devon. The extended discussions permit misreading and misunderstanding among the three, and help to create still other possible conclusions to the narrative about Diana's early experience of her brother's and their nurse's deaths: infanticide—or is it euthanasia? Suicide?

In this E version Diana also discovers a note in her teddy bear's, Boff's, stuffing, presumably a confession by her Welsh nurse (Nain) that she had, in mercy, taken Edmund's life to spare him an unloved future; now she is taking her own, throwing herself down the three-floor staircase. Diana tosses the note into the fire, but on the second thought that it might have been a plant by her neurotic mother, she tries to retrieve it to study the handwriting. Only one word remains: "Peace." This incident of the second thought seems a tantalizing improvement over the apparently earlier account in version I. There Diana has no recourse: she has flushed the note down the toilet.

West reveals the flinty edge of Diana's critical insight, her approving view of euthanasia, and her cynical attitude toward maternity. In the following scene, Jo has already developed but not admitted an erotic interest in O'Dea, though he remains characteristically apart. Parish needs have called him out on this stormy night, and the two women talk by the fire. Diana asks,

" . . . Has he given you the impression that he considers me a bitch?"

"No, to the contrary. It needs a bitch to smell one."

"Darling, how mutual!" she exclaimed. "But, have you given him the word, then?"

Jo made a face, refusing to reply.

"I wouldn't be angry if you had, darling? A much lower assessment of my—my transcendence might even be a relief, since as you wisely imply, we're all rather bitches, practical or not, as the case may be. On mere Freudian terms, how can we be anything else, considering our natural condemnation to physiological rut? I dunno. Ideally, we should all be polyandrous with prerogative for euthanasia. Men keep on dying, anyway . . . Are you also in love with Dea?"

"While I haven't directly asked myself that particular question, under the circumstances, I confess I did rather take to Dr. Freeman," Jo replied, carefully cool.

"Freeman?" Diana said, absently. "But he can't give away any babies?" [Dea's friend Freeman suffers impotence from a war wound.]

"There are hundreds of babies being born every day, darling."

"Yea, man! But Freeman—he mightn't particularly want to go through the necessary motions?"

"Oh, I dunno? He didn't strike me like that. One can usually tell. They say emasculation can sometimes encourage, rather than the opposite."

"When did you see Freeman?" she asked, not quite able to keep a note of possessiveness out of her voice. "When I was out with Dea. Have you ever asked Dea?"

"No," she admitted grudgingly. "Never that much interested," she added, moving her chest to release a belch, like a pigeon rumbling its crop. "We might even make a civilized foursome?" she suggested. "Dea and Freeman see eye to eye. If you hurry I can wet-nurse your foundling."

"Oh, don't be a pig, darling" Jo protested defeatedly. "We don't have to act sea-lawyers, after all these years" (698–699A).

Jo disappears from the R, and in some apparently early versions (F and G, for examples), she has no lesbian relationship with Diana, being simply a close girlfriend from school.

Jo Sollas-Hutton had . . . decided to keep her sex-life in one compartment, rather than risk mental and emotional dependence, which she
looked upon as a sort of contamination. But Joe was a total and natural
autocrat . . . and she had seemed born with a natural and unpossessive
attitude to sex that was no more romantic than satisfaction over a good
meal. . . . Jo had been her touchstone since childhood . . . a friend who
possessed all the feminine shrewdness and little of the bitchiness. Their
association was a love, a quiet intimacy without friction. Jo had said once:
Good thing, Di, neither of us are nowhere near a lesbian (G, 14-16).

The social boundaries are pushed in F, nevertheless, by Jo's having
had a satisfying love affair with a black man. Diana has only this comment on race relations:

I fully accept my white heritage, all of it, bad and good. I refuse to drag
it under the feet of the coloured man, or use it as a sack to pull over his
head. I am as good as he is, such as I am. He is good as I am, such as he
is. If we agree, we can go forward together. I have no sense of colour bar.
I want the man, neither colour, caste or rank........(Q fragments, 176).[9]

Homosexuality seems to have presented a more difficult taboo for
West to address. In the E version, probably an early one, O'Dea explains
that it's "a sort of imbalance of soul, but not a wrong" (347). In the K
version, also apparently an early one, Diana is still firmly heterosexual,
saying she

had tried making love with a school girlfriend, but it was all rather
pathetic and embarrassing. . . . You can't really beat a man . . . he's
made for it—just as we are (404).

A fragment among the Q alternates shows how far from participating
Diana still is, as she studies unrecognized lesbian relationships in the
parish:

Let not the thighs' fond junction submit to male assault . . . I suppose it's
feasible, provides some satisfaction for after all they know each other's

capability more intimately than men. I'd love to see them at it. Were
I not so abnormally normal two lefts might make an almost-right, sans
seedtime and harvest and after all there are various engines to be had
to simulate the boil climax and conclusion and even so there could
be a kind of love and love's always at risk and worth a risk of loveless-
ness and numb loneliness. I can't help wondering if old John Garret
Moore might wreck another table if he knew his darling's predilection.
Never having heard of lesbos altho'abnormally hungry for news of any
fornications, the parish, including Ana, sees no harm in the association
and old John's apparently proud of it and Cynthia [John's daughter]
as predator guarantees the social innocence. Probably Ruth Thomas
[the organist] has put more than two together but mum's her word and
god's her handy man (Q-alternate, 457).

In the E text, another early version, Diana's bisexuality presents itself
unabashedly, but in ways that compromise Diana's gender, her gentility,
even her integrity.

> Diana had settled herself in her chair, feet spread ungracefully to fire
> since they were always chill, and sucking her [ice-lolly] with a sort of
> childishly careful greed.
> "My, you're a sight for tired eyes, darling," she said lazily. "Wonderful.
> Funny, always when at your best you made me wish I were a man and
> having you. You're really a very mateable woman" (E, 687).

It is hard to shake the sense in E that she has never moved beyond
an adolescent pleasure in flaunting and therefore in exaggerating a devi-
ance, rather than that she maturely embodies and accepts a difference.
Correlatively, there is an impression of the author's merely putting on
a mask of femininity — to say nothing of the mask of lesbianism, which
seems even less successful with this comment — rather than truly imagining this woman's thought. Yet it must be granted that in a hostile time,
West was making a bold and conscientious try.[10]

By the R, however, Diana is both more mature of mind and candidly ambivalent about her sexuality. West has achieved more ease with

the feminine persona, and Diana stands a solid, plausible creation. Jo eventually admires O'Dea's strength, intellect, and character to the point where she begs him to impregnate her. In some versions, she wants neither lover nor husband, but would like to bear a child. Why she could not approach this objective with Diana's help, is not satisfactorily clear, Diana's unorthodoxy in other respects being by this time firmly established. In kindness to Diana, Dea and Jo are indeed concealing until after the birth the plan to undertake the socialist project for juveniles at Jo's estate in Devon. However, the unhappiness O'Dea has created by denying intercourse between himself and his wife while she is pregnant (a traditional taboo, one that helps the reader to measure Dempsey's offense in the novel's conclusion, and not an attitude for which one could with fairness fault Dea or his creator), is nurtured by a conventional jealousy when Diana accidentally sees and misreads her husband's parting from an unsolicited embrace by Jo. He is gently and firmly refusing Jo's request, but Diana never learns this truth.

Some of these people, events, and ideas almost disappear in Diana's monologue in the R; subdued references to them become merely the allusive flotsam of Diana's thought, as she reveals an ever more precarious sanity. In this way, without full disclosure of their story, Nain and the cretin, infant brother, Edmund, ghost Diana's memory and affect her present through her fears that her own child will be abnormal. His handling of these memories in the plot and characterization also dramatically illustrates West's changes of mind about his female protagonist. In an early account like the F, her anticipation of a defective birth is explicit (590). At Delia Dempsey's campfire in K (an early, pica typescript) Diana declares Delia's sleeping baby "sweet" and begs to hold it, "just to know what it feels like" (#3, 676). Diana has begun to lactate. Despite Delia's worries that the scour will make her baby ill, Diana starts to nurse it. With the combined pain of her own contraction and the biting of the child, Diana drops the baby (K679). West does not make her recollect Edmund, or suggest a malevolent or even an unconscious attempt to re-enact his death.

In an early Q fragment, however, Diana tells Delia that she once held a child "tightly till it stopped" (47). She muses, "You can make

yourself forget, y' know," as her own pain makes her push the baby off
her knees and Delia dives for the child to save it from the fire (47). In
the Q Alternate, Diana "slyly" bribes Delia to let her hold Delia's wailing
child (613). The narrator discloses that "its inarticulate crying sound[s]
like vicious commination" and she "suddenly hat[es] it" (612A).

In the E treatment of this scene, apparently later than K, Diana has
become a more complex woman, though not a very sympathetic one.
West's marginal note for revision at this point reports "Diana confesses
to murder of Edmund just by holding him tightly in her arms. Nain —
substitute. Killed two people" (927–928). So Diana carries the guilt from
her childhood of having caused both her brother's death and the suicide
of their nurse. T and P explain that the Dempsey child's "cry is now two
cries for Diana, the heard one scorching her hearing with the memory
of an earlier one until she can hardly tell . . . which . . ."(P, 53). By the
probably later I of 1977, "for Diana the crying is the same thing as her
own pains which would wail like that had they a voice . . ." In distraction,
not in hatred, Diana drops the child (I, 402).

The same scene in the R (613), which would seem to be the last
long version of Actaeon,[11] glosses an earlier disclosure that when she was
a child, Diana had tried to stop her brother's crying by stifling him with a
pillow (R, 429), but her address to this baby is no longer modified by the
adverb "perfidiously." Diana, indeed, recalls her brother and his crying
at this moment, but her own situation is dire and she elicits the reader's
sympathy as she "hears a loud cry and sees herself falling, the moon slipping down the sky . . ."(613).

The rector's wife has been seen in the fields that afternoon by some
boys out ferreting, and when Ana finally gets this word, she sends the
estates steward Ferris, down the road with the Bentley to look for their
mistress. He finds the tinkers' fire in time for Diana's delivery. Eventually
he and Mrs. Dempsey get her into the car. Ferris desperately, incompe-
tently, speeds toward home with Diana and child. A black bullock —
important to those ancient, sun-worshipping Kerrymen from whom
Dea, through his mother, descends, and whom West has earlier evoked
through the seanchai's tales — collides with the car in the fog-shrouded
road, rolling the Bentley into the ditch. Only the baby survives.

So the R version concludes. Other accounts vary. The early E, for example (and unsurprisingly), shows Diana guilty again of infanticide. Crazed by the accident, she finally discovers Ferris is only stunned and can be roused to go for help. Moved in and out of consciousness by the wailing child still lying between her legs, she covers it with a pillow and stifles the noise. Diana survives the car wreck, and

> wakes up with a dry mouth and a dull pain hammering in her head. . . . Up the road strong lights are fixing as day the hazy hedges. A car's coming. She thinks a moment and then, almost unconsciously, lifts the pillow off her quiet child and puts it behind her head as the car stops, the figure of a man jumping out (E, 1033).

The mature, married O'Dea of Actaeon may be a surprising outcome of the boy in an earlier part of the ur—say, of the thirties' novel, Wall—but West follows no obligation to make their developments seamless. Stories are made. Beginnings and endings are arbitrary. Nowhere does he insist these protagonists are the same, even when the names recur. He says only that "all these characters are part of me."[12] Within the limits of their own, unusually connecting stories, these respective characterizations serve the purpose of helping West work out his ideas and develop his craft. West decides, for example to take away from the man in Actaeon the artistic talent exaggerated in the boy in Wall. He emphasizes instead O'Dea's intellectual, historical, and spiritual studies. O'Dea becomes the unconventional Church of Ireland clergyman, still philosophically sympathetic to the artist, but recognizing that he, himself, is not one, needing Diana all the more as complement. Diana's regard for him is plausible, for he is both irritating and endearing, misunderstanding yet generous. Bright and independent, Dea has managed to avoid being trapped by adolescent or adult sexuality. Now, at mid-life he is ready to marry and knows at once he has met the right woman.

Diana's awakened sexuality, her admiration of her husband and her distress over him, her adjustments to parish people and their ways, as well as her spiritual and intellectual discontents exacerbated by immediate pregnancy are all filtered through her Orphean imagination.

From vulgar to sublime, we walk—we waddle through the dusks. We like the dusk: it can't see us, people just goodnights with sightless eyes, distance not measurable, all voices grey. We count the lights for interest, the land's rheumed eyes spying on the dark: odd how darkness manifests so many hidden dwellings that day can't see.

The rectory lights as one, Ferris' lodge as two, we count all lights that we can see, an odd total comforting, an even one catastrophe. We try to ignore the hill-topping cars but sometimes cheat the change the even into odd and then regret it, guilty that fate will recognize dishonesty. If we regain the rectory gates with an even number, we'll linger or walk a little more until we find an extra odd one, then close our eyes and hasten home. Altho' much walking brings a dull pain into the small of our back, frightening us, we can't stand still at night; it becomes an uncomfortable lurking and invites some passer-by to ask us our intentions. Ferris the old abortion lurks. I've seen him about his lodge, a shadow in his shadows as if his dracula has the better of him.

We dwaddle through the days, thinking un-thinking non-thinking re-thinking, looking for something we never knew we had and know we never had; reading scraps of this and that, even the print on toilet-paper sans any interest or satisfaction, sentences without sense, the single printed words disowning their associates and changing into symbols for something else, arguing the opposite way of what we see, the broken bits invoking different images. Then we doze and dream the words as they float about and sound themselves and change themselves by adding random letters fore and aft, the alterations so coarse that we wake up embarrassed and hope we haven't been overheard. We know it's all a game but doing it's believing it like a gambler with a sure-fire horse or hand of cards. I remember playing my mind similar tricks when a child, burying an apprehension or misdeed under a better fable, avoiding due punishment by contorting my excuses with quite extraneous but quite logical explanation so the mentor's mind chased my hounds and let my hare go free. Come to think of it, my later poetry may have had similar motives: preaching to myself like gate to post to silence the creaks of old remorse for something done or undone long years before.

Unless Dea has lived a totally blameless life I can't understand it when he implies he has no remorse and speaks as if his past belongs to some other for whom he's not responsible and even that in face of his evident helpful responsibility for others' shortfalls. He always says forgive oneself to let oneself live on in better fashion instead of using new experience to mourn the past's sour milk—all very well, there could be ruthlessness involved, the velvet glove disguising the iron fist: hardened homicidal criminals are supposed to be unremorseful altho' he looks at the meaning of criminal, splitting it between the mere law-breaker and the psychopath, a word I dislike since law-breakers are recoverable, psychopaths damned. He always interprets common words and sayings according to his total view, saying we use words at secondhand oblivious of their substance and reality. But be that as it may, are good and bad so close together in us all that right and wrong are interchangeable and almost indiscriminate, no one aware of change or good or harm until the action gives the social evidence to society which then proceeds to judge the right or wrong according to its own ideas of right or wrong, the judgment itself quite liable to be right as wrong or vice versa, the national norm an awful prejudice and preconception, a kind of unwritten constitution of mere rumour that would stoop to covert criminality to save the appearances of discredited appearances...

Christ I dunno. I'll never understand—anything, nor national rights nor wrongs, nor rights nor wrongs religious that can saint one man and burn another, hosannah the twin of crucify, hanging the sibling of enoblement. In France the frogs eat snails as cockneys catch eels and Scots shave in whiskey the way old beauties bathed in ass's milk, Chinese cook birdsnests, cheddars like cheese, Germans have beerfeasts and Irish gaelic yams, Jews won't talk to swine and Moslems keep geishagirls in heaven called houris the singular hour. I'll preach a bran-new faith and keep a stud of big-boned males in paradise and make 'em chew our wood and drink our water.

When I asked Dea what he thought of Moslemism as rival to his christianity he said it was an amalgam of Greco-judean gnosticism and satisfied a certain kind of intelligence.

But is it a real faith?

Yes much as if simplistic christianity, I suppose. Anyway, our science is almost totally arabist—Allah into cosmic machine.

But was Mahomet a genuine prophet?

Yes and no . . .

What's that mean?

He had certain clairvoyance that was akin to Swedenborg's while his theology was an echo of the old hebrew monotheism but even Sufi gnosticism doesn't realise his importance to christianity.

Altho' I'm lost I persist and he makes matters worse by saying that Mahomet opposed cold intellectualism with emotionalism...

Then he says laughingly that I have pagan piety, Arthurian piety and I don't know if this is a paving stone or a bunch of shamrocks and making me see Hauley vividly with its legend that it was one of Arthur's many seats. God he can scare me sometimes. Am I his lady of Shalott, my mirror full of moving shadows. I'd rather be his Shalott than his Maud by god...

When I wanted more, impatient with his frustrating chinks, he said it was all too vast a subject for five minutes, making me bite my tongue to keep from asking him why the hell he had brought it up in the first place until remembering it was I who started it.

Godknows I'm not interested in religion and only so appear since he is so involved and so seldom discusses personalities and convivial commonplaces and there's little left in the filing cabinet. His attitude whether meant or not is similar if not the same to any cleric past and present who metaphorically hums and haws when layfolk ask close questions on his craft, every damn one of them seem linked in masonic secrecy. I remember reading reports of letters between two early old fathers when one warned the other to be careful about giving the groundlings too much information on the subtleties of their faith with the implication that the latter might know as much as they did: power again—I've heard the self-same sentiment in Westminster. Secrecy and power—don't educate, indoctrinate like all the little Kremlins and praise the social goose for all its golden eggs. At times I'm so indigested with unsaid challenge that my heart beats in my throat and starves my breathings...

Disgruntled winter's imperceptibly retreating even if winter here is only sunless wetness of long time, spring ruthlessly maturing, larks already singing descants to the dawns quite often high enough for cloud to hide them so their disembodied melody feathers down earth like starry song. Daylong the rookery's loud with garrulous argument as mated couples watch spare males compete for wives, the married males loudly possessive. Their evening dance gets later every day. It used to be at two in windraked racing winter-skies and now it's held at three and will soon be four then five then six and more, five minutes more each day as if they had a clock to tell their ritual time. And still these sombre clouds of starlings flee darkness home without a thought of pairing. I now watch for them every evening and hold my breath to wish them, drive them on their way and feel like borrowing Clancy's shotgun to hurry them.

Dea's going on with this farming plan — the new monasticism, labour and prayer, saving the old Irish soul at expense of my sanity. When I challenge him he always quite humbly explains and I can feel sorry for him, for his worried concern about the world's greedy ways. I know this world's a greedy place, a sump of human failings, a pyramid of fleas, envy a natural habit, good fortune grudged, others ill-luck a cause for celebration. Knowing so I've kept aloof, self the best master of one's revels until old time himself appears and murmurs enough's enough...

It's what's living's all about and no one goes naked and unarmed bar decent folk like Angus born sacrosanct sans need for guile and needless of self-protective fear...

Doubtless Dea loves me I assume or else he grins and bears me with or without the sex, which puts me at emotional and practical disadvantage. I may even be his shirt of hair to mortify his mind for goodness sake when many another lesser man would call me his pro-verbial pain in the ass.

I know how love might feel beyond the sexual bar tho' never felt it in or for myself — the so-called total lostness in and for another as in literature — for me an emotional prison despite the hollywood hedonics: fists in the gob and smacks on the kissers, the undertone of violence similar. I've never watched a living love-affair nor seen nor read a fictional one without asking how much old fuxing was involved. Ironically, like Dea himself, I've always tried to see the human being without the

spurious increment of fux despite its passionate importance. As usual
he goes further and claims the sexual act is over-emphasized because it
can hardly be mentioned without invoking sexuality whereas in better
philosophical terms it's one of the few activities in life when pleasure
and desire are momentarily balanced—animals procreate, men experience. And women experience the results more ways than one I silently
add. . . (R, 576a–582; R disk, 476–479).

Pregnancy—unwanted but only casually prevented—eventually
foments or perhaps licenses her derangement. Her behavior is unusual,
but to the reader it is poignantly explicable.

Christmas is coming and I am very fat: grey flurries of wet snow falling
the way the wind wants to make its dance viable, spectral mornings
white and beautiful, cleansed and calm, this weary land just black
and white—black trees and roads, white fields, all autumn's waste disguised unter a pewter sky. Blackly gigantic against the pallor, Dea's
herm sports a cap of snow that makes its height seem endless against
the white horizon. I bet it moves about at night and wails in rock-fall
gaelic for its lost estate.
    I read both nativities as I've always done; why I don't know, perhaps
because poor dear Nain solemnly read them aloud on every christmas
eve. I now see that the two accounts really seem to describe the births
of different children, one in a house with attending notables, the other
in a stable with attending hinds, one persecuted, the other not—Luke's
gentle story and the savage tragic Matthew with its refugees. On the
evidence if evidence and not interpolation Dea's theory seems the
better bet rather than saying Matthew and Luke described the self-same
thing in different ways with the silent implication that one or the other
made a bad mistake which on the face of it is hardly possible and if
the whole four gospels are post-christian concoctions, the concoctors
made a confusing job of it indeed. It's really extraordinary that over
centuries theologians roman and otherwise have stared at the contradictions without better explanation—no wonder their churches are
now so rickety. When I ask Dea again he nods and says there it is, that

Jerome and the new constantine church buried the infancy gospels in order to create an oversimplified creed for the imperial masses in lieu of worked-out paganism. Were I christianly involved, I'd be hopping mad and I accuse him of the lie's extension since after all he runs with it irrespective of whatever he personally knows. All he says is patience and the truth will slowly reappear. Like psychologists, I think that theologians are brainwashed by theologians to preserve the appearances much in the same way as politicians replace the dreadful human truth with diplomatic fables convenue.

Irrespective of my indifferent atheism or a-religion-ism, I obey the seasonal sentiment and decide to go to church, jesus and/or christ here or there, admitting that the nostalgia does create a kind of sharing and benign neighbourliness, makes people hide their natural envy and say happy christmas to one another as if they meant it.

Dea held a midnight service followed by eight o' clock communion, coming home for a cup of coffee and going off again for a children's service on his bicycle, leaving the Ben for me. I don't know where he finds his energy. He can rest for fifteen minutes flat, sleep like an infant and rise refreshed. Work satisfaction I suppose. My work is worry while his is blandly social, meeting people all the time, straightening bent souls like Father O'Flynn. I only meet Ana, Lord, Ferris, Clancy, Angus strangers and myself and self is antisocial.

Old Ferris horsed us to the service, creeping over snow-patches with eggs in his mouth, squeezing his eyes as the downy snowflakes rush at him and die as rain on the windscreen, the Ben dictating to him as usual. He is really an old horse man. I heard him talking to the car while grooming it. If a rear wheel kicked him he would shout whoa. To give him due, Ben is spotless inside and out.

Poems O God as seen on old palimpsests: trees walking through snow, a red cock pheasant burning snow, a rusty fox stalking a feeding blackbird along a snowy hedge. A lovely tawny hare lopes up the road ahead of us, stops, stands up then runs a little more, squirming Ferris in his seat as he swallows protective spittle and likely to sain himself against his orange grain in lieu of spitting out as Ana looks at me and whispers god-save-uz...

Why should a nervous hare be so suspected: the buddha had a hare
and it has been a sacred sign for millenia from china through the bible
to peru, painters crouching it at Mary's feet, painters also poets those
days like honest Brueghel's terrible magi and Bosch's awful prelates—no
honest radicals any more . . . (R, 507–509; disk, 411–413)

Soon in the R, Diana's journal stops.

My world or what I think is world is upsidedown or downside up in
vacant sphere of time or space which is the shape of time that causes
all effects in life and loneliness and ergo life and loneliness is time
between the minor poles of dusk at dawn and dusk and evenset and
slowly breaks us on the wheel that spins then stops then spins again,
grinding existence down to dust that blows away to nothingness and
total peace where Dea insists his Christ resides in timeless glory in
ever-resurrection.

Until that time or timelessness I'll never know. . . The everlasting
never never never when time is nevermore (R, 596; R disk, 493).

O'Dea is called out on a pastoral errand. Leaving the parsonage and
the tea Ana prepares for her, Diana wanders distractedly into the pasture
and into the jeopardy of the tinkers' camp near the river. A third-person
narrator—either her freely conjecturing offspring (the author of the
novel according to some pseudonyms), or an arbitrary omniscience, a
vividly descriptive and aurally keen persona of West—completes the
tale. In the early sections West employs a simple past tense; in later ones
he adopts a dramatic present. Diana reviews the fixed focus of O'Dea's
temperament, so contrastive to her own, and yet the complementarity
of their individual natures. Singly or married, they nevertheless fall short
of the necessary spiritual evolution. This limited progress remains West's
point. The baby survives, the produced child perhaps their most measurable contribution toward the "becoming" dynamic. The necessary
karmic process goes on. (See the appendix for the conclusion to Actaeon
in the R version.)

The Actaeon onion-skin typescripts sit on the copier in West's London study, 1989. PHOTO BY JOHN M. EYLER.

So West describes individual and social progress. The Denis Dempseys of the world will enjoy, alas, a long ascendancy. Yet he offers clues for economic, civic, spiritual, and cultural advancement and tries to establish supportive continuities for the future with the past. The sheer bulk of the Actaeon effort (the stack of onionskin pages stood floor to table high in the sorting), the many revisions over six decades, and the evolution of the telling itself, show the writer struggling again and again for the best way to make this vision intelligible, to "agree"—as he would transitively cast the verb—the idea and the form. Neither prophet nor artist can retire the quest. West, like the Ancient Mariner, held a purpose that was both artistic and spiritual. He was keenly aware that if he, too, were to grow old in the reiterative, unsuccessful effort, he must accept this karmic fate.

ENDNOTES

1   Maurice Leitch's "Other People" included West in a seven-minute segment 1
    September 1965. British Broadcasting Company.

2   ACW in interview with Meirion Edwards 29 April 1970, BBC.

3   ACW to Timothy O'Keeffe, early March, 1963?

4   ACW to Charles Davy, 3 November 1965.

5   West tells Davy he is "not an article man," 3 November 1965. He did not retain
    copies of as many of his own letters to Charles Davy as seems to have been his
    usual practice, though Davy's habit of responding point-by-point to his correspon-
    dent's letter often indicates West's content. Unfortunately, Davy's collection of
    their letters has not been saved, according to Davy's son, Richard (RD to ASE,
    16 May 1995).

6   EJ to ACW, 1968 or 1970? Professional reviewers can sound just as clueless: ".
    . . The life of Christopher MacMannan makes escapeful reading. The author
    overwrites a bit, but at least you know where you are and what the place looks
    like. . . . " *Pittsburgh Press*, 22 March 1970.

7   O'Brien, 30.

8   This fragment bears a Dublin address, 7 Eldon Terrace, South Circular Road,
    which West probably held briefly before the War. It was later crossed out and
    replaced with 56 Meyrick Park, Belfast, where he and Olive lived in 1941.

9   Box 13, page once numbered 6y. West introduces the topic of race in some stories
    set in America, Embryon, for example. He mentioned that he was indebted to a
    black man in America for saving his life, in a "Questionaire [sic] on Anthony C.
    West," [c. 1980]: Did I ask him why was he a negro? No, I did not. I kissed him."

10 Novelist Jack Cady deplores the critical expectation that a writer's language
    should conform to the reader's contemporary, politically correct usage, *The
    American Writer* (New York: St. Martin's Press, 1999), pp. 144–145. West includes
    "pansy" in the vocabulary in "The Upper Room," wherein the narrator also dis-
    parages "bum-boys." In the next decade after his story's first publication, how-
    ever, he read Maurice Leitch's *Liberty Lad* with great respect and appreciation,
    sending Leitch a ten-page, studied response to the book, 8 December 1965. West
    registers no special sympathy, personal or political, with its homosexual subject.

11 The M versions may be late-eighties attempts to rewrite the short story that Obo-
    lensky saw in the fifties.

12 ACW in taped interview with Audrey Eyler, July, 1986.

Chapter Nine

1980 MALCOLM CLOSE: NEEDING NO BOEING NOR ROCKET

As he had dreamed aloud to Christine Countess of Longford, West did consider going back to Ireland. In June of 1977 on a trip to Belfast to see his sister Dorothy, he had enjoyed a welcome from a number of Irish writers and supporters of the arts, North and South, whom he admired: Michael Longley, Seamus Heaney, John Kilfeather, who later, in 1983, called West William Carleton's truest descendant and the North's most important contemporary writer,[1] Roy McFadden, Peter Fallon, David Marcus, John Boyd, Ted Hickey and Elizabeth Crum, and John Hewitt among them. With some of them he had occasional reasons to correspond. Hewitt showed him Jack Foster's extended and gratifying assessment of West's work in *Forces and Themes of Ulster Fiction* (1974). In 1981 West was elected to the Irish academy of artists, "Aosdana."

Other encouragements — invitations, miscellaneous publications like the Irish Arts Council's printing of "An Irish Bull" in *Drumlin* or the 1984 *Dictionary of Literary Biography Yearbook*'s solicitation of West's tribute to Liam O'Flaherty affirmed to him a respected literary identity. The Irish reissuings of his early fiction made him appreciative of home as well as hopeful about unpublished typescripts. Poolbeg Press came out with another *River's End* as *All The King's Horses*, "The Monocrats" and "The Upper Room" being discarded and "All The King's Horses" being joined with the others: "River's End," "Not Isaac," "The Turning Page" (the retelling of "Myself and Some Ducks"), "Song of the Barrow," "Narcissus unto Echo," and "No Fatted Calf." By mid-decade there was a gratifying reissue of *The Ferret Fancier* by O'Brien (1983) as well as a paperback by Blackstaff (1985) of *As Towns with Fire*.[2] Despite these successes, however, there seemed to be financial preclusion to publishing any new and lengthy works.

MacGibbon & Kee, who had published the original *Towns* in 1968 and had also accepted Naked to Laughter,[3] agreed back in the early seventies to publish The Casual Comedy, if they could they share costs with an American counterpart. When Simon and Schuster decided against the long typescript, MacGibbon withdrew. In the spring of 1978 Comedy's appearance was still expected, however, and *The Honest Ulsterman* published an excerpt in anticipation.[4]

Howard Samuel at MacGibbon & Kee had been enthusiastic about West's work, but with the organizational change following his accidental death, the interest in it diminished. Still, letters show that someone at what had become Hart-Davis MacGibbon retained hope of a cooperative publishing of The Casual Comedy as late as 1981. The correspondence goes on between West and a variety of editors or representatives. Tim O'Keeffe, with whom he kept in touch until at least 1980, had left the company in the mid-sixties. In April 1981, however, West responded to a Miss Parkin:

> . . . *Despite the praise of your critic, after so long a lapse since doing that MS, I'm seeing/thinking many flaws and misses, especially around the Jonty character; also the lack of folk-matter, which in 1920 was almost Iro-Tudor, before wireless, TV, and EEC. I would like to re-write quickly, cutting here and there, tightening and inserting a little and if the book's as good as your critic's opinion, it is worth this extra effort.*

He asked to withdraw The Casual Comedy for some months.

West had paid off what indebtedness existed from advancements and courtesies. He was retrieving his copyrights and manuscripts: The

Casual Comedy, Naked to Laughter, and The Mowin' Man, a long, "wild attempt to get away from the he-said-she-said"[5]. This effort corroborates posited dates for that momentous switch that occurred in the narrative arrangements for the Actaeon story: He may well at 61 have been thinking his "lively" days were running out, but the agility of his imagination in assuming Diana Hauley's perspective and adopting her first-person narration, in the last decade and a half of his life, was keen. The I version, marked "Done again, 1977" took on a new vitality, and her persona as well as O'Dea's became convincing.

Basically, West was blessed with good health. In 1954 he had weathered a severe bout with pleurisy, and it is true that he was prone to migraine headaches. For a time in the sixties he had been feeling especially low and had written a naturopathic doctor for help, confessing that he knew he should quit (he never did—shreds of Golden Virginia were strewn throughout the typescripts) the "four ounces" of tobacco he was rolling for himself every week, but he hoped for some additional relief for what he described as a "dullness." Some earlier Weleda prescription and anadins (perhaps the iron supplement and honey he refers to in a letter to a Dr. Krause[6]) were not doing the job. He was keenly tuned to a relationship between his artistic production and his body, and had long ago abandoned alcohol.

> Big meals heavy me unbearably, and I can only work into the artistic sphere on an empty stomach, until I get dizzy and tired. . . . I often get migraine, although not so often as heretofore. (I do an arm-exercise every morning). As usual, ideas come down thick and fast before an attack, none of which are very violent.[7]

He noticed a further distinction between his philosophical and his creative self. In the former, he felt "quite wide awake." It wasn't a shortage of ideas, but an inability to "satisfactorily incarnate them . . . an odd feeling of impotence." Nor did he feel deprived of "actual writing energy." He confessed that the long period of "financial insecurity, which affects the family more directly than it does me, . . . [nevertheless] saps my creative drive." He had repeated the message he would reiterate throughout the years when there were dependent children and hope for a consistent market.

> *I may have certain things to say to this generation that could be of some value . . . I'm quite willing to flog myself for the next twenty years. I assure you I'm not after temporal fame and fortune. I just want a living so I can keep on writing till I disincarnate again.*[8]

West had considered some of the educational options through which writers conventionally financed and promoted their art. The ur suggests that as a very young man West may have tried oral presentation and that he early confronted the loss of credibility in having no formal degree.

Generously they applauded and the curate blew his nose and stood up, thanking Stephen for a novel and entertaining evening and feeling sure all had greatly enjoyed the talk and that to him personally it was a privilege to be given the opportunity to listen to a brilliant interpretation of an old folk-tale presented in an unorthodox and lively manner and that they should as a result know more about the ways of the devil and as Stephen had said, the devil known is better than the devil unknown.

He then said a brief closing prayer and the club members scuffled out. . . .

Hamilton was obviously and genuinely impressed by Stephen's range, asking him if he had taken a degree.

"No more'n Adam," Stephen said. "Sweat and thistles!"

"Ha, very interesting," Hamilton commented, withdrawing himself at once from knowledge not bought over legitimate counters.

Stephen could not blame him, thinking that the political world alone was sniving with half-feathered thinkers who climbed the cliff of fame on steps cut by their tongues' tireless activity, quite apart from the sense in what they said. But he had tasted the warmth of a unified faith, naive as it was; it had governed his early childhood when life had been warm and whole and each day a new day........

"Well," he explained, "some men collect postage stamps, some old books, some women, some money—this sort of stuff is my spare-time work" (Fox in a Trap, a story excised from Room without a Door, #2B: 243, 244).

When the Welsh Arts Council invited him to participate in a writers-in-the-schools program,[9] however, West had explained that he'd like to assist "serious, would-be writers," but because he'd like to "get down to the literary bone. . . scores of other men much more competent and informed . . . [would be better able] to discuss general literary trends and past and current productions."[10]

Late in his career he had considered being a writer-in-residence at a university. By the end of the sixties his artistic achievement and his self-confidence had been established enough for him to apply for a University of Wales Gregynog Fellowship at Aberystwyth and for a short term at Berkeley. Neither materialized, but both applications show his typically modest proffering of his own ability and achievement. He told the warden at Gregynog that his present work might be his "major opus or, possibly, [his] major flopus." He said he could not "expect that my kind of writing will make much money, at least, not while I'm alive. I have never compromised by writing with one eye on the 'big time.'"[11]

To Professor Thomas Parkinson, West identified himself as

one who has little or no writer-pride in the general sense . . . [but who] seem[s] to have a genuine if small name in the US, in England, and in Germany. I know enough to know that I've still much to learn and any contact with keen open students would probably benefit me more than it might benefit them."[12]

Parkinson eventually turned him down, saying the reduced budget and the commitment to establish an ethnic balance on the staff precluded their bringing West in for a term.[13]

In 1970, talking with Meirion Edwards on BBC Radio 4[14] about his life and writing, West had described his chosen insecurity as a necessary fortifying against the "hedonism of the artist": "I need the worry, I need to be near the wall. . . . I have to be the hungry fighter all the time, otherwise I won't fight." A little less worry about finances would, nevertheless, have been a relief, to body if not to soul, and a university term could have provided stimulating contacts and encouragement as well.

He was still vigorous enough in the beginning of his last decade and trusting enough of his capacity for physical labor, however, that the old hope of establishing a cooperative farm had not died. In the early to middle years of the sixties West had been involved in a "green island" plan whose dissolution now seems paradigmatic. The letters exchanged with Baroness Uslar about her estate, Paradise House in Gloucestershire, illustrate some features of the pattern familiar after the Elin case. At first the situation, as the correspondence describes it, looks promising. The baroness has land with buildings, money, and anthroposophical sympathies, but West explains to her that the timing for him is not right. She persuades him, nevertheless, to advise her about the property and some charitable disposition of it and even to become a board member for the Trust she wishes to establish for its future. Recommending a builder to her, as well as a Welsh couple whom he trusted to manage the place,[15] West offers advice and cautiously explores board membership. In the letters he describes his own dreams (did ever an artist so extol a midden?).

> . . . *Every effort should be made to establish a head of compost—say, ten tons to the acre and further, to establish a year's compost in the 'bank.' For this you need one person to be conscious of it, one who will do the sprays and take responsibility and who should be equipped with all necessary mechanical aids. He must know all the various methods for handling the different manures and plant residues. Much of this has been done in Germany and merely means that the established methods be studied. There should be composts for grassland, for root-crops, etc., and special therapeutic composts for sick areas. The compost yard is the first thing. It must be made a living and organic radiating centre for the whole farm.*[16]

The letters to Uslar show again the karmic patience of his efforts as idealistic reformer, farmer, and writer.

> *Ideally, I would like to obtain, say, 150 acres of neglected land . . . and*

build it up. This implies the need for a considerable capital sum to cover
the building-up years, quite apart from the high costs of stock and equip-
ment. I can recruit suitable people but I would not consent to move until
I could reasonably foresee at least four or five years ahead, and hope
to conclude successfully the first rhythmic seven years. Seven is a key
number in farming. I'm 53 now and I can't work as hard as I did after the
war although, thank God, I'm still very fit.[17]

An earlier paragraph reveals sources of some of his judicious skepticism:

Confidentially: (I don't want to add more critical fuel to the general fire
of inside gossip in the Society.) My opinion of so-called attempts by the
various B/D pundits over the past 20 years is very low. On several occa-
sions I tried hard to work creatively and as selflessly as I could but ulti-
mately, I was always frustrated by egotisms and personalities who could
afford to keep a foot in the bourgeois camp while dipping the other one
in vaguely general Anthroposophy. X was just hopeless, almost pathetic.
He even had the nerve to tell me that Y's Farm was the only BD farm in
Britain; while Y told me himself that he had compromised, using igno-
rant paid labour and artificals. I think that Z was a paranoic—he had
had access to thousands of pounds at one time and wasted them. Miss Z
of King's Langley seemed the only one with, at least, the right attitudes,
and her separate B/D foundation, before the merger, was much better
than X's bland journalistic approach. (She offered me, incidentally, the
Kings Langley property in 1950, but I couldn't accept because I could
see no way to finance it and keep it going; and in any case her acreage
was much too small. I suggested to Dr. Heidenreich [CC priest] that he
should take it over for the Community. . . .

I'll move immediately I see a clear way, but if I can't do it this life,
then (DV) I'll do it in the next one![18]

West was very experienced with people and their utopian projects by
this time,[19] and while he carefully preserved his vision, he simultaneously
and consistently demonstrated his idiosyncratic toughness and practical
expertise.

*Out of what experience I've managed to collect over these anxious years I
will never now say much different to the following: A projected BD farm,
of any size, must have sufficient capital to cover everything for the first
three years. This has been one of the weaknesses in many English undertakings: big plans but capital only sufficient to get started and thereafter,
compromise after compromise until final defeat. The Agricultural Course
is also one of Steiner's profoundest social documents, I believe, and so
one must try to establish a full and fraternal association from the very
beginning. This has been the second weakness in many attempts—the
full use of people but only half the human responsibility on the part of
the initiators. . . .*

*Understudies should also be immediately established and all knowl-
edge and experience should be discussed and shared since no one knows
the day and the hour. The first big cycle to be slowly established is one
of seven years and if the first three years are carefully managed, income
should be there on the fourth. I do not accept the excuse that BD is
uneconomic in these times. That is a fable convenue put out by folk with
one foot in artificials and the other in a bank overdraft. To my knowledge, I don't think there is one full B/D farm in England.*

*N___ started his experiment with £50,000 and lost £20,000 he says
on the farm, over about nine or ten years, altho' he still seems all right
with his investments. I told him way back to get the human thing right
and to build up the compost but he knew better—to £20,000 worth! I
have no longer the patience to deal with such people.*

*Herbs, shrubs, trees and overall ecology must firstly be seen to and
if even one person 'listens' to a place over three years, he will begin to
have his doubts and queries answered. There is no capital in farming
save fertility. Worms must be encouraged and worm-cultures established.
Accounts must be kept and a full record of development daily written
and all the people concerned must be kept aware of the finances. It's no
use having big crops against a background of human frustration and
discontent. The Luciferic/Ahrimanic element, the one these times have to
reckon with, can only attack through the human element, and therefore,
one must be sure as far as possible that the people concerned are reasonably happy.*

Wages as such wouldn't be paid, rather a living allowance according to need, profits to be ultimately shared, with a proviso that a fund be created out of profits to further more developments, perhaps on other farms. The whole person must be taken up in a kind of marriage and a real community created.

If ever I get any capital, this is the way I'll try and do it. A green island, as Pfeiffer [an Anthroposophist leader] said, which would if possible, include school and church, every 'cultural' aspect in agriculture recognized. I think, D[eo] V[olente], I could do it, using every modern aid and trick of the trade and I'd like to write the first seven years up with photographs and graphs and . . . analyses. We know now how the bacteria work in cycles and we know that if the soil temperature can be raised by even one degree that growth becomes earlier and later, the growing season extended. Even outside BD there is a wealth of uncoordinated knowledge.

Hasten slowly as, I believe, Goethe said: three years working on to the first seven. The implication is, in failed or half-failed BD'ers, that Dr. Steiner was in this not quite economic, and I know he never, never disregarded the economic factor in human life. He recognized the value of materialism, as such.

Cropping is easy: British farming in a reasonable locality is easy. Stock-keeping is more hazardous, since it enters into the astral life and you'd need a wise and patient man for this.

It should be possible that after seven years of devoted work, a sabbatical year rhythm be established whereby one person or family could have a year's holiday to travel and to collect more knowledge and information.

I'm not being idealistic. I'm being hard-headed and practical, malice to none. This is my ideal but God knows if and when I'll ever be able to bring it about. I would look for a derelict place of sufficient size and try and recruit at least one competent carpenter. Ahriman strikes at us through capital shortage. Let me know your reactions sometime. Godbless.[20]

The baroness seems to have been soundly impressed, at least in their early exchanges. She wrote him of her pleasant surprise that a bearded artist could be so unpretentious, practical, and a man with whom "one could pray."²¹ That was before she began her apparently typical changing of mind, and before the construction began to require expenditure she would not pay. A terrible rift developed between her and her builder. Jesus' special tie with carpenters not withstanding, the rapport between Uslar and the young craftsman whom West recommended grew brittle, and by November 27, West was offering to arbitrate.

West wrote immediately to the couple he had also recommended for the market-gardening and farming positions to warn them, urging them to keep their "doors open [to] avoid heartbreaks."

> *I see the whole thing clearly; the confusion between mere personal ideas and Steiner ideas, the former the really operative ones and the latter merely oil to remove some of the inevitable friction. This is not Anthroposophy, this is common split-mindedness, but the difficulty is, when working with it, that one never knows which horse is being exercised. . . .*
>
> *I had very similar problems in Ardleigh and I thought at one time I could just ignore them and convince the ____s that the only way to do hard work was to work hard. But this became, actually, an embarrassment to them. They had an income and were bored and only wanted some ritual work and a lot of talk. [Another patron/employer?] was similar: everything was expensive, wages were high, work was long and yet, the whole family could fly out to Europe for a mountain holiday. To see energy and some idealism just being used like an old sack can eventually be frustrating and heartbreaking.²²*

Another matter had developed, however, to reduce West's persuasiveness with the baroness. She had just read "River's End", and apparently finding its sexuality too explicit and its language too vulgar, had raised criticisms West would not accept. West's response was unusually full. The incident and the response underline at more than one level the integral relationship between West's art and life. They show, obviously, that at the practical level, the published fiction affected the acceptability to his employer of the agricultural consultant. They also emphasize that although he wrote with an intention to alert moral responsibility, he refused with moral fervor to be programmatic and proselytizing; he respected an incompatibility of art and philosophy. Finally they show West acknowledging an impossibility for an artistic neutrality, given, as he also describes in this response, the use to an anthroposophical "clair-cognative" like himself of words and "the 'naming' of ideas [as] a kind of religious exercise."

It is a fact that a writer should be the last person to defend his own work—a published story is a kind of foundling, a kind of crust cast upon the waters.

Someone has said, wisely enough: realism is not showing real things, but in showing things as they are. As a now established twentieth-century writer, I am committed to challenging our shocking social attitudes and, relative to my talent, the only way I can do this is realistically to describe these mental/physical attitudes and to try to point to their moral effects. I do try, whenever possible (literature and philosophy being two different functions and, indeed, art-wise, enemies) to insert the thin end of the anthroposophical wedge. On the other hand, I refuse to plagiarize Anthroposophy, as I suspect many would-be poets and writers are doing, using Dr. Steiner's high inititate precepts in a merely intellectual and spiritually inexperienced way.

I do accept your criticism on the values you give it, but I couldn't accept it as a generally valid criticism for many reasons—which would take five more pages to enumerate. Making due allowance for one's consciousness and limitations, one can, at best, only try to begin to build a kind of bridge towards the in-coming pneumatological and etheric consciousness of our increasingly Michaelic age. You quoted the opinions of a man of 80, and also of a 30-yr-old spinster. Well and good, they are entitled to their opinion, but nevertheless, I'd have to talk to them in order to find out just how experienced they are in the minor art of criti-cism/appreciation, in light of their general experience and psychological content. I'd be inclined to say that any serious work must, to be valid at all, mean all things to all men, its impact relative to the observer's . . . experience. . . .

As a professional writer, one is always between the devil and deep

sea, the onus being that, to exist at all, one has firstly to attract and
please a publisher, while trying not to lose one's soul. . . .
    Although the Freud [influenced] critics praised these stories on
their face value, I as writer, had intended them to be a direct criticism
of our common ways and values and manners, and of the destructive
influence that one generation sees fit to inflict upon the next: (the sins of
the parents spreading over the generations!) And, in the main, sexually-
speaking, I didn't think I'd gone beyond say, Chaucer, the myths, Shake-
speare, and even the Bible.[23]

He withdrew from Baroness Uslar's project, as he had from others
and would do again, yet bio-dynamic farming remained an approach
he insisted could work, no matter how many times he had been disappointed. In the next decade, West wrote to Charles Davy about human
and agricultural lessons learned:

Michael Hall wrote me, asking me down. I returned a 'passive' reply,
since at this point how [could] anyone concerned . . . afford to capitalize
what I might envisage, community-wise; and I'm 61 this year and can't
expect to be lively for much longer.[24]

I've worked on several places where the 'whole man' was wanted, but was
only finally recognized for his 'elbow grease.' . . . Duffy, for instance,
when he had the backing of Lord Glentanar, in Aberdeen, employed a
hard core of Scottish labourers under a hard, practical, wage-earning
bailiff, plus a scatter of ill-used students. Even that didn't work and Glen-
tanar pulled out, which was a great pity, although between us, Duffy
was a very strange man, god rest his soul. I feel that it just isn't enough
to look at soil and plant anthroposophically—the human being who is
concerned must be apprehended anthroposophically as well. If the right
kind of consciousness is created in such an agricultural enclave, and if
the people concerned protect the idea of the continuity then, granting
the necessary skills, good BD farming must result, along with a sense of
human fulfillment and progress. And if all the factors, human and prac-
tical, are kept in balance, the result must be economic. I pin my faith on

the creative, constructive potentials in human association.[25]

My father likes my help and company. Sometimes he talks about the land and that we could manage, were we to buy a few more acres. I don't encourage him. I love the land, he doesn't, except as a possession, as a miser can only see gold's colour as an attribute of value. He uses the land as a source of vegetable and animal product to satisfy his living needs, much as one would use a whore. Like all the others, he sows a few shillings and reaps a few pounds, the cackle of a laying hen and the noble mating of a bull are cash considerations and, like all the others, he also works because he is scared of going bankrupt, socially and financially. (As *Towns with Fire*, Blackstaff, 61)

Up in the hills, watching his own small movement against the titan-molded boulders dropped there by ancient ice: great rocks as skulls, bones of the dying earth flensed by fierce weathers. The blessed hills do not demand understanding. The sun melts behind the crests, dropping dull cassius shadow in the lee and away to the north the Donegal uplands move slowly to the sky, the sun slashing last-lost wastes of light across the pits of brown shadow, dusk flowing into the low valleys. . . . Pale potato faces with slow eyes. . . . You womb-wet bastards! Off the diddy, onto the bottle! Have your free pees in exchange for costly liquids! But I will go and find a spade and I will start walking till I come to a green field and I will dig in it. . . .(*The Native Moment*, 85)

In the mid-seventies, the Wests had finally initiated formal plans for a cooperative community and proceeded with legal organization. A statement drafted 18 April 1972 explains that the "West Project has been simmering for at least twenty-five years" and may now be "coming to a boil." Ability, rather than status, would determine assignments and authority, experts immediately taking on understudies; remuneration, "based on actual needs and given in cash and kind," would be determined by discussion and consensus. They aimed at fraternity without paternalism.[26] The Wests, with Ormond and Irene Edwards, along with Ormond's friend Michael Dixon, planned in 1973 to pool capital and make an application for the Artos Association to be eventually a self-supporting, non-hierarchic group, possibly with a Christian Community center under the same roof; it would maintain a market-garden and a small farm. For a while it looked as though they might obtain a Franciscan monastery in Essex sixty miles east of London.[27] They talked of fostering twenty-five teenagers, helping them into adulthood with responsibilities and guidance. Key staff would include "farmer, market-gardener, builder-handyman, housekeeper/cook, bookkeeper (the books must be dead accurate), plus semi- and unskilled help, temporary or permanent."[28] They had tried to activate their Artos plan with the old monastery, but the hopes for the Essex priory fell through. Finally, in 1975 the Artos Agricultural and Housing Association Limited was incorporated 26 November, its solicitors Royds Barfield, 46 Bedford Square in London. The Artos Biocrafts and Trading, Limited, with R. Williams Asquith & Company in Gwynedd as its accountants, listed Anthony C. West as its acting organizer. The ARTOS "Preliminary Statement"[29] explains that

> Anthony and Olive West have recently sold their business and are, consequently, relatively free at the present time. They both have considerable experience in idealistic ventures and in commercial trading: Anthony West is experienced in farm management and in organic farming. They have given the Charity some capital, in the form of building land [its potential value listed as £10,000]. And it has been suggested that, initially at any rate, they assume direction of the Enterprise, apart from being Sponsors of the Charity.
>
> The scheme is intended to be a creative, practical and self-subsistent attempt in living-together. There will be no hidden clauses, all aspects and issues openly discussed, all opinions respected for their relative validity. Nor will there be any racial nor sectarian overtones.[30]

Apart from the recognizable detailing of "three independent /interdependent realms or spheres . . . the cultural/religious; the rights/justice; and the economic," these applying to individuals as well, there is no stated allegiance to any idea that is identifiably and exclusively anthroposophical or Christian Communal. Artos's (the term is Greek for "bread")

"Preliminary Statement" used almost no anthroposophically specialized vocabulary; the group recruited known anthroposophists and members of the Christian Community because they already tended to share such sympathies.[31] Yet anyone with the appropriate resources and compatible sentiments would have found a warm reception. There is no mention of religion; the premise that "human beings can be most content and productive when their common needs are met and their unique contributions as individuals thankfully acknowledged" promoted wide inclusiveness. The group wanted

> non-exploitative autonomy, shar[ed] work and pool[ed] skills under an agreed system of rights that . . . guarantee[d] cultural freedom . . . [that] allow[ed] the individual genius to benefit all: in short, co-operative responsibility instead of the prerogatives of power.

Moving from Wales in 1975, the Wests went to a place that Michael owned, 102 Ballingdon Street in Sudbury, Suffolk. There they continued to nourish their plan to develop the Artos community. West steadily hoped for an opening where his agricultural dream might be applied, even as he realized an increasing limitation on his own participation. In 1977 Olive purchased a whole foods shop in Battersea, the Wests living above the shop itself. In 1982 she signed it over, like the Wales properties, to Artos. West was not ready to abandon his green dream.

He engaged in yet one more big effort to establish a co-operative farm. Late in 1979 he writes Davy from Wales[32] that he is exploring the possibility of Artos's joining Barbara Sinclair's place, "Llwyn Teg," with the Anthony Mathews farm, Artos supplying the necessary capital. A year later, he writes that he is again building compost in Wales, and Davy wishes him well on this farm project.[33] Although he has endured many disappointments with people and their plans to live communally, his talk about the land varies little between the 1980s and the 1940s.

> I came down here [Carmarthen, Dyfed, Wales] in August and have worked seven days a week ever since, just working eating sleeping, which is therapeutic. I'm pretty fit again and back to my usual ten stone.[34]

> ... I have evolved a very personal philosophy covering my relation-
> ship to the soil, with malice to none, but therein I am practical, not
> mystical. I can do most jobs on a farm from milking cows to mainte-
> nance. My Met experience in the RAF, for which I had to do an intensive
> course, convinced me that farming started with the subsoil and ended
> somewhere above the tops of our loftiest clouds. I am dead scared that our
> individualistic land heritage may drift into the maw of land nationaliza-
> tion.[35]
>
> I like farming. I tried to bring back no-longer operated farms to a
> state of fertility. You read a lot about agriculture and the way the world
> is going now: the ecology is being ruined, and all these entrepreneurs are
> just making a fast buck. I knew what was happening before the War. The
> arid steppes were increasing into the Ukraine; they had no respect for the
> earth—or the fish, or the whales. Not Communism, not Reaganism—the
> real thing is the food element. The land is all we've got, really.[36]

"Llwyn Teg" as it turned out, wasn't any closer to his ideal. The
Wests had put the Battersea shop up for sale in order to give Sinclair and
others a chance. They hoped something would grow from their effort,
but by March 1981, West was concurring with Davy that the times were
not yet right for the three-fold social scheme: "I'm beginning to feel now
that all my hammering at this idea may have to keep till the next time."[37]

It is hard to be sure exactly how many times they went through similar disappointment. The record in the seventies alone would have been
discouraging: Charles Davy had sent West his sympathy on 5 December
1973 when negotiation for the project in Essex had failed. On 29 July
'74 Davy expresses his hope that Artos will succeed in taking on Kings
Langley Priory, a place which had been offered to West back in 1950,
but which he had then been unable to afford.[38] A letter early in the new
year, 26 January 1975, includes Davy's good wishes on the progress of a
communal scheme, the Sudbury project in Suffolk, which again didn't
materialize.

In 1982 West sailed once more to Ireland, this time with Jocelyn and
Simon, for reunion with the one remaining member of his immediate
family, his sister Dorothy. The dream to move back to Irish soil gradually

West visiting Donegal, 1982. WEST FAMILY COLLECTION, PHOTOGRAPHER
UNKNOWN.

faded with his health. He had expressed an intention to find a botan near
the sea in Wexford or Cork,[39] but a slight stroke in 1981 had intervened.
The Wests moved back to London. He would not, as it turned out, move
again. He offered sympathy to Davy for Doris Davy's illness and en route
to generalized comments about their recent, again disappointing experience in Wales, he alluded to his own new caution.

> *It is an odd feeling after a lifetime of taking it for granted when this old
> body refuses to obey one. I had a slight experience of this in July, which
> taught me more respect for all the subtle balances and connections that
> work for long years, until. . . . It's a comforting thought . . . that physical
> loss can be spiritual gain. Even so, it is neither simple nor comfortable,
> and when one observes the young ones burgeoning into life, one envies
> them their great days, remembering, seeing oneself in careless springs
> when the earth was new again and life only for the living of it. . . .*
>
> *The Threefold awareness would have given us a legitimate means
> to develop without the inevitable bickering and personal (egotistic)
> opinionations that still bedevil groups who come together, albeit with all*

the good will in the world. Unfortunately, we could never bring it into operation.[40]

Never one to lament what couldn't be changed about his circumstances, he accepted the grim contrast. His chair in the sitting room afforded an axle-high view of the sidewalk in the Oakfield Road off the Penge High Street. His window-wells filled with the litter dropped by passers-by, and his ears were all day assaulted by the belching and grinding of trade lorries. Corncrakes and curlews, alas. Yet he told Olive shortly before he died it was all right; this was where he was content to be. As he had once explained to Tim O'Keeffe,

> *. . . I wouldn't be expecting the change in environment to decrease my own insufficiencies or insights. I walk through the world every day, anyway. . . . The soul doesn't need a Boeing or a rocket.[41]*

He continued to write, and while necessarily detaching himself from any more such projects, he still held out hope for cooperatives, not counting as losses the Wests' own investments of personal acquisitions and land. Until the early eighties the Wests were trying to sell the Artos Charity's North Wales building lots: 3 and ½ acres with full planning permission for 32 dwellings and the Charity was asking £29,000."[42] On 23 August 1982 West wrote Charles Davy,

> *Confidential for the moment: we have managed at long last to sell the Welsh Building lots, and Olive signed over the Battersea shop and freehold to the Charity prior to sale. The Charity will soon have about 50,000 pounds in hand, once all debts are paid. Unfortunately, it is not sufficient to buy a farm and we'll have to decide how best to use the money in some other way.*

Artos remained a legal entity after West's death, and Olive, along with other members, continued to explore its possibilities.

> *. . .I gather up the tools as he walks back to the house. . . . With my*

West at his desk in Malcolm Close, 1983.
WEST FAMILY COLLECTION, PHOTOGRAPHER UNKNOWN.

back to the sun I look across the drowning parish, all the little hills and copses shining joyously in the light's lee, the barrier shadows thickening behind them. The beauty of it heals the loneliness he left with me and makes me strong again. It doesn't much matter what people say or, even, how they say it (*As Towns with Fire*, Blackstaff, 63).

The land was lovely, the shapely well-fed trees proclaiming its long fertility: no trees like this in Ireland except around landlords' asylums. It was odd how the remnant Celt seemed quite indifferent to the poems that were trees when once they had been sacred and untouchable things: arboriculture—one of the few activities for which the landlord deserved some gratitude.

  . . . This patient land would take its darkening days, life dying away under great star-sighing nights, naked to frost's fierce possession, flat field and rim of flying hill sculpted in stellar snows and yet still lovely, composing landscaped lines to make each separate scene a masterpiece. This atmosphere of England, this noumenon, so real it was almost tangible, seen. Touch soil and hear history (*As Towns with Fire*, Blackstaff, 374–375).

He worked in the garden when he had light for the relief it gave him. Molly was surprised at his skill. Some folk are born with spoons in their mouths, he said. I was born with this, instead. He held up the spade. Culture's first instrument and maybe, even, the final one, when all these swashers have buckled themselves out of existence (*As Towns with Fire*, Blackstaff, 452).

As his health diminished, West saved his energy for his prose. In 1984, bending to kiss Olive goodnight, the farmer-novelist slipped on a glossy magazine,[43] fell, and fractured the head of his left femur. The accident put him in hospital for surgery to insert a supporting plate. It took a year to recover from this setback, and he coped with residual pain and lameness thereafter.[44] An even bigger blow came that same year to the Wests. In December their second son, Jeremy, severely depressed, ended his life by jumping from his London window. To West the experience that began after life was

> the joining of ninety to ten percent, the vast expansive experience of creation, beginning with life's retrospect and increasing to 'nebular' consciousness. . . . The first impact of the 'ninety per cent' is rather like a confused dream, before all the life's images settle into order. And there's this moment, eternity, of great remorse, even in normal death, for which no word has been coined: suicides have a frightful time; hanged criminals almost as bad since, in one way, they are also suicides, inasmuch as they knew they'd be hanged for certain actions, and they have betrayed their humanity by the supreme act of egotism, whatever the circumstances. God is not the judge—we judge ourselves.[45]

Through the measure of his writing life that was devoted to presenting resurrection, lies also some gauge of such grief as he must have confronted. Confined now to the house by his own ill-health, and stricken with this news, West remained, nevertheless, at the typewriter,

West being interviewed in 1988, Malcolm Close.
PHOTOGRAPHER, JOHN M. EYLER.

revising still The Casual Comedy and The Lady Actaeon. Four years later, both were on his desk when he died.

A friend, Fazil, from Iraq and his Danish wife, Inge, whom West met in the sixties at the Bangor University campus, remembered him with affection and hoped in 1988 that West might turn his long study of gnosticism into a formal book.

Thanks for generous cheque. It arrived in the nick of time for I'm forced to buy an expensive electric typewriter in the hope that it will improve my typing which has deteriorated over the last seven years due to the effect of a partial stroke in 1981, which was due to overwork, worry and self-neglect in Wales...I have a long MS of what is my last novel to type.

I'm 78 this July and am coming to the end of this life. My mind is still unaffected, thank God, and I sleep and eat well, even if I do have to hobble about on sticks.[46]

In the first place, Inge, I fear you overestimate my abilities. I wouldn't be much use to Mr. Mann. From his view point, I do not profess to be an intellectual academic. I am, at best, a self-taught creative artist with certain random intuitions based on the ideal of tolerance and independent self, who tries to look and live and let live, malice to none. . . freedom of thought for all, although I still become angry at man's inhumanity to man which, in the long run, is always negative and time-consuming, despite the propaganda in apparent justification.

In the second place, I'm now approaching the end of this particular tether. I have already outlived my allotted span.[47]

Cathcart Anthony Muir West died of heart failure in his study at Malcolm Close in London, 19 November 1988.[48] Olive had gone out for groceries. Enlightened and artistic changes are discernible in West's writing over the decades as he experiments with narrative techniques and as he makes an equal place in his art for women, but his quest, his spiritual commitment, steadily reinforced by these efforts, was undeterred. His statement at the break-through point of his writing career in the late fifties, with an emending of the number of children, could have been the same in 1988:

I'm a writer. Fiction. Trying, I suppose, to bridge this widening gap between mere subjective 'fiction' and true fiction, in the sense of the valid fairy story. Although I served in the past war, it taught me, finally, the witless waste of planned violence as means to ends, and I know that we'll have to spend probably the next thousand years learning . . . [that] if we are to survive, man must become christly, Christianity becoming utterly catholic, in the fullest and most liberal and in-sighted meaning of that good and harassed word, catholic. The fundamental and basic equation has never changed; modern extrapolation misnaming slow metamorphic processes as dogmatic changes, still stubbornly refusing to see, for instance, the Goethean concept of metamorphosis, as distinct from change . . .

I have nine children, sir, and now nine times I have seen that first, moving great resurrection from crawl to perpendicular: that epochic first step. That, God knows, is almost all the evidence required."[49]

ENDNOTES

1   "The Arts in Ulster," *The Belfast Review*, Winter, 1983.
2   Blackstaff kindly put my first letter through to West. I remain grateful.
3   ACW to Roger Schlesinger, Hart-Davis, MacGibbon Limited, 25 March 1977.
4   #57, 69.
5   ACW to RS, 25 March 1977.
6   ACW to Dr. Krause, Stuttgart, 22 February 1961.
7   ACW to Dr. Engel, 18 February 1963.
8   ACW to Dr. K.
9   1 July 1970, box 1, Arts II.
10   ACW to Arts Council, 6 July 1970.
11   ACW to Gregynog Fellowship committee, 1 September 1969.
12   ACW to Thomas Parkinson, 27 January 1969.
13   TP to ACW, 20/19/ [sic] 1970.
14   Wales, 29 April.
15   Mona and Garth Hatherly, to whom he dedicated the London edition of *The Ferret Fancier*.
16   ACW to Baroness Uslar, 3 July 1963.
17   ACW to BU, 17 March 1964.
18   BU to ACW, 17 March 1964.
19   In a letter of May 61 he had said to Charles Davy, *"I've had considerable contact with these high BD'ers—plenty of good warm talk but little sweat. I always tried to point out that the agricultural course was not just a packaged formula, similar to the one now printed (with trace-element content) on bags of artificial manure . . . that compost heaps just didn't grow like toadstools . . ."*
20   ACW to BU, 3 July 1963.
21   BU to ACW, 25 May 1964.
22   ACW to Garth and Mona Hatherly, 11 October 1964..
23   ACW to BU, 27 November 1964.
24   ACW to CD 5 April 1971.
25   ACW to CD, 12 October [1971?]

26 Autobiographical documents, box 1.

27 ACW to Peter [Imhoff?], 10 February 1973, Bio., Domestic, commercial corresp.

28 ACW to Andersons, 17 November 1978, Box 1, Biog.\ Aid to Friends.

29 Box 20, Artos & projects

30 Box 20, Artos & projects

31 In an earlier effort, West received a letter from associate Jeffrey Gilmin[?], 29 July [1963?] from Forest Row, Sussex, introducing his friend Leonard Sjoberg. "He has a great deal of biodynamic — farming — gardening experience . . . regarding the 3-fold aspect — He is one of us." Real Estate, box 1.

32 ACW to CD, 26 November 1979.

33 CD to ACW, 20 December. 1980.

34 ACW to Michael Longley, 3 December 1980.

35 ACW to MacDonald Hastings, Editor, *Country Fair*, 2 December 1[9]54.

36 ACW, interview with ASE, Tape#1, July 1986.

37 ACW to CD, 12 March. 1981.

38 ACW to BU, 17 March 1964.

39 ACW to C.Briain, 30 December 1981, Aosdana.

40 ACW to CD, 23 December. 1981.

41 ACW to TO'K, 20 April 1961.

42 ACW to Shaykh Fadhlallah (Haeri), 25 April 1982.

43 Miriam West supplied this sad detail, enjoying, nevertheless, the irony. She didn't say whether it was *Esquire*. Taped interview with AE, 29 July 1992.

44 ACW to Inge Haeri, 3 March 1988.

45 ACW to TO'K in a draft for his response to O'Keeffe's letter of 1 April 1961.

46 ACW to IH, 25 February 88.

47 ACW to IH, 3 March 88.

48 His body was cremated in Beckingham, and his ashes were scattered at the site. Olive West died in 2001.

49 ACW to an unidentified correspondent, page two, from a letter written between September 19, 1954 and November 1961, Autob., box 1.

CHAPTER TEN

EPILOGUE

BIOGRAPHER LYNDALL GORDON HAS SAID of the career of T. S. Eliot, "The more I found out about Eliot's life, the more it appeared that life and work were, in this poet, inseparable. For the patterning of the poetry on the familiar model of spiritual biography was reflected in a life that was, to a curious degree, patterned itself, almost as though Eliot's life were an invention complementary to his work."[1] Yeats's similar integration of life and art has been magisterially charted.[2] The appearance of such an impulse, its intensity, and its powerful consequence surely can be no surprise here. Preceding chapters of this study have demonstrated that Anthony C. West was an artist with parallel attention, purpose, and comprehensive scope. He was not imitative in method or thesis of these great fellow artists, though allusive evidence shows West knew Yeats's poetry well. Nor did West try, like Eliot, to shape his life to some aesthetic idea. West sought rather to understand the spiritual import of his experience and to wrap it, to embody it, aesthetically. To him one's life's ultimate design was divinely purposeful, if not entirely knowable, and eternal. Through fiction he steadily labored to show it, charting the universal soul's—and his own soul's—evolutionary progress. He stayed West, intent upon his quest, despite relentless personal and critical jostling. In this summary chapter we not only review the significant aspects of this evolution and the story of West's autobiographical fiction, but we also see his career more clearly in its Irish critical context.

Writers usually work for name-recognition. Especially in the earliest years of his publishing, West even tried to avoid it. Though early impelled to write, and not yet philosophically articulate about the threat of ego, he seems never to have been motivated by personal vanity. Ironically, when he eventually agreed to publication of his real name, he appeared an imposter. That letter from the American Anthony West marked an extreme instance of a problem long of West's own making. How significantly, a reader may legitimately wonder, may that obscured identity have reduced his reputation? When O'Faolain published the first half of his ducks story (presented by *Esquire* as "The Turning Page") in 1942, West had used the pseudonym, "Michael MacGrian."[3] It was several years before his real name or even this most frequently employed appellation resurfaced for Irish fiction readers. "MacGrian" had covered him in *The Bell* and "Terence O'Reilly" for his first accepted story, five years earlier, "The Scythe" (published in *Ireland Today*[4]), but many names turned up in his files, appearing on his agricultural or local press contributions and on manuscript drafts and submissions. Unsurprisingly, his practice of assuming various writing identities created inaccuracies in formal listings of his works and has made the compiling of a complete bibliography difficult, if not impossible. Had he relied exclusively upon his own name, he would still have been plagued by readers' confusing him with several other authors named West. Throughout his career, West probably received little help through his name.

There was the related problem, as it more than once explained his retaining a nom de plume, that West's frank, if poetic, language about sex drew the attention of the censors. Not only did they cancel the conclusion to "Myself and Some Ducks" in *The Bell*; *The Ferret Fancier* was banned in the 1960s. Even in the mid-1980s, the library in Cavan was keeping all his books in a case, disclaimer attached, off-limits to casual browsers.[5] What may have been the ultimate effects of censorship upon West's familiarity and availability to readers? Brian Fallon has dismissed the assumed wide consequence of the official Irish censors. It is hard, after all, to find an Irish writer of name who did not tangle with censorship, and the banned list among authors outside the country has been a who's who of the rest of the world's prominent writers, from Malraux to Maugham.[6] Censorship of publication and the banning of books, Fallon points out, often did not stop an author's sale or distribution in Ireland. Nor did the censors stop all discussion of ideas or the vocal and visible objecting to bigotry and foolishness; furthermore, censorship afforded unpaid advertising for the authors. Fallon may be right that despite its embarrassing activity, the long-term negative influence of the Censorship of Publications Board on the general development of Irish writing has been exaggerated. He might additionally have claimed an oyster-and-irritant effect on much writing that did emerge during and after those years. These observations notwithstanding, the fact remains that West did not see a published conclusion within that magazine to the first and much-lauded story he sent to *The Bell*,[7] and the best known of his published novels, *The Ferret Fancier*, encountered similar obstruction.

We have seen that he experienced further alienation at a personal level. West left Ireland several times—with disappointment but without rancor or bitterness—to live elsewhere. One may well ask just how limiting to his literary career were his separation from his homeland and his settled isolation? More than once, West tried to set himself and then his family up in Ireland, but found the milieu unwelcoming ("like being sane in an insane asylum"[8]) for establishing his writing or his domestic life. Inhospitable conditions are portrayed in autofiction deriving from these periods: "Myself and a Rabbit," *The Native Moment*, and sections (especially the Mourne trip of the American edition) of *As Towns with Fire*. It is hardly disputable that the geographic variety of his experience gave a richly stimulating, picaresque quality to his fiction. As has been documented in the previous chapters, most of his narratives were lived, at the very least, at a geographic level. He was deeply attached to Ireland's landscape. Settings of West's childhood in Down and Cavan were evoked in *Rebel to Judgment* (1962), *The Ferret Fancier* (1963), *Wall* (unpublished novel), and *As Towns with Fire* (1968). His teenage years in Cavan formed the setting for Jonty's life as well in The Casual Comedy.[9] West's North American years were nineteen to twenty-five

(1930–1936); Naked to Laughter (unpublished novel) and many novella versions of a narrative called Embryon (unpublished), as well as the published novellas Swineherd and The Monocrats, grew from them. West did briefly return to Ireland after his six years in North America, and lived for a time on the money he made trapping and selling eels, an experience that anchored The Native Moment (1959). Giving up the eel business for ecological and humane reasons, he hoofed and biked, trying numerous regions all around Ireland, from Donegal to Kerry to Dublin, and even the Channel Island of Sark. From these places came settings or experiences for still-unpublished novels: Wall, The Casual Comedy, Room without a Door, and The Lady Actaeon.

One could ask to what extent literary Ireland—past and present— exerted an affective force upon West's sense of a professional self, or on his practical career and reputation? We have seen that West studied the island's ancient history assiduously. He talked about it with awe and profound respect. Notes filled the margins of the scholarly texts in his library. Features of ancient Breffni became integral at stages of the Actaeon narrative. His denials of paying much attention to the contemporary writing scene are relatively true. He had been early schooled in the Romantic poets and familiarized himself with the work of Yeats and Joyce. Although he was a quick study of people and publication, and one who didn't forget much he had encountered, he was no literary junkie, hanging on reviews and dropping names. His isolation was partly that of the autodidact; part of it was due to poverty; mostly, it was chosen concentration. Reviewers, naturally enough, compared him to other writers: Beckett and Joyce for his heft and his focus on the artistic youth,[10] Kavanagh and Hardy for his rustic settings and characters,[11] Behan ("without drink"[12]) for his verve, D. H. Lawrence for his sensuality,[13] and Dylan Thomas for his word music.[14]

High praise tends to raise expectations for subsequent performances, in one's self as well as in one's critics. The "best-ever" response to "River's End" from Esquire's Arnold Gingrich in 1956, like Sean O'Faolain's superlatives in 1942, was the kind of praise any artist might hope to die with. O'Faolain had trumpeted "Myself and Some Ducks" as the most "original, fresh, and beautiful in concept and in style" to appear in that magazine. He called it the work of the "most tremblingly sensitive imagination that had yet ventured into . . . Irish life." It's hard to imagine a greater blow than to have had its conclusion canceled by the censors.

More than a decade earlier,[15] *Esquire* had enthusiastically published six of his stories. Several of his *Esquire* shorts were collected in his first book, *River's End and Other Stories* (New York: McDowell Obolensky, 1959).[16] In Ireland some small West pieces had found welcome after the war: several stories on British Broadcasting Corporation radio, a handful of poems in *Rann*. The most significant among these post-war Irish publications ("On Killing a Sheep" in *Irish Writing,* 1953) became "Not Isaac" in its later, international appearances. In 1946, thanks to O'Faolain's endorsement, West was the recipient of a Rockefeller Atlantic award. His star appeared just this side of the middle of the century, with multiple re-issuings of his books on both sides of the Atlantic.[17] After London editions in 1963 and 1968, respectively, by MacGibbon & Kee, two most prominent New York houses—Simon & Schuster and Alfred A. Knopf— brought out novels three and four, *The Ferret Fancier,* 1963, and *As Towns with Fire*, 1970. West appeared to be securing a reputation in England and in the States. In Ireland he was gaining attention as well. In the middle 1970s, West was singled out by J.W. Foster as the only Ulster fiction writer to supply the combined qualities Foster found missing in other story writers from the North: "seriousness, psychological perception, poetry, a variety of modes (including realism), an unabashed and evocative celebration of love and sexuality and an ability to straddle the sectarian divide."[18] Mark Storey echoed Foster's praise for West's serious, poetic evocation of a rural Irish childhood noting its "astute Wordsworthian echo"[19] (170).

In the 1980s, as Michael Bromley reported, Ireland had "rediscovered" West's "meticulously written and descriptively powerful novels." West was "rapidly emerging as a cult figure of Ulster literature,"[20] where a second Irish renaissance had begun in the North.[21] John Kilfeather lauded West as the "truest descendant" of William Carleton, "incontrovertibly" Ulster's greatest prose writer.[22] In *The Irish Times* he celebrated West and *Towns*: He is "an autodidact, his novel . . . ego-centered in the tradition of the great prototype *The Portrait of the Artist.* . . .Genius is stamped on every page."[23] Cahalan, Welch, and Martin, among the annotating cataloguers and literary historians of the late 1980s and 1990s, noted his merit and achievement.[24]

Attention to West then declined. The Irish literary establishment began to neglect him. By the late 1980s and '90s many of the wide surveys made no mention of him.[25] Patricia Craig, loudly unforgiving of his depiction of women, rejected him in her Northern Ireland collections.[26] Deane in *Field Day* merely listed *The Ferret Fancier* as one of "numerous Bildungsromane" (III, 940).[27] Richard Kirkland mentioned West only as a recipient of Arts Council money.[28] Robert Hogan included him, but was inspired to heights of gratuitous invective.[29] Though in his longer summary he gave West a nod, Jeffares was cursory and misleading.[30] Colin Graham obliquely referenced West to make a negative point, but apparently without full awareness, as he did not further discuss or index him.[31]

Anthologists, of course, are challenged by a multitude of choices, and the hoard of good stories they are forced to leave out must disappoint; the omission of West, however, was sometimes pointed.[32] Sean McMahon excluded O'Faolain's own favorite[33] in choosing *The Best of the Bell* (1978). Rust Hills and his committee, honoring Arnold Gingrich with "Sixty Years of *Esquire* Fiction," left unmentioned the story Gingrich thought the best.[34] The writer regarded as the "most strapping talent in contemporary Ulster, perhaps Irish, fiction,"[35] was omitted, as just noted, by Patricia Craig from *Images*[36]and from *The Rattle of the North: An Anthology of Ulster Prose* (1992). Given his early success, his revival, and his fifty years in print, West's place in the pantheon would seem to have been secured, but it has been long in coming. In 2012, thirty-eight years after John Wilson Foster's affirmation in *Forces and Themes in Ulster Fiction*, George O'Brien gave West fair notice in *The Irish Novel, 1960–2010* with an insightful reading of *As Towns with Fire*. The contrast between West's promising success and his subsequent disappearance has been great. Multiple features of West's context and character—feminist objection, a too common name, autodidacticism, geographic isolation, unlucky timing, and discomfort created by esoteric

Christian thought— may all to some degree have contributed.

Continuing our summary of these affective possibilities, we have seen that West had landed in London and was experimenting as a play-wright, just in time for Chamberlain's declaration of war. His first piece, called "The Window", scheduled for production at a small theatre near Marble Arch, was canceled, and the theatre itself never reopened.[37] He joined the war effort. He married an English woman, Olive Burr, in 1940, and in 1941 they tried briefly to establish life and work in Belfast, but again he found the context unsupportive. Olive soon pregnant, three people to feed, and the Nazis threatening the world, West found practical and intellectual reasons to enlist in the Royal Air Force. South Africa for training, and the English Midlands for flying duty—both places, along with Ireland (it's Christopher MacMannan's last view before his plane crashes) appeared in As Towns with Fire (1968). The War, West said, took ten years of his life. Not until Towns could he finally write it behind him.

He had thought for a while it would be practical and possible to wait out the war at home near Belfast, and recent study suggests he per-haps would eventually have found a congenial context there for writing. Fallon challenges the picture of isolation, provincialism, and Church-in-glove government understood to have followed Ireland's official neu-trality during the war.[38] By the late 1950s and 1960s, artistic repression indeed may have been little stronger in Ireland than it was in England, France, or the States:[39] O'Faolain had become the first Arts Council Chairman; Behan was riding high, and Beckett's Godot was brought to Dublin.[40] Strong new voices[41] in several literary genres were being heard by the early 1960s in the North (especially in criticism, drama, and poetry).

But West's decision to enlist in the Royal Air Force had put him in training far from Ireland and subsequently stationed him in Lincoln-shire. Olive had no ties to remain in Ireland without him. By the end of the war, his parents were both dead, and the ties to family in Ireland were significantly weaker than claims West was considering in England. The Wests now had four children and decided to try a communal living project in Shropshire, West managing the gardens and selling the vege-tables to profit the group. We have seen that his numerous Bio-dynamic,

socialist living experiments had little more success in establishing themselves than the hold on literary establishment. The Wests separated from
the first one, Albrighton, by 1950. West was lucky then to settle his family
in a rent-free house in Wales. As a pacifist by now, he had yet, as a writer,
to come to terms with his war experience. His eyewitness of war's damages to human sensibilities inspired the Wales-set novella (unpublished)
he usually called The Jewel in the Snout, or Circe, which gained plausibility from West's knowledge of pig-farming and of Welsh rural life.
Although West lived parts of three decades in Wales, his writing mind
was more frequently in Ireland. He explored the experiences of his childhood, youth, and early adulthood, avidly followed the newspaper reports
of his homeland, and passionately researched its ancient history. He
kept framing his ideas and creating his characters with unsentimental
retrospection in that Irish context he knew best, Ireland remaining his
geographical and cultural focus.

While the absence of a sympathetic, stimulating, liberal writing culture might drive an artist into exile, there was no escaping the heft of Ireland's twentieth-century literary context. Naturally, professional readers
measure a writer coming on the scene by comparative reference to other
writers; writers, themselves, are attentive to new company, anxious about
influence and succession. It has been understandably difficult to write
in the shadow of Ireland's literary notables and Nobels. What were the
effects of this legacy for West? Did comparisons intimidate or misrepre-
sent him? West's life overlapped by almost thirty years that of the great
leader of the Irish literary renaissance, Yeats, but the Celtic Twilight had
faded by the time West began to reach self-consciousness as a writer. He
could not avoid their presence or the comparisons, but there is no evidence that he brooded about or begrudged his compatriots. He showed
from very early work an independent spirit. He traveled his own road.
His first published novel, *The Native Moment*, gave a respectful nod to
both Yeats and Joyce.

The Native Moment registered his appreciative awareness of his
inheritance through Simon Green, a country-nurtured poetic spirit, a
reading, feeling, Yeatsian soul. Though the novel charted Simon's day
in Dublin, Simon was temperamentally no Leopold Bloom. Protagonist

and plot actually began with West's own situation. Neither the rusticity nor Simon's contrastive language[42] was a Twilit pose, and the now grown-up fancier of ferrets presently kept company with an eel on what only in a superficial way could seem Red Hanrahan's Bloomsday. West knew intimately the life of eel-catching, and the circumstance of the abused Tamar, who chooses a fiery death before Simon gets around to acting on his intention to rescue her, was created from the fate of a fourteen-year-old girl West had known.[43] Although his father's job as butler-valet on the Anglo-Irish estates of Moyallon and then of Farnham gave West a special window on aristocratic life, and though he spent some years in the cities of Dublin, London, and New York, he felt a stronger son-of-the-soil kinship to Patrick Kavanagh, born in 1904 and growing up thirty miles away in County Monaghan, than to any other Irish writer.[44]

Did he lose through a narrower identification with Ulster? Though his earliest sense of place would have had no political border, this identity seemed to please him retrospectively in his adulthood and to increase, understandably, after his important critical attention from Foster. His literary models in childhood and adolescence were mostly English writers, Shakespeare, and nineteenth-century novelists and poets. (He did pay special notice to the Brontës, whose father had been a Prunty near Loughbrickland, the same area where West's mother, Ellen Clements, was born.) Had he desired camaraderie among, or even thought about sharing a perspective with other Northern writers, a coterie would have been difficult to find. Not until the 1960s did a sense of literary community develop in the North.[45] In the first half of the twentieth-century, it tended to be Dublin or London that gave Irish writers visibility, and writers from the southern counties of the island dominated the literary scene.[46]

West became aware of them gradually, but there is no record that he ever paid imitative attention to fiction writers of the North—to older or younger contemporaries like Kavanagh and Michael MacLaverty, or to predecessors from Carleton to Shan Bullock to Patrick Boyle.[47] To be sure, childhood and adolescent discovery also appeared among their themes,[48] but as Foster long ago pointed out, West's treatment of the rural, Bildungsroman 'awakening' was substantially different. Did the

individuality of his themes or some other aspect of his use of this genre
negatively affect his reception?

Because in Ireland the inheritance of the land marked the important transition to a young farmer's manhood, crises of love and marriage
tended to be deferred and created social rather than sexual problems.
Ulster's typical "rural fiction, then, [did] not depict [the Bildungsroman's] three great forms . . . the initiation into sexuality, the questioning
of religious faith, and the discovery of literature and art" (Foster, 117).
West, however, explored all three. Foster was right about the existence
of this contrast and its prominence, although he could then have had
little information to help him appreciate its cause or extent. Foster was,
of course, aware only of Simon's and MacMannan's experiences, not
knowing them as parts of a continuum explored in The Lady Actaeon,
the vast, highly individual and mostly unpublished work through which
West managed to "stay West."

For George West's children, the question of inheriting land was
moot; there was no property to inherit. If the fact separated his son from
fiction writers in the North it also contributed to an atypical freedom
to explore sexuality, faith, and art. His protagonists' revelatory experiences began very early. Sexual awareness had come to West precociously,
concurrent with the acquisition of language, early even for a boy who
roamed barns, woods, and pastures. West incorporated its consciousness
with all the stages of physical and spiritual growth he wrote about: life in
his pram, pre-school visits to teachers, evocative sexual play invited by the
house maid and primary ventures into the woods, Sunday School terrors
of damnation. Gradually, he explored it in restless adolescent dreaming,
hitch-hiking across the United States and Canada, eel-catching for sales
in Dublin, as well as events of marriage, parenthood, middle-age, and
the writing life. The impetus for the author's probing of sexuality seems
to have resided in features of West's own experience and in his quest for
a bigger "Truth," rather than in a conscious awareness of distinguishing
his novels and stories from those of other writers, North or South.

Similarly, West's patterns of spiritual questioning and artistic discovery also had their genesis and implication in his own life. To continue
interrogating and understanding his reception it becomes helpful at this

point to compare him with two other novelists among Irish contemporaries who were also moralists or Truth-tellers. Francis Stuart earns first mention here, for he, too, despite a shelf of compelling novels, has experienced neglect. He was but lately (and still with objection) instated in Aosdána. His fiction was forceful, much more prescriptive than West's, with heavily religious, even theological themes. His premises, like West's, were didactic, deeply serious, and Christian. He even wrote candidly in an "Afterword"[49] appended in 1994, that writing *Redemption* (1949) was (apropos Kazin's observation) his own salvation. One can wonder how much Stuart's moral fervor has negatively affected his reception by the Irish literary establishment.

The response to Stuart the artist, however, may still be so overshadowed by the outrage over his war-time broadcasts from Germany that the measure of his moral fiction cannot yet be taken. The case of another twentieth-century Irish writer, still writing, may therefore offer more help. His reception is not obviously complicated by politics. He does not repeatedly approach his plot from a single and systematic theoretic or philosophical position, as both Stuart and West tended to do; he enters more readily into the "pure" story-telling challenge of assuming narrative masks. Yet he, like them, is more moralist than traditional Irish storyteller or seanachíe. For a period, the treatment of Anthony C. West paralleled the critical reception of William Trevor, about half a generation younger than West. Trevor was not born in the North, but was, like West, long in receiving his due in his birth-land.[50] Both writers were praised in their literary beginnings by discriminating and prominent professional readers, and then skipped over or dismissed by many of the academic surveyors and analysts of Irish literary history and culture.[51]

One wonders whether it has been for different reasons, after all, that Stuart, Trevor, and West incurred this treatment. All three writers confronted separation from the home written about, geographical, political, or cultural. Trevor's sense of being the involuntary outsider[52] does not match Stuart's or West's chosen exiles, but all three were Truth-tellers who suffered similar alienation. James Cahalan observed in 1988, as Martin had also and earlier chided,[53] that writers like West were neglected because they fell outside the mainstream of Roman Catholic

fiction from Joyce to Brian Moore.[54] Very likely. Additionally, the moralist's became an ostracizing posture in the post-colonial critical climate.
Stuart, Trevor, and West may have turned an alienated position to artistic
advantage, but their having done so insured no fit with critical fashion in
the late twentieth-century. Entertainers often had more welcome than
novelists bearing an earnest message.

There was a significant parallel in West's and Trevor's Truth-telling
compulsions. Trevor, as Denis Sampson shows, developed strategies
for hiding within his prose. Wanting "to be unknown apart from his
writing"(292), he generally suppressed his own voice, deferring to the
voices of his many characters. Though many novels had appeared before
he ventured into prose that was obviously autobiographical,[55] it was
during the 1970s Trevor experienced an epiphany[56] when "memory came
to be . . . the moral and imaginative anchor of his writing"(Sampson,
292). Even when Trevor disappeared into his characters (Samson, 293),
however, he could still be discovered in his particular choices, like his
settings (281), or in the aggregate, in the creation of characters who were,
like himself, fiction-makers.[57] The autobiographical inspiration is finally
affirmed in the essays of *Excursions in the Real World* (1993).[58] Through
memory both Trevor and West offered the crucial access to moral truth.
Neither one looked back in sentimentality or escape, but each looked
back at himself "in order to see more than himself."[59] Both West and
Trevor would agree with Beckett that memory of "real people and real
places" helped get at the "Truth" that matters in artistic creating.[60] Both
Trevor and West, while self-effacing, relied in their fiction upon recollection, upon personal memory.

Though he was like Trevor in having been reluctant to parade himself, West by contrasted evidence of even the earliest fragments,[61] realized
intuitively the artistic potency and potential of autobiography as a creative tool. While he insisted on the artistic freedom to adapt or to revise
experience, or the right entirely to fabricate it, he faithfully focused
on one questing soul—his own, despite the variety of protagonists. He
recorded his questing in the huge ur-narrative, which he subsequently
exploited for the basically auto-fictive stories and novels; often he let
these stand alone on internal and self-supporting plots. His published

works comprise some of them (the evolutionary and spiritual relatedness of his four published novels demonstrated at length in *Celtic, Christian, Socialist*[62]). His unpublished fictions have also been featured in this present book. Here we have explored their relatedness, virtually all his fictions being, like icebergs, small chunks from the enormous ur glacier. In contrast to Trevor, who attempted to disguise himself through greatly varied plots, characters, and settings, West early adopted pseudonymity instead, and eventually social and geographical isolation. There could be no stopping of the relentless quest.

Sexual discovery and identity, an appropriation of history, literature, and art, and the acquisition of spiritual understanding are all gradually perceived and achieved rewards of the quest in West's ur narrative. The creative, artistic impulse to write had begun for West, himself, when he was close to the age of the fancier of ferrets, but West's personally important fusion of the aesthetic commitment with his spiritual one developed after his return from North America. Simon's experience, especially in *The Native Moment*, led toward that next merger seen in Christopher, a would-be poet, in *Towns*. The Lady Actaeon, explored and made accessible through this study, advances this union through the marriage of a poet to a rector.

West steadily made artistic use of his own spiritual journey. When he was the age of Simon Green in *The Ferret Fancier*, he was still deeply affected by Calvinism,[63] Orange-ism, and the Evangelical Quaker Sunday school of childhood instruction; we saw that these influences were modified by his new life among Catholics at age eleven, when his family moved to Cavan. The published novels trace the young protagonist's steady sorting out of bigotry from belief, and the unpublished ones also advance this progress. A spiritual re-direction of West's thinking occurred to him in New York, between ages twenty and twenty-five, when he encountered Anthroposophy, the teachings of Rudolf Steiner. West was self-educated, having no university experience and slightly less formal schooling than did most Irish people of his generation.[64] Wordsworth had nurtured the young West artistically and philosophically, but a more important feature of this literary relationship may have resided in the German Romantic thought that influenced them both.[65] As Wordsworth

absorbed thought of Goethe, West also took affective instruction from
this German mind, filtered through the transcribed lectures of Steiner,
charismatic teacher, who was himself a product of intensive Goethean
studies.[66] In his fiction, West meant eventually to embed pertinent Christian and anthroposophical teachings so deeply that no reader need trip
over them. He acknowledged that art, while it was supremely serious,
would be jeopardized, nevertheless, by ideas that hadn't been thus integrated. That is not to say he successfully obscured the didactic impulse,
or that though the psychology, realism, and other qualities carried them
along, many of his readers could offer an informed sympathy for the
ideological substructure of his thought.

Steiner taught a system of patient, karmic progress of the soul: people
carried into their lives a destiny conditioned by previous existences. West
had met this idea, of course, in the "Intimations Ode," but he could
make new sense of it after he began to study anthroposophical, along
with New Testament, teachings. Present and ongoing destiny could be
affected, Steiner taught, by choices and attitudes adopted now. Anthroposophy was spiritual study, a quest for spiritual knowledge, compatible
with Christian practice. Steiner had been baptized a Roman Catholic,
and his break with contemporary Theosophists lay in the credence he
continued to give Jesus Christ and Christianity. Anthroposophy even
depended upon the "warmth" that religion and ritual, simultaneously,
were able to infuse into it.[67] Steiner appropriated esoteric medieval history and theosophy selectively, Zoroastrian imagery as well as the Mystery
of Golgotha. He concentrated his gentle teaching in editing a journal,
giving public lectures, advising socialistic and religious communities,
and establishing Waldorf (or Morningstar) schools, which advocated an
integrative physical, aesthetic, and intellectual education of the child.
He proposed a tripartite application of socialism for the economic aspect
of life, democracy for its civil aspect, and individualism to promote its
spiritual dimension, while he claimed Jesus Christ, an incarnation of
Zarathustra, uniter of the spirits of Hermes and Moses, as the antidote
to the dominating ego. Eastern bodhisattvas anticipated Christ, one of
them Gautama Buddha, who showed that when a person dies, the spirit
returns to the "Universal Spirit" or Logos. This Logos—or Wisdom, or

Creative Force—had become flesh in Christ.[68] Cosmic, spiritual truths Steiner thought to be platonically mirrored in epochal, cultural, and individual ones. Perception of the ultimate, spiritual reality, he taught, was apt to be blocked by the ego; ignoring the ego's threat produced the world's social and economic distress. Thus West nurtured the "egoity" or "egoism" of the aspiring soul-self, and distinguished it from obstructive, negative "egotism."

There was no anthroposophical teaching of original sin (a significant departure for West from his Calvinist beginning). A person's great individual effort thus lay in seeking, in willing, the soul's evolution from egotism into love. This effort was manifested in a conscious subduing of the ego and in assisting others to bear their karmic obligations. Simon, Adam, and Christopher—West's protagonists—are witnessed at various stages of a karmic journey. None of them is ultimately successful in the quest; each must resign himself to hope for the next stage of the present life or for another incarnation. West's reviewers sometimes objected to his major character's aimlessness or his ambivalence,[69] describing this feature as a fault in plotting. If the sections of his life-narrative that have been published have evoked in readers a sense of incompleteness about the character or desultory wandering, West has achieved part of his intent. He contended that the earthly pilgrimage remained unfinished for most souls, neither extremity, neither birth nor death, posing finitude. The karmic progress continued.

West was recognized for his integrity, and for the depth and breadth of his themes. His recurrent subject was this dubious progress of the modern, questing soul, paralleled by the dubious progress of this modern evolving planet. Rural Ulster was where he had begun his own journey, and it remained the typical setting for his published fiction. When he had progressed through young adulthood, beyond Christopher Mac-Mannan's years and into middle age, West began to question whether there were historical and spiritual connections, potentially helpful, between an ancient Irish gnosis and these esoteric Christian teachings. The Irish scholarship that interested him most profoundly, therefore, was archeological and anthropological. On the subjects of Irish antiquity, Celtic history and prehistory, mythology, excavation and exploration, he read everything he could find, from Eleanor Merry (*The Flaming Door*, 1936) to Alwyn and Brinley Rees (*Celtic Heritage*, 1961).[70] He wrote letters of inquiry to experts on the topics of his research.

At the university library at Bangor, he absorbed volumes and kept hundreds of pages of notes, which he typed out. To incorporate his research into his art, he then put all his notes aside, he said, and without looking back at them, he wrote through to the end of the current versions of the two very long fictions he continued to revise until he died: The Casual Comedy ("an indictment of landlordism" he called it) and The Lady Actaeon.

The significant motive in his historical research remained his hope to find evidence for Ireland's "Participation"—he would sometimes capitalize it—in an ancient, universal spiritual knowledge, whose vestiges, as he identified them, were rapidly disappearing in modern life. West wondered whether Ireland might longer have preserved this knowledge if "religion had never come into it"(and he felt religion would not have been needed if the Irish landlord had "consented to live with and help the people instead of exploiting them"[71]).

Was it this increasing knowledge and enthusiasm that widened the distance between himself and his critics? Did his raising spiritually premised questions discourage his readership? Was it the fault of an increasing secularism that West was edged out of recent anthologies? It seems unlikely that the embedding of non-centric or traditional spiritual views in his work could wholly explain the failure of a twentieth-century writer with West's talent to become and remain a familiar literary figure of his century. Spiritual interest, even an esoteric one, had been no unusual thing among early twentieth-century writers. Theosophical study was common among the literati and intelligentsia from the late nineteenth century through the first half of the twentieth.[72] Yeats strongly defended his magic, and AE (George Russell) his visions. E. M. Forster's Wilcox men of *Howards End* do not respect the spirits of the Welsh hills and come, significantly, to ruin. Nor should this penchant have discouraged mid-century sales in America. Among West's American contemporaries in the 1950s and 1960s, Ayn Rand was commanding much attention with best-selling ideologic fiction, and anthroposophical ideas like West's seem to have motivated Saul Bellow.

While he was cited with writers like John Montague and Sam Hanna Bell for challenging an ugly side of Northern Protestantism,[73] West as artist and as ordinary citizen firmly insisted upon religious indepen- dence:[74] Although his wife joined the Christian Community (a group originally advised by Steiner), West refused to become a member of it or of any other. Foster commented that MacMannan in *Towns* was effective "as an embodiment of the racially and nationally ambiguous Ulster Prot- estant, and in his death becomes an ironically 'con-ascending' Christ." These observations may have validity, yet it would be misleading to call West a "religious" writer.[75] He was Protestant by birth and childhood instruction, and he privately devoted himself to esoteric Christian study, but still, as the mature artist, viewed his artistic identity as something apart from sectarian interests. The root of his writing was profoundly spiritual, but meditative rather than mystical. His novels raise serious questions and imply resurrective hope, but preach no theological dogma.

Because he recognized that unmuted didacticism would compro- mise art, a great challenge lay in making the fiction carry at once the threat of the ego, a hope of resurrection, the evolutionary movement of individual and humanity, and the implicitly (or at least traditionally) contradictory sense of the ending required by art. He felt largely unsuc- cessful at this complex goal, although he thought his story "Narcissus unto Echo" came closest to achievement. Here, at the moment of death in his hospital bed, protagonist Stephen Muir is able to connect all the dots of memory: images from his early idyllic life on his aunt's farm, of his sexual awakening with its loss of innocence and paradise, and of incestuous guilt in the family evidenced by physical and mental defor- mity. He can finally celebrate their integration—in his understanding— and move into his next evolutionary existence with peace and hope.

Choices made can become impediments. It is apparent that Cath- cart Anthony Muir West battled consequences of his course, from the bizarre trouble over names, to more predictable effects of exile, geo- graphical isolation, and gender antagonism. Yet his extraordinary adven- tures through bold moves like emigration, exile, and enlistment also fueled inspiration. West faithfully maintained the quest; he consciously suppressed narcissistic egotism; without apology, he stayed focused on his Diana-vision; he unreservedly embraced the Ancient Mariner's obligation to tell.

Yeats has insisted that the artist's "life is an experiment in living and those who come after him have a right to know it . . . [in order to appreciate that his art] is no rootless flower but the speech of a man; that it is no little thing to achieve anything in any art, to stand alone perhaps for many years, to go a path no other man has gone, to accept one's own thought when the thought of others has the authority of the world behind it . . . to give one's own life as well as one's words (which are so much nearer to one's soul) to the criticism of the world."[76] These chapters of *Staying West* have been offered as a yet another forum for Anthony C. West to extend his story, another bridge from this Son of Éiru to his readers.

ENDNOTES

1   Quoted by Thwaite, Batchelor, 210. Bib: Batchelor, John, ed. *The Art of Literary Biography*. Oxford: Clarendon Press, 1995.

2   Hazard Adams, *The Book of Yeats's Poems* (Tallahassee: Florida State University Press, 1990). Bib: Adams, Hazard. *The Book of Yeats's Poems*. Tallahassee: Florida State University Press, 1990.

3   Sometimes permitting inference of a Roman Catholic identity, sometimes Protestant (as he was born and reared), sometimes English or Welsh, but usually just preferring anonymity for better focus on the writing, West often employed pseudonyms on his submissions, among them: Terence O'Reilly, John or Tom Whitfield, Trefwr, John Mongan Russel, Mary Mongan Russel, Brigid Russel, Adam McAdam, Michael Maturin, Anthony Morris, John Kells, and John Dreame. Michael MacGrian appeared most often.

4   See note above; "Myself and Some Ducks," *The Bell*, IV, 4, 253–265 (second installment censored); "The Scythe," *Ireland Today*, May 1937, Vol II, 5, 43–47.

5   I had to ask to see them. Reviewers like Vincent Lawrence and the anonymous author (Ciaran Carty?) of "Dialogue," *Sunday Independent*, 6 November 1983, p. 15, allude also to the banning of *The Ferret Fancier* in Ireland in 1963.

6   Brian Fallon, *An Age of Innocence: Irish Culture 1930–1960* (Dublin: Gill & Macmillan, 1998), 203.

7   The magazine's editor, Sean O'Faolain, was front and center in attacking the Board. Terence Brown discusses O'Faolain's role in his *Social and Cultural*

History; Robert Welch (*Oxford Companion*) blames the printers, presumably the conduit to the Board.

8 ACW to Gail Leeson, 28 April 1963.

9 Only a small part of this novel appeared in *The Honest Ulsterman*, number 57, 1977, page 69, anticipating a publication that never occurred.

10 Elizabeth Jennings, e.g., reviewing *River's End and Other Stories*, *The Listener*, 15 September 1960, p.439. Matthew Hodgart compares *As Towns with Fire* to Beckett's *Murphy* for its power and energy, unidentified source, 5 May 1961. It was natural, though not for long helpful, for reviewers of *The Native Moment* to invoke Joyce because West also claimed twenty-four hours in Dublin and attention to a growing artist. See Robert C. Healey and James Stern, who seem to have held it against him that West was not attempting another *Ulysses: New York Herald Tribune*, c.22 May 1960; *New York Times*, 4 December 1959. Harvey Curtis Webster, on the other hand, appreciates differences between West and Joyce: *Saturday Review*, 12 December 1959. As to Continental or American comparisons, John Davenport invokes Dostoevsky: *The Observer*, 30 April 1961, p.29; *The Long Island Catholic*, Rabelais, 3 November 1965; Thomas F. Curley, Teilhard de Chardin in *Commonweal*, 71:501, 29 January 1960. James G. Murray in *The Long Island Catholic*, 11 March 1965, and Paul A. Johnson, *Beaumont Journal*, Texas, 5 March 1965, think of Salinger; the *Oxford Mail*, 11 August 1960, and *Time*, 9 April 1965, suggest that West may be the Irish William Faulkner. Simon reminds Anne O'Neill-Barna of Huck Finn, *New York Times Book Review*, p. 4, 21 March 1965.

11 John Kavanagh, *Irish Post*, 12 November 1983, and Joan S. Hall, Houston Post, 7 June 1970.

12 William Bittner, about *As Towns with Fire*, *The Miami Herald*, 21 June 1970.

13 Charles Brady sees West as "a more dour" Lawrence, *Buffalo Evening News*, 13 March 1965; the British Broadcasting Company reviewer as an equally honest one, "World of Books," 4 May 1963.

14 Chad Walsh agrees with British reviewers that there is something of Dylan Thomas's vision in West's: *New York Herald Tribune*, 4 April 1965; Granville Hicks is another of a number who cite Thomas, Saturday Review 27 March 1965, p. 24. Many of the reviews (most are clippings sent to ACW from agents, editors, and friends) of West's publications are listed in the appendix. See Box 19 of A. C. West's papers, "General Reviews and Notices." Bibliographical notations on his clippings are frequently incomplete, although some of the omitted data I have been able to supply.

15 *The Bell*, IV, 4, July 1942, 253–265.

16 "River's End" included, besides the title story, "The Upper Room," "Not Isaac," "The Turning Page," "Song of the Barrow," "Narcissus unto Echo," "No

Fatted Calf;" *The Monocrats*, a novella, completed this volume. In London, by MacGibbon & Kee, 1960; German translations were offered by Fischer and Kindler verlags, 1962, 1963. See Box 2, Letters, Geisenheyner and Crone.

17   The list of his publications I have been recovering may be found in the appendix. West, himself, for reasons discussed in this study, kept neither a comprehensive tally of his publishing achievements nor a complete shelf of the works themselves.

18   John Wilson Foster, *Forces and Themes in Ulster Fiction* (Totowa, New Jersey: Rowman and Littlefield, 1974), 258.

19   Mark Storey, "'Bewildered Chimes': Image, Voice and Structure in Recent Irish Fiction," in *Across a Roaring Hill*, eds. Gerald Dawe and Edna Longley (Belfast and Dover, New Hampshire: Blackstaff Press, 1985), 161–181.

20   Michael Bromley, "The Quiet Revival of Anthony West," *Belfast Telegraph*, 20 March 1985, 14.

21   "The Group" of young writers who collected in 1963 around Philip Hobsbaum, English poet and lecturer at Queens University, Belfast, included Edna Longley, Robert Longley, Derek Mahon, and Seamus Heaney. David Lehman with Donna Foote, "A Literary Flowering in Ulster," *Newsweek*, 2 June 1986, 74D, F.

22   John Kilfeather, "Hard Men to Follow," *The Belfast Review*, Winter, 1983. He cites Carleton's "energy and honesty and humour," and offers a connection, too, of Carleton's "straddling . . . deep divisions . . . [of] the Ulster psychic landscape" (Foster, 17).

23   John Kilfeather, "Somewhere up in the Clouds above," *Irish Times*, 20 April 1985, "Weekend 5."

24   James M.Cahalan, *The Irish Novel* (Boston: G. K. Hall, 1988). Robert Welch, *The Oxford Companion to Irish Literature* (Oxford: The Clarendon Press, 1996). It is regrettable that Welch lacked current information for his entry, as West had been dead eight years by this publication date. Augustine Martin, *The Genius of Irish Prose* (Cork and Dublin: The Mercier Press, 1985). Martin asserts that all West's work deserves to be better known, and wisely points out West's contribution in showing through his adolescent protagonists that sexual repression was not just a Roman Catholic problem (135). See Barry Sloan, *Writers and Protestantism in the North of Ireland: Heirs to Adamnation?* (Dublin and Portland, Oregon: Irish Academic Press, 2000), 279–285.

25   Brown, Terence. *Ireland's Literature* (Totowa: Barnes & Noble, 1988), *Ireland: A Social and Cultural History 1922–1979* (London: Fontana, 1981); Neil Corcoran, *After Yeats and Joyce: Reading Modern Irish Literature* (Oxford and New York: Oxford University Press, 1997); Seamus Deane, *Short History of Irish Literature* (London: Hutchinson, 1986) and the *Field Day Anthology* (1991); Terry Eagleton, *Crazy John and The Bishop* (Cork: University of Cork, 1998); *Exiles and Emigres* (1984); *Heathcliff and the Great Hunger* (London: Verso,

1995); Brian Fallon, *An Age of Innocence: Irish Culture 1930–1960* (Dublin: Gill & Macmillan, 1998); Declan Kiberd, *Inventing Ireland: The Literature of the Modern Nation* (London, 1995), W.J. McCormack, *Ascendancy and Tradition* (1985), *Burke to Beckett* (1994), *The Battle of the Books* (Gigginstown, Mullingar: Lilliput Press, 1986); Roger McHugh and Maurice Harmon, *Short History of Anglo-Irish Literature: From its Origins to the Present Day* (Dublin: Wolfhound Press; New York: Barnes and Noble, 1982); Patrick Rafroidi and Terence Brown, *The Irish Short Story* (Gerrards Cross: Colin Smythe, 1979); Susan Sailer, *Representing Ireland* (1997): Gerry Smyth, *Decolonization and Criticism* (1998); Eibhear Walshe, *Sex, Nation, Dissent* (New York: St. Martin's Press, 1997); Norman Vance, *Irish Literature: A Social History* (Cambridge: Basil Blackwell, 1990); Alan Warner, *A Guide to Anglo-Irish Literature* (Dublin and New York: Gill & Macmillan, St. Martin's Press, 1981): These have widely surveyed Irish literature, but do not cite West.

26 Patricia Craig, *The Rattle of the North* (Belfast: Blackstaff Press, 1992) and *The Oxford Book of Ireland* (Oxford and New York: Oxford University Press, 1998). See also note 27 below.

27 Seamus Deane, et. al., *The Field Day Anthology of Irish Literature*, III (Derry: Field Day Publications, 1991).

28 Richard Kirkland, *Literature and Culture in Northern Ireland Since 1965: Moments of Danger* (London and New York: Longman, 1996).

29 *Dictionary of Irish Literature* (Revised and Expanded Edition), II (London: Aldwych Press, 1979 and 1996, 1228–1229. "Old Boys, Young Bucks, and New Women: The Contemporary Irish Short Story," *The Irish Short Story*, ed. James F. Kilroy (Boston: G. K. Hall), 169–215.

30 Not in the *Pocket History of Irish Literature*, Dublin: O'Brien, 1997, but in *Anglo-Irish Literature*. (New York, Schocken Books, 1981). He mentions West's attention to adolescence, noting exuberance of style; then he criticizes *Towns* for being a formless war novel, contrasting it by proximity and praise to W. S. Gilbert's *Bombadier* (1944). West, as I have detailed in *Celtic, Christian, Socialist: The Novels of Anthony C. West* (Rutherford, Madison, Teaneck, New Jersey: Fairleigh Dickinson University Press, 1993) and further explain, here made no pretension of offering a generic "war novel" (44–71).

31 *Deconstructing Ireland: Identity, Theory, Culture* (Edinburgh: Edinburgh University Press, 2001), 47. O'Faolain, of course, knew better of whom he spoke when he wrote in "Signing Off," "People have made fun of our factual pieces" but couldn't resist giving "the slightly mischievous examples 'Myself and Some Ducks' and 'Myself and Some Rabbits.'" The original citation is Graham's (47). West's titles often made him a soft target.

32 West was omitted even when Bolger could give a place to Sam Hanna Bell

and John Broderick, and Kiely had included one from Boyle that surely must have raised a cry from some feminists. Dermot Bolger, ed., *Picador Book of Contemporary Irish Fiction* (London: Pan Books, 1993); "Go Away, Old Man, Go Away," Benedict Kiely, ed., *Penguin Book of Irish Short Stories* (Hammondsworth, New York: Viking, 1981); Colm Toibin, ed., *Penguin Book of Irish Short Stories* (London and NewYork: Viking, 1999); David Marcus, *The Irish Eros* (Dublin: Gill & Macmillan, 1996).

33 "I always felt you were the most exciting and promising writer I got in *The Bell*." Sean O'Faolain to ACW, 22 October 1945.

34 *Lust, Violence, Sin, Magic: Sixty Years of Esquire Fiction*, ed. Rust Hills, Will Blythe, Erika Mansourian (New York: Atlantic Monthly Press, 1993). The title may portend a cynical maturity that West's story about sexual awakening and the departure of childhood would distort. Although "The Turning Page" surely is about a loss of magic, love is conspicuously missing in the title's list.

35 Foster, *Forces and Themes*, 258.

36 Bromley takes Craig to task for leaving West out of the Northern Ireland Arts Council's celebratory book, *Images*, published in March 1985. Kilfeather ("Somewhere . . . ") is also critical of her judgment, objecting to her reply to the *Belfast Telegraph* that she found West's writing "turgid, humourless and sexist." I find him neither turgid nor humorless, but I understand her indignation about the representation of women. Further study of West's work, as I have argued here, discloses a story that has to mitigate feminist ire.

37 West made several attempts at play-writing. In *The Bell* introduction, O'Faolain mentions an Abbey production by West, though I have not located it.

38 Fallon, 216; John Kilfeather, *Irish Times*, 20 April 1985

39 Fallon, 205–210.

40 Fallon, 264.

41 Among them were Edna Longley, Michael Longley, John Montague, Brian Friel, Derek Mahon, John Hewitt, and Seamus Heaney.

42 James Stern found Simon's philosophizing in "pure Oxford English" unaccountable and therefore irritating, *New York Times*, 4 December 1959.

43 ACW to Audrey S. Eyler, Interview, 1986.

44 ACW to Patrick Kavanagh, 10 April 1961. With such mental and artistic stimulus as early exchange with Kavanagh would have afforded, he mused, his thinking might have been earlier and more productively directed.

45 Philip Hobsbaum's literary group at the Queen's University Belfast marks the change after mid-century.

46 In his pleading for the Republic's, especially Dublin's, cultural vitality of this period between 1930 and 1960, Fallon has little to say about those Irish writers from the North who were then making themselves known in Dublin and London.

He does cite Forrest Reid in a list of the original members of the Irish Academy of Letters, and in another list of contributors to the *Irish Statesman* (45, 82). Their names could have swelled the defense he makes: Besides Reid, Stephen Gilbert, Brian Moore, St. John Ervine, Joyce Cary, Jack Wilson, John Broderick, Lynn C. Doyle, and Janet McNeill along with other writers whom John Wilson Foster has cited or explored in *Forces and Themes*. After the war, despite the novels emerging from yet other Northern writers, like *Tarry Flynn* in 1948 (West's later reading of it prompted his appreciative letter to Kavanagh in 1961); *December Bride* by Sam Hanna Bell in 1951; *Honey Seems Bitter*, 1954, and *There Was an Ancient House*, 1955, by Benedict Kiely; and *A Child in the House* by Janet McNeill in 1955, the attention still focused on Dublin. MacNeice, Kavanagh, Kiely, and Hewitt, at least, would seem to have been approved by Dublin and so have received Fallon's "undivided" attention.

47   John Wilson Foster's *Forces and Themes in Ulster Fiction* is still the best discussion of many of these writers. I have also talked about approaches and achievements of some of them, contrastive to West's in *Celtic Christian Socialist*, pp. 25ff.

48   Foster compares Cary's *A House of Children* with Reid's *Apostate* on the subject, for example. He shows that they (unlike West) are "nostalgic about childhood," seeing it as "a falling-off from a prior state of beauty, order and graciousness" (197).

49   See Chapter 1, Overview . . . , Endnote 19.

50   Douglas Archibald, "Introduction," *Colby Quarterly*, XXXVIII, 3, September 2002, 269–279.

51   See Archibald's summary of Trevor's fate at the hands of the Irish literary establishment, 269–271.

52   Archibald, 276.

53   See n. 15 above.

54   *The Irish Novel*, 296. This kind of neglect, it is fair to note, has recently been addressed: Colin Cruise's study of Forrest Reid in Walshe's *Sex, Nationalism, Dissent* (1997); Patrick Grant's *Breaking Enmities: Religion, Literature, and Culture in Northern Ireland*, 1967–1997 (1999); and Barry Sloan's *Writers and Protestantism in the North of Ireland* (2000).

55   *Excursions in the Real World*, 1993. Sampson suggests that these essays are probably all the autobiography Trevor is inclined to offer (280).

56   Beckett incorporates this autobiographical moment in *Krapp's Last Tape*.

57   Robert Tracy, "Telling Tales: The Fictions of William Trevor," *Colby Quarterly*, XXXVIII, 3, September 2002, 295–307. Tracy explores the "engaging parallel " that marks Trevor's fiction-making and that same "obsessive activity of his . . . characters:" He shows Trevor's stories and novels as a collective "meditation" on fiction-making, on his art's varied motives—escape, protection, romance, control,

malice, revenge, guilt, perversion—its features, and its liabilities.

58 See Sampson, 281, where the work of Dolores MacKenna is also cited in this regard: *William Trevor: The Writer and His Work* (Dublin: New Island Books, 1999), 28–58.

59 Arno Karlen, "Surviving Ireland," *The Nation*, 200: 486, 3 May 1965.

60 Denis Sampson, "'Bleak Splendour': Notes for an Unwritten Biography of William Trevor," *Colby Quarterly*, XXXVIII, 3, September 2002, 292; Sampson quotes from Trevor's *Excursions in the Real World* (Toronto: Vintage, 1993), 172–173.

61 See Law Office narratives, for example.

62 Fairleigh Dickinson University Press, 1993. At that time, not having examined all of the nearly 35,000 pages West left, I was unaware of the scope of this narrative.

63 See especially Sloan, n. 51, who explores insightfully the impact of Calvinistic theology on Simon Green of *The Ferret Fancier*.

64 Fallon, *Innocence*, 206.

65 I have discussed this relationship at length in *Celtic, Christian, Socialist*.

66 At twenty-one (1882) Steiner edited *The Scientific Writings of Goethe in Kürschners Nationalliteratur*. In the 1890s he regularly collaborated at the Goethe-and-Schiller Archives and edited the Sophia edition of Goethe's scientific writings. In 1897 he published Goethe's Weltanschauung. Johannes Hemleben, *Rudolf Steiner, A Documentary Biography*, East Grinstead: Henry Goulden, 1975, 156–157.

67 Rudolf Steiner, Lecture in Basil, 1917, quoted in Hemleben, p.134.

68 Rudolf Steiner, *Three Streams in the Evolution of Mankind* [Six lectures at Dornach, 1918] (London: Rudolf Steiner Press, 1965), 123. See *Celtic, Christian, Socialist*, which explores the effects of Steiner's teaching on West's fiction.

69 See Pearl Schiff, review of *Towns, Boston Globe*, 2 April, 1970; New Yorker, 46:98, 30 May 1970; Webster Schott, *New York Times* review, 5 April 1970 for readers who objected to Christopher's inadequacy.

70 For more on his application of Irish legend to his published fiction see *Celtic, Christian, Socialist*, beginning with a note on his library, pp. 38–39.

71 ACW to Davis [?], 9 September 1977. See Schaffner correspondence.

72 John Tebbel's account of the spiritualism of John and Elliott Macrae of E. P. Dutton & Co., illustrates. The firm could be proud of having skeptics like Max Beerbohm and Samuel Butler on its list, and simultaneously be the largest publisher of occult books in the United States. *A History of Book Publishing in the United States*, Vol. IV, New York & London: R. R. Bowker Company, 1981, chapter 13. Fallon reminds the reader that Yeats's esoteric interests reflected a "characteristically twentieth-century motif" (271).

73 Foster, 274, 284; Anthony Bradley, "Literature and Culture in the North of

Ireland," in *Cultural Contexts and Literary Idioms in Contemporary Irish Literature*, ed. Michael Kenneally (Totowa, New Jersey: Barnes & Noble, 1988), 36–72.

74   "I am a-political and non-sectarian, out of a protestant background, for what it was worth." ACW to C. Day-Lewis Fellowships, 2 Mar 78.

75   "I suppose I write out of a Christian consciousness but not in any naive churchly sense." ACW to Ms. Hodgart, 27 Jul. '74.

76   W. B. Yeats, quoted by Seamus Heaney in *Preoccupations: Selected Prose, 1968–1978* (New York: Farrar, Straus, Giroux, 1980), 100–101. The "rootless flower" (splendor in the grass, indeed) may have its root earlier than Wordsworth, though it appears to be his image for the poet Tennyson, Yeats, and others have appropriated. Yeats is said by Richard Ellmann and Charles Feidelson Jr. (*The Modern Tradition*) to have been referring to Lionel Johnson in 1907.

1910   Cathcart Anthony Muir West born south of Belfast at Moyallon, Guilford, 1 July.

1921   Family moves to Farnham, Cavan.

1929   West emigrates to the United States.

1935   West returns to Ireland. "The Personality of Bedell [Bishop of Kilmore and Ardagh, 1629–1642]," *Ardagh and Elphin Gazette* of Kilmore parish, September. "The Scythe, " Terence O'Reilly, *Ireland Today*, May, II, 5, 43–47.

1938   West lives on Sark, Channel Islands.

1939   West moves to London. 20 Nov. *John O' London's Weekly* offers nine guineas for first British serial rights to "Farewell to a Kid." "The Window" is scheduled for production at Torch Theatre near Marble Arch. War erupts. He works with ambulance squad.

1940   West marries Olive Mary Burr, 15 January in London. They move to Belfast and work for Navy Army Air Force Institutes.

1941   Michael John is born. West enlists in the Royal Air Force.

1942   "Myself and Some Ducks," Michael MacGrian, *The Bell*, IV, 4, 253–265 (second installment censored). The Air Force sends him to South Africa for training in navigation and meteorology; he joins Pathfinder unit, Squadron 627. Mary is born.

1943   Moves family to Lincolnshire cottage next to airbase.

1944   Bronwen is born.

1946   "Myself and a Rabbit" Michael MacGrian, *The Bell*, XI, 4, 860–872. West is demobilized. He receives a Rockefeller Atlantic Award of L250. Jocelyn is born.

1947   "Myself and a Birth" Michael MacGrian, *The Bell* XIII, 4, 47–57. The Wests move to Albrighton in Shropshire. Jeremy Paul is born.

1949   "Two Sonnets: January, February," *Rann*, 4, Spring. Christopher
        Terence is born.

1950   "Bees and Saturn" *Notes and Correspondence*, Anthroposophical
        Agricultural Foundation, New Series, #1, Spring. Ardleigh project
        begins. Brigid is born.

1951   BBC, Northern Ireland, presents "The Half Crown." West moves
        family to Elmbank in North Wales.

1952   "Fable" *Rann* 16, Summer.

        "Four Prayers," "Like a Flame that Burns Quietly," *Rann* 16,
        (Summer). Miriam Margaret is born.

1953   "On Killing a Sheep," Michael MacGrian, *Irish Writing*, #25, 16–19,
        72.

        "Spring Song," *Rann*, #18

        "Love Song," *Rann*, #20.

1954   "Blackthorn" Michael MacGrian, *The Christian Community*, VIII,
        #11, 12, November–December, 142.

        "Myself and a Rabbit", Devin Garrity, ed., *44 Irish Short Stories*
        [much-shortened version: four of thirteen pages].

        "And Where Did You Go, Lord?" Michael MacGrian, *The Christian
        Community* IX, #3,4, March–April, 35–36.

        "Song for the Hills," Michael MacCrian [sic] *The Christian
        Community*, IX, #11, 12, November–December, 161–164.

        "The Sick Deer," Michael MacGrian, *The Christian Community*, IX,
        #7,8, July–August, 112–113.

        Farmer's Boy article #2 accepted by *Country Fair*, London. 28 July:
        #'s 2,3,4,6,7 on file (name "John Whitfield").

        "A Farmer's Boy," Tom Whitfield, *Country Fair*, X, July, 70–71.

        Stephanie Ellen is born.

1955   Sees this period as a significant "break-through" time in artistic
        and spiritual development. In early fifties sends out more than sixty
        stories.

1956   "Farmer's Boy: New Style," Tom Whitfield, *Country Fair*, X, March,
        59–60.

        "Narcissus unto Echo" *Esquire*, May.

"The Turning Page" *Esquire*, December.

"Lament For Judas," Michael MacGrian, *The Christian Community*, X, #3,4, March–April, 34–40.

"Except Ye Become" Michael MacGrian, *The Christian Community*, X, #11, 12, November–December, pp. 150–154.

1957   "Song of the Barrow," *Esquire*.

"River's End," *Esquire*.

"Not Isaac," *Esquire*.

"The Marriage Feast," Michael MacGrian, *The Christian Community*, XI, #9, 10, September–October, 123–129

"River's End" in *Best Stories of 1957*, ed. Robert Oberfirst.

1959   *River's End and Other Stories*, New York: McDowell and Obolensky.

The Native Moment, New York: McDowell Obolensky, Toronto: George J. McLeod Limited.

Move to Bryn Afon in Penmon.

1960   "Gun-play," *Esquire*, September.

Swineherd, *The Evergreen Review*, Spring, II, 8, 16–21, 202–237.

"All the King's Horses," *TransAtlantic Review*, 5, London, December, 57–68.

"A Sweet Mouse-Trotting Cup," 21 April, in *First Person*, ed. Morton Elevitch.

The Native Moment, London: MacGibbon & Kee, 24 Apr.

"The Fairy Midwife," *The Colorado Quarterly* IX, 3, 253–261.

The Native Moment, published in pbk by Hillman-MacFadden, New York: Bartholomew House.

"Myself and a Rabbit," *Irish Stories and Tales*, New York: Washington Square Press.

1961   Move into Maelfa in Rhiwlas. Katherine Sarah Antonia is born.

1962   *Rebel to Judgment*, New York: Obolensky.

"Looking for Bridie," *Audience* 8, Cambridge, Massachusetts, Winter, 11–41

"Not Isaac" and "The Upper Room" published by Fischer (date uncertain).

River's End & Other Stories, Frankfurt: FischerVerlag.

"As Queenbees Soar" *The Second Coming*, I, 3, 20.

1963   *The Ferret Fancier*, London: MacGibbon & Kee.

Rebel to Judgment, pbk. New York: MacFadden.

English paperback edition of *The Ferret Fancier*? [see letter to Lyn Hughes, 24 Apr. 70]

The Ferret Fancier, New York: Simon & Schuster.

L'Istante Nativo, Milan: Valentino Bompiani and Co.

River's End and Other Stories, Munich: Kindler Verlag.

1964   Simon Gwyon is born.

1966   Letter to editor of [*The Observer*?] published re: Papal decision on birth control, nd [between 1966 and 1969, from Bryn Goleu].

"Morning's Twilight," [Review of McGahern's *The Dark*] *The Nation*, 7 November, 488–490.

The Native Moment. London: Four Square, New English Library paperback. April. [Dedicated "To My Grocer, L. G. W."]

River's End & Other Stories. London: Four Square (Barnard's Inn, Holburn), October.

Move to Bryn Goleu in Llanberis.

1967   "Farewell to a Kid," Michael MacGrian, *Threshold* #21, 66–73.

1968   *As Towns with Fire*, London: MacGibbon & Kee.

Excerpt from *Towns* in *The Irish Press*, Saturday, 26 Oct, "New Irish Writing," ed. by David Marcus.

1969   "The After Vacancy," London *Vogue*, December, 63–81.

1970   *Towns* reissued by A. Knopf, NY.

BBC interview at Bryn Goleu, April.

"Llanberis" by Trefwr, *Caernarvon and Denbigh Herald*, Friday, 15 May.

1971   "Not Isaac" and "The Upper Room" translated in Berlin. Move to a house in the High Street in Llanberis.

1972   Receives bursary for writers from the Arts Council for Northern Ireland.

1973   Essay on Emil Bock in *The Christian Community*, 12 August [?].
        Group starts the Artos charitable association.

1975   Move to Sudbury, Suffolk. Artos gains legal identity.

1974   John Wilson Foster gives West's fiction the first extended critical
        study in *Forces and Themes in Ulster Fiction* (Totowa, New Jersey:
        Rowman and Littlefield).

1977   *The Casual Comedy* excerpted in *The Honest Ulsterman*, No. 57, 69.
        The Wests move to Battersea. Receives a second grant from the Arts
        Council of Northern Ireland.

1978   "An Irish Bull," *The Drumlin*, Autumn, ed. Dermot Healy, 72–75.

1979   "Song of the Barrow" *In The Country*, ed. Eileen Buckle and Derek
        Lord, London: New English Library, 166–174.

1980   "Not Isaac" in *Bodley Head Book of Irish Short Stories*, ed. David
        Marcus; London, Sydney, Toronto: The Bodley Head. Goes back to
        Wales for Llyn Teg experiment.

1981   *All the King's Horses*, Dublin: Poolbeg Press, paperback.

        Letter "from a Lover of God," *Nuradeen*, I, 2, March–April, 20. West
        becomes a member of *Aosdana*. They move to 19 Malcolm Close,
        Penge, in south London.

1982   Paperback of *Bodley Head Short Stories* issued.

1983   *The Ferret Fancier* reissued in Sept., Dublin: The O'Brien Press,
        London: Allison & Busby, Devin-Adair. Makes last trip to Ireland,
        July.

1984   "Tribute to Liam O'Flaherty," *The Dictionary of Literary Biography
        Yearbook*. West falls, fracturing his left femur. Surgery and slow
        recovery confine him. Jeremy's death, 5 December.

        As Towns with Fire, Belfast: Blackstaff; London: Allison & Busby,
        paperback.

1988   Cathcart Anthony Muir West dies 19 November and is cremated at
        Beckenham, his ashes scattered at the site.

GUIDE TO PUBLICATIONS BY ANTHONY C. WEST*

1937   "The Personality of Bedell [Bishop of Kilmore and Ardagh, 1629–42]," *Ardagh and Elphin Gazette*, Kilmore parish.

1937   "The Scythe," [pseudonym] Terence O'Reilly, *Ireland Today*, II, 5, May, 43–47.

1939   20 Nov. *John O' London's Weekly* offers 9 guineas for first British serial rights to "Farewell to a Kid," [publication unverified].

1942   "Myself and Some Ducks," [pseudonym] Michael MacGrian, *The Bell*, IV, 4, 253–265 (second installment censored)

1946   "Myself and A Rabbit," *The Bell*, XI, 4, 860–872.

1947   "Myself and A Birth," *The Bell* XIII, 4, 47–57.

1949   "Two Sonnets: January, February" *Rann*, 4, Spring.

1950   "Bees and Saturn" *Notes and Correspondence*, Anthroposophical Agricultural Foundation, New Series, #1 (Spring).

1951   BBC, Northern Ireland, presents "The Half Crown" [plus "Freight"? "Shoeshine Boy"?]

1952   "Fable" *Rann* 16, Summer.

"Four Prayers," "Like a Flame that Burns Quietly," *Rann* 16, Summer.

1953   "On Killing a Sheep" [pseudonym] Michael MacGrian, *Irish Writing*, #25, 16–19, 72.

"Spring Song" *Rann*, #18

"Love Song," *Rann*, #20.

1954   "Blackthorn," *The Christian Community*, VIII, #11, 12, November–December, 142.

1955   "Myself and a Rabbit," Devin Garrity, ed., *44 Irish Short Stories* [four of thirteen pages].

"And Where Did You Go, Lord?" *The Christian Community* IX, #3,4 (March–April), 35–36.

"Song for the Hills," Michael MacCrian [*sic*] *The Christian Community*, IX, #11, 12 (November–December) 161–164.

"The Sick Deer," *The Christian Community*, IX, #7,8 (July–August), 112–113.

"A Farmer's Boy" article #2 accepted by *Country Fair*, London (28 July),

"A Farmer's Boy," Tom Whitfield, *Country Fair*, 9 (July), 70–71. Numbers 2,3,4,6,7 on file (name "John Whitfield").

1956 "Farmer's Boy: New Style," Tom Whitfield, *Country Fair*, 10 (March), 59–60.

"Narcissus unto Echo," *Esquire* (May).

"The Turning Page," *Esquire* (December).

"Lament For Judas," Michael MacGrian, *The Christian Community*, X, #3,4 (March–April), 34–40.

"Except Ye Become," Michael MacGrian, *The Christian Community*, X, #11, 12, (November–December), 150–154.

1957 "Song of the Barrow," *Esquire*, (28 January)

"River's End," *Esquire* (March).

"Not Isaac," *Esquire* (September).

"The Marriage Feast," Michael MacGrian, *The Christian Community*, XI, #9, 10 (September–October), 123–129.

"River's End" in *Best Stories of 1957*, ed. Robert Oberfirst.

1959 *River's End and Other Stories*, New York: McDowell and Obolensky.

The Native Moment, New York: McDowell Obolensky, Toronto: George J. McLeod Limited.

1960 "Gun-play," *Esquire* (September).

Swineherd, The Evergreen Review II, 8, (Spring) 16–21, 202–237.

"All the King's Horses," *TransAtlantic Review*, 5, London (December), 57–68.

1961 "A Sweet Mouse-Trotting Cup," *First Person*, (21 April).

The Native Moment, London: MacGibbon & Kee.

"The Fairy Midwife," *The Colorado Quarterly*, IX, 3, 253–261.

The Native Moment, paperback, Hillman-MacFadden, New York: Bartholomew House.

"Myself and a Rabbit," *Irish Stories and Tales*, New York: Washington Square Press.

1962   *Rebel to Judgment*, New York: Obolensky.

"Looking For Bridie," *Audience*, 8, Cambridge, Massachusetts (Winter), 11–41.

Stories: "Not Isaac" [?] and "The Upper Room," Frankfurt: Fischer Verlag. See 1971.

River's End & Other Stories, Frankfurt: Fischer Verlag.

"As Queenbees Soar" *The Second Coming*, I, 3, 20.

1963   *The Ferret Fancier*, London: MacGibbon & Kee.

Rebel to Judgment, paperback, New York: MacFadden.

Ferret? English paperback edition [see letter to Lyn Hughes, 24 Apr. 70]

The Ferret Fancier, New York: Simon & Schuster.

L'Istante Nativo, Milan: Valentino Bompiani and Co. [Via Senato, 16].

River's End and Other Stories, Munich: Kindler Verlag.

Rebel to Judgment paperback [?] by MacFadden [?] via Obolensky.

[Essay in *The Golden Blade* symposium? Proof sent to ACW by Charles Davy, 3 October?]

1966   Letter to editor of *[The Observer*?] published re: Papal decision on birth control, n.d [between 1966 and 1969, from Bryn Goleu].

"Morning's Twilight," [Review of John McGahern, *The Dark*], *The Nation*, 7 (November), 488–490.

The Native Moment. London: Four Square [New English Library], paperback, (April).

River's End & Other Stories. London: Four Square (October).

1967   "Farewell to a Kid," pseudonym: Michael MacGrian, *Threshold*, 21, 66–73.

1968   *As Towns With Fire*, London: MacGibbon & Kee.

Excerpt from *Towns* in *The Irish Press* (26 October), "New Irish Writing," ed. by David Marcus.

1969   "The After Vacancy," London *Vogue* (December), 63–81.

1970   *As Towns with Fire*, New York: Alfred A. Knopf.

BBC interview at Bryn Goleu (April).

"Llanberis," pseudonym: Trefwr, *Caernarvon and Denbigh Herald*, (15 May).

1971   "Not Isaac" (translation) in `Anders is der Glans des Mondes' *Evangelische Verlagsanstalt*, Berlin. [also "The Upper Room"?]

1973   Essay on Emil Bock, *The Christian Community* (12 August)? [see Charles Davy to ACW].

1977   Excerpt from The Casual Comedy [see p. 69: full publication was anticipated in Spring, 1978), *The Honest Ulsterman*, 57.

1978   "An Irish Bull," *The Drumlin* (Autumn), 72–75.

1979   "Song of the Barrow" *In The Country*, ed. Eileen Buckle and Derek Lord, London: New English Library, 166–174.

1980   "Not Isaac" in *Bodley Head Book of Irish Short Stories*, ed. David Marcus, London, Sydney, Toronto: The Bodley Head.

1981   *All the King's Horses*, Dublin: Poolbeg Press, paperback.

Letter "from a Lover of God," *Nuradeen*, I, 2 (March–April), 20.

1982   *Bodley Head Short Stories*, paperback.

1983   *The Ferret Fancier* reissued, Dublin: The O'Brien Press, London: Allison & Busby, Devin-Adair, Connecticut.

1984   "Tribute to Liam O'Flaherty," *The Dictionary of Literary Biography Yearbook*.

1985   *As Towns With Fire*, Belfast: Blackstaff; London: Allison & Busby, paperback.

*After 1956 West usually wrote under Anthony C. West. There are some exceptions, notably his piece in *Threshold*, 1967, and the local article on Llanberis, 1970. Corrections or supplements to this list are welcome.

SELECT BIBLIOGRAPHY

Archibald, Douglas. "Introduction." *Colby Quarterly* XXXVIII, 3, September 2002, 269–279.

Bonaccorso, Richard. "The Ghostly Presence: William Trevor's Moral Device." *Colby Quarterly* XXXVIII, 3, September 2002, 308–314.

Brown, Terence. *Ireland: A Social and Cultural History 1922–1979*. London: Fontana, 1981.

Brown, Terence.. *Ireland's Literature*. Totowa: Barnes & Noble, 1988.

Cahalan, James M. *The Irish Novel*. Boston: G. K. Hall, 1988.

Cahalan, James M. *Modern Irish Literature and Culture, A Chronology*. New York: G. K. Hall and Toronto: Maxwell Macmillan, 1993.

Corcoran, Neil. *After Yeats and Joyce: Reading Modern Irish Literature*, Oxford and New York: Oxford University Press, 1997.

Craig, Patricia. *The Rattle of the North*. Belfast: Blackstaff Press, 1992.

Deane, Seamus. *Field Day Anthology of Irish Writing*. Derry: Field Day Publications, 1991.

Deane, Seamus. *A Short History of Irish Literature*. London: Hutchinson, 1986.

Eyler, Audrey Stockin. *Celtic, Christian, Socialist: The Novels of Anthony C. West*. Rutherford, New Jersey: Fairleigh Dickinson University Press, 1993.

Eyler, Audrey Stockin. "The Old Made New Again: Imagery in Two Stories by Anthony C. West." *Eire-Ireland*, Fall 1985, 52–64.

Eyler, Audrey Stockin. "Piques in Darien: Anthony C. West and his New York Publishers." *Eire-Ireland*, Fall, 1992, 49–66.

Fallon, Brian. *An Age of Innocence: Irish Culture 1930–1960*. Dublin: Gill & Macmillan, 1998.

Feather, John. *A History of British Publishing*. New York: Croom Helm, 1988.

Foster, John Wilson. *Forces and Themes in Ulster Fiction*. Totowa, New Jersey: Rowman & Littlefield, 1974.

Gingrich, Arnold. *Nothing But People: The Early Days at Esquire, A Personal History, 1928–1958*. New York: Crown Publishers, 1971.

Graham, Colin. *Deconstructing Ireland: Identity, Theory, Culture*. Edinburgh: Edinburgh University Press, 2001.

Heaney, Seamus. *The Place of Writing*, Atlanta: Scholars Press, 1989.

Heaney, Seamus. *Preoccupations, Selected Prose 1968–1978*, New York: Farrar, Straus, Giroux, 1980.

351

Hemleben, Johannes. *Rudolf Steiner, A Documentary Biography*. East Grinstead: Henry Goulden, 1975.

Hills, Rust.Will Blythe, and Erika Mansourian, ed.. *Lust, Violence, Sin, Magic: Sixty Years of Esquire Fiction*. New York: Atlantic Monthly Press, 1993.

Hogan, Robert. *Dictionary of Irish Literature* (Revised and Expanded Edition) II. London: Aldwych Press, 1979 and 1996.

Hogan, Robert. "Old Boys, Young Bucks, and New Women: The Contemporary Irish Short Story," in *The Irish Short Story*, ed. James F. Kilroy, Boston: G. K. Hall, 1984, 169–215.

Jeffares, A. Norman. *Anglo-Irish Literature*. New York: Schocken Books, 1982.

Kazin, Alfred. "The Self as History," *Telling Lives: The Biographer's Art*, Marc Pachter, ed., University of Pennsylvania Press, 1981.

Kiberd, Declan. "Aosdána: A Comment," *The Crane Bag Book of Irish Studies*. Dublin: Blackwater Press, 1982, 783–784.

Kiely, Benedict, ed. *Penguin Book of Irish Short Stories*. Hammondsworth, New York: Viking, 1981.

Kirkland, Richard. *Literature and Culture in Northern Ireland Since 1965: Moments of Danger*. London and New York: Longman, 1996.

Korda, Michael. *Another Life: A Memoir of Other People*. New York: Random House, 2000.

Korda, Michael. *Making the List: A Cultural History of the American Bestseller, 1900–1999*. New York: Barnes & Noble, 2001.

Madden, David. *Rediscoveries*. New York: Crown Publishers, 1971.

Mahon, Sean, ed. *The Best of the Bell*. Dublin: The O'Brien Press, 1978.

Martin, Augustine. *The Genius of Irish Prose*. Cork and Dublin: Mercier Press, 1985.

McHugh, Roger, and Maurice Harmon. *A Short History of Anglo-Irish Literature from its Origins to the Present Day*. Totowa: Barnes & Noble, 1982.

O'Brien, George. *The Irish Novel 1960–2010*. Cork: Cork University Press, 2012.

Pelaschiar, Laura. *Writing the North: The Contemporary Novel in Northern Ireland*. Trieste: Edizioni Parnaso, 1998.

Pierce, David, ed. *Irish Writing in the Twentieth Century: A Reader*. Cork: Cork University Press, 2000.

Reynolds, Paul R. Jr. *The Middle Man: The Adventures of a Literary Agent*. New York: William Morrow & Company, 1972.

Sampson, Denis. "'Bleak Splendour': Notes for an Unwritten Biography of William Trevor," *Colby Quarterly* XXXVIII, 3, September 2002, 280–294.

Sloan, Barry. *Writers and Protestantism in the North of Ireland: Heirs to Adamnation?* Dublin and Portland: Irish Academic Press, 2000.

Somerville-Large, Peter. *Irish Voices: Fifty Years of Irish Life, 1916–1966*. London: Chatto & Windus, 1999.

Storey, Mark. "'Bewildered Chimes': Image, Voice and Structure in Recent Irish Fiction." In *Across a Roaring Hill*, ed. Gerald Dawe and Edna Longley. Belfast and Dover, New Hampshire: Blackstaff Press, 1985, 161–181.

Steiner, Rudolf. *Christianity as Mystical Fact.* New York and London: G. P. Putnam's Sons, 1914.

Steiner, Rudolf. *Discussions with Teachers.* London: Rudolf Steiner Press, 1967.

Steiner, Rudolf. *The Education of the Child in the Light of Anthroposophy.* London: Rudolf Steiner Press, 1965.

Steiner, Rudolf. *The Nature of Anthroposophy.* New York: Rudolf Steiner Publications, 1964.

Steiner, Rudolf. *Three Streams in the Evolution of Mankind.* Dornach Lectures, 1918. London: Rudolf Steiner Press, 1965.

Steiner, Rudolf. *Woman and Society.* Lecture at Hamburg, 17 November 1906. London: Rudolf Steiner Press, 1985.

Tebbel, John. *Between Covers: The Rise and Transformation of Book Publishing in America.* New York: Oxford University Press, 1987.

Tebbel, John. *A History of Book Publishing in the United States, IV The Great Change, 1940–1980.* New York: R. R. Bowker Company, 1981.

Tracy, Robert. "Telling Tales: The Fictions of William Trevor." *Colby Quarterly* XXXVIII, 3, September 2002, 295–307.

Welch, Robert. *The Oxford Companion to Irish Literature.* Oxford: The Clarendon Press, 1996.

West, Cathcart Anthony Muir. Papers. These include correspondence, autobiographical documents, published and unpublished works and notes, conversation notes, and interviews. West's papers were originally purchased by the University of Surrey, St. Mary's College, Strawberry Hill, Twickenham, and later acquired by Linen Hall Library, Belfast, N.I. At West's request, I had sorted them in his study after his death in 1989, indexed them, boxed them, and deposited an accompanying description with St. Mary's College library. My work since has been done through my photocopies of much of the collection, copying kindly permitted and assisted by Olive West. I have observed here the classification of the originals, making notes, however, about the inevitable later discoveries that altered earlier conclusions of the sorting.

Versions of The Lady Actaeon

The typescripts bear various titles, among them The Garden Party, Naked to Laughter, Memento Mori, The Stone in the Ring, The Stone and the Ring, Ring Around Stone, The Shapeless Stone. Concluded order of composition, earliest probably dating from late 1930s:

Some Q fragments
C
B
A,G,H,K
D, M
E
F

I (1977)
J
L
N,O,P,Q,S,T
R (1980s)
M (1980s)

The following versions are complete or nearly so (the others have been severely frag-
mented. The R and T versions incorporate their title pages into the fiction, with
Diana's and O'Dea's child grown and offering the record:

M - Anthony C. West, Memento Mori (short story).

E - Anthony C. West, Naked to Laughter, 1033 pages.

P - (Diana's journal with son's Postscript) The Stone in the Ring, 533 pages.

R - Mary Mongan Russel, Ring Around Stone, 654 pages.

T - John Mongan Russel, The Stone in the Ring, 560 pages.

The E is the most explicit, most psychologically motivated and philosophically
explained, most connected, clearest, and longest. It is probably a fairly early version.
It seems to be one he did after receiving Obolensky's suggestions (K + A?). West was
understandably dissatisfied with its he-said-she-said conventionality. The later, more
subtle R has been used for most citations in this book.

Reviews and Notices of Published Works

Unless starred (*), these clippings—forwarded by his agent, his publishers, or his
friends—turned up among West's papers. I have supplemented bibliographical information where possible.

River's End and Other Stories / All the King's Horses

Anon. *The Guardian*, 12 August [1960].

Anon. *Oxford Mail*, 11 August 1960.

Anon. *Richmond Times-Dispatch*, no date.

Anon. *Smith's Trade News*, 6 August 1960.

Duchene, Anne. No source, 12 August 1960.

Hicks, Granville. *The Saturday Review*, 5 July 1958.

Jameson, Storm. No source, no date.

Jennings, Elizabeth. *The Listener*, 15 September 1960.

Kennedy, Maurice. No source, no date.

Laws, Frederick. *Daily Telegraph*, 2 September 1960.

Noville, Constance. *South Wales Echo*, 13 February 1957 [re: "River's End"].

Ronan. *The Herald*, 10 September 1981.

Spark, Muriel. *The Observer*, no date.

The Native Moment

Adams, Phoebe. *Atlantic*, 205:99, January 1960.*

Anon. *Kirkus*, 27:797, 15 October 1959.*

Barrett, M. L. *Library Journal*, 85:304, 15 June 1960.*

Curley, T. F. *Commonweal*, 71:501, 29 January 1960.*

Davenport, John. *The Observer*, 30 April 1961.

Healey, Robert C. *New York Herald Tribune* book review, p. 9, 22 May 1960.

Hodgart, Matthew. No source, 5 May 1960

Hughes, Riley. *Catholic World*, 190:384, March 1960.*

Kelly, Bernard. *Penrar* [?] *Post*, 31 January 1960.

Stern, James. *New York Times* book review, p. 64, 6 December 1959.

Urquart, Fred. *Sunday Telegraph*, 30 April 1961.

Webster, Harvey Curtis. *Saturday Review*, 42:19, 12 December 1959.

Rebel to Judgment

Anon. *The New Yorker*, 38:171, 29 September 1962.*

W[ickenden], D[an]. *New York Herald Tribune* books, p. 7, 2 September 1962.*

Levin, Martin. *New York Times* book review, p. 42, 16 September 1962*

Pippett, Aileen. *Saturday Review*, 46:56, 19 January 1963.*

The Ferret Fancier

Adams, Phoebe. *Atlantic*, 215:160, April 1965.*

Anon. *Beaumont Journal*, Beaumont, Texas, 5 March 1965.

Anon. *Library Journal*, no date.

Anon. The New York Times summer list, 6 June 1965.

Anon. *The New Yorker*, 41:187, 20 March 1965.*

Anon. *The Observer*, 21 July 1963.

Anon. *The Oregonian*, Portland, Oregon, 21 March 1965.

Anon. *The Tablet*, 5 November 1983.

Anon. *Time*, [c. 9 April 1965].

Anon. *Times* [London] *Literary Supplement*, p. 181, 15 March 1963.

Anon. *Ulster Arts* [?], Northern Irish Arts Council, 1972.

Brady, Charles A. *The Buffalo Evening News*, 13 March 1965.

British Broadcasting Company. "World of Books," 4 May 1963.

Campbell, Kerry. *The Belfast Review* (Winter), 5, 1983.

Christine Countess of Longford, *The Irish Times*, 8, 9 March 1963.

Crumpler, Reva. *The Times*, Louisville, Kentucky, [1965?].

Francoeur, Robert A. *Best Sellers*, 25:13, 1 April 1965.

Glacken, Brendan, *The Irish Times*, 26 November 1983.

Hicks, Granville, *The Saturday Review*, 48:23, 27 March 1965.

Jackman, F. P. *Worcester Sunday Telegram*, Massachusetts, 14 March 1965.

Johnson, Paul A. *Beaumont Journal*, Beaumont, Texas, 5 March 1965.

Karlen, Arno. *The Nation*, 200:486, 3 May 1965.

Kavanagh, John. *The Irish Post*, 12 November 1983.

Kisor, Henry D. *Wilmington Morning News*, 19 March 1965.

Lawrence, Vincent. No source or date [c.1983].

Murray, James G. *The Long Island Catholic*, 11 March 1965.

O'Neill-Barna, Anne. *Chicago Tribune*, No date [1965?].

O'Neill-Barna, Anne. *New York Times Book Review*, p. 4, 21 March 1965.*

Raphael, Frederick. *The Sunday Times*, 17 March 1963.

Richardson, Maurice. *The New Statesman*, 65:349, 8 March 1963.

Thornburg, Barry. No source [1965].

Walsh, Chad. *New York Herald Tribune Book Week*, p. 18, 4 April 1965. *As Towns with Fire*

Anon. *Columbus Dispatch*, 26 April 1970.

Anon. *The Irish Herald* [San Francisco], March 1986.

Anon. *Newtownards Spectator*, 21 March 1985.

Anon. *Phoenix Arizona Gazette*, 18 April 1970.

Anon. *Playboy*, No date.

Anon. *The Times* [London? 1968?].

Anon. No source, 26 March [1970].

Berthelsen, John. No source [Sacramento], 19 April 1970.

Bittner, William. *The Miami Herald*, 21 June 1970.

Bracken, Beatrice [pseud. for Beryl Grwffyd]. "Man in Armour." [unpublished] .

Bromley, Michael. *The Belfast Telegraph*, 20 March 1985.

[Carty, Ciaran?]. *The Sunday Independent*, 6 November 1983.

Curley, Arthur. *Library Journal*, 95:1505, 15 April 1970.*

Curtis, Jack. *Monterey Peninsula Herald*, 28 March 1970.

Hall, Joan S. *The Houston Post*, 7 June 1970.

Healy, Dermot. *Fortnight*, 18 March 1985.

Kelly, Frederic. *New Haven Register*, 12 April 1970.

Kilfeather, John. *The Belfast Review* (Winter), 1983.

Kilfeather, John. *The Irish Times*, 20 April 1985.

Kiniery, Paul. *Best Sellers*, 30:36, 15 April 1970.*

Lask, Thomas, *New York Times*, no date.

Little, E. L. "Irish Poet's Saga," No source, no date.

O'F. P. *Irish Democrat*, 9 July 1985.

O'Keeffe, Timothy. "About a bicycle? Prose fiction since Joyce." No source, no date.

Oldberg, Karl. *Independent . . . Journal* [?], 10April 1970 [?].

Sachs, Sylvia. *Pittsburgh Press*, 22 March 1970.

Sandrof, Nancy. *Worcester Telegram*. 12 April 1970.

Scannell, Vernon. *New Statesman*, 76:588, 1 November 1968.*

Schiff, Pearl. *The Boston Globe*, 4 February 1970.

Schott, Webster. *The New Yorker*, 46:98, 30 May 1970.

Schott, Webster. *New York Times Book Review*, 33, 5 April 1970.

Excerpt from R version of The Lady Actaeon, Ring Around Stone

(It opens with Diana's last diary entry)

... From vulgar to sublime, we walk—we waddle through the dusks. We like the dusk: it can't see us, people just goodnights with sightless eyes, distance not measurable, all voices grey. We count the lights for interest, the land's rheumed eyes spying on the dark: odd how darkness manifests so many hidden dwellings that day can't see.

The rectory lights as one, Ferris' lodge as two, we count all lights that we can see, an odd total comforting, an even one catastrophe. We try to ignore the hill-topping cars but sometimes cheat the change the even into odd and then regret it, guilty that fate will recognize dishonesty. If we regain the rectory gates with an even number, we'll linger or walk a little more until we find an extra odd one, then close our eyes and hasten home. Altho' much walking brings a dull pain into the small of our back, frightening us, we can't stand still at night; it becomes an uncomfortable lurking and invites some passer-by to ask us our intentions. Ferris the old abortion lurks. I've seen him about his lodge, a shadow in his shadows as if his dracula has the better of him.

We dwaddle through the days, thinking un-thinking non-thinking re-thinking, looking for something we never knew we had and know we never had; reading scraps of this and that, even the print on toilet-paper sans any interest or satisfaction, sentences without sense, the single printed words disowning their associates and changing into symbols for something else, arguing the opposite way of what we see, the broken bits invoking different images. Then we doze and dream the words as they float about and sound themselves and change themselves by adding random letters fore and aft, the alterations so coarse that we wake up embarrassed and hope we haven't been overheard. We know it's all a game but doing it's believing it like a gambler with a sure-fire horse or hand of cards. I remember playing my mind similar tricks when a child, burying an apprehension or misdeed under a better fable, avoiding due punishment by contorting my excuses with quite extraneous but quite logical explanation so the mentor's mind chased my hounds and let my hare go free. Come to think of it, my later poetry may have had similar motives: preaching to myself like gate to post to silence the creaks of old remorse for something done or undone long years before.

Unless Dea has lived a totally blameless life I can't understand it when he implies he has no remorse and speaks as if his past belongs to some other for whom he's not responsible and even that in face of his evident helpful responsibility for others' shortfalls. He always says forgive oneself to let oneself live on in better fashion instead of using new experience to mourn the past's sour milk—all very well, there could be ruthlessness involved, the velvet glove disguising the iron fist: hardened homicidal criminals are supposed to be unremorseful altho' he looks at the meaning of criminal, splitting it between the mere law-breaker and the psychopath, a word I dislike since law-breakers are recoverable, psychopaths damned. He always interprets common words and sayings according to his total view, saying we use words at secondhand oblivious of their substance and reality. But be that as it may, are good and bad so close together in us all that right and wrong are interchangeable and almost indiscriminate, no one aware of change or good or harm until the action gives the social evidence to society which then proceeds to judge the right or wrong according to its own ideas of right or wrong, the judgment itself quite liable to be right as wrong or vice versa, the national norm an awful prejudice and preconception, a kind of unwritten constitution of mere rumour that would stoop to covert criminality to save the appearances of discredited appearances . . .

Christ I dunno. I'll never understand—anything, nor national rights nor wrongs, nor rights nor wrongs religious that can saint one man and burn another, hosannah the twin of crucify, hanging the sibling of enoblement. In France the frogs eat snails as cockneys catch eels and Scots shave in whiskey the way old beauties bathed in ass's milk, Chinese cook birdsnests, cheddars like cheese, Germans have beerfeasts and Irish gaelic yams, Jews won't talk to swine and Moslems keep geishagirls in heaven called houris the singular hour. I'll preach a bran-new faith and keep a stud of big-boned males in paradise and make 'em chew our wood and drink our water.

When I asked Dea what he thought of Moslemism as rival to his christianity he said it was an amalgam of Greco-judean gnosticism and satisfied a certain kind of intelligence.

But is it a real faith?

Yes much as if simplistic christianity, I suppose. Anyway, our science is almost totally arabist—Allah into cosmic machine.

But was Mahomet a genuine prophet?

Yes and no . . .

What's that mean?

He had certain clairvoyance that was akin to Swedenborg's while his theology was an echo of the old hebrew monotheism but even Sufi gnosticism doesn't realise his importance to christianity.

Altho' I'm lost I persist and he makes matters worse by saying that Mahomet opposed cold intellectualism with emotionalism. . . . Then he says laughingly that I have pagan piety, Arthurian piety and I don't know if this is a paving stone or a bunch of shamrocks and making me see Hauley vividly with its legend that it was one of Arthur's many seats. God he can scare me sometimes. Am I his lady of Shalott, my mirror full of moving shadows. I'd rather be his Shalott than his Maud by god . . .

When I wanted more, impatient with his frustrating chinks, he said it was all too vast a subject for five minutes, making me bite my tongue to keep from asking him why the hell he had brought it up in the first place until remembering it was I who started it.

Godknows I'm not interested in religion and only so appear since he is so involved and so seldom discusses personalities and convivial commonplaces and there's little left in the filing cabinet. His attitude whether meant or not is similar if not the same to any cleric past and present who metaphorically hums and haws when layfolk ask close questions on his craft, every damn one of them seem linked in masonic secrecy. I remember reading reports of letters between two early old fathers when one warned the other to be careful about giving the groundlings too much information on the subtleties of their faith with the implication that the latter might know as much as they did: power again—I've heard

the self-same sentiment in Westminster. Secrecy and power—don't educate, indoctrinate like all the little Kremlins and praise the social goose
for all its golden eggs. At times I'm so indigested with unsaid challenge
that my heart beats in my throat and starves my breathings . . .

Disgruntled winter's imperceptibly retreating even if winter here
is only sunless wetness of long time, spring ruthlessly maturing, larks
already singing descants to the dawns quite often high enough for cloud
to hide them so their disembodied melody feathers down earth like starry
song. Daylong the rookery's loud with garrulous argument as mated
couples watch spare males compete for wives, the married males loudly
possessive. Their evening dance gets later every day. It used to be at two
in windraked racing winter-skies and now it's held at three and will soon
be four then five then six and more, five minutes more each day as if
they had a clock to tell their ritual time. And still these sombre clouds of
starlings flee darkness home without a thought of pairing. I now watch
for them every evening and hold my breath to wish them, drive them on
their way and feel like borrowing Clancy's shotgun to hurry them.

Dea's going on with this farming plan—the new monasticism, labour
and prayer, saving the old Irish soul at expense of my sanity. When I
challenge him he always quite humbly explains and I can feel sorry for
him, for his worried concern about the world's greedy ways. I know this
world's a greedy place, a sump of human failings, a pyramid of fleas, envy
a natural habit, good fortune grudged, others' ill-luck a cause for celebration. Knowing so I've kept aloof, self the best master of one's revels until
old time himself appears and murmurs enough's enough . . .

It's what's living's all about and no one goes naked and unarmed bar
decent folk like Angus born sacrosanct sans need for guile and needless
of self-protective fear . . .

Doubtless Dea loves me I assume or else he grins and bears me with
or without the sex, which puts me at emotional and practical disadvantage. I may even be his shirt of hair to mortify his mind for goodness
sake when many another lesser man would call me his proverbial pain
in the ass.

I know how love might feel beyond the sexual bar tho' never felt
it in or for myself—the so-called total lostness in and for another as in

literature—for me an emotional prison despite the hollywood hedonics: fists in the gob and smacks on the kissers, the undertone of violence similar. I've never watched a living love-affair nor seen nor read a fictional one without asking how much old fuxing was involved. Ironically, like Dea himself, I've always tried to see the human being without the spurious increment of fux despite its passionate importance. As usual he goes further and claims the sexual act is over-emphasized because it can hardly be mentioned without invoking sexuality whereas in better philosophical terms it's one of the few activities in life when pleasure and desire are momentarily balanced—animals procreate, men experience. And women experience the results more ways than one I silently add . . . (R, 576a–582; R disk, 476–479).

Christmas is coming and I am very fat: grey flurries of wet snow falling the way the wind wants to make its dance viable, spectral mornings white and beautiful, cleansed and calm, this weary land just black and white—black trees and roads, white fields, all autumn's waste disguised under a pewter sky. Blackly gigantic against the pallor, Dea's herm sports a cap of snow that makes its height seem endless against the white horizon. I bet it moves about at night and wails in rock-fall gaelic for its lost estate.

I read both nativities as I've always done; why I don't know, perhaps because poor dear Nain solemnly read them aloud on every christmas eve. I now see that the two accounts really seem to describe the births of different children, one in a house with attending notables, the other in a stable with attending hinds, one persecuted, the other not—Luke's gentle story and the savage tragic Matthew with its refugees. On the evidence if evidence and not interpolation Dea's theory seems the better bet rather than saying Matthew and Luke described the self-same thing in different ways with the silent implication that one or the other made a bad mistake which on the face of it is hardly possible and if the whole four gospels are post-christian concoctions, the concoctors made a confusing job of it indeed. It's really extraordinary that over centuries theologians roman and otherwise have stared at the contradictions without better explanation—no wonder their churches are now so rickety. When I ask Dea again he nods and says there it is, that Jerome and the new constantine church buried the infancy gospels in order to create an over-simplified creed for the imperial masses in lieu of worked-out paganism. Were I christianly involved, I'd be hopping mad and I accuse him of the lie's extension since after all he runs with it irrespective of whatever he personally knows. All he says is patience and the truth will slowly reappear. Like psychologists, I think that theologians are brainwashed by theologians to preserve the appearances much in the same way as politicians replace the dreadful human truth with diplomatic fables convenue.

Irrespective of my indifferent atheism or a-religion-ism, I obey the seasonal sentiment and decide to go to church, jesus and/or christ here or there, admitting that the nostalgia does create a kind of sharing and benign neighbourliness, makes people hide their natural envy and say happy christmas to one another as if they meant it.

Dea held a midnight service followed by eight o' clock communion, coming home for a cup of coffee and going off again for a children's service on his bicycle, leaving the Ben for me. I don't know where he finds his energy. He can rest for fifteen minutes flat, sleep like an infant and rise refreshed. Work satisfaction I suppose. My work is worry while his is blandly social, meeting people all the time, straightening bent souls like Father O'Flynn. I only meet Ana, Lord, Ferris, Clancy, Angus strangers and myself and self is antisocial.

Old Ferris horsed us to the service, creeping over snow-patches with eggs in his mouth, squeezing his eyes as the downy snowflakes rush at him and die as rain on the windscreen, the Ben dictating to him as usual. He is really an old horse man. I heard him talking to the car while grooming it. If a rear wheel kicked him he would shout whoa. To give him due, Ben is spotless inside and out.

Poems O God as seen on old palimpsets: trees walking through snow, a red cock pheasant burning snow, a rusty fox stalking a feeding blackbird along a snowy hedge. A lovely tawny hare lopes up the road ahead of us, stops, stands up then runs a little more, squirming Ferris in his seat as he swallows protective spittle and likely to sain himself against his orange grain in lieu of spitting out as Ana looks at me and whispers god-save-uz . . .

Why should a nervous hare be so suspected: the buddha had a hare

and it has been a sacred sign for millenia from china through the bible
to peru, painters crouching it at Mary's feet, painters also poets those
days like honest Brueghel's terrible magi and Bosch's awful prelates—no
honest radicals any more . . . (R, 507–509; disk, 411–413)

My world or what I think is world is upsidedown or downside up in
vacant sphere of time or space which is the shape of time that causes all
effects in life and loneliness and ergo life and loneliness is time between
the minor poles of dusk at dawn and dusk and evenset and slowly breaks
us on the wheel that spins then stops then spins again, grinding existence
down to dust that blows away to nothingness and total peace where Dea
insists his Christ resides in timeless glory in ever-resurrection.

Until that time or timelessness I'll never know. .The everlasting
never never never when time is nevermore (R, 596; R disk, 493).

* * *

. . . Sphinx-like, Mrs Delia Dempsey sits on a log before her fire that
brightly glows in the shade of the sheltered peaty hollow, her sleeping
child stretched across her thighs, its heavy head in the crook of her left
arm.

Around her camp circles the waste of tumbling heathered bog, its
far circumference fusing to the grey rim of wind-raked sky on which a
bleached bonewhite half-moon waits patiently to shine her borrowed
light when the sun decides to go. . . .

Looking at nothing nor blinking, Mrs Dempsey could be taken for
one of the bog's old corpses cured over centuries by the acid peat, the
fire-glow bronzing her bedouin-brown weathered face and cruelly goi-
tered neck, the pale eyes heavily lidded, the skin stretched tightly across
the bones, two deep charcoaled lines etched down to the mouth-corners
from the roots of the beaked nose, large ears with silver rings the size
of shillings in the pierced lobes, the hair scraped up under a man's old
cap, the feet in old brown shoes tied once with scraps of lace, a square of
grey blanket shawling her shoulders over a faded green blouse fastened
once across her chest by one large safety-pin, the small brown hands
absurdly deft and shapely, a broad golden ring on the wedding finger
put there by the great O'Dempsey himself, four thousand year-long days

ago: sphinx-woman for sure and well-abused by harsh hopelessness and uncharitable time.

The child is large, with a bloated belly and high conical head above the ears, its little hands hooked together as it sleeps and sparsely clad for the time of year—only a wash-shrunken jersey that doesn't reach its navel, the nether end covered by a patch of loose grey blanket matching the mother's shawl.

Behind them is the dark triangle of their tent and behind the tent a small spring van with delicate rubber-tyred wheels, its box a bright yellow with false panels framed by bright red lines, the garish colours discordant against the environment's neutral monochrome. Under the cart sleeps the lurcher dog among a set of harness and behind it hang a few tatty bits of washing on a string tied to two saplings.

The dog grumbles a suspicious growl and Mrs Dempsey lifts her head with indrawn breath to listen, hearing only the movements of the donkeys until a form appears on the lane above her and says good evening . . .

Hough! she coughs with a start, looking up at a small pale-faced woman with a head of tangled coppery hair and wearing a long dark-blue quilted coat that covers her from throat to foot, the wakened child starting a costive wail. She can't hear what Diana says and watches the latter come down the slope into the hollow and move round the fire to sit opposite on a step cut into the soft bank and hold out her hands to the warmth. The child now in full voice, she absently unfastens the safety-pin in her blouse and puts it in her mouth, lifting a lank smoke-brown dug, pinching the nipple between first and second fingers and guiding it to the child's open mouth. It seizes the teat, worries it and complains before it starts to suck, the mother holding its big head in place with her left hand, staring at Diana with obvious puzzlement and asking flatly: Whur ar'y'headin' fur?

Before Diana can reply, a drift of acrid smoke blinds her as another pain begins to sear through her back and loins. She shuts her eyes and fists her hands tightly against smoke and pain and waits for them to pass, Delia closely watching and stating from a distance: Ye're havin' t'panes . . .

I'll be all right, Diana whispers as the pain reaches its height and begins to ebb.

Hagh! Y'shud b' makin' yr'way hoam, Delia states firmly, prising the teat out of the baby's mouth and automatically changing it over, giving it the second teat and replacing the used one as if they were both dummies and didn't belong to her at all. Have ye cum far? she asks.

Diana nods.

There is silence until the child exhausts the second teat and whines again. Delia lifts it under the arms and jigs it on her knees, changing its cry into angry hiccoughs, then slinging it under her left arm and staring its bare backside at Diana, a breath of rancid urine drawn off the movements by the rising air over the fire. The pink backside seems like an irate face, the kicking legs its arms, the mother seemingly oblivious to the noise that fills the hollow as if with vituperative despair. The crying is invoking a reluctant memory in Diana that she doesn't want to know, Delia's indifference angering her as if the latter were wilfully teasing her. Can't you make it stop? she demands impatiently.

Delia glances at her with hardened eyes, resenting the interference but not answering as a horsehoofed train gallops across the cooling distance. She removes the safety-pin from her mouth and pins the blouse together again, then fumbles in a skirt pocket and produces a small cigarette butt which she places carefully between pursed lips, bending to the fire and selecting a charred twig, uses it for a match, pincers the butt between forefinger and thumb and drawing several deep lungfuls before it is exhausted and then saying flatly but forcefully, each word with its own little wisp of smoke: I t'ink, missis, ye'd better be makin' yr'way hoam.

Let me stay a little longer, Diana pleads.

Dis is no place at all in your state an' I doan't want trubble.

You would like me to die somewhere else, Diana says vindictively.

Doan't be sayin' dat! Delia protests. 'Tis unlucky.

Death needn't be so luckless?

Ye'll be havin' t'po-lice at uz!

A tap tap tap sounds on the road and she glances round . . .

You're expecting someone?

Me husban' . . . she says shortly, then demanding sharply: Where's your man?

Diana keeps silent.

D'ye have wan at all?

Diana nods.

He mus'b'a quare feller littin' ye out like dis. Diana nods again.

Hagh . . . she says, rising and going to her tent and filling a small three-legged cauldron with potatoes, tipping water over them from a chipped white enamel pail, returning to the fire and settling the pot in a nest of ashes. All this with her right hand, the child under the other one. Standing over the fire, she says as if the solution suddenly struck her: Tell ye what, missis, whin Dinnie gits here we'll tackle an ass an' take ye hoam. Where d'ye live?

Diana hardly hears as she waits the onset of another pain that gathers in the distance and swells towards her like a tidal wave, a flush of blood-warm water bursting from her and quickly cooling round her thighs. She locks her hands together and sways back and forth, Delia watching her with dispassionate sympathy then returning to her log and jigging the child on her knees.

The pain's departure fills Diana with gratitude. She breathes deeply and wipes the sweat of her forehead with a handkerchief, her hand coming on a lipstick in a pocket of the dressing-gown. She offers it to Delia as a kind of thank-offering for her own relief.

Delia looks at him, at Diana and at the distance between them before she rises and goes into the tent, returning with a strip of blanket which she fastens on the child for a napkin and then lights the candle off the fire, the drops of melting tallow momentarily brightening their faces and accentuating the slow creep of dusk. Returning to her tent, she drops some hot grease on an old cracked saucer and sticks the candle on it then rummages in a soapbox and finds a half-empty half-pint of whiskey. Pulling the cork with her teeth, she holds the child's unruly head and carefully tips some whiskey into its open mouth. It gags and shudders. She pats it on the back until it regains its breath and offers it more and it takes the second swallow like a seasoned toper. Measuring the whiskey in the bottle against the candle, she gives it two more mouthfuls, corking the bottle while throwing an eye on Dempsey, then laying the child on its sack of straw and tucking a blanket around it, patting it gently on the shoulder until its eyelids heavy and finally close. She hides the whiskey again in her box, under her own private possessions which, oddly, Dempsey has never once disturbed: a rosary, a small ivory crucifix that has been blessed in Rome, several holy postcards, a big pebble from Lough Derg where she had made the pilgrimage as a girl albeit to sell religious mementos, a bent-stem pipe that had been her father's and a faded photograph of him standing between two horses, the big bone button off the fancy coat she had worn at her wedding, the child's caul done up in brown paper and an old bronze brooch big as a door-hinge that she had found in the bog, an article worth more than all Dempsey's donkeys although neither of them knew it.

Dempsey meditates by the fire, his body weary, the drink and the warmth dozing him. Cold streets with shaving winds sharpened on the corners, damp butts stored in the peak of his cap to dry them out; people warmly clad and fleshed, cars going by worth hundreds, shops with more money in their windows than the bank of Ireland, tills in the pubs jangling joyously and oceans of amber swallows in shining bottles, publicans with fat hands, rings on their fingers, women with round arses and the legs and bodies of women young and old, fine clothes and fur coats and big feeds in eating-houses with great smells tasting the air: moneyless in a land of money, the lack of it a bankrupt's interest and when he had any he didn't know he had it until it was spent: the emancipated physical man, free man beyond society, a man like the wind that blows where it wants, who can only use his freedom to complain about it and envy the unfree and never to know alas that his world could be as splendid as his most exotic dreams.

He can see only his misery and scheme to escape it: the ass and cart worth ten pound, the asses maybe another tenner—sell out and skip, clean heels. The thought is so loud in his mind that he glances craftily at Delia in case she might have overheard it, the sight of her calling her his jailer: a prisoner he is, the wide land his jail, an old dry wife his jailer fit only to breed idiots, poor the day he had been honest enough to ring her. Whom god has joined Dempsey . . . the priest warned, making sure he had the pound before he said it.

Shoite . . . he mutters defeatedly.

Wha . . . ? Delia asks.

Nottin . . . he mutters guiltily, turning away from her reading eyes in case she sees his treason. Sell out and skip, over the water, meet up with a fresh woman like this one with the milk-white thighs . . . Did ye fine it yit? he asks.

I'll say ef'I do! Delia snaps, hoping she will to save her possession of it and at that moment seeing it in the grey ashes at the edge of the fire. Pretending to rake the spot with a bit of stick, she presses the ring into the peat with a thumb and spreads ashes over it.

What d'ye say it's wort'? Dempsey asks.

I dunno what it's wort'!

What'd she say?

Arragh, she was bletherin' somet'in 'bout it bein' t'popes, Delia said compulsively, desperate now to maintain her duplicity.

Jaysus, it cud be wort' money, Dempsey surmises. Mebbie tin poun'?

How t'hell do I know?

Twenty pound, thirty, forty, fifty—sixty whole pounds in his head . . . Ye're rale schmart an' no fucken mistake, he condems.

Delia doesn't reply, pretending to give up her search, looking worriedly at Diana and telling him again to harness an ass . . . Ef she comes t'harm we'll be blamed.

What'd we do? he demands rhetorically. We didden ax her? Is der anyt'in' t'ate?

Der's taters ef they're not biled t'mash.

She uses the tail of her skirt to drain the pot and he hunkers by it and gingerly lifts a potato, juggling it from one hand to the other, blowing on it, asking: Any fucken salt atsilf?

She rummages in the tent and finds him a packet of salt and with skillful fingers he peels the potato, pinches salt over it and haws through a mouthful to cool it. Delia reaches to the top of the bank and finds two tin plates, handing him one and they settle down to their meal, eating skins and flesh and hawing their breaths round the hot mouthfuls, seemingly so unaware of Diana that they could have forgotten her. When he is satisfied, he hands his plate to Delia and she again asks him to harness the donkey.

Y'haven't a drap'a tay? he asks.

Catch t'ass an' I'll bile t'kettle. Day cud be sayin' we hurted hur?

Two agin wan . . . he replies, finding a butt in his cap and lighting it as Delia fills the small blackened kettle from the pail. The cockerel flaps in her face. She curses it and bats it away and it cockles with brave terror, Dempsey looking around nervously and up the silvered stretch of road. Delia's backside fills the mouth of the tent and he uses the opportunity to take a long swig of his liquor, the shock of it making him hiccough, his eyes watering.

Hamstrung by darkness, the cockerel staggers about, blundering as moth towards the fire. Dempsey throws it aside, driving it across the fire with swift stench of singed feathers. Dancing to the burning, it doodles sideways across the road into the briers the far side, pushing into them as if ashamed, its weeping tailfeathers in full view.

Delia settles her kettle on the fire and goes back to the tent. Marking her position, Dempsey drops on a knee and reaches out a sentient hand to touch Diana's bush, its softness fusing the witless alcohol to his lust. He snatches the hand away and pretends to stir the fire as Delia returns with a George the Fifth coronation tea-caddy and two cracked mugs. He watches her, wanting to touch Diana again but invisibly restrained by her wirey will, drawing a deep breath and swallowing a stone in his throat. Delia leaves the fire and goes round the tent and he takes several more mouthfuls of his stimulant, measuring what's left and taking some more. The spirit scalds his stomach but begins to make him new and brave, his common care evaporating, his drugged lust rising until it will break the bonds of self-protectiveness and Delia's obdurate will. He runs a hand over his genitals like a man cocking a gun. What's keepin' ye? he calls to identify her position and her voice answers from the bog where she is trying to catch a donkey. Moving swiftly, he kneels by Diana, opening his trousers with his left hand and slipping a finger into the moist vulva, fondling his penis and feeling its slow enlargement as it grows into a law unto itself.

Delia stumbles back without a donkey and only remarks him when she reaches the fire. Gware dat! she growls dispassionately as to a dog, clouting him on the side of the head and dunting him sideways with a knee. He keels over beside Diana and looks up at her, his instinctual if not physical fear of her very real. Turning over, he crawls a yard before he rises as Delia puts a hand on Diana's forehead, then leaves her for the tent, to return with the whiskey bottle. Vaguely careless-conscious, Diana shudders against the raw taste of the whiskey, turning her head away.

Dempsey watches across the fire, the spirit now freezing his mind on this one conviction. He has no knack for beauty, his existence educating him to value only the simple possession and non-possession, his natural wit for pity never instructed, taught to live see and breed as a beast . . . He has only lust's envy and its blind seed-throe for extreme sensation. . . . thickening his must and he grasps his phallus in his fist as if testing its readiness. . . .

Delia is trying to move Diana's body round so her shoulders may lie against the peaty bank. She calls to him over her shoulder to get the cart ready. His silence draws her eyes and she sees he is cold-drunk and knows what he is like in that condition, can burst a bare fist through a plate-glass window, burst an innocent man's nose with his head or even meet his teeth in his own tongue. She isn't afraid of him, is only fearful for him now in case he harms them both by harming this unwanted and unknown woman.

His intention now his total dream, he takes a blind step towards Diana as Delia stands up and moves between them, advising quietly: L'ave her be. He tries to press past her, one foot in the fire as if it isn't there.

L'ave hur be I tell ye! she shouts, leaning against him. He pushes her aside as her voice rises into a lilting shout:

Jaysus Dinnie ye'll have us all in jail!

He shakes his head against her noise. She pushes him roughly away and he falls on his back against the slope off the road from which he rebounds like a spring. They writhe and struggle, the wirey Delia no match for him.

Mother'a'god. . . she mutters hoarsely, grasping his penis. Forgetting to hit her, his hands drop to protect his totem and, kindly as she can, she pushes against him and they lean into each other for a long moment, the Torry dog standing in the tent door, trembling and whining at the rage it alone can see.

Dennie god-damn ye . . . she wheezes, trying to penetrate his trance. He grasps her wrists and tries to break her grip and only hurts himself and as if steering him with a tiller, she slowly backs him up unto the road where he grasps her throat, cruelly squeezing with both hands and forcing her backwards until she has to let go. Thrusting her down the slope, he goes to Diana, kneeling at her feet, taking her ankles in his hands and widening her legs, running his hands along the napes of her thighs and gently parting the lips of her orifice with his thumbs. Delia has come behind him, slipping her right arm round his neck and pulling him back, falling backwards with him, her head touching the edge of the fire with a whiff of singed hair. He tries to break her grip but she locks her legs around him, the two of them rolling about as one. . . .

Diana makes a long groan that rises to a shout, the dog now barking on the fight and disturbing the asses in the bog and one after another they all give tongue as if nature herself had arranged an ovation for the birth.

Dempsey masters his exhausted wife and stands up, breathing hard, the rigid penis cowled by the shreds of his shirt-tail. He returns to Diana and stares down at her uncomprehendingly, at the child lying in the creche of her thighs, his lust suspended.

Delia comes behind him and shoves him away. This time he doesn't object. She kneels by Diana, telling her: It's a foine girl glory be t'god . . .

Fetch uz a blankit! she shouts at Dempsey.

Wha . . . ? he asks bemusedly.

A blankit ye bleddy fule!

Obediently he stumbles to the tent and returns with a brown army blanket. Delia snatches it and spreads it over Diana, telling her: Doan't move, achula. Kape still now. Ye'll be all right.

Diana nods, breathing deeply and gratefully, the pain expelled at last, muttering: Keep it . . . Give it—give it to the little people. . . .

Husha now husha . . . Delia comforts, looking round for Dempsey.

He sits on her seat by the fire in a daze. She hurries into the tent and finds a twist of twine and a pair of scissors. Returning to Diana, she measures the twine into two lengths and cuts it, putting the pieces across her mouth and lifting the blanket, taking up the heavy cord and judging the length of it, her actions apt and precise. Then, tying the strings very tightly on the cord a couple of inches apart and about six inches from the baby's navel, she cuts the cord between the strings and satisfies her self the ends aren't leaking then gently lifts the child and puts it on the mother's breast, tucking the blanket around them.

Vaguely observing them, Dempsey is more concerned with the mortal war inside himself, the moonlit world running round his head, his spirit-inspired elation now a numb emptiness, Delia's activities mean-ingless. She picks up his old cap and throws it on his knees, saying: I hope yr'satisfied ye basthard, adding in kindlier voice: Go an' tackle t'ass an' we'll git her out'a here. He doesn't answer, staring across the fire at a brightness of light that seems to dance the birches about.

Jaysus . . . he mutters as Delia sees two great white eyes coming down the road.

Ferris stops the car above the camp, more to ask for information than to find anything. He gets out and the first sound he hears is the new cry of the child before he sees the vague forms below him round the fire.

My god . . . he mutters, feeling weak. What—what's goin on? he asks Dempsey who stares up at him with open mouth.

Agh, fuck off . . . he mutters tiredly.

She's all right! Delia assures. It's a foine healt'y choile!

My god . . . Ferris mutters again, his mouth dry.

Turn t'moter an' we'll git hur int'it, Delia instructs as Diana groans and begins to labour again, twisting and turning under the blanket. Delia goes to her and lifts the child, wrapping it in the blanket and handing the bundle to Dempsey, telling him to hold it. Automatically, he obeys and holds the child against his chest with an arm.

Pressing her hands on Diana's abdomen, Delia encourages: Dat's right, m'chree. Bear down now, bear down . . . as Diana grunts and groans,

her hands grasping the earth beside her for purchase. Come an now.
Kape pushin . . . Delia encourages, taking her hands and holding them.

His eyes fixed on Diana's thighs, sensations of fear and curious
revulsion running over them, his maleness interested, his oldmaid's soul
offended, Ferris sees the afterbirth come away, a great clot blackened by
moonlight lying between Diana's raddled thighs as his legs give way, his
body slipping down the bank to the edge of the fire. Neither Dempsey
notices him, Dennie swaying on his seat, the child quiet in the crook of
an arm, Delia sopping the blood with the towel and telling Diana over
and over that she is fine . . .

Ferris is temporarily overcome, but as he recovers from his faint,
Delia enlists his help to get Diana and her baby into the car. He promises
to report her services to the rector.

Delia nods and watches the car snail away, Ferris grinding his gears,
the exhaust fumes lingering in the cool air, the rear lights not seeming to
move at all and then blinking out around a corner, the quiet moonlight
returning to the night.

There is a fine red rug on the ground. She picks it up, hiding it with
her body from Dempsey, bundling it together and looking for a place to
hide it, stuffing it under a gorsebush, suddenly aware of her aching body
after his abuse.

He sits by the fire bent over his knees, half-dozing, his elbows slipping off his thighs and threatening to keel over his body into the fire.

Ye'll be fallin' int't'bleddy fire, she says loudly to wake him.

He looks up at her, asking: Wha . . . ? He puts the cap back on his
head and makes himself more secure, muttering: Agh, fuck it . . . closing
his eyes and leaning on his thighs again.

Dead weary, Delia is hardly able to believe that anything untoward
has happened. The moonlight shines the dark blob of the afterbirth
which the dog is slyly approaching and she watches, waiting for it to
come within distance of a kick and hitting it with the side of her foot.
It yelps and retires to its bed under the cart. She sees the whiskey bottle
and treats herself to what's left of it.

Passing Dempsey on her way to the tent, he looks up, asking:
Whur—whur—whur's she?

She doesn't answer. Finding an old newspaper in the tent, she spreads it on the ground and lifts the chill-warm placenta onto it, parcelling it up and then wondering what to do with it, superstition as much as hygiene advising her to dispose of it safely. The parcel is unsafe, the blood rotting the newspaper and she goes back to the tent and reluctantly appropriates a threadbare blanket and uses it for an extra wrapper. Taking Dempsey's poacher's spade, she digs a two-foot hole in the soft peat and gives the placenta to the bog. Back by the fire she scuffles mould over the remaining blood and thinks about the ring and plans to return it, knowing her midwifery will be rewarded, Diana's ill wind blowing some good.

She then begins to worry about the ring, unsure of its location, blaming herself for not using the sacrosanctity of her box. Dunno whet I wuz t'inkin' about . . . she mutters aloud.

Wha . . . ? Dempsey asks, groping in the lining of his cap for a butt and lighting it off an ember, the sudden lungful of acrid smoke coughing him so much that he retches as a sudden squawking comes from the bushes. The starving dog has found the cockerel. It gets free and spurs its adversary bravely. Dempsey jumps up, cursing the dog, which now has the cock under its forepaws and plucks the feathers off its back, the squawks slowly lowering into terrored exhaustion. He hits the animal with a full kick up the tail, lifting it off the cock with a bright yelp. It scurries to the safety of the cart and watches him between the wheel spokes.

Catching the cock, he locks its wings and stands on the road looking round the milky night, coming to himself, stretching and flexing his arms, the gyved cock crouching beside him under the nether weight of the twisted wings. Delia watches him, wondering if she dare risk a search for the ring, sitting down on the log and trying to remember its exact location in the few square feet of trash and ashes at her feet.

Dempsey picks up the cockerel and tosses it into the tent, returning to the fire and asking her: Make uz a drap'a tay?

Why don't ye go t'bid . . . she comments. When she rises he sits on her log and pokes the fire absently with a stick, watching unseeingly the heat's distillation of lemon orange rose and purple flames as the fuel's long-stored salts return to the chill night air.

When in the tent she hears him singing, chanting mainly on three or four notes since there is little music in him although he can always win a few coppers from bitter old rebels at the fairs and from equally bitter orangemen over the border with the opposite sort of song, sentiment the earning factor not the song.

> How hard is me fartune
> An' vane me repinin'
> T'sthrong rope a'fate
> Fr'dis young neck is pinin'
> Me strenth is deeparted
> Me chiks sunk an' salla
> Whoile I languish in chanes
> I't'gaol a' Cluanmella . . .

The singing alerts her, knowing his habit of singing to himself when thinking about something else. She fetches two mugs with pinches of sugar and tea in them, fills them from the kettle and gives him one. He looks at the black brew, protesting: Arragh, giv'uz a drap a'milk?

Der's on'y a drap fr't'choile i't'marnin', she objects.

Gwan . . . he insists, nodding to the tent.

She looks at him a moment without spite boycott affection or blame then fetches a half-pint bottle of blue milk, serving him a meagre spoonful, not taking any herself. He cups his hands round the mug and blows on the liquid before taking a careful sup, the hot tea falling down his gullet like acid. Delia sits on Diana's seat and they drink the tea in silence. When he finishes he hands her his mug and goes beyond the fire to pee, examining the penis where it stings him, his small hands with their pointed fingers suddenly tender and kindly for this his finest and only genuine possession, the fondling slowly rising it with each pulse to its majority. He tests the painful socket and then lets the organ support itself.

Ye'll be spillin' dat wit' too much handlin', Delia comments laconically. He looks at her, tossing up his mind whether or not he will have her, the penis urging, his mind declining. He listens to his mind and presses the penis up against his belly, doing up a couple of buttons, complaining: Y'fucken hurted me.

Aye! she exclaims derisively. An' where'd we be if ye got int'hur?

What ar'ye sayin'? he asks, frowning.

Niver mine . . . she mutters, unsure if he is playacting or really not remembering his attempted assault.

What ar'ye talkin' about? he insists. What wuz t'moter doin'?

She refuses to answer in case his ignorance is genuine, swilling out the mugs from the kettle and taking them back to the tent. They both sit over the fire and stare into it.

Whet wuz I doin'? he asks suddenly.

Nottin'. . . she answers, thinking he may have also forgotten about the ring.

They both sharpen their hearing as they hear faint crackling sounds, Dempsey asking: Whur's dat fucken rabbit?

Whur y'leff it, Delia replies.

Dat fucken dog . . . he says starting up and going to his sack in the tent, emptying and sighing an extravagant fuck me.

What's it? Delia asks.

D'bleddy dog! Jaysus, I'll kill it!

Y'shud'a hung it up.

Arragh, hang me arse! Torry! Here! he shouts.

The hungry dog, wisely taking the threat at face value, slinks out from under the cart and makes for the free bog, leaving the hind half of the rabbit neatly chewed as if it had been chopped by a cleaver. Dempsey crawls under the cart to salvage the remains and doesn't reverse far enough on hands and knees and knocks his head on the cart bottom as he straightens, whirling the half-rabbit into the night and mouthing a string of curses. A hand on his head still teary with blowhard, he trips on a shaft and falls on his face, lying there stiff with rage and shouting his blasphemous chant to the deaf earth.

Taking advantage of his mishaps, Delia searches for the ring, digging into the peat with a bit of stick. Dempsey goes to the tent and fumbles through the sack for the hedgehog, shouting: T'fucken hedgepig's gone as well!

See Torry an it . . . Delia suggests.

Torry me arse . . . he retorts, rolling over the turnips and potatoes in hope one of them might be the hedgehog in disguise.

Ded y'fine it? Delia calls to mark where he is as she digs away with her stick, sieving the plocks of peat in her fingers.

Whet ar'y'afther? Dempsey asks above her, startling her.

T'oul ring she give me, she blurts, realizing she has put her foot in it when he asks: Whet ring? He had forgotten in his ecstacy of lust.

Der 'tis, he says, bending down quickly before she can ask where and snatching the ring in a handful of the peat, opening his hand and picking out the ring in finger and thumb.

Giveuzit! Delia demands hoarsely, enraged with her own stupidity. He ignores her, holding up the ring and watching its green answer to the fire's glow.

Y'darn't flog dat! she protests.

Why doan't y'shet yr'gob, he says coldly.

I'll tell ye, den, I'll tell ye . . . she hisses. T'bleddy guards'll be afther it an' axin' uz queskins!

Dey'kin ax whet t'fucken loike, he says carelessly.

Where't'hell cd'ye flog dat—heh? she demands. An' it wort' mebbie tin poun'? Heh? She jerks her sharp face nearer with each heh and he thinks he could hit her with his fist and, her impotence the equal of her chagrin, she can only watch him fondle the ring with his disincarnate pickpurse fingers.

Ef dey come lukin' fr'it I'll bleddy-well tell, she threatens bitterly. He glances at her as if neither hearing nor seeing her.

He is remembering having seen green rings with smaller stones in jewelers' shops and priced at thirty pounds and more and one in Limerick he had seen that was valued at two hundred and fifty and, looking at the ring on his palm, he puts the larger figure on it, seeing the amount in his hand instead of on the ring and immediately beginning to dreamspend it. He looks at his fuming disadvantaged wife and sees nothing save his own rankling repugnance—the mulish image of his own malevolent frustrations, blaming her for the poison in his time and life. A terrible sickness of hatred smoulders in him, every failure of his own commission

her solid fault; a poor deal her fault, a good one also her fault because
he had to lie to make it poor, his own lies so self-convincing that he has
long lost any notion of falsity and truth. As sole begetter of his misery,
nothing is her due, deprivation her keep, starvation her diet, a clout her
caress, curse her endearment. . . .

He wants to throw these things at her, the words scalding his throat,
his need to choke her where she sits possessing him, making his skin
prickle like the expectation of a fuck, a strong nerve knocking in his
solar plexus like a knuckle on a door and, watching him, she doesn't
know that there is nothing between her and death bar the whisper of his
subconscious fear.

He closes his fist tightly over the ring and in his mind he kills her.
She lies there by the fire. He is faced with the problem of her disposal.
Looking around and listening to the secret night, he finds a long pole of
a stick and goes into the bog to find a deep hole. Stones, pile stones on
her—no stones about. Dig a grave in the bog. In a few days it will be the
same as the rest but turf saves things like the old leathery man he found
the day he also found the ring-brooch with the long pin, frightening
himself. He comes back to the camp for his spade. . . .

Faraway, the child whimpers in the tent, startling him. He had forgotten it. Child and the mother. . . .

Delia watches him, trying to read him, suggesting mildly: Ef we
tak't'ring up i't'marnin', dey'll cominsate us.

He starts, her voice dowsing his dream, shrugging and pretending to
think, spitting out, saying: D'ye t'ink so?

Aye, she agrees, thinking he is moving her way. Gimmie t'ring an'
I'll go i't'marnin' wit' t'chile?

Her threadbare guilt insults his general expectations but he remains
silent.

Godsaveuz, we c'do wit' a fiver. . . she muses.

An' we c'do wit' t'fucken Irish Sweep! he jeers, angry because her
modest figure doubts his superior valuation, as if she were aware of the
latter and was selling him short.

An itchy silence falls between them, each mind chasing its expectations in secret in totally divergent directions. A slender shaft of moonlight

shoots from a twiggy bow and strikes Delia's face, lighting the life-bruised features, poignant manifest for want's bitterness and poverty's long ache of greed, Dennie's face in shadow—the face of a man could he but see it beyond his harrassments and self-protective vanity that sustained his persecution mania as reason for being alive at all, the thing he sees as wife and woman revolting him since, like a mirror, she matches the deformations of his poverty. By blaming her, as he would blame his dog for being hungry, he can disown his own contribution to their condition.

Heartlessly, he matches her against his notional appreciation of the Bideen Bawn, remembering her fleshless body with bones like harrow-pins, breasts like an ass's ears on a frosty night, a clammy bag of skin for belly, unpadded pubic arch that rowels his own and all the while dis-counting her constancy and grateless for the many times she had backed him, pulling him out of trouble when he was too drunk to know black from white and disremembering the fresh young girl going the roads with him and proud of his jaunty boast of life.

What d'ye t'ink? she asks.

Wha . . . he says, wilfully absently, her persistence enraging him, her being there enraging him: any time he manages to forget her she comes at him again, forcing him to acknowledge her.

The quenchless cockerel tries to fight the tyranny of its locked wings, crippling out of the tent towards the firelight. Impulsively he reaches down and grabs it, unhooking the wings, taking the yellow legs in his left hand and swiftly pulling the neck across a thigh, so violently that the combed head comes away in his hand, the elastic skin slipping down the red stump of the neck pointing about like a finger, the failing pinions draughting wide airs across the fire and blowing smoke and ash into Delia's face.

A distant donkey brays the night and the Dempsey beasts reply, sawing their doleful way through their atonal poem. Delia looks up, crossing herself for safety and ignorant of the worse threat that stalks her. Dempsey feels his rough jowls and says he will shave. Shave i't'marnin'? she suggests.

I'll fucken shave whin I fucken want . . . he says, fetching a mug of slimey soap and a small paintbrush and a cut-throat razor from the tent.

Pouring a little hot water from the kettle into the mug, he lathers his face which the moon sets in spectral silver, and whets the razor on a palm and seeing himself drawing it across her throat. He shaves by feel, cursing as the blunt tool pulls the stubble out by the roots. Pluck dat fucken cock afore it's coul, he orders, mouthing the words as he stretches the skin round his lips.

She picks the bird up, running a hand through the warm luxury of its feathers. He knows she waits to see what he is going to do. Physically she has no restraint, only her stubborn will constraining him and he will never break it unless by destroying her.

Tomorrow . . . He wipes his face on a rag and dreams in a corner of his mind where Delia's will can't go, putting Bideen Bawn and his vague memory of Diana together to build such a paragon of passion and lechery that his own virility would need to be samsonian to match it, the soaring height of the dream the exact opposite of the depth of his repugnance for Delia, the difference urging him to finish her as he slowly dries the razor.

The child whines in its sleep and across the fire he thinks he sees a female figure painted by moonlight on the night. He stares at her, a coldness in his belly, muttering Jaysus . . .

She seems to smile at him as she drifts past the fire and stands over Delia, laying a hand on her shoulder, then bending over and kissing her head.

Who's dat? he whispers.

Wha? Delia asks, catching his fright. What ar'ye sayin'?

Nuttin . . . he mutters.

It's coul, Delia mutters, shivering.

Go t'bed, he advises quietly, trying to think about what he thought he saw, looking round the mottled ring of moonlight and shadow.

I'll pluck t'cock furst, Delia says.

Go ye t'bed. Her practical decision enrages him again but he keeps silent as she rises, picking up the razor and shaving mug on her way to the tent, returning with a sack of feathers and sitting down again to pluck the bird, her hand making small rapid frupping sounds, frup frup frup . . .

Thinking her occupied, he stretches and goes behind the tent. She hears him breaking sticks for some moments and then there is silence. She waits for his reappearance with the firewood and when it doesn't happen, she stands up and sees him making off.

Dinnie! She feathers the word in him, stopping him, his obedience maddening him.

Dropping the cockerel, she is up on the road in three strides, warning him quietly: I shwear t'god, ye're goin' nowheres wit'out me.

Whur t'hell d'ye t'ink I cud be goin' dis time a'night? he bluffs.

Gimmie dat oul ring now! she demands. I'll see t'it.

He looks at her, scratching his cheek with his left hand as, secretly, he stiffens his right arm and swings a swift open-handed slap against the side of her head, staggering her sideways. She recovers, cursing as she comes at him. He sets himself in a boxing stance, dancing about, feinting in and out, hitting her lightly several times on the face as she swings wild blows at him. She manages to land a sound one that sings his left ear and coldly, he times himself and hits her a hard right, felling her. She lies there, sobbing with rage. He threatens her with a foot and wisely, she keeps still.

Satisfied by her unconditional surrender, he looks up the moon-blighted road and starts along it as though he is worried about being late, walking smartly, back straight, head up, the light feet slipping along, swaggering slightly because of his shoes, mincing along his jerusalem road.

Dinnie! she screams after him, kneeling on the road like one praying his return. He pays no heed. Come back, y'basthard! He twitches his neck. Besotted with rage, she scrambles to her feet, roaring: Y'hure's git!

The good dog Torry comes out from under the cart and slinks after him as Delia shouts: Gwan! Gwan now y'fucken git! as if urging him away.

He stops, turns round to shout something and sees his dog, deciding to punish it for its thievery, calling and slapping a thigh: Gud dog! Here!

Although trembling and distrustful, it goes to him, dragging itself along the ground. He goes back and grasps the scruff of its neck, making a fist for it. It cowers down, trembling, not struggling. He stops the blow,

changes it into a rough fondle of the head, saying crossly: Gwan home!
G'ome now! Saddened by the rejection, it turns with dropped tail and
snails back to the cart.

In her wallow of impotence Delia chews curses like mouthfuls of
gravel: Git! Fuckin git! Gwan now! I'll git ye, y'basthard! She snatches
up a stone and throws it after him ineptly.

He stops, turning, filling his lungs before he roars, slowly, clearly:
Sinn . . . fucken . . . Fein! Up the I R Rah . . .

The brave phrases fly into the night across the moon-tranced bog,
invoking the ghosts of old spent battlecries that are now meaningless
expletives and disturbing the wayworn donkeys again, inspiring them to
offer up their bucolic orison as if they mimicked Dempsey's meaningless
catcalls.

Delia hardly hears the hullabaloo in the noise of her recriminations,
running out of breath as the concerto ends in wailing sighs. Breathing
deeply, she slowly comes out of her rage into the aching heaviness of
her weary body and gazes vacantly across the old bog's waveless sea, its
hollows black, its ridges silvered where the moon false-frosts the heather,
an early snipe drumming to the dark with a gentle sound that enhances
the lunar calm.

Basthard. . . she mutters, trying to think what Dempsey will do—sell
the ring or else give it back to the big house. Unaware of his superior
valuation and also unaware of his vague knowledge of the ring's ownership, she thinks she will follow his own pattern and bluffing his trustless
reputation will sell the ring for a pound for drink, robbing her in all ways.

Basthard . . . she mutters again, bitterly regretting the loss of so much
money that could have been hers in all honesty had he but listened.
Bleddy stewpid git! she shouts at the night, her impotence almost as sore
as her deprivation.

Fuckin' git . . . she mutters and then suddenly and ironically begins
to worry for him, seeing him in the barracks and being asked to explain
how he came by the ring. T'bleddy amadaun . . .

Back at her tent she reconsiders and grants him his cunning quota
of prudence that pound to penny would guide him to the rectory with
his story and would take advantage of her care for Diana, pocketing the

reward and disappearing until it was spent. Hure's fucken git! she shouts, out of herself again with rage.

I'll git t'basthard yit, she tells herself, making up her mind. I'll bleddy foller him. . . .

She hastens to the cart and finds winkers and reins and stalks a donkey. The longsuffering beasts are canny, their relative freedom better than any human intention. They don't run away, they just offer her their rumps, no matter which way she approaches them. Calling gud neddy come neddy, she approaches one after another but they don't believe her, bucking her away with maidenly squeals and swiftly pivoting when she endeavours to grasp their heavy heads. Moving quietly from one to another with her neddy gud neddy, she tries to pounce to no avail.

Basthards . . . she admits defeatedly and considers, thinking she could walk but can't leave the child nor contemplate carrying its sodden weight. She tries again and every beast presents its triggered heels. Despairingly, she throws herself on one, lying across its back. It bucks and canters off with her and she can't get a leg across it, grasping its topknot with one hand, the other around the curve of its belly. Sensing her weakening purchase it stops and turns swiftly right-round and decants her. Basthard . . . she shouts, leaping up in a rage and grasping the nearest tail, only to be towed stiff-kneed for yards, presenting in profile a strangely articulated being in the half-light's antiquity as if a beast were hauling a captured female to its pound, creation all reversed. She has to let it go.

On her way back to the tent, she charges an unsuspecting donkey, its head in a birch bush, embracing its neck along with wirey branches. It lunges away with preterhuman strength, the sprung branches whipping her face. In momentary blindness, she stumbles on a tussock and falls flat into an old boghole, sinking a foot in greasy mud and scared she will sink deeper. Clawing her way out, she lies on firmer ground, exhausted and rancid with impotent rage. Fuck ye all . . . she shouts, beating the bog with her fists. Gits! Hure's fucken gits . . .

Cynically serene, the relucent moon drifts through a frond of cirrus and sports a momentary halo of cold blue, a poet's moon on a pigeon-breasted sky, its beauty adding careless if not unkindly insult to her misery, transforming her shroud of glar into a refulgent habit enriched with mystic artifacts of old silver. Mumbling her releasing plaint or prayer of broken curses against such purposeless injury, she labours to her hogan, autochthon bog-birthed in an unmagical time, going home to her hovel to wait for nothing and nothing, blackfaced—the white eyesockets staring as a skull's.

As if taking full advantage of her preoccupations, the cunning dog has scoured the camp, finding the half-plucked cockerel. Like its master, it looks about and listens, then tenderly picks up the cock by the breast-bone and trots off with a high head, moving swiftly along the shadow-hachured road and not stopping for a quarter-mile.

Back at the low fire Delia thinks about brewing a mug of tea but can't make the effort. Although her life, like any other's, is relative to its own exigencies and can still see hope where others would find but utter hopelessness, the misery of this night has frayed her stubborn will to a single strand, the soiling of her poor clothes almost the final straw.

Agh-a-nee aga-a-nee . . . she moans, bowing her head under the weight of her despair. She tries to squeege some of the mud with the edges of her hands, the low night wind chilling her wet body. The sack of feathers reminds her belatedly of the cockerel and its absence tells her where it is.

Torry! she calls in anger, then less so, softening the name: Torry, gud dog . . . whistling, putting two fingers in her mouth and wheeping piercingly, the wheeps arrowing almost visibly over the void of the bog. She waits, listening, but neither whistles nor their echoes persuade the dog's return.

Basthard . . . she mutters defeatedly. Min asses an' bleddy dogs ef der's any hure's differens . . .

She slowly strips, wiping her face with her blouse and the miracle-making moon declares she is beautiful, describes a fair woman to the myopic night. Unhooking her skirt, she lets it drop round her feet and again the moon discovers a beauty that no man would see. Shivering with cold, she fills the enamel pail from a little spring that somehow preserves its healthy purity from the bog's contamination, and washes by the fire, finding an old shift in the tent and pulling it over her wet body with difficulty. Dropping the soiled garments into the pail, she swirls them about, dissolving most of the mud and then renewing the water for them to soak overnight. As she makes her bed the blanket suddenly reminds her of the red rug from the car, and she searches a good five chilly minutes before she finds its hiding place. Its soft richness seems to feed her cold starved body, the moon saying she is no longer an anonymous tinker, changing the red into royal purple and naming her a cowled madonna.

In its slow sleep-drift her mind moves after Dempsey, her rancour changing to a kind of remote compassion, leaving his last assault to wander along the track of her life with him when he was a better man than now, her mind flying over a thousand miles of road and visiting as many fairs, his recklessness a young excitement. She sighs, crossing herself, scrambling a prayer together to the Great Mother, her friend in a heaven of Zeus males, asking Her to make Dempsey come back with the ring because she couldn't go to the big house to claim her recompense without it. T'basthard . . . she mutters, angry again then crossing herself again and making the effort to overcome the comfort of her gathering warmth, she scrabbles in her box for her rosary and talks to it bead by bead in the gloom until sleep takes her prayer away, the beads dropping from her fingers.

The moon rests on the western hills, made large and amber by the mists of earth, darkness growing against her departure, the old bog becoming a world's-end waste at the end of time as Torry the well-fed dog comes sniffing round the tent, half-waking Delia. She listens, asking: Dat ye Dennie? hoping to see his form in the tent's triangle of faint light, disappointedly identifying the dog: Hagh, y't'eivin' basthard . . . she snarls drowsily, dog and Dempsey the one thing in her mind. Glutted for once in its life, Torry curls up by the dying fire as a wandering breeze cools the moon's secession and night proclaims her stars.

* * *

The new night is soundless, the sinking moon meshed in the tall firs beside the rectory, their movements making her struggle for release and silent the silver-paved highway the great O'Dempsey half-trots along as moon-pollen flours the old face of Ireland, her four seas mining silver on her shores, her lakes and rivers silver, her mountains, her passionate poverty-enriched past counting as a fairyman's notion of wealth. The big green ring in his pocket, his talisman to fortune, he doubles its value as he goes, each yard of his way creating compound interest on his mythic capital, spending far more than he has and driving himself into still greater bankruptcy.

He ghosts along on the uppers of his heels, a Midas in the making with touch of gold, consenting neither to toil nor spin, a man of seven sins with a mind like a fox or a rat, a natural trespasser dreaming of unattainable ease and luxury much as any other ten million citizens rich and poor who, like him, would pawn what they assume to be their souls to the devil for a guarantee of power and plenty: poor Dempsey, prisoned creature of his dictatorial dreams, his blindman substitute for living, with heaps of spanish wealth waiting for the lifting around the next corner in a land of milk and honey.

T'heels. Clane pair af focken heels . . . Denis the rich absconder tells himself, his self-conviction better than his bone.

The bone-dry rattle of a distant goodstrain sounds very near. He gets into it and rides to freedom, a big whole Afton in his mouth instead of rancid cap-dried butts reclaimed from gutters.

Erin go bleddy braw! shouts General Dempsey of the IRA, drawing his revolver and firing a shot in the air. Dat's t'bleddy sthuff! he commends himself, shooting a fearful shadow with forefinger and thumb.

But dream as he may, scattering the legions of his poverty with stout delusions, his acutely poacher hearing misses no small sound: a rabbit's spastic movement in a sheugh, ducks up near the moon, the scringing sounds of grazing cattle, complaint of peewit, fox-bark, a blackbird's scarlet warning for a hunting stoat. Brave as he is or as he thinks he is, he never took to night, its universal covering hiding a thousand other things and hazards as crafty as himself, making his footpad thieveries an exquisite torment, darkness while hiding him also dressing every shade and shadow in the uniform of an apprehender.

He stops and helps himself to a mouthful of methyolated courage, the silence closing round him like a threat. Kicking a loose stone, he grabbles on the road for it, putting it in a pocket as ammunition against attack for nine times in ten he can throw a stone with uncanny accuracy, hitting the target before the missile leaves his hand.

. . . Dis country's fucked an' finished . . . muses His Reverence Father Dempsey to his pastoral shade, the only thing in his creation with wit enough to listen without argument. Aye, it agrees, der's fuck-all here an' slow starvation. Dey'd fucken walk all over ye . . . muses Monsignor O'Dempsey with great wisdom, the clerical atonym due to his coat, the gift of a distant kinsman who thinks he might well be The Dempsey, chief of the lost clan, telling him "dilis" is his motto which means true or beloved.

Proscribed outcast then running from himself, briefly appointed by the sovereign anonymity of night to ancient privileges and powers, a very distant cousin to a big general in the war, connected to Niall of the Hostages who gave a drop of blood to the king of England; a proud man well-made and blooded as night-time cows are grey whom heredity has betrayed, blood-linked to Europe's nobility, wild-goose as ugly duckling in a tinker's midden; an active man well-turned on the lathe of time — nor time nor even circumstance his enemy, no enemy extant so hurtful as himself.

Thickened by moonlight, starvation shadows lurk in hostile concentrations of trees, the long backs of hedges fencing fears as the moonlight makes monsters up for fun. Up t'fucken ribils! cheers Commandant Dempsey to his craven army and whistles a few bars of the Soldier's Song, the rhythm not the melody.

Fuck ye! Dukes Dempsey shouts at a cat-eared owl that baulks at sight of him, its fawn-white underbody feathering a sudden cross in the moonlight. Dukes is a nom de cabaret for his ability not to refuse a fight and he spars a few moments with his fright, breaking its nose with his head and bending its balls with a dirty knee and walking bravely on, refusing to look back and give the following shadows the benefit of his nervousness although they tickle the nape of his neck.

Cock'a't'fucken walk . . . the Lord of old Kilsuan endears himself for courage to pass through the next dark tomb of trees, now his own sole leigeman, no other left to swear him fealty save himself to self. . . .

Aye, a bit af an oul song now . . . announces Dennie the Prick, an

ancient and autochthonous rank with all the rights and responsibilities
associated with seignorial prerogative on account of the more than life-
size of his ichthyphallus which, four pints alee, he can exhibit as the
land's finest dildo to a selective quorum of hag-ridden but otherwise
respectable burgers too old for such athleticism, their phallicism a nostalgic memory.

Ooooh lhist t't'tale af a pire Oirish harapur

An' schorn nat t'notes frum his oul wit'ered han' . . Dat's t'boy,
Dinnie. Ye're all der yit!

Thus self-assured he unwinds the spools of his thinking to kite his
milvine dreams, the dearest occupation bar real or imaginary coition of
ninety nine in every hundred citizens between a royal breakfast and a
soldier's supper as known in the army.

Money . . . thinks Dempsey the financial impressario. I have dis ring.
What's yr'offer? Wha . . . fine poun'? Five poun' me arse! D'ye t'ink I'm
an amadaun?

Doan't go, Dinnie, he says. We can make a dale.

I till him t'be quick about it . . . Ye're nat t'on'y wan.

Fifty? he says.

Fifty fivers says I.

Ye're a hard man, he says but it's a dale . . .

He followed himself into Phonsey Flannigan's with his creeping
smile, his belly so big he can only reach his counter with his fingertips.

I'll be havin' a dubble malt an' a pint t'chase hur Mister Flannigan
if ye pl'ase, he hears his doppleganger say.

An' can ye pay, Dinnie?

Shlap down a fucken fiver. He gaups at it, t'eyes fallin' out'a his head.

An' t'row me twinty Aftons whin ye're at it.

Are ye dere, Dinnie. Yis me boy I'm here!

Give t'boys a roun' af pints Mister Flannigan.

Yis Mister Dempsey he says.

Dacint man, Dinnie!

Slainte, Dinnie, slainte . . .

She's at t'dure. I goes out an' where ar'we goin' she axes me.

Englan' says I. Git yr't'ings packed up.

D'ye mane it Dinnie?

I man more'n day says I . . .

At this juncture he walks over a bullock lying on the road, falls over it onto the verge as the beast tries to rise. Petrified, he lies still for an eternity, not daring to move until it dawns on him the devil hasn't decided to run away with him. He rises, checking the safety of his bottle and kicks the beast, hurting his foot inside the wet limp shoe and filling the night with his homemade rosary of curses. In the following silence that heats his heart he imagines he hears a distant wail and blames the owl but, limping on, he hears it again as his fear fixes on an ivy-clad oak, the leaves scratching the breeze, patches of moonlit-lichened bole shaping a tall white woman in a shining coat. Jaysus . . . he mutters, feeling his neck-hairs stiffening, blaming the tree for the cry and running for fifty yards.

Uncorking his bottle and crossing himself with the cork, he takes a long swig, his breathlessness choking in the middle of it, spilling the spirit down his neck and chest but feeling better. He finds a butt, strikes a match with a thumbnail and lights the loose alcohol about himself so he suddenly glows in blue flames like St Elmo himself. Bottle in one hand, he beats himself with his cap in the other, dancing about and setting fire to his bottle so he has to drop it, the flames scorching his shaved cheeks and neck.

Whoo . . . he sighs and gropes on the ground for his bottle. It hasn't broken and he finishes what's left of the spirit and throws the bottle against a tree in disgust, going on silently on the cat-soft balls of his feet, now weary nervous and hungry, his sight challenging every shadow. He tries to rake over the ashes of his mind's foolfire for another spark of dream but dreams by their nature are illusive and his hollow belly rumbles its emptiness for fact. He thinks about food for several hundred yards: bacin sassages bread an' tay . . . he tells himself, now more concerned with his inner man, fondling the green ring like a latter-day Aladdin. Thinking about looking for a hayshed to shorten the night, he sees a figure standing by the kiosk at the rectory gates and goes on the grass verge, stalking it to discover who it is before it sees him.

Ana has made herself a cup of tea and watches the lazy clock as she drinks it, the sweet stimulant calming her worst inarticulate fears. She knows Fallon's Road well, that it ends in a track through the bog. She has often used it as a shortcut to her home beyond Lough Suan and her mind follows Ferris on his way and sees the returning Diana in his lights, the thought so real that she feels weak with relief.

Giving him five more minutes to turn around, she hurries down to the gatelodge. The three ways are empty, stretching quietly into the quiet empty night, nor sign nor sound of any car on any road. Waiting and listening, she thinks he could have got back and taken Diana on to Ballysuan Infirmary without stopping at the rectory. Looking at the telephone kiosk, she considers calling the infirmary again and realises she hasn't any money. The silence, the delay, her helplessness and distrust of Ferris' competence combine to frighten her again. She blames herself for not going with him, seeing Diana in labour on the roadside, maybe bleeding to death on the roadside . . . Jesus Christ . . . she mutters, sobbing, the thought making her sweat, her tears shining the moonlit land's silvery mirage.

Dempsey ghosts out of the shadows, his sudden appearance startling her. Jaysus, ye freckened me! she complains.

It's a nice saft night, he placates, trying to see her in the gloom.

Did ye come far? she demands.

Aye, a fair bit, he replies reluctantly, disliking any sudden question.

Did ye see anyt'ing?

What—what loike, now? he asks, her urgency advising him to be careful.

A big moter wit' an oul man in it?

Noh . . . he says after a pause, pretending to think about it, his denial three-quarters of the truth for he but vaguely remembers Ferris and the car.

Ye didn't see a woman?

Well noh . . .he lies with nice inflection of surprise. Noh, I—I don't t'ink so . . . his second denial a disavowal of his inebrious debauchery.

Ye didden hear anyt'ing atself? Ana demands desperately, her voice breaking.

Well . . . nottin' out'a t'way like, he replies innocently. Whet—whet wd'ye be lukin' for now?

Ignoring the query, Ana cocks her hearing to the sound of an approaching car and mutters thank god as Freeman pulls up beside them, the bright lights robbing Dempsey of his redoubtable anonymity and blinding all escape.

O'Dea gets out of the car, followed by Father O'Connor. They listen as the tearful Ana tumbles out her story, clinging to the hope that Ferris must have returned since he couldn't go on.

He may have taken her to the infirmary, Freeman interposes, going to the kiosk.

Who is this man? O'Connor asks as Dempsey tries to inch away. What's your name?

It's—it's Reilly sur . . . mumbles Dempsey, touching his cap.

He says he'as jes' come up t'road an' niver saw anyt'ing, Ana explains.

You didn't see a car? O'Dea asks less fiercely.

Noh, father, noh . . . Dempsey denies as the green ring burns a hole in his pocket.

Aren't you called Dinnie, O'Dea asks him.

Yis father Iyam . . . he mutters, touching the cap again, equal amounts of fear and guilt contending in his stomach, the sight of two priests two too much.

Freeman returns with a negative answer and they look at each other. They decide that Ana and O'Connor return to the rectory while O'Dea and Freeman investigate Fallon's Road.

Fearing further involvement, Dodger Dempsey backs slowly into the shadow, slipping across the road and sliding down into the opposite sheugh, forcing a way through the hedge into the field behind as he tells himself: T'heels Dinnie. T'fucken heels . . . as he melts into the dark.

The bullock lying in the middle of the road stops Freeman. He toots the horn and it tries to rise and fails. O'Dea gets out to see what ails it, discovering it has a broken foreleg. Hearing a faint cry, he recognizes the vague oblong shape of the big car thirty yards or so down the sloping field. They jump the sheugh and clamber over the damaged hedge, running to the car which lies on a side, the dimming headlights still on.

The child is alive and apparently unharmed but Freeman quietly tells O'Dea that Diana and Ferris are dead. Wrapping the rug round his daughter, O'Dea just nods as she cries faintly: Lah a-lah a-lah . . . as if she were praising the unutterable name of God (R, 607-636; R disk, 502-543).

* * *

Postscript: My mother and Ferris were both dead when they got the car out of the ditch, Ferris with a broken neck. Even though the police found the car-tracks at the camp, Mrs. Dempsey at first denied involvement and Dempsey couldn't be found until he tried to sell the green ring to a suspicious publican in another town. When the whole story finally emerged, my father refused to prosecute and installed the Dempseys in a small cottage, giving Mrs. Dempsey a small annuity for the rest of her life.[1]

ENDNOTES
  1   This Postscript combines versions from P1 and Q fragments. Photo 35 (Actaeon onion-skins)

Index

WEST CHARACTERS CITED